STUDIES IN HISTORY, ECONOMICS AND
PUBLIC LAW

COMMENTARIES ON THE CONSTITUTION
1790 - 1860

# COMMENTARIES ON THE CONSTITUTION
## 1790–1860

BY

ELIZABETH KELLEY BAUER, Ph.D.

*NEW YORK*
RUSSELL & RUSSELL · INC
1965

TO
*my mother*
*and*
*to the memory of*
*my father*
*this book*
*is*
*gratefully and affectionately*
*dedicated.*

# ACKNOWLEDGMENTS

PROBABLY no book has ever reached its publisher without the efforts of many persons other than the one whose name appears on the cover. This book is no exception. I should like first to acknowledge my indebtedness to Columbia University for the fellowship under the benefits of which I began this work, and to Professor Henry Steele Commager who proposed the subject and guided my research. Valuable suggestions were given by Professors Dumas Malone and John A. Krout of Columbia, Arthur Whitaker of the University of Pennsylvania, and Lawrence A. Harper of the University of California. Dr. Tracy Randall Kelley and Eugenia Halvorsen Eaton aided in editing the text. Mrs. Eaton, Dr. Ethel Kime Ware, Grace Hutchison Larsen, and Dr. Ursula Schaeffer Lamb assisted in verifying elusive references in eastern libraries. Virginia Pierce Kelley, Amy Freuler Schirmer, and Blanche Nilson helped in preparing the various manuscripts, and Harriet Siegel Nathan gave valuable aid in proofreading. Greatest thanks go to my mother, Elizabeth Worley Kelley, and my husband, Frederick William Bauer, for unfailing support and understanding during the years this book has been in preparation. To these friends and family whom I have named and to countless other librarians and professional and personal friends go my deepest gratitude.

E.K.B.

BERKELEY, CALIFORNIA
AUGUST 1951

# PREFACE

THE study of commentaries on the Constitution of the United States occupies a position midway between the fields of history, political science, and constitutional law, and therefore partakes of the characteristics of all three. The present volume has been prepared from the historical standpoint as a contribution to the history of American political thought. It is not a technical study of the evolution of constitutional law, as such. The authors discussed were all lawyers who cited precedent to establish the validity of their conclusions. Some of them unconsciously touched upon the nascent field of political science, but in the view of present-day experts their efforts were minor and they have been criticized for an undue dependence upon the past.

Some knowledge of the lives of the men who wrote law books assists in humanizing the law. The late Harlan F. Stone, once dean of the law school at Columbia University, and former chief justice of the United States, in his introduction to *Men and Books Famous in the Law* by Frederick C. Hicks, said that it is necessary to study the men as well as the books in order to " give to law study its human interest and to increase its real value." It is apparent that one of the major reasons for the decline of the commentaries in public knowledge was the adoption of the case method in the training of lawyers. Dr. Hicks' volume was regarded by Dean Stone as a contribution toward counteracting the disadvantages inherent in this highly objective inductive method. It is hoped that this study may serve a similar purpose.

In order to bring a survey of the formal interpretation of the Constitution before the Civil War within the confines of a single volume, it has been necessary to accept certain limitations. Admittedly, acts of Congress and presidential pronouncements throw light on the meaning of the Constitution. Furthermore, judicial decisions are partially creative and are, therefore, the most important official interpretations of the Constitution.

9

These edicts, however, have grown out of the daily operations of the Government, have often been studied, and are available to anyone willing to read through the records of Congress and the reports of the United States Supreme Court.

There is another medium for the interpretation of the Constitution—the "formal commentaries." These volumes were in part summaries of the official pronouncements. Although they favored one or another interpretation of controversial points, they were designed to be expository. In the mid-twentieth century, the majority of the pre-Civil War commentators are unknown to college students and even to legal students. Most libraries do not have full collections of the most important, let alone the minor ones which were prepared for high school students and the general public.

This study, therefore, is presented with the hope of opening a relatively neglected field in the history of American political thought. Moreover, the commentaries present a good systematic development of the two major schools of constitutional interpretation before the Civil War. They illustrate the early divergence between the North and South in theoretical discussions of the nature of the Union, and eventually lead to the constitutional justification of Southern secession. The nationalistic school found full expression in the Marshall-Story decisions of the Supreme Court, but the states rights school had no spokesmen of comparable weight in that tribunal. The debates in Congress often called forth statements of sectional attitudes, but the circumstances inherent in debate usually precluded considered and systematic analyses of all the phases of the two basic attitudes to be found in the commentaries.

There are necessarily omissions. In the first place, only commentaries published in book form have been included. This study does not embrace speeches, pamphlets, magazine or newspaper articles. Argumentative tracts, such as the *Federalist Papers,* and the works of Congressional spokesmen, like Webster and Calhoun, have received relatively little space, as falling outside the main confines of this study. And finally, the works of foreign observers—Tocqueville, Martineau, and others—have been excluded. Also, with certain exceptions appearing in the footnotes, all of the material used has been published. The primary concern has been with volumes that were read during the period in which they were written. The final section does no more than suggest some of the uses and effects of the commentaries. A comprehensive study would require more time, space, and information than are available and even then would be inconclusive.

With these limitations, this study attempts to place the commentaries on the Constitution in their historical setting, to trace the lives of the men who wrote them, to compare them with respect to a few major theories, and to sketch the uses to which they were put when men were aware of their existence.

# TABLE OF CONTENTS

# PART I

## INTRODUCTORY

# CHAPTER I
# THE NATURE OF THE COMMENTARIES

COMMENTARIES as a form of legal literature have a history many centuries old. It is difficult, if not impossible, to point to a single commentary on law with the assurance that it is the "first" work of its kind. Probably examples can be drawn from any people who have possessed a formalized system of law, at least as far back as the Greeks and the Romans.[1] Difficult as it is to trace relationships, there is a clear connection between the first great English legal writer, Bracton, and one of the medieval school of glossators, Azo. In a work which was " Romanesque in form, English in substance," Bracton undertook to systematize the precepts of the common law under the headings to which the jurists of his day were accustomed.[2]

From the American standpoint, the most momentous of all the English commentaries is that of Sir William Blackstone (though that of Sir Edward Coke earlier was relied upon as the standard exposition of English law). The significance of this work lies largely in the time when it was published. Blackstone lectured at Oxford as Vinerian Professor of English Law between 1758 and 1766, and is responsible for the innovation of regarding the Common Law as a proper " academical " study. Blackstone, like Bracton five centuries before, attempted to put the common law into the divisions which were considered essential by contemporary legal thinkers.[3] Another similarity between these two men which sets them apart from other writers on the same subject, is that their systematizations of English

1 John M. Zane, *The Story of Law* (New York: Ives Washburn, 1927), chs. ix, x, xi.

2 Frederick Pollock and Frederic William Maitland, *The History of English Law before the Time of Edward I*, I (Cambridge: 1895), 186. Bracton, writing about 1250, copied Azo's form of summary of the numerous glosses that had been made of Justinian's Code and Institutes.

3 Max Radin, *Handbook of Anglo-American Legal History* (St. Paul, Minnesota: West Publishing Company, 1936), p. 287.

law were intended to be intelligible to other persons than practitioners.

Blackstone published his *Commentaries* between 1765 and
1769. The first American edition appeared as early as 1771-72,
and achieved immediate popularity. Fourteen hundred copies
were subscribed in advance, though at least a thousand copies
of the English edition had previously been imported into the
colonies.[4] " There is no doubt that, for many early American
lawyers, Blackstone was the Common Law, because, for one
thing, they often had no other book." [5] The confusion of the
revolutionary period in the United States, and the strong movement to repudiate everything English, were followed by a return to English precedents in support of the effort then being
made to establish an American system of jurisprudence. Obviously, the *Commentaries* of Blackstone were in ideal form for
immediate use.[6]

An important criticism of Blackstone's work may be made
here, since undoubtedly it had an influence in the development
of the American practice of law. Among the great commentaries on the English legal system, that of Blackstone, though
the last and most influential, was least abreast of its own time.
Blackstone was really describing the law of a generation or
more earlier.

> Scarcely a suggestion is found in Blackstone of the epoch-
> making changes which the labors of his own contemporaries
> were effecting in the law. We are carried rather to the be-
> ginnings than to the middle of the eighteenth century, to the

4 Charles Warren, *History of the Harvard Law School and of Early
Legal Conditions in America*, I (New York: 1908), 142. See also Charles
Warren, *A History of the American Bar* (Boston: 1911), pp. 178-179.

5 Radin, *Handbook of Anglo-American Legal History*, p. 287.

6 Alfred Zantzinger Reed, *Training for the Public Profession of the Law*,
Bulletin No. 15 of the Carnegie Foundation for the Advancement of Teaching (New York: 1921), pp. 110-111.

first stirrings of the Age of Enlightenment rather than to the result of the illumination.[7]

Furthermore, Blackstone was recognized even by his successors in office as " an anti-republican lawyer." [8] The first volume of his *Commentaries* was evidently written before 1765 and contained nothing aimed directly at the colonists. But material changes were made in the discussion of the relations between the colonies and Parliament in the later editions.[9]

Several of the early American commentators with whom we shall be dealing recognized the difficulties and endeavored to point out those subjects on which Blackstone's treatment was deficient, biased against the American form of government, or antiquated. But revising and annotating Blackstone, however important in the early years, did not solve the problem, and though it was not at first clearly recognized, a distinctively American systematization of the common law was a desideratum. It could not be attained overnight, and in the interim the

7 Radin, *Handbook of Anglo-American Legal History*, p. 278. *Cf.* footnote by James DeWitt Andrews in his edition of *The Works of James Wilson*, I (Chicago: 1896), 15: " That Blackstone, in common with others of his time, drew largely upon his imagination, and was not faithful to the accurate delineation of the subject he treated, is nowhere in the English language pointed out more clearly or forcibly than in the writings of James Wilson." Andrews also asserts that Blackstone's opinion with regard to the sovereign power of the people over their constitution, which Wilson criticized, has " been pronounced by the highest judicial authority to have been founded in his zeal to sustain the dignity of his subject, rather than in the sober reflection of a jurist." See the observations of Judges in Stockdale *v.* Hansard (1839), 9 Ad. and El., s. c. 36 E.C.L. 118-121.

8 Wilson, " Introductory Lecture. Of the Study of the Law in the United States," in Andrews, *Works of Wilson*, I, 19.

9 Andrews notes that " The situation of Blackstone should always be regarded when judging him. He was the protégé of Mansfield, who was then in Parliament, and an avowed advocate of the extreme legislative right of Parliament over the colonies; the first volume came out in November, 1765. In February, Pitt and Mansfield made speeches on opposite sides of the colonial question. The second edition of Blackstone's first volume containing the necessary changes appeared in November, 1766. See Stockdale *v.* Hansard (1839), 9 Ad. and El. 1-36, E.C.L.R. pp. 70-118-120-1." *Works of Wilson*, I, 19 note.

United States came to a general acceptance of Blackstone almost without knowing it. The laity had the general idea that American law was constructed by legislatures, within the framework of the Constitution. The bench, on the other hand, was constantly confronted with the practical necessity of rendering decisions on cases not covered by legislation. Reason and abstract justice were felt by many to be but slender reeds; safer support was precedent. Before 1789 there were no published American law reports, so judges were driven back to English decisions. The availability of Blackstone's compilation at that time, therefore, encouraged the continuation of the authority of the common law in America.

Meanwhile, another effort to solve the same problem—codification of law by legislative enactment—was in progress, especially in the early years of the federal period and again between 1820 and 1850. Several states took steps in this direction,[10] encouraged by authorities who were familiar with French law. Jeremy Bentham (1748-1832), one of the "great seminal minds" of Anglo-American law, was the chief exponent of codification in the early period. Edward Livingston brought Bentham's influence to America, when he drafted a Code of Procedure which was adopted by the Louisiana legislature in 1805.[11]

Among the strongest agencies working against codification were the commentaries, which made the law accessible and applicable to American circumstances. Paradoxically, two of the commentators who believed most wholeheartedly in the establishment of codes of law, wrote volumes which worked most strongly in the opposite direction. The writings of Kent and Story, by making the common law available and comprehen-

10 Francis R. Aumann, *The Changing American Legal System: Some Selected Phases* (Columbus: Ohio State University, 1940), pp. 122-127.

11 *Ibid.*, pp. 123-124. Livingston followed this code with another complete one on Crimes and Punishments, Criminal Procedure, Evidence and Prison Discipline (which was not adopted in full, but was "an unfailing fountain of reforms"). See *North American Review*, XVII (Oct. 1823), 242-268, for a comprehensive review of this criminal code.

sible, rendered codes unnecessary.[12] And even before Story and Kent wrote, St. George Tucker—though a friend of Jefferson, the great opponent of the common law—had prepared an edition of Blackstone with notes, applicable to conditions in the United States in general and Virginia in particular. So the common law was soon available in many forms—English and American decisions (as soon as the latter came to be published, around 1800), the English original of Blackstone, the Americanized version of St. George Tucker, *A General Abridgment and Digest of American Law* (which Nathan Dane began in 1800 and published in nine volumes between 1823 and 1829), Kent's four volumes of *Commentaries on American Law,* published between 1826 and 1830, and the series of commentaries on various legal subjects published by Story between 1832 and 1845.

There is much evidence that most of the commentaries on the Constitution were not prepared by scholars and jurists who enjoyed leisure. There is a direct connection between many of the political events of the period and the efforts to make the meaning of the Constitution clearer, but not always between the amount of spare time a man had and the number of books he wrote. For example, Story was encouraged to write his *Commentaries* not merely by the requirements of his position at Harvard, but because he felt that the nullification argument then being elaborated in South Carolina needed to be answered.[13] In fact, the two years, 1833 and 1834, just following this controversy, saw the publication of more new works on the Constitution than had appeared in any previous ten-year period.

And there is another relation in which the commentaries had great practical significance at the time in which they were written. In several instances, they formed an integral part of the new system of legal education that was developing in the United

12 Aumann, *Changing American Legal System,* p. 125.

13 *Cf.* Joseph Story, *Commentaries on the Constitution of the United States* (Boston: 1833), sec. 1906. South Carolina is not mentioned by name, but the reference is clear.

States. The time-honored method for the training of lawyers had been akin to the apprenticeship system in the trades. A young man entered the office of a lawyer as a clerk, using his spare time to read such standard tomes as Coke on Littleton and Blackstone. Occasionally, ambitious parents sent their sons to England to study law in the universities.

University instruction in professional law in the United States is generally considered to have been initiated at William and Mary College in 1779.[14] Jefferson, as Governor of Virginia, was responsible for the reorganization of his *alma mater* in such a way as to provide for the establishment of six faculties, each represented by a single professor. The lectures on law, based in large measure upon Blackstone, were delivered by Chancellor George Wythe, one of the most eminent of Virginia's lawyers.[15]

Chancellor Wythe's lectures were not printed, but the published lectures of his successor spread the influence of the Wil-

14 Occasionally, one sees a claim that Columbia began law instruction in 1773. However, John Vardill (1749-1811), who was appointed professor of natural law in King's College, December 28, 1773, never actually held the post. He sailed for England almost immediately for his ordination. See the article on Vardill in the *Dictionary of American Biography* by Milton Halsey Thomas.

15 John Marshall, attending the school in 1780, has left notes on Wythe's lectures, showing that they were a mere running commentary on legal heads, arranged alphabetically. Albert J. Beveridge, *The Life of John Marshall*, I (Boston and New York: 1916), 174. But in 1784, Governor Jefferson told President Stiles of Yale that Blackstone was the basis of the law lectures. Franklin B. Dexter, ed., *The Literary Diary of Ezra Stiles*, III (New York: 1901), 126. Wythe was Professor of the School of Law and Police. Bishop James Madison, president of the college (not to be confused with the President of that name), occupied a chair which included Moral Philosophy and the Laws of Nature and Nations. The field of international law was thus made a subsidiary to ethics, one of the four branches of philosophy. Lyon G. Tyler, *Early Courses and Professors at William and Mary College*, An address before Alpha Chapter, Phi Beta Kappa, Dec. 5, 1904 (Williamsburg: 1904); Letters of John Brown to his uncle, William Preston, published as " Glimpses of Old College Life," *William and Mary College Quarterly*, IX (October 1900), 80; Warren, *History of the Harvard Law School*, I, 169 *et seq.*; "Laws and Regulations, 1837," *Bulletin of the College of William and Mary*, XI (1917), no. 2.

liam and Mary law school through the entire United States. St. George Tucker, assuming Wythe's position in 1789, continued to use Blackstone as the basis of his lectures, explaining that he had had no time to devise a classification of his own. According to Reed,

> the *Commentaries,* with notes adapting it to American usage, provided for the time being a sufficiently satisfactory textbook of American law. Tucker's work, published in 1803, fixed the Blackstone tradition in this country, and by ostensibly compressing all legal knowledge within the covers of a single book, undoubtedly discouraged the organization of law schools elsewhere. It made the apprenticeship method of teaching law practicable and sufficient.[16]

Experiments in formal legal education were conducted at various points in the newly united states, notably at the College of Philadelphia, later to become the University of Pennsylvania, and at Columbia College (formerly King's College). Although Wilson and Kent were unquestionably able men, they were unsuccessful in attracting the large groups of students necessary to make a university law school an accepted center of training. David Hoffman's efforts at the University of Maryland some twenty years later were also disappointing.

It was really not until Joseph Story became Dane Professor of Law at Harvard University that the new system of legal education set out to become the chief means of educating lawyers that it is now. And under the requirements made by Nathan Dane when he endowed the professorship, Story published a series of commentaries on American law, mentioned above, which did more than any other single factor to establish a distinctively American system of jurisprudence, based upon the English common law.

There is, as may be expected, a marked connection between the commentaries on the Constitution and court *dicta* elaborating our constitutional law. The commentators made court deci-

16 Reed, *Training for the Law,* p. 117.

sions the basis of their discussions of constitutional points. As time passed, the courts came to cite the commentaries as authority for further decisions, which, in turn, were incorporated into later commentaries, or revisions of earlier ones, as additional refinements in interpretation.

Textbooks on law, both British and American, were cited in America more rapidly after their publication than in England. The reason for this is practical—the expansion of the United States created a situation in which both lawyers and judges had to use the common law without sufficient training in it, or without adequate reports and other literature in the field. Hence there was an early reliance on Blackstone, and on Kent and Story as soon as they became available. At the time that textbooks in American law were being called upon frequently in American courts, a rule still prevailed in the English courts that, with a few definite exceptions, textbooks could not be cited.[17] Such a rule in the American courts would have increased the difficulties of judges and lawyers materially, and it is no longer binding practice even in England.[18]

The commentaries thus grew out of a definite need in the early American legal situation. Nor were they disconnected with political events. In order to show the relationship of the commentaries to the period in which they were produced, it will now be our purpose to examine them in their historical setting.

17 Radin, *Handbook*, pp. 303-304. The exact rule was never clearly formulated. *Cf.* Percy H. Winfield, *The Chief Sources of English Legal History* (Cambridge, Mass.: 1925), pp. 253-256, and W. S. Holdsworth, *Sources and Literature of English Law* (Oxford: 1925), pp. 134-238.

18 *Loc. cit.* See *infra*, ch. ix, for a discussion of the use of the commentaries as authorities in Supreme Court cases.

# CHAPTER II

# THE COMMENTARIES IN THEIR HISTORICAL SETTING

A BRIEF backward glance over the years from the adoption of the Constitution to the Civil War is all that we are permitted in introducing the commentaries and their authors. These were the formative years during which men were laying the foundations for our national organization as we know it today and seeking the answers to many of the questions which arose as the result of the establishment of a new political unit.

The general outlines and many of the details of this period are familiar enough. But in looking back from the vantage point of the present, it is extremely difficult to maintain an unbiased attitude. Today, those events and persons which stand out most clearly are those which shared in the ultimately victorious nationalizing movement. The school child learns about Washington and Lincoln first; and if he was a Northerner or Westerner of the last generation, may even have memorized the peroration of Webster's reply to Hayne long before losing himself in the intricacies of the Virginia and Kentucky Resolutions, the Hartford Convention, and the nullification controversy. In secondary school, the child may learn of Marshall, Calhoun, Jackson, and Webster, of the issue of slavery, and of sectional differences. In college, he may encounter the names of Wilson, Story, Lieber, and Kent, if he studies the social sciences. But he rarely has his attention directed past the political giants who occupy such a large place in the accounts of the pre-Civil War era.

To put our study of these lesser lights into proper focus, it is necessary to introduce them as contemporaries of those who are better known. Often they were able to increase the glory of the more popular figures—as, for example, when Story,[1] Dane, and Kent all helped to sustain Webster's brilliance in the Senate.

---

1 Story is certainly not a lesser light. The emphasis here is on the fact that Webster is more popularly known today than is Story.

The first generation of political thinkers was led by Hamilton and Jefferson, whose opposing views on the nature of the union they wished to build, served to mark out the main lines of controversy for the ensuing half-century and more. Hamilton, with his associates, Madison and Jay, succeeded in producing so skillful a series of arguments, that the *Federalist* was used to sustain all shades of opinion for years to come. James Wilson and Nathaniel Chipman, both of whom wrote during Washington's first administration, helped in the establishment of the nationalizing or federalist line of reasoning. Jefferson, on the other hand, wrote no commentary of his own. His spokesmen were John Taylor of Caroline, whose contributions will be discussed subsequently, and St. George Tucker, who in 1803 produced the first systematic presentation of the states rights position.

The developments along national lines during the early years of the federal period did not come unopposed. Jefferson's arguments with Hamilton in Washington's cabinet were among the earliest expressions of the constitutional opposition. The states themselves spoke in the Virginia and Kentucky Resolutions, claiming a right later to be elaborated, to determine the constitutionality of the federal laws. And Tucker's work, published in the year of Marbury *v.* Madison (1803), shows that a Southern judge was teaching in a Southern law school a different theory of the Constitution from that expounded by Marshall.

It will quickly be noted that this early line of demarcation between the Northern nationalists and the Southern states rights advocates was not consistently followed, especially in the first part of the period. Already, the reader may have recalled instances of Northerners who proclaimed the rights of the states, Westerners who plotted secession, and Southerners who argued for the maintenance of the strength of the national government. This inconsistency was not unnoticed by contemporaries. As interpreted by one of our commentators,

> *States rights and state sovereignty,* are expressions coined for party purposes, often by minorities, who happen to be dissatisfied with the measures of the General Government, and

as they are afterwards used, they produce only state delusion. In this business each large minority has had its turn.[2]

During the temporary period of nationalistic sentiment in the South at the time of the War of 1812, few spokesmen remained loyal to the original tenets of Jeffersonian Democracy and narrow construction of the Constitution. One of these few was Jefferson's philosopher friend, John Taylor of Caroline, whose four works on government appeared between 1814 and 1823. Taylor is one of the most consistent thinkers in the history of American political thought, and though his writings are difficult to read, they are essential documents in the study of the Jeffersonian theories. Taylor's death in 1824 left a serious gap; had he lived another decade, he might have been of real service to the South in the nullification controversy.

Historically, the decade of the 1820's is generally thought of as an era of transition. The commentaries written during this period also seem to show a transitional character. Thomas Sergeant of Philadelphia compiled the first volume of purely constitutional cases in 1822. The fact that a second edition appeared in 1830 may be taken as an indication that it found favor with the bar. Another welcome work was the first constitutional text on the college and law school level by William Rawle, a book which is still of considerable interest. In spite of his admiration for Washington, and his self-professed Federalism, Rawle closed his analysis of the Constitution with a definite recognition of the right of states to secede from the Union. The warm reception accorded the volume, both north and south, would seem to show that the idea of secession was not then so " monstrous " as it was later denounced as being. Rather, it was presented as the logical end result of a system of reasoning followed by one who had seen the American states break away from the mother country. In the same year that James Kent published the first volume of his famous *Commentaries on American Law* (1826), Thomas Cooper of South Carolina,

2 Nathan Dane, *General Abridgment and Digest of American Law*, IX (Boston: 1829), App., pp. 32-33, sec. 23.

writing as a political scientist, presented another exposition of the Southern viewpoint.

These works appeared just before the North-South tension crystallized in the nullification controversy—a crisis to which the commentators quickly responded. Although the bulk of Nathan Dane's *General Abridgment and Digest of American Law* was published earlier, the Appendix to the ninth volume, giving the author's interpretation of constitutional history, was prepared especially as an addition in 1830.[3] Other reactions to the nullification controversy followed quickly. Andrew Jackson's Proclamation to South Carolina in 1832 contained a forceful statement of the sanctity of the Union, which came as a surprise to the particularists of that state. And John Quincy Adams, whose father had required three volumes to discuss his theories of the state constitutions,[4] presented his constitutional ideas in the relatively short compass of a Fourth of July oration in 1831.

The most extended reply to the nullifiers came from Joseph Story, whose momentous *Commentaries on the Constitution* issued from the press in 1833. Story leaned heavily on Dane for much of the historical part of his argument, and most of the subsequent commentators leaned on Story. William Alexander Duer, Nathaniel Chipman, and Peter Stephen DuPonceau were among those who followed Story in responding to the threat to the Union, and Story himself prepared his ideas in various forms so that they would reach the widest possible audience. David Hoffman, whose work was more closely connected with the establishment of better curricula in the newly developing law schools than with theoretical problems, was in agreement with this group. Perhaps if he had been able to carry out his original design, he, too, would have prepared lectures like those of Story and Kent, in which he would have elaborated upon this

3 The ninth volume was printed in 1829, and this section was added to some of the copies later.

4 John Adams, *A Defence of the Constitutions of Government of the United States of America, against the attack of M. Turgot in his letter to Dr. Price* .... (London, Boston, New York, Philadelphia: 1787-88, with several later editions). 3 vols.

agreement. Timothy Walker's introductory volume in American law was published a few years later (1837), but the section on constitutional interpretation seems to show in part, at least, the effect of the same stimulus.

Southerners, meanwhile, were apparently content that Calhoun should be their leading spokesman. His authorship of the South Carolina Exposition was a secret until 1831, shortly before he resigned from the vice-presidency and succeeded Hayne in the Senate.[5] Thus Calhoun gained the opportunity to battle with Webster personally in the great forensic contests on the floor of the upper house. During the succeeding years, he developed, in even more precise terms, the ideas of the South—state sovereignty, nullification, concurrent majority, and their corollaries.

Not all of the commentators sided outspokenly with either the North or the South. In 1837, Henry Baldwin, an associate of Story and Marshall on the Supreme bench, published a volume in which he asserted his intention to take a third line of approach to the interpretation of the Constitution, one neither liberal nor strict. Baldwin was unique in his effort, but does not appear to have been entirely successful in steering a middle course. Others made no claim to such objectivity, nor did they think it desirable. Abel Parker Upshur, whose critique of Story's *Commentaries* was written in the same year in which Baldwin wrote, finally published his monograph in 1840. It was definitely a pro-states rights argument, as were the three volumes of lectures prepared by Henry St. George and N. Beverley Tucker early in the 1840's. And simultaneously with the Tuckers, William Alexander Duer of New York published a set of lectures, setting forth the nationalist interpretation. E. Fitch Smith's heavy tome (1848), was declared to be in support of strict interpretation, but is not so argumentative in character.

Discussion of the Constitution during the "fitful fifties" centered around the debates over the Compromise of 1850, the

5 Hayne had been elected governor of South Carolina in 1832. Calhoun appeared in the Senate early in 1833.

Kansas-Nebraska Act, and the Dred Scott decision. George Ticknor Curtis, a devoted admirer of Webster, and a former student of Story's, wrote a constitutional history from the Websterian standpoint shortly before the Civil War, but oddly enough, he did not support Lincoln during his difficult years of leadership.

The outbreak of the Civil War found the North and South with other elements of strength than economic and military. Each had evolved a fully-developed body of constitutional doctrine, and each section was able to justify its actions in the light of its own interpretation of the Constitution. Our purpose is to examine the contributions of the commentators in the exposition of the major points in this controversy.

A commentator is, by definition, one who expounds, or makes explanatory or critical notes upon a text. Not everyone, then, who wrote on the Constitution was a commentator. For the purposes of this study, works have been selected which present, in general, an orderly analysis of the Constitution and the philosophy underlying it. Some, of course, are far more orderly than others. All of them elaborate a rather definite point of view.

Many authors and statesmen whose works are normally included in histories of American political thought are mentioned only briefly. For example, the *Federalist Papers* of Hamilton, Madison, and Jay, generally considered to be the earliest commentary on the Constitution, are not discussed in detail because they were issued as campaign documents urging ratification, rather than as an analysis of a system already in operation.

Again, John Marshall is usually thought of as a commentator *par excellence,* but his interpretation of the Constitution is contained in his series of constitutional opinions. He did not write a formal commentary, contenting himself with full agreement in the views expressed by Story.[6] Marshall's best opinions were collected shortly after his death and published under the

6 See letter of Marshall to Story, in William W. Story, *Life and Letters of Joseph Story,* II (London: 1851), 655, and Story's statement, *ibid.,* II, 273-274.

title, *The Writings of John Marshall, Late Chief Justice of the United States, upon the Constitution of the United States,*[7] a book frequently cited as *Marshall's Commentaries.*

To take examples from the political arena, Daniel Webster and John C. Calhoun have long represented the opposite poles of Northern and Southern interpretation. Webster evidently intended to write a formal statement of the views which he had often and ably expressed in debate. He did not do so, but left the task to his friend, George Ticknor Curtis, whose work we shall discuss subsequently. Calhoun prepared two brief expositions of his school of thought—*A Disquisition on Government,* and *A Discourse on the Constitution and Government of the United States*—both of which were published posthumously,[8] and which cannot be called systematic analyses when compared with such a work as Rawle's, for example.

And finally, the principal works of Francis Lieber, the great pioneer political scientist, are peripheral to the commentaries. He was known to support the nationalist interpretation of the Constitution, but his only direct statement on the subject, written before the Civil War, was contained in two lectures delivered in the winter of 1860-61, entitled, *What Is Our Constitution,—League, Pact, or Government?* [9] These lectures are not included in our study, but we shall have occasion to mention Lieber's discussion of sovereignty, which has been considered the earliest full analysis of the subject in the United States.

With these men as a part of the background rather than on the main stage, we may proceed to a consideration of the lawyers and teachers who wrote the formal commentaries on the Constitution.

7 (Boston: 1839). There have been several later editions.

8 These two essays form Volume I of *The Works of John C. Calhoun,* edited by Richard K. Crallé (Charleston: 1851).

9 (New York: 1861), 48 pp. An address on secession, written in 1851, was appended to the printed pamphlet. The lectures had been delivered in the law school of Columbia College.

# PART II

BIOGRAPHIES OF THE COMMENTATORS

# PART II
## INTRODUCTORY

As a group, the commentators on the Constitution of the United States represented one of the most highly educated sections of society. All were members of the intellectual élite of their times. Yet today, the names of very few of them are known to Americans.

In the filiopietistic spirit of the period, the works, or " life and letters," of a few of these men were prepared for the public. This was true for Chipman, Wilson, Kent,[1] and Story. In recent years, full-length scholarly biographies, using primary source materials, have been written for Kent, John Taylor of Caroline, and Thomas Cooper. But the five volumes of Justice Wilson's *Life and Letters* still await a publisher, and the records of Justice Story's life are yet to be analyzed.[2]

The thought of such future obscurity would probably have been depressing to many of the commentators. At the times in which they lived, they were generally admired as brilliant ornaments of bench or bar. Nathan Dane, who drafted the Northwest Ordinance, compiled the first digest of American Law and founded the first really successful chair of law in an American university, was declared to have earned glory enough for one man in one age. John Quincy Adams asserted that Liberty and Law were " associated till the judgment day with the name of Nathan Dane;" and it was one of Webster's periods that the authorship of the great Northwest Ordinance would make that name " as immortal as if it were written on yonder firmament, blazing forever between Orion and the Pleiades." Yet within fifty years from his death, scarcely a single collegian knew his

1 See *infra*, ch. iii, note 159 for explanation of the reason why Chancellor Kent's great-grandson prepared his *Memoirs and Letters*.

2 Burton Alva Konkle, who died late in 1944, did the work on Wilson. Professor Henry Steele Commager has a study of Story in preparation.

name, his digest had been superseded, and the honors for writing his famous statute had been given to another.[3]

A similar lament has been made by a recent scholar on the fate of Nathaniel Chipman, who died a recognized authority on law and political institutions—

> yet few writers on these subjects have made use of his contributions to American thought. He wrote our first treatise on the principles of government, but less able and consistent writers are much better known. He settled some of the most difficult legal questions in the troublous days following the Revolution, but is never mentioned among our great jurists. He was Chief-Justice of his state, federal judge, United States Senator, and professor of law, but not even a portrait can be found in the scenes of his latest labors. Although his political writings were highly praised by Jefferson himself, both they and he have been forgotten.[4]

Another man all but forgotten until about a century after his death was James Wilson, signer of the Declaration of Independence and the Constitution, and member of the first Supreme Court, as well as a faithful servant of the Continental Congress, the Congress of the Confederation, and his state of Pennsylvania. Only recently have scholars begun to realize the enormous contribution he made during the formative years of our history as a nation. After ignoring him for ten decades, they have begun to wonder whether he was second to Madison in the Constitutional Convention, or actually his intellectual superior.

How can such able, constructive thinkers sink so rapidly into oblivion? The writer of a recent sketch on Chipman says that he " was too modest to make for himself a conspicuous place in the memory of his countrymen." [5] A Wilson apologist claims

3 Henry A. Chaney, " Nathan Dane," *The Green Bag*, III (Dec. 1891), 548.

4 Roy J. Honeywell, " Nathaniel Chipman, Political Philosopher and Jurist," *New England Quarterly*, V (July 1932), 555.

5 *Loc. cit.*

that the Justice was too reserved to become a popular leader like Jefferson, or a symbol like Hamilton, while a critic argues that he was lacking in judicial detachment by reason of his consuming interest in practical concerns, and therefore could not reach his goal of establishing the basis of an American jurisprudence.[6]

In the light of these selected instances, it would appear that the lives of the commentators constitute a neglected field, and one which should be re-examined if their contributions to the development of a distinctively American system of jurisprudence are to be understood. It has not been thought advisable to attempt lengthy analyses, nor have all of the commentators been included in the following chapters. Rather, thirteen of the most significant men have been selected and their lives compared. These thirteen have been divided according to the section of the country where they lived and worked, or with which they seem to be most closely identified. The first six are from the Middle States and are more or less a "middle" group. In the works of Wilson, Kent, and Hoffman, the exposition of the Constitution was only a part of a larger endeavor. In constitutional interpretation, these men, together with Duer and DuPonceau, generally agreed with the nationalists. Rawle most clearly represents the middle viewpoint that one might expect to find in this area. The four New Englanders and the three Southerners stand for the opposite poles of interpretation.

These men have not been selected because of the worth of their commentaries alone. All of them except Rawle, Dane, and Taylor were directly connected with the newly developing system of legal education in schools instead of lawyers' offices. Thus they had a double influence through their own personal teaching efforts as well as through their writings.

6 Julian P. Boyd in the *Dictionary of American Biography*. On the other hand, Simeon E. Baldwin, president of the American Bar Association and later of the American Historical Association, said that Wilson was "the real founder of what is distinctive in our American jurisprudence." Lucien H. Alexander, "James Wilson, Nation Builder," *The Green Bag*, XIX (Jan.-Apr. 1907), 143.

The life span of these thirteen commentators as a group covered the years 1742-1858. One or another of them witnessed all of the stirring events from the days of the Stamp Act Congress and before to the period of tension just preceding the Civil War. Their backgrounds, life experiences, and observations were important formative elements in the writing of their commentaries, and thus will constitute a sound foundation upon which to build the analysis of their writings.

# CHAPTER III
## COMMENTATORS OF THE MIDDLE STATES

THE first commentators to be discussed are the representatives of the middle Atlantic states. Though James Wilson, William Rawle, and Peter Stephen DuPonceau are the only members of the Philadelphia bar whom we shall be able to study in some detail, the work of Thomas Sergeant,[1] also of Philadelphia, should not be overlooked. His volume on *Constitutional Law* (Philadelphia: 1822) was the first compilation of court decisions on the Constitution, and proved to be useful to the bench and bar.  Another Pennsylvanian, Henry Baldwin,[2] who

1 Thomas Sergeant was born in Philadelphia, Jan. 14, 1782. After graduating from the College of New Jersey (Princeton) in 1798, he entered the law office of Jared Ingersoll. He was admitted to the bar June 8, 1802. From 1812 to 1814, he was a member of the Pennsylvania House of Representatives. In 1814 he was appointed Associate Justice of the District Court of Philadelphia. From 1817 to 1819, he served as Secretary of the Commonwealth, and subsequently had to submit to an examination of his activities while in office. He was State Attorney-General from 1819 to 1820, and Postmaster of Philadelphia from 1828 to 1832. On Feb. 3, 1834, Sergeant was appointed Associate Justice of the Supreme Court of Pennsylvania, and continued on the bench until his resignation in 1846. "During his judicial career, he was the chief expounder of the limited equity jurisdiction of the court; and he was of great service in bringing this into a convenient and intelligible shape." He resigned because the new Constitution called for the election of the judges rather than their appointment by the governor. He returned to a highly successful practice at the bar, which he maintained until 1850.

Sergeant succeeded DuPonceau as Provost of the Law Academy from 1844 to 1855. He was a member of the American Philosophical Society and was for many years one of the trustees of the University of Pennsylvania. In 1812 he married Sarah Bache, granddaughter of Benjamin Franklin, by whom he had four children. He died in 1860, "leaving behind him an honorable fame as a lawyer, a politician, and a private citizen." *Memorial Biographies of the New England Historic Genealogical Society*, IV (Boston: 1885), 72-75. See also the article on Sergeant in the *Dictionary of American Biography*, by Julian P. Boyd.

2 Henry Baldwin (1780-1844) was born in New Haven, Connecticut. He graduated from Yale in 1797 and studied law under Alexander J. Dallas. In 1799, he began to practice in Pittsburgh, Pa., stopping there

eventually became an associate of Story and Marshall on the Supreme Court, also prepared a commentary expounding theories which will be taken up in chapters vi and vii of this work.

James Kent and William Alexander Duer have been selected as the representatives of the New York bar. The author of the voluminous *Commentaries on Statute and Constitutional Law,* E. Fitch Smith, has not found place owing to the paucity of information on his activities.[3] His work was designed as a pro-

---

while en route to Ohio. The personal library which he accumulated was said to be one of the finest in the West. In order to make an adequate living, he and the other successful lawyers practiced in several counties, traveling from one county seat to another on horseback, with their legal papers and a few books in a sack thrown across the saddle. Baldwin and two of his closest friends became the leaders of the Democratic-Republican party in Pittsburgh. Their zeal stopped at nothing until one of the triumvirate was killed in a duel over politics. In 1816, Baldwin was elected to Congress, and was twice re-elected. He is remembered as a strong advocate of protection when he served as chairman of the Committee on Domestic Manufactures.

Baldwin was appointed to the Supreme Court in 1830, after he had zealously supported Jackson in 1828. He is regarded as at his judicial best while on the circuit. On constitutional questions, he followed Marshall at first, but later became somewhat unpredictable in opinion. *Cf. Pennsylvania Law Journal,* III (1844), 330-332; Daniel Agnew, Address to the Allegheny County Bar Association, December 1, 1888, Sketch No. 8 on Henry Baldwin, *Pa. Mag. of Hist. and Biog.,* XIII (Jan. 1889), 23-29; M. Flavia Taylor, "The Political and Civil Career of Henry Baldwin, 1799-1830," *Western Pennsylvania Historical Magazine,* XXIV (March 1941), 37-50; article on Baldwin in the *Dictionary of American Biography* by Lindsay Rogers.

3 The following is all the information on Smith that the present student has been able to assemble. Between 1843 and 1866, he edited 17 volumes of *Reports of Cases Decided in the High Court of Chancery,* by the Rt. Hon. Sir John Leach (and others)..., vice chancellor of England (1826-1852) with notes and references to American decisions. Smith was elected county judge of Ontario County, New York, in 1845. Alden Chester, *Legal and Judicial History of New York,* III (New York: 1911), 142. According to the preface to the Constitutional *Commentaries* (p. vi), he was a counsellor-at-law at the time he wrote and had followed "the humbler walks of a private professional life." A pamphlet in the New York Public Library indicates that Smith was the nominee for alderman for the 18th Ward in 1851. In October of that year, the Committee of the 18th Ward Temperance Alliance sought his agreement to four propositions which they favored.

test against " the progress of the political pestilence of excessive and unconstitutional legislation," [4] and its emphasis is upon the constitutional restrictions on the legislative power.

Finally, David Hoffman receives extended biographical treatment because of the significance of his efforts at the University of Maryland.

### JAMES WILSON

Wilson, Kent, and Story share the honor of being the best-known expounders of the nationalist interpretation of the Constitution, though each differed from the others as to methods of interpretation.   Kent and Story have been linked in fame since the days when both were determining cases and writing commentaries. During that time, most of the first half of the nineteenth century, Wilson was little known, though lawyers were aware of his great contributions to legal thought, and his celebrated decision in Chisholm v. Georgia was well remembered. It was not until almost the centennial of his death that Wilson began again to command the attention of historians and legal theorists,[5] who have at last restored him to his rightful position among " the Fathers."

James Wilson was born September 14, 1742, at Carskerdo, near St. Andrews, in Scotland,[6] of " godly parentage "—Wil-

---

He promised enforcement of no-Sunday-drinking laws, removal of polls from places where liquor was sold, and suppression of illegal money contributions by candidates for office to promote their election. But he would not agree to the fourth proposition—compulsory prohibition. In his opinion, the common law provided all the relief needed. He placed great emphasis on moral character and said that he did not want the vote of anyone who did not trust in it.

4 Smith, *Commentaries on Statute and Constitutional Law* (Albany: 1848), Preface, p. vii.

5 Hampton L. Carson in his review of Andrews' edition of Wilson's *Works* (1896), wrote, " It is greatly to be regretted that no adequate biography of this truly great man has ever been prepared. It may now be too late." " The Works of James Wilson," *The American Law Reporter and Review*, Vol. 44, O.S. (35, N.S.), (Oct. 1896), 633.

6 Andrew Bennett in his *James Wilson of St. Andrews* (St. Andrews: J. and G. Innes, Ltd., [1928]) has written a short popular biography (81

liam and Aleson (Lansdale) Wilson.[7] Little is known of his
early life, except that he was educated as if intended for the min-
istry.[8] After grammar school study and a short period at St.
Andrews University, he went to the University of Glasgow
while Adam Smith was rector, and from there to the University
of Edinburgh to sit under some of the greatest minds in Scotland.[9] Professor John Stevenson taught him logic and Professor
Adam Ferguson, moral philosophy.[10] From Dr. Hugh Blair he
learned rhetoric and laid " the foundation of the celebrity which

pp.) of St. Andrews' most illustrious son. Bennett comments on the fact
that Wilson has not achieved the fame he deserved in his adopted country,
and is scarcely known at all in his birthplace. There are no citations of
sources in the little volume, and there are various errors (such as " Chisholm
v. South Carolina "), but the picture drawn of Wilson is sympathetic and
interesting.

7 Names from Paul Edward Sloane, *The Background of the Constitutional Ideas of James Wilson* (Master's thesis, University of California,
Berkeley: Feb. 1945), pp. 25-26. The same conclusion was reached by
Julian P. Boyd, author of the article on Wilson in the *Dictionary of American Biography*, who used the five-volume unpublished manuscript of the
*Life and Letters of James Wilson* of Burton Alva Konkle. Konkle was one
of the foremost Wilson scholars prior to his death late in 1944. Other writers
have suggested that Wilson's father might have been any one of a number
of gentlemen, including a professor of astronomy at the University of
Glasgow. See Alexander in *The Green Bag*, XIX, 4-5.

8 Burton Alva Konkle, *James Wilson and the Constitution*, The Opening
Address in the official series of events known as The James Wilson Memorial
... delivered before the Law Academy of Philadelphia on Nov. 14, 1906
(Philadelphia: 1907), p. 7. Robert Waln, Jr., concludes that Wilson's father
was in good circumstances because of the education that young James received. J. Sanderson, ed., *Biography of the Signers of the Declaration of
Independence*, VI (Philadelphia: 1823), p. 113. His mother was a devoutly
religious woman, and it was undoubtedly she who insisted upon his education for the clergy. Letter of Mrs. Aleson Lansdale Wilson to James Wilson,
July 25, 1791. This letter and some other manuscript materials were loaned
by Mr. Konkle to Paul Edward Sloane for his Master's thesis on *The
Background of the Constitutional Ideas of James Wilson*, p. 26.

9 Alexander in *The Green Bag*, XIX, 5. Hume and Adam Smith were
also among the literary coterie around Edinburgh. Konkle, *James Wilson
and the Constitution*, p. 7.

10 Alexander in *The Green Bag*, XIX, 5.

he subsequently acquired, as a powerful orator, and almost ir-resistible logician." [11] He may also have absorbed some of the teachings of St. Andrews' great political scientist, George Buchanan. Two hundred years before Wilson lived, Buchanan wrote in his *De Jure Regni,* that all power resided in the people, and that rulers should be upheld only so long as they looked after the well-being of the people.[12] In fact, the entire intellectual atmosphere in Scotland during the second half of the eighteenth century was one in which " historical and political thinking was jumping over the narrow walls of nationalism." Some men, at least, were thinking in international terms. In such an atmosphere the reasoning was sure to develop that should help American colonists in their search for a theory of imperial decentralization.[13]

At 23, then, Wilson set sail for America, on borrowed

11 Waln in *Biography of the Signers,* VI, 114.

12 Buchanan's book was suppressed by Parliament in 1584, but became a standard in the days of the Long Parliament and contained doctrines afterward adopted by John Milton. William F. Obering, in his *Philosophy of Law of James Wilson* (Washington, D. C.: Catholic University of America, 1938), presents a learned discussion of the similarity between Wilson's views and those of the medieval scholastics, especially Aquinas, Grotius and Bellarmine. Many of these ideas came to Wilson via Richard Hooker, whose eight books of *Ecclesiastical Polity* he knew well. Also, Obering contends that Wilson learned much of medieval political theory through the common law which " was animated, and, in the lines of its development, guided by the philosophy of the Schoolmen." He quotes Maitland and Pollock (*History of English Law,* 2nd ed., I, 133-134) as follows: " It is by ' popish clergymen ' that our English common law is converted from a rude mass of customs into an articulate system, and when the ' popish clergymen,' yielding at length to the pope's commands, no longer sit as the principal justices of the king's court, the creative age of our medieval law is over .... English law, more especially the English law of civil procedure, was rationalized under the influence of the canon law." See especially Obering's introduction, pp. 5-17. Along the same lines is the pamphlet by May G. O'Donnell, *James Wilson and the Natural Law Basis of Positive Law* (New York: Fordham University Press, 1937), 40 pp.

13 Randolph G. Adams, *Selected Political Essays of James Wilson* (New York: Alfred Knopf, 1930), p. 6.

money,[14] but equipped with a liberal education which was to serve him well. At the time of his arrival in New York, there was much excitement over the passage of the Stamp Act. Thus, he " received his first impression of America in an atmosphere of indignation against threatened invasion of cherished rights and stubborn purpose of resistance." [15] In October, the Stamp Act Congress gave Wilson opportunity to observe the delegates at first hand. This experience seems to have led him to make his home in Philadelphia, where he could be near such a man as John Dickinson.[16]

Early in 1766, Wilson became a tutor in Latin in the College of Philadelphia, his examination in Latin setting a new record in the college.[17] He then won a Master's degree, but did not intend to teach. Rather, he wanted to read law under the brilliant Dickinson, who, after considerable negotiation, accepted him as a student.[18] He was admitted to the bar in November

14 According to Waln in *Biography of the Signers*, VI, 113, Wilson's father lost heavily by the " same passion for speculation, which that son unfortunately inherited." After his father's death, his mother remarried, and must have been in difficulties, as Wilson frequently sent her money from this country even when he needed it himself. These early financial reverses caused the interruption of Wilson's studies at Edinburgh in 1765 and prompted him to take up bookkeeping. Apparently, Wilson had been thinking of coming to America for some time before he made the trip, particularly since a relative was established as a merchant in Philadelphia. Sloane, *Background of Constitutional Ideas of James Wilson*, p. 50 *et seq.* Bennett in *Wilson of St. Andrews*, p. 6, points to evidence that Wilson made his decision to come to America while he was at Glasgow.

15 Bennett, *Wilson of St. Andrews*, p. 10.

16 Konkle, *James Wilson and the Constitution*, p. 8.

17 *Ibid.*, p. 9. Konkle also thought that Wilson was a tutor in King's College during the three months he was in New York. Sloane, *Background of Constitutional Ideas of James Wilson*, pp. 62-63.

18 Konkle, *James Wilson and the Constitution*, p. 10. Wilson studied from the first two books of Blackstone which were available in 1767. When he went to Philadelphia, he got a loan from an uncle in Scotland, using as security some land which he bought almost as soon as he came to America. Sloane, *Background of Constitutional Ideas of James Wilson*, pp. 50, 56-57.

1767, just a month before his preceptor began to publish his famous *Farmer's Letters*.

Wilson set himself up in Reading, Pennsylvania, moving soon to Carlisle, where he quickly had the largest local practice. The Revolution found him established there as a leader in his profession. During these years, Wilson spent his spare time investigating for himself the problem already perplexing many Americans—" What is the relation of Parliament to the colonies?" While it was the prevailing opinion that Parliament could not tax the colonies, it was generally admitted that Parliament had certain supervisory rights. Wilson's conclusion was that the colonies were subject only to the Crown and not at all to Parliament.

> Many will, perhaps, be surprised to see the legislative authority of the British parliament over the colonies denied *in every instance*. Those the writer informs, that, when he began this piece, he would probably have been surprised at such an opinion himself; for that it was the *result,* and not the *occasion,* of his disquisitions.[19]

Wilson's views were not published at the time (1769), because the non-importation agreement was dissolved before they were ready for the press, and " it was then judged unseasonable to publish them." [20] Seasonableness came in 1774, when it was learned that counsels of moderation had failed in London and the series of " Intolerable Acts " were fanning fiery colonial tempers to fever heat. Consequently, the pamphlet came out just in time to be distributed among the delegates to the First Continental Congress, and by them must have been carried into every American colony. Wilson's arguments went far towards

19 Advertisement to paper " On the Legislative Authority of the British Parliament," dated August 17, 1774, in Andrews, *Works of Wilson,* II, 503.

20 *Loc. cit.* One reason for the comparatively recent revival of admiration for Wilson is that historians and political scientists have suddenly recognized the close similarity between Wilson's ideas and the present constitution of the British Commonwealth of Nations.

convincing the colonists that revolt was legal, and that in revolt they would not make themselves rebels.[21]

At this point, emphasis may be placed on certain ideas propagated by Wilson with extraordinary acuteness and foresight. In denying the authority of Parliament over the colonies, he affirmed " that all the different members of the British empire are distinct states, independent of each other, but connected together under the same sovereign, in right of the same crown " [22] —a description applicable to the British Commonwealth of the twentieth century. Wilson was convinced that the colonial assemblies were the constitutional equals of Parliament, a conclusion which proceeded naturally from his ideas of the equality of all the members of the British Empire.

Wilson accepted the concept of unconstitutionality of laws and mentioned it in his address of January 1775 as though it were so well known that it need not be discussed.[23] This theory, a development of American jurisprudence, unknown to Parliament and to English lawyers (who could not comprehend how Parliament could pass an " unconstitutional " act),[24] became a major political barrier between the mother country and the colonies.

It was during the Revolutionary period that Wilson first expounded the idea that later he would develop insistently—the hypothesis that power came first from the people and that, there-

21 Alexander in *The Green Bag*, XIX, 7.

22 Andrews, *Works of Wilson*, II, 542, note 1. In regard to trade, a problem which seriously worried his contemporaries, Wilson suggested that the power of regulating the trade of the Empire might be added to the royal prerogative and the king exercise it. *Loc. cit. Cf.* also Adams, *Essays of Wilson*, p. 13.

23 Speech in Convention of Pennsylvania, January 1775. In Andrews, *Works of Wilson*, II, 556-557. Later, Wilson was to insist that this power of judicial review did not go far enough—that judges should also have " revisionary power " to pass on bills in the process of enactment. Max Farrand, ed., *Records of the Federal Convention of 1787*, II (Rev. ed., New Haven: Yale University Press, 1937), p. 73.

24 Adams, *Essays of Wilson*, p. 14.

fore, they alone were sovereign. In his Address to the Inhabitants of the Colonies, February 13, 1776, he said,

> That all *Power was originally in the People—that all the Powers of government are derived from them—that all Power, which they have not disposed of, still continues theirs*—are Maxims of the *English* Constitution, which, we presume, will not be disputed.[25]

Wilson had so far advanced in popular fame that he was elected with Franklin to the Second Continental Congress, and was re-elected successively in November 1775, July 1776, and March 1777.[26] He was superseded at the election of September 1777, mainly because a rival political party had come to power.

Wilson was among the group which, at first insisting that America could be free without being independent, turned to independence only as a last resort. The Pennsylvania delegates were expressly forbidden to vote for independence by instructions from the state Assembly and until these were rescinded on June 14, Wilson was bound to obey them regardless of his own opinions.[27] Nor were the Pennsylvanians the only delegates so circumscribed. Wilson joined with a group of leaders in postponing the vote until the restrictive instructions of the various states could be removed. Meanwhile, the committee to draft the declaration was appointed, in order that there might be little delay when the desired unanimity was attained.[28]

25 Reprinted in *ibid.*, p. 106.

26 Wilson had not been re-elected on Feb. 5, 1777, various new delegates being chosen to supersede him and other signers of the Declaration of Independence. However, the force of public opinion and the urgent request of General Washington returned Wilson and George Clymer to Congress. Alexander in *The Green Bag*, XIX, 105.

27 Konkle, *James Wilson and the Constitution*, pp. 15-16.

28 Full explanation, giving, perhaps, too much credit to Wilson, by Alexander in *The Green Bag*, XIX, 7-9, and in Konkle, *James Wilson and the Constitution*, pp. 15-17. Alexander claims to print for the first time the document signed by the members of the Second Continental Congress and dated June 20, 1776, certifying that Wilson acted only under instructions in postponing independence. When the resolution for independence was

Wilson served diligently in the Continental Congress. He was put on most of the important committees, and was constantly engaged in writing reports, besides negotiating with Indians in the West and conferring with generals in their camps. On January 30, 1777, moved by the many admiralty appeals coming before it, Congress decided to appoint a standing committee to hear them, rather than designate a special committee for each appeal. Wilson was made chairman of this Committee on Appeals, and thus became the presiding officer of the first supreme federal Court of Appeals having a semblance of permanency— an ancestor of the present Supreme Court.[29]

Though Wilson held the rank of Brigadier-General and Director-General of the Philadelphia militia, he was at no time in the field. Rather, he concentrated upon the administrative work of Congress and organizing the conduct and supply of operations.[30]

After his retirement from Congress, Wilson settled down to an extremely lucrative practice in Philadelphia. For five years, he was not seen in the halls of government where he had done so much to secure the independence that he had helped to declare.[31] In the interim, as a private citizen, he rendered the na-

adopted, July 2, 1776, all the states except New York concurred. New York finally agreed on July 15. See John H. Hazelton, *The Declaration of Independence, Its History* (New York: 1906), especially chapters viii-ix. An interesting sidelight on Wilson-inspired changes in the text of the Declaration was given by Jefferson in a letter written Dec. 4, 1818. " When the Declaration of Independence was under the consideration of Congress, there were two or three unlucky expressions in it which gave offence to some members. The words ' Scotch and other foreign auxiliaries' excited the ire of a gentleman or two of that country "—and were quickly stricken out. *Ibid.*, p. 178.

29 Alexander in *The Green Bag*, XIX, 101-104. A second committee for the same purpose was appointed May 8, 1777, and Wilson was retained as chairman.

30 During the British occupation of Philadelphia, he lived in Annapolis, Maryland. Bennett, *James Wilson of St. Andrews*, pp. 30, 32.

31 Wilson was not popular with the common people of Philadelphia, apparently because of his huge land speculations at a time of poverty, and a legal way of thinking which they could not understand. The affair of " Fort Wilson," Oct. 3, 1779, in which Wilson's house was attacked by an armed

tion many services, not the least of which was the maintenance of close relations with America's chief ally, France. On September 15, 1779, the French minister plenipotentiary notified Congress that Wilson had been constituted Advocate-General of the French nation, " in order that he may be charged with all the causes and matters relative to navigation and commerce." [32] Wilson eventually offered his services free to the French government [33]—quite a concession, for at the time he commanded higher fees than any other lawyer in Philadelphia. The treaty of 1778 with France had provided that commercial relations and a consular system were to be established, and it devolved upon Wilson to draft the agreement for France in 1780. The outline of jurisdiction and procedure of courts in international commercial causes, as well as an elaborate consular system which he drafted, later became the basis for the system adopted by the United States.[34]

Beginning in 1779, Wilson maintained an active correspondence—often in cipher—with the American commissioners in France. Also, he devoted himself to the study of finance, an expression of his concern over the instability of the currency. He drew up a plan for a national bank in 1780 and made extensive " Observations on Finance." [35] Closely associated with Robert Morris, whose legal adviser he was, in the organization of the Bank of North America, he was appointed one of the directors

mob, is an indication of this fact. Waln in *Biography of the Signers*, VI, 145-152. See also John F. Watson, *Annals of Philadelphia and Pennsylvania in the Olden Time*, enlarged by Willis P. Hazard, III (Philadelphia: 1877), 286-287. Wilson served again in the Congress of the Confederation in 1783 and from 1785 until the dissolution of that government. Alexander in *The Green Bag*, XIX, 138-139.

32 Alexander in *The Green Bag*, XIX, 108.

33 Waln records in the *Biography of the Signers* that the King of France gave Wilson the "princely remuneration" of 10,000 livres in November 1783, for his services. VI, 127.

34 Alexander in *The Green Bag*, XIX, 109.

35 *Ibid.*, XIX, 137. These manuscripts are among the *Wilsonia* of the Historical Society of Pennsylvania.

by Congress on December 31, 1781, and at the same time became counsel for the Bank.[36]

In 1785, Wilson developed another theory destined to be of supreme importance in the interpretation of the Constitution. This was the doctrine of implied powers, which he invoked to support the incorporation of the Bank of North America by the Continental Congress.[37] The Articles of Confederation had no specific provision for chartering a bank, and all unenumerated powers were reserved to the states. But, asked Wilson, could any state charter a Bank of North America for all the states? Obviously not; neither had any state ever had such a power. Therefore, the lack of express delegation to the Congress did not mean that the states retained a power they had never had. Rather the authority in question belonged inherently to an independent nation.[38]

It was in the Federal Convention that Wilson made his greatest contribution to his adopted country. Pennsylvania appointed seven delegates, any four of whom were authorized to represent the state. Wilson was the strongest member of this group, and one of the strongest men in the convention as well.[39] He was forty-five at the time, and was regarded as among the ablest lawyers in America.

36 *Loc. cit.*

37 This report was used by Hamilton as the basis for his report to Washington on the constitutionality of the first Bank of the United States.

38 Reprinted in Andrews, *Works of Wilson,* II, 549-577. Adams notes in his *Essays of Wilson,* p. 18, note 6, that Professor Jesse S. Reeves objects to calling this "the 'doctrine of implied powers,'" because he says it goes much farther. It should be called, he believes, a 'doctrine of inherent sovereignty.'" The Bank had been chartered by the Congress of the Confederation and later by the state of Pennsylvania, where it was located. Wilson prepared his "Considerations" when a bill came up in the Pennsylvania legislature (and eventually passed) to repeal the state act granting the charter. This argument was directed toward demonstrating that the charter from Congress was all that was necessary.

39 Madison is generally rated as the Number One man in the convention, though some more recent students are beginning to claim the title for Wilson. See Adams, *Essays of Wilson,* p. 20.

Tall and large featured, his nearsightedness compelling the use of glasses and adding a touch of sternness to his appearance, he had won the respect of many but the affection of few.[40]

In the early stages of debate over the various plans for constitutions submitted to the Convention, Madison and Wilson were prominent advocates of a strong central government.[41] In general, Wilson favored the popular election of both the executive and legislators. For ratifying the Federal Constitution, he supported popularly chosen conventions in each state, and, with Pinckney, suggested ratification by less than the whole number of states.[42]

Wilson's participation in the Federal Convention may be traced in detail in Max Farrand's admirable *Records*. Exceedingly active in debate, he had an opinion on every important issue. As a member of the Committee on Detail, he was responsible for much of the final form of the Constitution.[43]

Farrand's judgment of Wilson, made after more than ten years of study in the records of the Federal Convention, is as follows:

> Second to Madison and almost on a par with him was James Wilson. In some respects he was Madison's intellectual superior, but in the immediate work before them he was not as adaptable and not as practical. Still he was Madison's ablest supporter. He appreciated the importance of laying the foundations of the new government broad and deep, and he believed that this could only be done by basing it upon the people themselves. This was the principal thing for which he

40 Max Farrand, *The Framing of the Constitution of the United States* (New Haven: 1913), p. 21. "'James the Caledonian,' as he was sometimes called, was rather a tribute to his character and his oratory than a mark of popularity." *Loc. cit.* See, however, *infra*, p. 53.

41 Farrand, *Framing of the Constitution*, p. 81.

42 *Ibid.*, pp. 80-81.

43 *Ibid.*, p. 126.

contended in the convention, and with a great measure of success.[44]

Alone among the large Pennsylvania delegation to the Federal Convention, Wilson was chosen to sit in the state convention called to ratify the Constitution. Wilson's first defense of the Constitution was made at a mass meeting in Philadelphia. Here he replied to all the false charges brought against the new instrument and sought to make clear just what its purposes and terms were.[45] At the convention, all the speeches were recorded stenographically, so Wilson's have been preserved. Wilson's speeches and those of Chief Justice Thomas McKean were published in London in 1792 under the title of *Commentaries on the Constitution of the United States of America, in which are unfolded the principles of free government and the superior advantages of republicanism demonstrated.*[46]

Wilson was attacked with the most violent political bitterness for his stand on the Constitution, and together with Chief Justice McKean was burned in effigy at Carlisle, Pennsylvania.

44 *Ibid.*, pp. 197-198. Adams prefers Farrand's estimate to that of any of the other scholars on the Federal Convention. See *Essays of Wilson*, p. 19. Also see the surprisingly similar appraisal by George Ticknor Curtis in his *History of the Origin, Formation and Adoption of the Constitution of the United States; with Notices of Its Principal Framers*, II (New York: 1858), 520-521. In 1858, Curtis noted that Wilson was one of the ablest members of the Federal Convention, but was being ignored by historians.

45 Konkle, *James Wilson and the Constitution*, p. 27. Address reprinted in Adams, *Essays of Wilson*, pp. 151-160. *Cf.* Elliot's *Debates* (Washington: 1827-30), and J. B. McMaster and F. D. Stone, *Pennsylvania and the Federal Constitution* (Historical Society of Pennsylvania: 1888), *passim.*

46 All but fifteen of the 150 pages contained Wilson's speeches. It is believed that this is the first instance of the use of the title, *Commentaries on the Constitution of the United States.* Lucien Hugh Alexander in " James Wilson, Patriot, and the Wilson Doctrine," *North American Review*, 183 (Nov. 16, 1906), 971-989, has collected and reprinted encomiums of Wilson, including comments from James Bryce, who is said to have gained his insights into Wilson's theories of government from these *Commentaries.* McMaster and Stone in *Pennsylvania and the Federal Constitution* point out that only the speeches of Wilson and McKean were allowed to be printed. The full record of the debates was suppressed. (Pp. 14-15).

Called derisively " Jimmy," " Jamie," or " James de Caledonia "
—this latter being the inscription fastened to the coat of the effigy—Wilson still adhered to his principles and at last helped
win from the convention the ratification of the Constitution.[47]

When the requisite number of states had ratified, a great cele-
bration was held in Philadelphia on July 4, 1788. In the impressive procession, each of the thirteen states was represented by a
distinguished citizen, Pennsylvania by Wilson who also was
selected to deliver an oration at Independence Hall before (as
the reports have it) 20,000 listeners.[48]

When the United States Supreme Court was first constituted,
Wilson had suggested his own name to Washington as the most
logical appointee to the Chief Justiceship [49]—a suggestion in

47 Alexander in *The Green Bag*, XIX, 146.

48 *Ibid.*, XIX, 265. *Cf.* Francis Hopkinson's *Account of the Grand Federal
Procession, Philadelphia, July 4, 1788* ... (Philadelphia: 1788) for descrip-
tion of these festivities. The address is in Hopkinson's pamphlet and in
Bird Wilson, *The Works of the Honourable James Wilson, LL.D.*, III
(Philadelphia: 1804), 299-311.

49 Wilson wrote Washington as follows: "A delicacy arising from your
situation and character as well as my own has hitherto prevented me from
mentioning to your Excellency a subject of much importance to me. Perhaps
I should not even now have broke silence but for one consideration. A
regard to the dignity of the government over which you preside will naturally lead you to take care that its honors be in no event exposed to affected
indifference or contempt. For this reason, you may well expect that, before
you nominate any gentleman to an employment (especially one of high
trust), you should have it in your power to preclude him, in case of disappointment, from pretending that the nomination was made without his
knowledge or consent. Under this view, I commit myself to your Excellency
without reserve and inform you that my aim rises to the important office
of Chief Justice of the United States. But how shall I proceed? Shall I
enumerate reasons in justification of my high pretensions? I have not yet
employed my pen in my own praise. When I make those high pretensions
and offer them to so good a judge, can I say that they are altogether without foundation? Your Excellency must relieve me from this dilemma. You
will think and act properly on the occasion, without my saying anything
on either side of the question." Wilson to Washington, April 21, 1789,
*Calendar of Applications and Recommendations for Office under the
Presidency of George Washington* (1901) by Gaillard Hunt. Quoted in
Charles Warren, *The Supreme Court in United States History*, I (Boston:
1922), 33-34.

which Washington apparently did not concur, however high his opinion of Wilson as a lawyer. Wilson had to be content with an associate justiceship, the first position going to John Jay.[50]

Business was slow for the first Supreme Court, as it had to wait for cases to be appealed from the lower courts. Therefore, Wilson had ample time to assume another responsibility, that of professor of law at the College of Philadelphia, a newly created position. The establishment of a law professorship was made by the trustees at the suggestion of Charles Smith, son of the provost of the College, who had formerly been a student of Wilson's.[51] Smith had apparently planned to deliver the lectures himself, but the committee of three to whom the plan was referred thought otherwise. Wilson, one of these three,[52] prepared an outline for a course of law lectures which was made part of the committee's report.[53]

Wilson eagerly anticipated his first lecture on law, recognizing his opportunity to become the American Blackstone. It was delivered December 15, 1790, in the hall of the " Academy," and was a gala event.

50 Wilson supporters ascribe his failure to be appointed Chief Justice to the fact that Washington had already decided to appoint Thomas Jefferson Secretary of State. Jay had held that position under the Confederation, so had to be given an equally exalted place in the new government. Hence, he was made head of the Judiciary.

51 Francis Hopkinson, at a meeting of trustees, March 16, 1789, requested that a number of young gentlemen, students in law, who had formed themselves into a society for mutual improvement, might have permission to hold meetings in one of the rooms of the college. The request was granted, according to the *Minutes of the Board of Trustees*, II, 171. Hampton L. Carson, *An Historical Sketch of the Law Department of the University of Pennsylvania* (Philadelphia: 1882), pp. 8-9.

52 He had been a trustee of the College for several years and had taught English there between 1773 and 1779. Bennett, *Wilson of St. Andrews*, pp. 15-16. He resigned his trusteeship when he became a professor. Carson, *Pennsylvania Law Department*, pp. 13-14.

53 The outline was prepared in August 1790. Most of it is reprinted in *The Green Bag*, XIX, 266-268.

A distinguished and brilliant audience awaited the lecturer. The gallery was crowded with those citizens who had received tickets of admission from Judge Wilson himself: President Washington and his Cabinet, both Houses of Congress, the Supreme Executive Council, the members of the Assembly, the Mayor, Aldermen and Common Councilmen, the Judges of the Courts, citizens of mark and influence, and members of the bar, occupied the lower part of the hall,—" a polite assemblage; "—while the stately and powdered dames who clustered about Mrs. Washington and Mrs. Hamilton, of the Woodlands, by the interest they displayed, embarrassed the lecturer, who " never before had the honour of addressing a *fair* audience." [54]

Wilson's visions of being the American Vinerian sage were to be disappointed. Only his first lecture was published during his lifetime, the others after his death. The course was not completed. Of its three planned parts, the first was delivered in the winter of 1790-91, and a portion of the second, the following winter.[55] Shortly thereafter, the College of Philadelphia merged with another college to form the University of Pennsylvania.[56] A new law professorship was erected on April 3, 1792 and Wilson was appointed to fill the chair, but no lectures were delivered.[57]

Wilson's failure to shape a thriving law school at Philadelphia cannot be fully explained, though according to William Rawle's recollection many years later, the lectures did not " entirely meet the expectation that had been formed." [58] The fact that his fees were very high undoubtedly had something to do with it. Fees required of his office students were also above

54 Carson, *Pennsylvania Law Department*, p. 14. Quoted from the *Packet*, Dec. 15, 1790.

55 No degrees were conferred during Wilson's professorship. *Ibid.*, p. 18.

56 *Ibid.*, pp. 8-9.

57 *Ibid.*, p. 15.

58 Rawle, Second Address in *Two Addresses to the Associated Members of the Bar of Philadelphia* (Philadelphia: 1824), p. 44.

those asked by other members of the bar.[59] Scholars are usually impressed by General Washington's insistence that his nephew, Bushrod Washington, later a justice of the Supreme Court, study in Wilson's office, by-passing all the notable lawyers of Virginia. The originals of Washington's note for one hundred guineas and Wilson's receipt have been preserved.[60] But the advantages to be had at such a cost were slight. Mr. Wilson rarely went to his office except to consult his books, and the time spent on his students was small.

> Hence his intercourse with them was rare, distant, and reserved. As an instructor, he was almost useless to those who were under his direction. He would never engage with them in professional discussions; to a direct question he gave the shortest possible answer; and a general request for information was always evaded.[61]

He liked to dwell upon general principles and to deal with great governmental problems, and he refused to descend to the trifles, technicalities, and niceties of the law.[62]

Wilson's ideas on the Constitution are included in his *Lectures on Law,* as the three volumes of his works edited by his son were generally known. They were used by most of the later commentators and their authority was recognized in the United States Supreme Court. The volumes include all the lectures which Wilson had planned to deliver, though many of them reached the public only in printed form.

Judge Wilson's later years were clouded with projects which did not materialize. He was commissioned to make a digest of the laws of Pennsylvania, but had to give it up when the legislature refused to advance additional funds.[63] He commended

59 Carson, *Pennsylvania Law Department,* pp. 15-16.

60 Copy in Carson, *loc. cit.,* and *The Green Bag,* XIX, 266-267.

61 Waln in *Biography of the Signers,* VI, 171-172.

62 *Ibid.,* VI, 172.

63 He continued the project for some time, using his own funds, and assembled most of the pertinent material. He was, however, unable to complete the work.

himself to Washington to do the same service for the Federal Constitution, i.e., to set up principles that were consonant with the Constitution before they were called into operation. Washington's attorney-general advised against any such codification, and the matter was dropped.[64]

As a member of the Supreme Court, Wilson gave his greatest service in the case of Chisholm v. Georgia,[65] in which he enunciated the principle that a state could be called before the federal courts as a defendant. So great was the uproar against this decision that the Eleventh Amendment to the Constitution, in which the practice was specifically prohibited, was promptly adopted.

A contemporary remarked that Mr. Wilson on the bench did not equal Mr. Wilson at the bar.

> Late in life he became deeply involved in speculations in land, and his financial misfortunes deprived him of the equanimity of mind so necessary to the proper performance of the duties of a judge, but apart from this, his temper and habits of thought were those of an advocate, and his style . . . [was] diffusive.[66]

Wilson's involvements in the land speculations of the day were too complex to be discussed here. Suffice it to say that they were extremely widespread and complicated, and that when the bubble burst, Wilson was all but ruined. In 1797, he moved to Burlington, New Jersey, to escape an arrest for debt. In spite of talk of impeachment, he retained his place on the bench, though he decided to trade circuits with Justice Iredell in order that he might not have to try cases in Pennsylvania, where the rural districts were bitter against him. He died on August 21, 1798,

64 Julian P. Boyd in the *Dictionary of American Biography*. From Washington Papers, vol. CXVI, Library of Congress.

65 2 Dall. 419 at 453 (1793). The opinions of the justices were delivered *seriatim* at this time.

66 Carson, *Pennsylvania Law Department*, p. 13. Based on a remark by "Mr. Watson, in his Annals [I, 320], quoting the published opinion of Mr. Rawle." Rawle, *Two Addresses to the Philadelphia Bar*, p. 44. Also cf. Waln in *Biography of the Signers*, VI, 171.

at Edenton, North Carolina, Iredell's home, after suffering from a nervous disorder. Apparently the fact that he had been arrested for debt, at long last, was too much for his proud spirit.[67]

To estimate the character and contribution of Justice Wilson is extremely difficult, as scholars seem to vie in pointing out characteristics that are worthy of either high encomiums or severe censure. Burton Alva Konkle, whose huge manuscript still awaits a publisher, grew to admire Wilson tremendously; yet consulting the same material, Julian P. Boyd who wrote the article in the *Dictionary of American Biography,* concludes that the whole of Wilson's learned writings may be charged with the fault of special pleading because of his ambition for place and power and his avid desire for wealth. Yet his personal failings notwithstanding, Wilson remains one of the foremost thinkers of his time, and one to whom the present-day United States owes much.

### WILLIAM RAWLE

While Wilson was actively promoting the interests of the new government, another Philadelphian was establishing himself. William Rawle was born April 28, 1759, scion of a long line of distinguished gentry. The accidental death of his father when William was two years old, laid upon his mother the care of three small children.[68]

---

[67] Griffith J. McRee, *Life and Correspondence of James Iredell,* II (New York: 1858), 532-535. Alexander in *The Green Bag,* XIX, 274-275. Wilson did not tell his wife, Hannah, that he had been arrested, and she was at a loss to understand much of what he said while delirious. She was told after his death. Wilson's first wife, Rachel Bird, whom he married in 1772, died in 1786. He had married Hannah Gray in 1793.

[68] Thomas I. Wharton, "A Memoir of William Rawle, LL.D.," *Memoirs of the Historical Society of Pennsylvania,* IV, Part 1 (Philadelphia: 1840), p. 40. There is a biography of Rawle, based in part on Wharton's " Memoir," though with the emphasis shifted to the family home, Laurel Hill, by Thomas Allen Glenn, *Some Colonial Mansions and Those Who Lived in Them, with Genealogies of the Various Families Mentioned* (2nd series, Philadelphia: 1900), pp. 140-170.

Following the family beliefs, William was educated in Quaker schools, and was apparently a student at the Friends' Academy, a collegiate institution, when the Revolution broke out. The Rawles and their friends were Loyalists, and William's stepfather, Samuel Shoemaker, was the mayor of Philadelphia during the British occupation.[69] When the British evacuated the city, Mr. Shoemaker, also, had to withdraw,[70] so he left for New York in June 1778, taking William with him. William began the study of law under John Tabor Kempe, the British Attorney General, but " New York . . . in its then condition, did not afford sufficient opportunities and inducements for the study of a peaceful science." [71] As Rawle wrote in a letter,

> In the profession which I have chosen, it is impossible to obtain even a slender knowledge of essentials in the situation of things here. This every body agrees to; and the reason is, the military government which prevails; in consequence of which the still small voice of the law is seldom heard and never attended to.[72]

Oppressed by these circumstances, Rawle determined to go to England. One of his biographers thinks that Rawle's childhood Loyalism was due to his family, and that as he grew older, his admiration for Washington and Washington's cause made him waver from the political faith of his family. Furthermore, he was a Quaker, and held to their doctrine of non-resistance.[73] He stood, therefore, with one foot on religious principle when he said, " I have in no one instance taken a decisive part on either side." [74]

69 Wharton, " Memoir," p. 42. Mrs. Rawle married Shoemaker, a prominent merchant, on Nov. 10, 1767. Glenn, *Colonial Mansions*, p. 143.

70 On March 6, 1778, the State Legislature had declared Shoemaker and others guilty of high treason, and all their estates forfeited unless they surrendered by April 20 following. Shoemaker refused, and suffered the consequences. *Ibid.*, p. 145.

71 Wharton, " Memoir," p. 43.

72 *Ibid.*, p. 44.

73 Glenn, *Colonial Mansions*, p. 148.

74 Wharton, " Memoir," p. 51. Letter to his mother, Jan. 1, 1782.

Arriving in London in August 1781, William immediately entered the Middle Temple.[75] He alone of the commentators had the training of this venerable institution. We have no record of the particulars, but whatever young Rawle brought away with him from the Middle Temple was acceptable in America. He returned in January of 1783, declared his allegiance to the new American government,[76] and was admitted to practice in the Court of Common Pleas for the City and County of Philadelphia on September 15 of the same year. Less than two months later, he was married to a childhood playmate, Miss Sarah Coates Burge.

His early professional career was rather discouraging, according to his friend, Thomas I. Wharton. Not only had he to compete with Wilson, Lewis, and other prominent lawyers, but he had also to live down his early relations with the Loyalists. During the ten years between his admission to the bar and the time when he felt himself " rooted in his position, and assured of success," [77] Rawle met one of his future good friends, the young French immigrant, DuPonceau, whom we shall consider later.[78]

Rawle sided with Wilson in supporting the new Constitution, and even had a small share in facilitating the work of the Convention. As secretary of the Library Company of Philadelphia,

75 *Ibid.*, p. 45. Rawle kept journals of his stay in England and of his trip to the Continent, from which Wharton quotes. In addition to the ability to write easily, he could draw. His journals are illustrated with sketches of scenery and figures " very naturally delineated." Rawle's attendance at the Middle Temple is mentioned in E. Alfred Jones, *American Members of the Inns of Court* (London: 1924), pp. 180-181, and John Hutchinson, *A Catalogue of Notable Middle Templars with Brief Biographical Notices* (London: 1902), p. 203.

76 Glenn, *Colonial Mansions*, p. 167, quoting Prof. Vethake, but without citing source. *Cf.* Wharton, " Memoir," pp. 54-55.

77 Wharton, " Memoir," p. 54. On the other hand, David Paul Brown said that Rawle had been at the front rank of the Philadelphia bar from the first. " Eulogium upon William Rawle, LL.D.," delivered Dec. 31, 1836 (Philadelphia: 1837). This eulogy was reprinted in *The Forum*, I (Philadelphia: 1856). See especially p. 501.

78 *Cf. infra*, next section.

he signed the Company's letter inviting the delegates to use its collection of books.[79]

In 1789, he was elected to his one political office—membership in the state Assembly for the city of Philadelphia. He served his term only—a single year. In politics, Glenn describes him as a "decided Federalist," though Wharton tells us that Rawle did not approve all the measures of that party during its last few years in power.[80]

Rawle had come to know Washington in Philadelphia, and evidently made so good an impression that he was offered the attorney-generalship of the United States when the first President took office.[81] This position he declined, but was induced to accept the post of Attorney of the United States for the District of Pennsylvania, which he held from July 1791 until his resignation in May 1800. During his nine years of service, he was called upon to uphold the authority of the United States when it was challenged by two insurrections,[82] and in spite of his difficult position, retained the respect of all factions.

Since Rawle was convinced that his place was not in the political arena, he was content to stay by his profession, particularly as his own position in it grew lucrative. In 1808, Joseph Story described Rawle, arguing before the Supreme Court as

> quite a plain but genteel man, [who] looks like a studious, ingenious, and able lawyer. He argues with a very pleasant

79 Farrand, *Records of the Federal Convention*, I, 548 and note. Journal entry for July 7, 1787.

80 Wharton, "Memoir," p. 55; Glenn, *Colonial Mansions*, p. 168.

81 Brown in *The Forum*, I, 505. It seems likely that Rawle made Washington's acquaintance at the home of the elderly Dr. Franklin, who had organized a "Society for Political Inquiries." Washington was a member of this group, as were Rawle and Wilson. Wharton, "Memoir," p. 57.

82 *Ibid.*, pp. 55-56. James Wilson had called the situation of the Whisky Rebellion to Washington's attention by a letter stating merely the barest facts. *Cf.* Alexander in *The Green Bag*, XIX, 273. It was Rawle's duty to accompany the District Judge and the military on the Western Expedition in 1794 and prosecute the offenders after the insurrections in that year and in 1798 had been put down. Wharton, "Memoir," p. 56.

voice, and has great neatness, perspicacity, and even elegance. He keeps his object steadily in view; he distinguishes with care, enforces with strength, and if he fails to convince, he seldom spends his thoughts vainly.[83]

Rawle was elected one of the Trustees of the recently consolidated University of Pennsylvania in 1795,[84] when Wilson was still listed as professor of law. His part in legal education came later, and was to be indirect, as he did not lecture personally. In 1820, when the Society for the Promotion of Legal Knowledge and Forensic Eloquence was formed among the judges and members of the bar, Rawle was named vice president. Though the society was shortlived,[85] it gave an impulse to legal studies, especially to the Law Academy instituted under its patronage. Rawle was much interested in the Law Academy, and " delighted in promoting the progress and advancement of the rising generation." [86]

In 1820 or thereabout, Governor Hiester twice offered Rawle the position of Presiding Judge of the District Court of the City and County of Philadelphia. He was admittedly well-fitted for the post and would have enjoyed judicial life, but at this time the salaries of judges all over the United States were still

83 Story, *Life and Letters*, I, 162-163.

84 Wharton, " Memoir," p. 59. In a published lecture delivered in 1823, his second annual discourse as Chancellor of the Society of Associated Members of the Bar of Philadelphia, Rawle gave " interesting recollections of the worthies of olden time," including Mr. Wilson. Second of *Two Addresses to the Bar of Philadelphia*, especially pp. 43-44. *Cf.* Wharton, " Memoir," pp. 61-62. The Society of Associated Members of the Bar combined with the Law Library Company of Philadelphia, under the corporate name of the Law Association of Philadelphia. Rawle was elected Chancellor of the new group and continued in that office until his death.

85 The Society was incorporated in 1821, and dissolved because of an accident. The room in which the election of officers was to have been held was found locked, so no election took place. The Society was not revived and the Law Academy continued without it. P. S. DuPonceau, " Memoir of William Rawle," *Memoirs of the Historical Society of Pennsylvania*, IV, Part 1, pp 90-91.

86 *Ibid.*, p. 91.

so low as to keep many men from the bench. Mr. Rawle's income from his practice was considerably more than he would have received as a judge, and his domestic responsibilities were still heavy.

In 1825, Mr. Rawle published his *View of the Constitution of the United States,* his most important juridical writing. This seems to be the earliest work devoted entirely to the Constitution, in which the background, philosophy, and articles of that document are discussed systematically. It is the concise presentation of the material which gave the volume its widespread and long-lasting appeal as a textbook. Rawle himself prepared one revision, and shortly before his death, Dartmouth College applied to him for a third edition, a request which he did not feel able to grant.[87]

Though admittedly a valuable and able study, Rawle's *View of the Constitution* stirred up controversy. Rawle himself was a Federalist, but his studies in government had led him to the judgment that the Union was not irrevocable. His final chapter on " The Union " [88] includes a detailed statement that the right of secession was necessary to the fundamental right of a people to choose their own form of government. In spite of this concession to a doctrine inadmissible to the nationalists, the book was widely current in the North. It was used even in Justice Story's stronghold, the Harvard Law School.[89]

In several ways, Rawle may be considered as providing the transitional step between the North and the South. His *View* was published midway between the inauguration of the Federal Government and the outbreak of the War between the States. Though admitting the possibility of secession, he had Washington as his earthly model and he revered the Federal Union. A member of the Maryland Society for Promoting the Abolition

---

87 Brown in *The Forum,* I, 523. Dartmouth had conferred a LL.D. degree on Rawle in 1828.

88 Entitled " Of the Permanence of the Union " in the second edition (1829).

89 *Cf. infra,* ch. ix.

of Slavery, he was its president from 1818 until his death. On the other hand, as a moderate, he disapproved of the radical abolition societies formed in the eighteen-thirties.[90]

Like most of the commentators, Rawle was busy until near the very end of his life. In 1830, at the age of seventy-one, he was appointed a commissioner with Thomas I. Wharton and the Honorable Joel Jones " to revise, collate, and digest all such public acts and statutes of the civil code of this State [Pennsylvania], and all such British statutes in force in this State as are general, and permanent in their nature." The commission was instructed to consider and report what alterations and improvements were required therein.[91]

> During the four years of employment under this commission, his colleagues found him always ready for business, always prepared with his quota of work, always prompt in communicating his abundant knowledge, and equally disposed to receive the suggestions of others, and remarkably free from prejudice or tenacity of opinion . . . . Mr. Rawle joined in all the reports made by the commissioners to the Legislature, excepting the last; which was prepared and transmitted in March 1836, a few weeks only before his decease.[92]

In contrast with most of the other commentators, Mr. Rawle spent a quiet and retiring life. His friend, Wharton, has described him as an " accomplished jurist, a good scholar, and a person of great taste and great general acquirements." [93] He was not only learned in the jurisprudence of England and America, but was well versed in ancient and modern European law. Another eulogist, Brown, adds that " With Rawle, the law was but *one* of the elements in the proud structure of his emi-

---

90 Brown in *The Forum*, I, 511-513. This tribute was prepared under appointment of the Maryland Society for Promoting the Abolition of Slavery. Brown had read the twenty volumes and more of Rawle's *Journal.*

91 Wharton, " Memoir," p. 65.

92 *Ibid.*, p. 66. Rawle died on April 12, 1836.

93 *Ibid.*, p. 69.

nence. The whole circle of arts and sciences was tributary to his formation." [94] Although toward the end of his life, he was known to the legal profession as the " Nestor of the Philadelphia bar," [95] he coupled with this lofty distinction the human qualities which marked him in men's memories as a respected adversary and a valued friend.

## PETER STEPHEN DUPONCEAU

While Rawle's life was drawing to its close, his old friend, Peter DuPonceau, was still living vigorously in Philadelphia, teaching in the Law Academy. Since his arrival in America as a young man, in the midst of the Revolution, he had grown to be a most loyal citizen. Born Pierre Etienne DuPonceau on June 3, 1760, he later anglicized his Christian names, and is known in legal annals as Peter Stephen DuPonceau.

Pierre's youth was spent in the town of his birth—St. Martin's on the Ile de Ré, off the coast of La Vendée, France. His father came from a noble family, and at the time held a military command on the Ile de Ré.[96]

By the time he was six, Pierre had acquired good French and Latin vocabularies and was studying both at an excellent grammar school, and under private teachers at home.[97] Very

---

94 Brown in *The Forum*, I, 506.

95 Glenn, *Colonial Mansions*, p. 169.

96 Obituary notice by John Pickering, *Journal of the American Oriental Society*, I (1844), 162. The correspondence between Pickering and DuPonceau on law and "the most obscure departments of philology would alone fill a large volume." Andrew Preston Peabody, *Harvard Graduates Whom I Have Known* (Boston and New York: 1890), p. 53. See also Evart A. and George L. Duyckinck, *Cyclopedia of American Literature*, I (New York: 1856), 578. DuPonceau's brother was the Marquis DuPonceau. The latter visited the United States at about the time of the French Revolution, and seems to have been as positively royalist as our adopted countryman was republican. *Law Reporter*, VII (May 1844), 62. See also brief biography in Watson, *Annals of Philadelphia and Pennsylvania in the Olden Time*, III, 283-286.

97 DuPonceau to Robert Walsh, May 12, 1836, *Pa. Mag. Hist. and Biog.*, LXIII (April 1939), 195-196. *Amer. Law Mag.*, V, 2. DuPonceau's letters,

soon, he was busy learning English. He enjoyed Milton and Shakespeare so much that he never acquired a truly national fondness for the literature of France. His schoolmates called him " l'Anglois." [98]

Pierre did much as he pleased until he was thirteen, staying at home and reading. He was taught mathematics, geography, history, military fortifications, etc., by some of the well-educated recruits who offered to instruct the DuPonceau children in return for some easing of military discipline by Captain DuPonceau.[99]

Pierre's father had intended him to be a military engineer, but nearsightedness prevented him from entering the army. In 1773, he made noteworthy progress in the Benedictine College at St. Jean d'Angely; [100] and there, eighteen months later, upon the death of his father, and at the request of his family, he reluctantly undertook to become a priest. He soon tired of the college at Bressuire in Poitou, where the Bishop of Rochelle had put him as an instructor; so he fled to Paris.[101]

He had already absorbed some of the principles of the Reformation in the Ile de Ré, the population of which was half Protestant. He was led to abandon study for the priesthood, he

---

constituting an autobiography from his birth to 1783, are edited by James L. Whitehead for the *Pennsylvania Magazine of History and Biography*, vols. LXIII-LXIV (April 1939-April 1940). The information in the article in the *American Law Magazine*, V (April 1845), 1-33, was collected by Robley Dunglison from private letters of DuPonceau to his friend, Mr. Walsh, and to his granddaughter, Miss Garesché (i. e., the autobiography mentioned above), and was delivered as a public discourse before the American Philosophical Society, October 25, 1844.

98 DuPonceau to Walsh, May 12, 1836, *Pa. Mag. Hist. and Biog.*, LXIII, 195-196. *Jour. Amer. Oriental Soc.*, I, 163.

99 Narrative of Jan. 19, 1844, *Pa. Mag. Hist. and Biog.*, LXIV, 101. *Amer. Law Mag.*, V, 3.

100 DuPonceau was not happy there. *Cf.* narratives of Jan. 26 and 29, 1844, *Pa. Mag. Hist. and Biog.*, LXIV, 108-116.

101 Letters to Walsh, May 12 and 13, 1836, *Pa. Mag. Hist. and Biog.*, LXIII, 196-197. *Cf.* narrative of Feb. 3, 7, 9, 15, 1844, *ibid.*, LXIV, 243-261. *Cyc. of Amer. Lit.*, I, 578.

says, by religious scruples—and " to be perfectly candid, by a restless disposition, and a spirit of adventure, which made me see everything in bright colors before me." [102] He soon gave up Roman Catholicism, and after he came to America, worshipped at a Presbyterian church in Philadelphia.[103]

DePonceau arrived in Paris in 1775, and at fifteen, was earning a frugal living by translating English at so much a page (for professed translators), writing English letters for businessmen, and giving lessons in French and English.[104] In Paris, he met the Baron Von Steuben, who was looking for a secretary and interpreter. DuPonceau satisfied the Baron, so they sailed from Marseilles, arriving in Portsmouth, New Hampshire, December 1, 1777.[105] Many years later, he confessed,

> I shall not set up the vain pretension of having come to this country for the sake of freedom, or of a republican government. I was, it is true, a friend of liberty and hated despotism, but that was not my predominant passion at the time. My most anxious desire was that of travelling; I wished to see different nations, different men, different manners, and above all, to learn different languages, of which I was at that time, and ever since have been, extremely fond.[106]

In DuPonceau's opinion, he understood and could speak English as perfectly at the time of his arrival in America as he ever could afterwards.[107] He wrote,

> . . . . I was only astonished to find the milkmaids as learned in it as I was. My astonishment would hardly have been

102 *Cf.* letter of May 13, 1836, *Pa. Mag. Hist. and Biog.*, LXIII, 197. *Amer. Law Mag.*, V, 5.

103 *Jour. Amer. Oriental Soc.*, I, 162. *Cf.* letter to Anne L. Garesché, Sept. 22, 1837, *Pa. Mag. Hist. and Biog.*, LXIII, 331-332.

104 Narrative of Feb. 15, 1844, *ibid.*, LXIV, 260.

105 Letter of May 13, 1831, *ibid.*, LXIII, 199. *Cyc. of Amer. Lit.*, I, 578.

106 Narrative of Dec. 11, 1843, *Pa. Mag. Hist. and Biog.*, LXIII, 446. *Amer. Law Mag.*, V, 29.

107 *Jour. Amer. Oriental Soc.*, I, 162.

greater if they had spoken Greek or Latin. As the Baron [Steuben] could not speak one word of English, I accompanied him every where, and thus I was thrown at once into the first company in the land. I was pleased with every thing around me. We ate our first dinner at Governor Langdon's, and there we heard for the first time of the capture of General Burgoyne and his whole army. We hailed it as an omen of future success.[108]

DuPonceau visited Boston with Steuben and met there some of the leaders of the American Revolution. He was paid a rather singular compliment by Sam Adams, who asked him where he had learned his amazing republican principles. " In France," said DuPonceau. " In France! that is impossible." Then recovering himself, Adams added, " Well, because a man was born in a stable, it is no reason why he should be a horse." " I thought to myself," notes DuPonceau in his account, " that in matters of compliment they ordered things better in France." [109]

At Baron Steuben's request, DuPonceau was appointed a captain by brevet in the American Continental Army, February 18, 1778.[110] He accompanied Steuben on his movements until the winter of 1780, when he became ill in Philadelphia, and was left behind to complete arrangements for the publication of Steuben's famous " Blue Book." These new duties pleased DuPonceau.[111] He disliked military life, and was not qualified for

108 Letter to Walsh, May 1836. *Pa. Mag. Hist. and Biog.*, LXIII, 200. There are several references to DuPonceau's career as military secretary to Baron Steuben in John McAuley Palmer, *General Von Steuben* (New Haven: Yale University Press, 1937), *passim*. DuPonceau gives most of the known details of the Baron's trip from Paris to Valley Forge.

109 *Pa. Mag. Hist. and Biog.*, LXIII, 201. *Amer. Law Mag.*, V, 10.

110 *Amer. Law Mag.*, V, 10. When Steuben was commissioned a major-general and inspector-general of the army, DuPonceau was given, by courtesy, the rank of major. He kept this rank for the remainder of his military career, but it was as a captain of the infantry of the line that he received a pension until his death. *Ibid.*, V, 12.

111 Palmer, *General Von Steuben*, pp. 203-206. When DuPonceau was left behind in Philadelphia, it was not expected that he would survive his illness. His doctor wrote him, apologizing for not riding out four miles to visit him

active duties because of his nearsightedness.[112]

When DuPonceau left the army, Baron Steuben gave him a strong letter of recommendation to Congress, requesting that he be employed in some civil capacity. On July 25, 1781, he took the necessary oaths and became a " Citizen of the great commonwealth of Pennsylvania." [113] Of this occasion he says,

> Behold me, then, a citizen of the U. [sic] States, having entered with them into a solemn compact; to which I have faithfully adhered; and which I have never repented.[114]

Highly recommended by Steuben, Governor McKean, and Judge Peters, DuPonceau received on October 22, 1781, the appointment of secretary to Robert R. Livingston, then in charge of the department of Foreign Affairs.[115] He held the office until June 4, 1783. By the close of the war, he had decided on a career in law, so began his studies under William Lewis,

---

occasionally, on the ground that his disease was incurable and visits would do no good. "You are a philosopher," he said, "therefore, I have no doubt that you will hear this intimation as a philosopher ought to do." In the letter was enclosed a sealing wax impression of the goddess Hygeia, together with the observation that if it did no good, at least it was harmless. His concluding recommendations were to sleep in a stable and inhale the breath of cows. The letter disgusted the patient. Instead of succumbing, he says, " I wrote satirical verses on the consumption, and determined that it should not consume me." DuPonceau to Anne Garesché, Sept. 6, 1837. *Pa. Mag. Hist. and Biog.*, LXIII, 226-227. *Amer. Law Mag.*, V, 12-13.

112 *Jour. Amer. Oriental Soc.*, I, 163-164. Examples of the ludicrous mistakes he made because of his nearsightedness in *Amer. Law. Mag.*, V, 24-25. Though DuPonceau knew English, he was not familiar with military terminology, so that not long after he came to America, he was superseded in his primary job as interpreter by Washington's young aides-de-camp, John Laurens and Alexander Hamilton, who knew French, English, *and* military terminology. Palmer, *General Von Steuben*, p. 136.

113 Letter to Miss Garesché, Sept. 22, 1837, *Pa. Mag. Hist. and Biog.*, LXIII, 333. *Amer. Law Mag.*, V, 15.

114 Letter to Miss Garesché, Sept. 25, 1837, *loc. cit.*

115 *Cyc. of Amer. Lit.*, I, 578. Description of his appointment and duties in letters to Miss Garesché, Sept. 25 and Oct. 3, 1837. *Pa. Mag. Hist. and Biog.*, LXIII, 338 *et seq.*

whom he regarded at the time as " the most celebrated lawyer in Philadelphia, and perhaps in the United States." [116] In 1785, at the June term, Mr. Lewis moved for DuPonceau's admission as an attorney of the court of common pleas, and examiners were appointed to test his knowledge. The examiners were Rawle and Sergeant (father of Thomas Sergeant, the commentator). DuPonceau had already made Rawle's acquaintance when he advertised in the paper that he would exchange Valin's *Commentaries on the French Marine Ordinances* for Coke on Littleton. Rawle had answered the advertisement and the exchange had been made. On the occasion of DuPonceau's examination for admission to the bar, Rawle, intending to do him a favor, began by asking questions on the civil and maritime law. But DuPonceau was by this time far better versed in Coke on Littleton. Fortunately for the candidate, Sergeant directed questions toward this branch of knowledge, Rawle following his lead. Soon thereafter, DuPonceau and his examiner became good friends. The young Frenchman later expressed deep gratitude to Mr. Rawle for taking him as assistant counsel in an important case, thus giving him, says DuPonceau, " a standing at the bar which I could not have expected for many years to come." [117] DuPonceau was soon very busy, and later in 1785, on motion of Mr. Lewis, he was admitted an attorney of the Supreme Court of the state.

On May 21, 1788, DuPonceau married Anne Perry, and began forthwith to lead a more retired life.[118] In 1791, he was made a sworn interpreter of foreign languages,[119] a position which he held for some years.

116 *Amer. Law Mag.*, V, 17. DuPonceau's comment on Lewis is interesting, particularly since Wilson scholars contend that their subject was the best known lawyer in the United States at about this time.

117 DuPonceau, "Memoir of Rawle," *Memoirs of the Pa. Hist. Soc.*, IV, Part 1, pp. 80-83. DuPonceau adds that he was not the only man whom Rawle helped, "for benevolence was a strong trait in his character."

118 *Ibid.*, p. 84. *Amer. Law Mag.*, V, 18.

119 *Amer. Law Mag.*, loc. cit.

Extensive information is not available, but DuPonceau defended the Pennsylvania Constitution of 1776, which Wilson had violently opposed, and argued against the adoption of the Federal Constitution which Wilson had helped to frame.[120] Of this circumstance, DuPonceau later wrote, " I regret to say that I belonged to what was called the anti-federal party. I thought I was right: subsequent events have proved that I was in the wrong." [121]

Peter DuPonceau was relatively quiet while Wilson was at the height of his fame. True, he helped to welcome Citizen Genêt in 1793,[122] but otherwise he did not court excitement.

During the tense years from the turn of the century to the War of 1812, when party spirit was high, Rawle and DuPonceau usually found themselves on opposite sides. Nevertheless, so many causes were carried from Philadelphia to the Supreme Court of the United States that it became the custom for counsel, inevitably including pairs of opponents, to hire a stage and go to Washington together.[123] There were Ingersoll, Dallas, Lewis, Edward Tilghman, Rawle, DuPonceau, and other leading lights; and on the way there were many pleasantries.[124]

> Our appearance at the bar of the Supreme Court was always a scene of triumph. We entered the Hall together, and Judge Washington was heard to say " This is *my* bar." Our causes had a preference over all others, in consideration of the distance we had to travel. The greatest liberality was shown to

120 Ellis P. Oberholtzer, *Literary History of Philadelphia* (Philadelphia: 1906), p. 145.

121 DuPonceau, " Memoir of Rawle," *Memoirs of the Pa. Hist. Soc.*, IV, Part 1, p. 84.

122 J. Thomas Scharf and Thompson Westcott, *History of Philadelphia, 1609-1884*, I (Philadelphia: 1884), 473. Apparently based on primary sources, but lacks citations.

123 DuPonceau, " Memoir of Rawle," *Memoirs of the Pa. Hist. Soc.*, IV, Part 1, pp. 84-85.

124 *Ibid.*, pp. 85-86.

us, by the members of the profession, who usually attended that court. It was really a proud thing at that time, to be a *Philadelphia lawyer*.[125]

From Joseph Story we have pictures of the Philadelphia bar as he saw it while serving briefly in Congress. He was less complimentary to Mr. DuPonceau than he had been to Mr. Rawle:

> Duponceau is a Frenchman by birth, and a very ingenious counsellor at Philadelphia. He has the reputation of great subtilty [*sic*] and acuteness, and is excessively minute in the display of his learning. His manner is animated but not impressive, and he betrays at every turn the impatience and casuistry of his nation. His countenance is striking, his figure rather awkward. A small, sparkling, black eye, and a thin face, satisfy you that he is not without quickness of mind; yet he seemed to me to exhaust himself in petty distinctions, and in a perpetual recurrence to doubtful, if not to inclusive arguments. His reasoning was rather sprightly and plausible, than logical and coercive; in short, he is a French advocate.[126]

Shortly after the acquisition of Louisiana, President Jefferson offered DuPonceau the post of Chief Justice of the newly added territory. He was well qualified in Roman and especially in French law, but his position in Philadelphia was so good that he declined.[127]

Because of his knowledge of European languages and his familiarity with civil law, DuPonceau attracted many foreign

125 *Ibid.*, p. 86.

126 Story, *Life and Letters*, I, 162-163. Letter to Samuel P. P. Fay, Esq., Feb. 16, 1808. Later, Story had a much more exalted opinion of Mr. DuPonceau and his works, or else he considered the gentleman a better writer than orator (or else he was more complimentary in print than in private letters). In a note to his *Discourse Pronounced upon the Inauguration of the Author as Dane Professor of Law in Harvard University on August 25, 1829* (Boston: 1829), Story said, "Indeed, when one considers the liberal and acute spirit, which pervades all the juridical publications of Mr. DuPonceau, it is a matter of universal regret, that he has not exclusively devoted his life to the exposition of law, and particularly of the civil law." P. 47 note.

127 *Amer. Law Mag.*, V, 20.

clients, among whom were the diplomatic and other agents of the French government in the United States. He was engaged in numerous important causes that came before the courts of the state as well as the United States. The young nineteenth century saw many questions of international law come up, touching United States neutrality during the European war. American lawyers were, in general, not ready to handle these questions because most of them could not read French.[128] At about this time (1810), DuPonceau prepared an annotated translation of *Bynkershoeck's Law of War,* one of the best known of his works, because it introduced certain ideas new to American jurisprudence. DuPonceau was the first to suggest the application of the distinction between an absolute and a qualified neutrality to the case of the United States and France, considering our neutrality not to be absolute but qualified by the treaty with France of 1778. He was also first to announce the opinion that piracy might be committed on land as well as at sea, a principle later incorporated into an act of Congress.[129]

In politics DuPonceau started as an anti-Federalist, and then became a Jeffersonian Republican. Later, he claimed to be non-partisan.[130] Pickering appears to apologize for his old friend when he says that DuPonceau had much less deference for the opinions of Jefferson in after life,

> when he applied the power of his own intellect, and his matured experience to the examination of the great questions which agitated the union,—than during the fervid season of youth.[131]

Oberholtzer lists him with other well-known foreigners living in Philadelphia, " all of whom, as might be expected, were anti-

128 *Jour. Amer. Oriental Soc.,* I, 164.

129 *Ibid.,* I, 167.

130 DuPonceau, *Brief View of the Constitution* (Philadelphia: 1834), Preface, p. xviii.

131 *Jour. Amer. Oriental Soc.,* I, 165.

English radicals." [132] DuPonceau himself explained his attitude toward Great Britain as follows:

> I have said, I believe somewhere, that I had come to this country an *Anglomane* which feeling was produced by my enthusiasm for English literature, particularly poetry. But the conduct of Great Britain during the war cured me of my Anglomania, and I soon shared in the sentiments that prevailed here. They have been hostile or friendly as political circumstances gave rise to them . . . . I love the country of my choice, and have no political attachment to any other. [133]

Occasionally, Mr. DuPonceau was consulted on constitutional problems that arose in other states than his own, and by persons in the British Provinces where the civil law was in use. For instance, in 1821, his advice was sought and followed in framing the Constitution of the new state of Alabama. [134]

DuPonceau was always interested in legal education. In 1820, the Society for the Promotion of Legal Knowledge and Forensic Eloquence was formed with the Law Academy as a branch and under its patronage. Chief Justice Tilghman served as the first president of the Society and DuPonceau was the first provost of the Law Academy. [135] The young men composing the Law Academy had been meeting together to improve their debating skills and to increase their legal knowledge. DuPonceau's interest was aroused when they requested him to address the group. In his talk, he suggested that they organize a more formal body, which would provide them with the learning which they were seeking. Thus the question arises as to whether or not DuPonceau was the actual founder of the Law Academy.

132 Oberholtzer, *Literary History of Philadelphia*, p. 133. Also listed are Mathew Carey, Alexander Wilson, John Bouvier, Joseph Priestley, and DuPont de Nemours.

133 Narrative of Dec. 18, 1843, *Pa. Mag. Hist. and Biog.*, LXIII, 450; *Amer. Law Mag.*, V, 30-31.

134 *Jour. Amer. Oriental Soc.*, I, 166-167.

135 *Amer. Law Mag.*, V, 20.

The two works that DuPonceau wrote on the Constitution, *A Dissertation on the Nature and Extent of the Jurisdiction of the Courts of the United States* (1824), and *A Brief View of the Constitution of the United States* (1834), were prepared as addresses to the Law Academy, and were intended to simplify some of the problems facing young students.[136]

The first of these two lectures was published in 1824, simultaneously with Marshall's decision in Gibbons *v.* Ogden. This work is somewhat aside from the specific study of the Constitution, in that the author is here more concerned with the application of the common law in the United States than with the construction of the Constitution as such. He was attempting to solve the problem of what constitutes common law jurisdiction, as several aspects of the question were still unsettled.[137] In his opinion, the common law did not occupy the position it held in England as the *source* of power or jurisdiction, but was rather the *instrument* through which the power was exercised.[138] Divorced from its power-giving capacity, the common law of England, as it existed at the time of the Declaration of Independence, was still the " national law of this country." [139] Modifications upon it were to be found in the federal and state constitutions, and in federal and state legislation.[140] Furthermore, the law of nations was a common law of the United States, " or a law common to them in their federate and national character." [141] Most of the commentators pleaded only for jurisdiction in the courts coextensive with the legislative authority, but DuPonceau went further, saying, " There are many cases in which the judiciary can act, nay, when it must

136 *Cf.* preface to both the works mentioned; also purpose stated in subtitles.

137 DuPonceau, *Jurisdiction of the Courts of the United States* (Philadelphia: 1824), p. xiv.

138 Ibid., preface, *passim.*

139 *Ibid.*, pp. 89-90.

140 *Loc. cit.*

141 *Ibid.*, p. 63.

act, on subjects which the legislation of Congress cannot reach." [142]

The *Brief View of the Constitution* was intended to be introductory to the more formidable tomes on constitutional law. In this treatise, DuPonceau aligned himself with the nationalists, despite his protestations of Jeffersonian Republicanism, and omitted discussion of some of the points of major concern to the South.

DuPonceau served as provost of the Law Academy until his death, and in his will, drawn in 1839, appended to his legacy to the Academy, a recommendation to his brethren of the bar that they take it under their special protection, to make it as useful as possible to the progress of the law.   He added,

> A law professorship has long been wanted in this city; several of the states have the advantage of us in this respect. I recommend this important subject to the consideration of the friends of the legal science, and who are desirous of making it redound more and more to the honour of Pennsylvania. [143]

Very popular with the junior members of the legal profession, DuPonceau was often consulted when they were about to publish an essay, dissertation, or review on legal subjects. According to his friend, John Pickering, many lawyers owed their written ideas to his mind, " as well as to the actual service of his pen." [144]

DuPonceau's interests were among the widest of any of the commentators. Always devoted to philology, he made a name for himself and for Philadelphia in the learned world by the publication in 1819 of his report on the *Structure of the Indian Languages of North America*. His object here was to give

142 *Ibid.*, p. 32. *Cf.* letter of James Madison to DuPonceau (August 1824) on this subject. Gaillard Hunt, ed., *Writings of James Madison*, IX (New York: 1910), 198-202.

143 *Amer. Law Mag.*, V, 23. See also *Pa. Law Journal*, III (1844), 297-299, for extracts of DuPonceau's will.

144 *Jour. Amer. Oriental Soc.*, I, 165-166.

America and Europe " just and philosophical views of the aboriginal languages of America." [145] DuPonceau was rewarded for his proof that philosophy could be applied to these primitive languages by election to many of the proudest societies of America and Europe.[146] According to one eulogy,

> There are few men in this country, or in Europe, who may justly be compared with Mr. DuPonceau in variety, amplitude and profundity of learning. Besides being a classical scholar of the most exact and critical kind, he had penetrated far into oriental literature. . . . He conversed or read in all the polite languages of Europe—in Italian, French, German, Spanish, Portuguese, and Swedish—with remarkable freedom. His written works are as instructive as his attainments were unusual.[147]

From the study of DuPonceau's autobiographical letters and other materials, Whitehead has come to the conclusion that his subject's greatest single ambition was to force Europe to recognize the worth of American literature, science, and scholarship. He took every opportunity to call such matters to the attention of his European correspondents, and did what he could to have American books reviewed in foreign publications.[148] His " Discourse on the Necessity and Means of Making our National Literature Independent of that of Great Britain " in 1834 anticipated various phases of Emerson's famous " American Scholar " address.

145 *Jour. Amer. Oriental Soc.*, I, 167-168.

146 Whitehead says that DuPonceau was a member of 23 American and 19 foreign learned societies. *Pa. Mag. Hist. and Biog.*, LXIII, 191.

147 *Western Law Journal*, I (May 1844), 380, quoted by the editor, Timothy Walker, from the *United States Gazette* (Philadelphia). It may be noted that his interest in languages carried him into the unknown field of Russian. At seventeen, when he came to the United States, he kept his journal in the French language, written in the Russian character. *Jour. Amer. Oriental Soc.*, I, 168-169.

148 Introduction by Whitehead to DuPonceau's letters, *Pa. Mag. Hist. and Biog.*, LXIII, 192. Whitehead finds in the letters important evidence of the advance of French culture in the United States during the period covered. *Ibid.*, p. 195.

DuPonceau's interest in music was scientific as he did not perform. He had a knowledge of counterpoint not often found among amateurs.[149] He enjoyed attending the musical soirées of Robert Walsh, editor of the *American Quarterly Review*, along with the other intellectuals of Philadelphia.[150]

In 1829, DuPonceau zealously attempted to introduce the production and manufacture of silk in this country. He considered the project feasible, and thought that the great economic gains to come from it would repay to the country his debt of gratitude. He presented a bill in Congress, but in spite of all his efforts, it failed to pass. Finally, after three years of work and the expenditure of $4,000, he admitted that he had been pursuing a phantom. In a letter to a friend, he said, " I awoke as from a dream, and consoled myself with the proverb, which says that the shortest follies are the best." [151]

An interesting picture of DuPonceau at the close of his life was given by Andrew Preston Peabody, who wrote,

> On my first visit to Philadelphia, Mr. Pickering gave me letters to Mr. Duponceau, also to Mr. John Vaughan, who had his apartments in the building of the Philosophical Society, and whose breakfast-parties held a distinguished place among the social institutions of Philadelphia. I was invited to one of those parties, and was seated next to Mr. Duponceau, who almost embraced me for love of his very dear friend from whom I had so recently come. He took me for an adept in matters in which I was hardly a novice. He had all the vivacity of a Frenchman of the ancient régime . . . A wizen-faced old man, with a countenance full of intelligence, with fluent speech in a slightly foreign accent, he talked not in, but on, unknown tongues, to me rather than with me; for he was beyond my depth, swimming freely where I could not begin

149 *Jour. Amer. Oriental Soc.*, I, 169.

150 Oberholtzer, *Literary History of Philadelphia*, p. 196.

151 *Amer. Law Mag.*, V, 25-26. Information from letter to Mr. Arthur Bronson of New York, and letter of July 29, 1837, to Mr. Warden of Paris, giving the " history of the silk bill."

to wade. He had in his coat a pocket lined with wash-leather and filled with snuff, with which, by the handful, he regaled himself at frequent intervals.[152]

His death came suddenly, when an attack of bronchitis unexpectedly took a turn for the worse. His mind was constantly active until his last illness, and he was always engaged in "reading, writing, or dictating, in projecting new works, or in devising some plan for the advancement of knowledge."[153] His last wish to see the June roses,[154] always given him on his birthday, was not granted, though his friends did all they could to fill his sick room with flowers. His much-mourned passing occurred early in the morning, April 1, 1844.[155]

### JAMES KENT

The future Chancellor James Kent was just a child during the stirring years of the Revolution, but the events of the period remained in his memory. He was born July 31, 1763, the eldest son of Moss and Hannah (Rogers) Kent. Following a family tradition, young James entered Yale College at the age of fourteen.[156]

Kent's freshman year was badly broken up, as the college was twice forced to evacuate New Haven in the face of the oncoming British. During the calamitous summer of 1779, when, among other depredations, the British burned his father's home,[157] Kent had an adventure which determined the course

152 Peabody, *Harvard Graduates Whom I Have Known*, pp. 54-55.

153 *Western Law Journal*, I, 379-380.

154 Letter to Miss Garesché, Jan. 2, 1844, *Pa. Mag. Hist. and Biog.*, LXIII, 454

155 *Amer. Law Mag.*, V, 28-29.

156 John Theodore Horton, *James Kent, A Study in Conservatism, 1763-1847* (New York and London: D. Appleton-Century Co., 1939), pp. 12-16. To date, Kent is one of the three commentators who have had the honor of an adequate recent biography. Horton's work is based on an exhaustive study of the sources, and contains a wealth of detailed information.

157 Stiles, *Diary*, II, 359. See for account of destruction.

of his life. He found a copy of Blackstone's *Commentaries* and was so fascinated by it, that he decided to become a lawyer. By the fall, when Yale reopened, Kent was eager to complete his classical studies so that he might begin his legal career. He found nothing in his regular classwork nearly so exciting as Blackstone—the only book which gave him a stimulating sense of intellectual adventure.[158]

On September 12, 1781, James Kent and his classmates received their bachelor's degrees.[159] Though the youngest gradu-

158 In later years, looking back on eighteenth century standards of undergraduate scholarship, Kent regarded them as contemptible, and his own acquisitions of knowledge as few and paltry. Kent to Thomas Washington, Oct. 6, 1828, Kent Papers, Vol. V (MS. in Library of Congress). Horton comments, however, that " when a boy of sixteen can become excited over a monumental treatise upon law, the fact is by no means a damaging commentary upon the intellectual training that he has received." *Kent*, p. 23. While Kent was at Yale, a professorship of law was suggested but not established, and the only law lectures were infrequent ones from the President. Stiles, *Diary*, II, 233; Horton, *Kent*, p. 31.

159 Stiles, *Diary*, II, 554-556. These exercises were the first since Stiles assumed the presidency of Yale. Kent did not serve in the Revolutionary Army. According to his great-grandson, who compiled his papers, it was doubtful that Kent would have wanted to be a soldier. A commission, dated Oct. 24, 1786, appointing Kent Paymaster No. 1 of a militia regiment of Dutchess County, is apparently his nearest approach to military service. William Kent, *Memoirs and Letters of James Kent, LL.D.* (Boston, 1898), p. 5.

The delayed compilation of the memoirs is explained by Benjamin D. Silliman, a New York lawyer, who knew the Kents. A note in his handwriting is tipped into the copy of the *Memoirs and Letters* owned by the law school at the University of California. " Judge William Kent, very soon after his father's death, told me that Judge John Duer had requested from him a loan of the Chancellor's letters and papers in order that he (Judge D. [*sic*]) might write his biography. Kent said that he had declined compliance with the request because it was his own duty and privilege to write the biography. He did not do so. He afterwards told me that he found the material inadequate for such a work as he should wish to write, and that the biography and life of his father were contained in the first eleven vols. of *Johnson's Reports*, and in the seven vols. of *Johnson's Chancery Reports* to July 13, 1823 [*sic*—should read July 31] when he became 60 years of age and under the state constitution then in force, that was the limit of Judicial life."

ate, Kent was one of the top scholars of the group which contained ten future judges, fourteen members of Congress, two state governors, and two college presidents.[160]

Following his graduation, Kent went to Poughkeepsie to study law under Egbert Benson, then attorney-general of New York. He found legal study both demanding and onerous, but, as Story was to do later, forced himself through the necessary course of readings.

Late in 1785, Kent returned to his old home town of Fredericksburgh to begin his career. Disappointed at his reception, he was back in Poughkeepsie six weeks later. While there, he had fallen in love with Elizabeth, the daughter of Colonel John Bailey, in whose home he had lived while studying law. Though Kent was but twenty-one and Betsy only sixteen, his appointment as junior partner in Gilbert Livingston's law firm made it possible for them to be married.[161] There was business enough for them to live in comfort, and to permit them to buy property. To Kent's mind, the acquisition of property and the dignity that went with it were all-important—a view sustained by his study of Blackstone. He had disliked the Revolution because of its threat to property, and he was ready for the arguments of the *Federalist Papers* for the establishment of a stronger government for the United States.[162]

In New York, Kent witnessed one of the closest contests in any of the states over the adoption of the Constitution. Governor George Clinton, his followers, and the yeomen farmers on whose support Clinton's power rested, were unanimously opposed to any instrument which would curtail the power of the state of New York.[163] On the other side were arrayed the aris-

160 Frederick C. Hicks, "A Man of Law as a Man of Letters," *New York Times Book Review*, May 27, 1923, p. 12. This article was written in honor of the centennial of Kent's retirement as Chancellor of the state of New York.

161 Horton, *Kent*, pp. 42-43.

162 *Ibid.*, p. 55.

163 Ernest Wilder Spaulding, *New York in the Critical Period, 1783-1789* (New York: Columbia University Press, 1932), *passim*.

tocracy, the speculators, the lawyers, such as Alexander Hamilton, John Jay, and Egbert Benson, and their clients. Kent's sympathies were immediately enlisted on the side of the Constitution and the aristocracy which supported it. The idea of a new government competent to protect property appealed to Kent as well as to those who had more to protect than he did.[164] He read the *Federalist Papers* with great interest, and even memorized long passages.[165] He had met Hamilton in Albany in October 1787, and their acquaintance ripened into friendship. For the benefit of the citizens of Dutchess County, Kent abridged the letters of Publius as they appeared and printed them in the local newspaper. When enough of the original had been published to form a small volume, Kent and Benson obtained a supply which they distributed among the freeholders.[166]

The history of the convention at Poughkeepsie is well known. The sessions lasted for six weeks, and for most of that time, the struggle seemed to go against the Federalists. However, when word came that New Hampshire and Virginia had ratified, and that the Constitution had been accepted according to its own terms, Kent, who had never missed a session even though he was not a delegate, noticed a rapid change in the tone and manner of the proceedings. Though Governor Clinton remained irreconcilable, enough of his followers deserted the anti-Federalist camp to secure ratification of the Constitution. Kent was as

164 Horton, *Kent*, pp. 54-55.

165 Kent to Washington, Oct. 6, 1828, Kent Papers, Vol. V. *Cf. infra*, note 183. *Cf.* the following from Kent's *Commentaries* (6th ed.), I, 241: The *Federalist Papers* "were read with admiration and enthusiasm as they successively appeared, and by no person more so than the author of this note, who made a fruitless attempt at the time to abridge them for the benefit of a country village print. No constitution of government ever received a more masterly and successful vindication."

166 James Kent to Elizabeth Hamilton, Dec. 10, 1832, Kent Papers, Vol. VI. Mrs. Hamilton had asked Kent for reminiscences of her husband, a request to which he responded promptly and in considerable detail. See Horton, *Kent*, pp. 56-57.

jubilant over the Federalist victory as if he had brought it about himself.[167]

Shortly after New York became a member of the newly constituted Federal Union, Kent was elected to the state assembly, even though the majority party in his own district were predominantly Clintonians. His constituents were apparently well pleased with his services in 1790, as they re-elected him in 1792.[168] However, the partisan feelings of the latter year convinced Kent that he should leave Poughkeepsie.[169] Furthermore, his partner, Livingston, was now one of his political opponents. Remembering the friends whom he had made among the leading lawyers in New York City while attending sessions of the legislature, Kent decided to move there. Thus, he and his family sailed down the river to the busy city in the spring of 1793.[170]

During his early months in the metropolis, Kent encountered only discouragement, and his meagre resources disappeared rapidly. The notification from Columbia College in December that he had been elected to the newly established chair of law at a stipend of £200 per annum, came as good news indeed.[171]

167 Details in letter from Kent to Mrs. Hamilton, as cited.

168 Horton, *Kent*, pp. 60-64, 67.

169 Horton explains the method whereby the vote of Otsego County was declared void, thus re-electing Clinton. Had Otsego's vote been counted, Jay would have been elected. Kent undertook to have the wrong righted, an activity which earned him the epithet, "ringleader of sedition in Dutchess." *Kent*, pp. 67-73. However, the Federalists were grateful to him. They tried to have him elected to the House of Representatives when he left the state assembly, but he was defeated by the Dutchess voters, who returned his brother-in-law, Theodorus Bailey, instead. *Ibid.*, pp. 73-74.

170 *Ibid.*, pp. 74-75. Kent's eight years at Poughkeepsie were important to his later activities. He read regularly and systematically, dividing each day into different kinds of reading. He was too poor to buy many books, but his brother-in-law, who lived next door, liked to buy them and Kent encouraged him. Hicks, "A Man of Law as a Man of Letters," *New York Times Book Review*, May 27, 1923, p. 12.

171 Horton, *Kent*, p. 87. The official notice is in the Kent Papers near the end of Vol. I. *Cf.* Frederick C. Hicks, *Men and Books Famous in the Law*

The course opened on November 17, 1794, with the young professor delivering an Inaugural Discourse in the college hall.[172] At first, Kent thought his efforts were to be successful, but he was soon disappointed. Horton suggests that the comprehensive character of the course may have been too professional for the students of arts and too academic for the apprentices-at-law. At any rate, the report that the lectures were well attended in December 1794 [173] was followed by the sad news in the next year that only two students had appeared. These two, the professor instructed in his office in a half-hearted manner.[174]

During the next few years, Kent occupied various and increasingly honorable positions. He was elected to the assembly again in 1796, and in the same year, was appointed a Master in Chancery by Governor John Jay.[175] In 1797, he was appointed Recorder of the City of New York, the highest position in the state judicial system below the Supreme Court.[176] Holding the

---

(Rochester, N. Y.: 1921), p. 140. Long afterwards, Kent wrote, " It was the character I had insensibly acquired as a scholar and a Federalist and a presumed (though it was not true) well read lawyer, that the very first year that I removed to New York I was appointed a Professor of Law in Columbia College." As quoted by Dixon Ryan Fox, " James Kent in Politics," *Columbia Alumni News*, XIV (April 27, 1932), 367. *Cf. infra*, p. 22, note 14, for data on Columbia's claim to priority in the establishment of a chair of law.

172 Available in the original printing. Reprinted in *Columbia Law Review*, II (May 1903), 330-343. Kent had spent the summer preparing himself to instruct in the law. James Kent to William Kent, April 5, 1847, Kent Papers, Vol. XI.

173 There were in attendance " seven students, and thirty-six gentlemen ... who did not belong to the college." Hicks, *Men and Books Famous in the Law*, introduction by Harlan F. Stone, p. 9.

174 James Kent to Moss Kent, Jr., Dec. 11, 1794 and Jan. 4. 1796, Kent Papers, Vol. II.

175 Kent had supported Jay against Clinton in the 1792 gubernatorial election, and was one of the most vociferous in charging the Clintonians with manipulating the election to suit their own ends. In 1795 he had supported Jay's treaty with England in the face of those who would " Damn John Jay " and thus deserved the appointments he received as a faithful party member and man of sound ability. Horton, *Kent*, pp. 106-110.

176 *Ibid.*, p. 111.

two posts of Master in Chancery and Recorder, Kent was glad to discontinue his practice at the bar. He preferred the activities of the bench.

In February 1798, the crowning appointment came—to the Supreme Court of New York. The pay was not high, but Kent had managed to win financial independence through prudent speculation in land and a lucrative practice during his five years in New York City.[177] Stopping first at Poughkeepsie, the Kents finally settled in Albany, where they made their home during the rest of the Judge's official career.[178]

Kent's appointment as a Justice of the Supreme Court of New York marks one of the turning points in the history of the American judiciary. According to John Duer, a contemporary, the Supreme Court had changed little from the time of the Revolution. The judges, while not ignorant or stupid, did not devote the requisite amount of study to the cases brought before them, and thus there were frequent unnecessary differences in opinion and inexcusably long delays.[179]

> It was seldom that the opinions of the judges, even in the most important cases, were reduced to writing, and as no reports were then published, and no records preserved of the grounds on which their decisions were placed, the cases were numerous in which they had no rules to direct, no precedents to govern them.[180]

Judge Duer, who made this observation, adds that this defective administration of the law had an unfavorable influence on the Bar, as the lawyers saw no need for careful preparation of the cases when the decisions of the judges did not inspire confidence.[181]

177 Kent to Washington, Oct. 6, 1828, Kent Papers, Vol. V.

178 Horton, *Kent*, p. 118.

179 John Duer, *A Discourse on the Life, Character, and Public Services of James Kent*, delivered ... April 12, 1848 before the judiciary and bar of New York (New York: 1848), pp. 33-34.

180 *Ibid.*, p. 34.

181 *Loc. cit.*

Kent was the first judge in New York to prepare written opinions on cases presented to him for decision.[182] He wrote,

> When I came to the Bench there were no reports or State precedents. The opinions from the Bench were delivered *ore tenus*. We had no law of our own, and nobody knew what it was. I first introduced a thorough examination of cases and written opinions.[183]

In these written opinions, Kent did not confine himself to cases and authorities cited in the argument. Rather, he included all the law applicable to the questions to be determined.[184] At first, his judicial brethren were quite overcome, since they could not oppose his conclusions, even if they disagreed. The weight of Kent's authorities was too heavy.

> Hence they at once understood and felt that their own position was materially changed: it was evident that they must either surrender to their junior brother—their junior in station and far their junior in years—the effective control and administration of all the important business of the Court, or if at all solicitous to maintain their own character and dignity, must follow his example.[185]

---

182 Chipman was the first judge in Vermont to record his opinions in writing. *Cf. infra*, p. 118, for note on his *Reports and Dissertations* (Rutland, Vt.: 1793).

183 Letter to Thomas Washington of Nashville, Tennessee, Oct. 6, 1828. Washington had asked Kent to tell him the secret of his success in life, and after repeated requests, Kent answered in full. He noted on the back of his retained copy, "It was fairly pressed out of me." Kent Papers, Vol. V.

184 As time passed, this research on the part of judges was to become impossible, due to the increase in the number of cases in litigation. Therefore, the judges have come more and more to rely on argument of counsel. See Benjamin R. Twiss, *Lawyers and the Constitution* (Princeton: Princeton University Press, 1942), *passim*.

185 Duer adds philosophically, "Fortunately for themselves and the public, it was upon the latter course that they resolved." *Discourse on Kent*, p. 35.

New York was one of the first two states to order official publication of court decisions.[186] The position of court reporter was created in 1803, but the first significant occupant, William Johnson, was not appointed until 1805.[187]

Though the other judges were forced to write out their opinions in order to maintain their dignity, still Kent retained his supremacy over them. This was particularly true after he became Chief Justice in 1804.[188] At first, each judge took his turn writing opinions in cases where all were in agreement, but gradually the task devolved upon the Chief Justice. In order to avoid arousing jealousy, he adopted the practice of writing *per curiam* decisions.[189]

While he was a member of the Supreme Court, Kent was required to hold Circuit Courts at the various county seats.[190] On the whole, he did not enjoy the long trips, though he often traveled with able lawyers and heard interesting cases. His home in Albany had more attractions than the wilderness of the " Land of the Leatherstocking." Furthermore, he could not take his library along on horseback, and stages were available only in the more settled districts.

186 The other state was Massachusetts. Aumann, *Changing American Legal System*, p. 77.

187 Apparently, Kent, who had been raised to the Chief-Justiceship in 1804, was instrumental in securing the appointment of his good friend, William Johnson, to the post. Kent, *Memoirs and Letters*, pp. 124-125. Johnson carried the reports back to the January term, 1799, using the copies Kent had kept of all his opinions, and the notes he had preserved of all important decisions. Mr. Caines published reports from 1803 until Johnson was appointed. Duer, *Discourse on Kent*, pp. 40-41.

188 Appointed by Governor Morgan Lewis, the retiring Chief Justice. Kent, *Memoirs and Letters*, pp. 120-121.

189 Kent to Washington, Oct. 6, 1828, Kent Papers, Vol. V. Harlan F. Stone, "James Kent, Judge and Chancellor," *Columbia Alumni News*, XIV, 366.

190 *Cf.* John T. Horton, "Western Eyres of Judge Kent," *New York History*, XVIII (April 1937), 152-166. Kent rode the circuit for sixteen years. *Ibid.*, p. 164.

Of law books he required none, as he usually decided all simple questions as they came before him, reserving his decisions only on the more complicated questions, until he could write his opinions. He frequently notes that he has brought home with him from his trip bundles of cases which will occupy him until the next term, to study and decide.[191]

Horton has commented more than once that Kent was extremely deferential to English law, applying it even when he doubted its justice in a particular case.[192] Though well versed in the civil law, Kent was primarily concerned, while a judge in the common law courts, with retaining and strengthening the English common law. Before his elevation to the bench, Kent had read and annotated most of the English reports, especially those in equity—which he could cite as precedents. He thus brought to his new post " methods of investigation and habits of study which made inevitable the rapid reception by his court of those legal principles and doctrines which were the fruit of some six centuries of English judicial experience." [193] Writing of the years prior to the War of 1812, when Anglophobia was prevalent, Kent said,

> English authority did not stand very high in those early feverish times, and this led me a hundred times to attempt to bear down opposition, or shame it by exhaustive research and overwhelming authority. Our jurisprudence was, on the whole, improved by it. My mind certainly was roused, and was always kept ardent and inflamed by collision.[194]

On February 24, 1814, Kent was given a second opportunity to create a system of jurisprudence. He was transferred from

191 Kent, *Memoirs and Letters*, p. 129.

192 Horton, *Kent*, p. 153. *Cf.* also, Vernon Louis Parrington, *Main Currents in American Thought*, II (New York: Harcourt, Brace, 1930), 197-198.

193 Stone, " James Kent, Judge and Chancellor," *Columbia Alumni News*, XIV, 366.

194 Kent to Washington, Oct. 6, 1828, Kent Papers, Vol. V.

the Supreme Court of Errors and Appeals to the Court of
Chancery and appointed Chancellor. He had been happy at his
previous post and disliked leaving it. As he wrote candidly,
many years later,

> The office I took with considerable reluctance. It had no
> charms. The person who left it was stupid, and it is a curious
> fact that for the nine years I was in that office there was *not
> a single decision, opinion, or dictum of either of my two
> predecessors* [Chancellors Livingston and Lansing], *from
> 1777 to 1814, cited to me or even suggested.* I took the court
> as if it had been a new institution, and never before known in
> the United States. I had nothing to guide me, and was left at
> liberty to assume all such English Chancery powers and juris-
> diction as I thought applicable under our Constitution. This
> gave me grand scope, and I was checked only by the revision
> of the Senate, or Court of Errors.[195]

Kent had been interested in the equity side of jurisprudence
ever since his early days at Poughkeepsie. His first post as
Master in Chancery for New York City provided him with the
practical experience needed to supplement the knowledge he had
gained from reading the English equity writers.

William Johnson followed Kent to the Court of Chancery,
continuing to report his decisions. Their joint efforts produced
the foundations for American equity, and in time, Kent was to
be recognized as the most famous of all the American jurists
who have held the ancient and distinguished title of Chancellor.[196]

195 *Loc. cit.* Kent was appointed by the unanimous vote of the Council of
Appointment. According to the *New York Evening Post,* Feb. 26, 1814,
" The supereminent talents, the indefatigable industry and stern impartiality
which for so many years have distinguished the presiding judge, will continue to exhibit themselves with equal lustre in the Chancellor." Quoted
in Horton, *Kent,* p. 199 note. Horton observes, however, that Kent's Federalist leanings had a great bearing on his decisions. *Ibid.,* p. 161.

196 *Ibid.,* pp. 200-201, 199. See references in Horton, " Western Eyres
of Judge Kent," *New York History,* XVIII, 153-154. Stone notes in his
article on " James Kent, Judge and Chancellor," that the more enlightened

As might be expected, Kent soon enjoyed an enviable reputation in England.[197] However, it should be noted that the English jurists were aware of Kent's activities even earlier, through the small volume of *Dissertations,* which contained the first three of the lectures he had delivered while professor of law at Columbia. According to Kent's great-grandson, the pamphlet was cited in *Brown's Treatise on Civil and Admiralty Law* which was published in England shortly afterwards. ". . . it is believed that this is the first reference made to an American law publication by a transatlantic writer." [198]

A provision of the New York Constitution, unchanged when that document was revised in 1821,[199] cut off Chancellor Kent's

---

conceptions of the English chancellors in modifying the rigors of the technically rigid eighteenth century common law, appealed to Kent's lofty principles of justice. He was eminently qualified by temper as well as knowledge and experience, to administer this branch of the law. *Columbia Alumni News,* XIV, 366.

197 Horton, *Kent,* p. 212 *et seq.*

198 Kent, *Memoirs and Letters,* pp. 63-64. James Kent, *Dissertations: Being the Preliminary Part of a Course of Law Lectures* (New York: 1795), 87 pp. Duer notes that the sale of the volume was not sufficient to defray the expenses of its publication—"a reproach to the taste and intelligence of the public of that day." He also said that he was unable to locate a copy at the time that he wrote. *Discourse on Kent,* p. 30. Today, copies are available in various large law libraries.

For an interesting comparison of Kent and Story on their reputations abroad and other phases of their careers, see John B. Cassoday, "James Kent and Joseph Story," *Yale Law Journal,* XII (Jan. 1903), 146-153. This article also presents a good analysis of Ogden *v.* Gibbons, 4 John. Ch. 150 (1819) and Gibbons *v.* Ogden, 17 John. 488 (1820). In this decision, Kent was later reversed by the United States Supreme Court.

199 Kent was a member of the Convention called to revise the New York State Constitution in 1821, representing the small but talented Federalist minority. On this occasion, his conservatism was most pronounced. He spoke feelingly against the extension of the suffrage, supporting the continued control of the landed interests. Such doctrines were unpopular with the Democrats, who were politically predominant in the Convention. Therefore, the sixty-year age limit on the members of the judiciary was retained in the new instrument—a clause which Kent tried in vain to erase. Furthermore, the Council of Revision was abolished as a conservative stronghold. This group, composed of the supreme court judges, the governor and the

judicial career in what appeared to be the most short-sighted manner. Promptly on his sixtieth birthday, July 31, 1823, he gave way to his successor. His last years had been unhappy ones. His stipend had been drastically reduced, the Democrats seeking to oust him from his position by this means before he reached the age limit. Then, the Court of Errors began reversing his decisions—a severe blow indeed. In 1820, he wrote to William Johnson, who was to resign as Court Reporter when the Chancellor retired, " There are but two sides to every case, and I am so unfortunate as always to take the wrong side." [200]

Though Kent's career was now apparently over, such did not prove to be the case. At first, he thought of opening a law school in Albany on the plan of the Litchfield School,[201] as he needed a source of income. However, his dislike for the " new dynasty in Albany " induced him to move to New York City, where he thought he might open an office as chamber counsel or " lawyer's lawyer." [202] Meanwhile, Webster had proposed that Kent be offered the presidency of Dartmouth, and in a letter to Story, had expressed the hope that the unemployed chancellor might be appointed to the United States Supreme Court.[203] However,

---

chancellor, was charged with examining bills from the legislature and vetoing them at their discretion. Kent had served on the Council since 1798, and had assisted in giving it the reputation for conservatism which it had attained. Fox, " James Kent in Politics," *Columbia Alumni News*, XIV, 367-368. *Cf.* also Parrington, *Main Currents in American Thought*, II, 197-199, for an interpretation of Kent's conservatism and its significance, and Horton, *Kent*, p. 161, for an analysis of the connection between Kent's conservatism, his Federalism, and his devotion to the English common law.

200 Kent, *Memoirs and Letters*, pp. 185-186.

201 Kent to William Johnson, Sept. 27, 1823, Kent Papers, Vol. V.

202 Kent to Washington, Oct. 6, 1828, *loc. cit.*

203 Vacancy due to death of Justice Livingston, March 19, 1823. Hicks, *Men and Books Famous in the Law*, pp. 147-148. William Wirt, Monroe's Attorney-General, urged Kent's appointment, also, writing, " Kent holds so lofty a stand everywhere for almost matchless intellect and learning, as well as for spotless purity and high-minded honour and patriotism, that I firmly believe the nation at large would approve and applaud the appointment." Wirt to Monroe, May 5, 1823. John Pendleton Kennedy, *Memoirs of the Life of William Wirt*, II (Rev. ed., Philadelphia: 1850), 135. In

Kent was requested to reassume his chair as professor of law at Columbia College, a position which had lain dormant since he had left it in 1795. He was persuaded to accept, but "exceedingly against [his] inclination." [204]

The ex-Chancellor immediately set to work preparing his lectures. He began his "imperfect and broken course" [205] in February 1824, intending to begin his " regular and habitual course " in the following fall.[206] At first, his students were numerous, but apparently new ones did not appear as the earlier ones completed their training. Before long, the Chancellor had " got heartily tired of lecturing " and abandoned it.[207]

Meanwhile, Kent had turned down a most interesting offer. Central College, soon to be converted into the University of Virginia, was in hopes that he could be persuaded to fill the chair of law which Dr. Thomas Cooper had been forced to resign in 1823 because of the outcry against his unorthodox religious creed. In explaining this amazing offer from the stronghold of Jeffersonian Republicanism, the following reasons have been presented:

> So great was his [Kent's] fame already and so enormous would be the distinction which he would give to the Law School, should he consent to take charge of it, that Gilmer at least appears to have been ready to sink all thought of his political convictions. As the communication between the two men was brief, and without result, it is not possible to say how far Jefferson would have approved the appointment of this

the Kent Papers, Vol. V, there is a letter from Moss Kent to William Kent, dated Jan. 25, 1827, which reads as follows: " Do tell me how he bore the disappointment in not receiving the appointment of Judge. It is no great loss, and I had rather, in future, that he should remain in private life."

204 Extract from resolution of the Trustees appointing him to the position in Kent Papers, Vol. V. Dated Nov. 3, 1823.

205 James Kent to Moss Kent, Jan. 16, 1824, Kent Papers, Vol. V. He gave two formal lectures a week and an additional one " more private for the matriculated Students only."

206 William Kent to Moss Kent, Jan. 28, 1824, loc. cit.

207 Kent to Washington, Oct. 6, 1828, loc. cit.

political heretic, mild, and reasonable, and academic as he was.[208]

Kent's influence as a teacher was not to end with the conclusion of his second effort at Columbia. As he later explained, ". . . it was my son that pressed me to prepare a volume of Lectures for the press. I had no idea of publishing them when I delivered them." [209] Thus, in 1826, at the age of sixty-three, Chancellor Kent set himself to reduce to writing the common law and equity jurisprudence of the United States, which he had expounded through so much of his judicial career. He began the project at his own expense, and had the first volume not met with a warm reception, the remaining three probably would not have appeared.[210] His original plan for two volumes expanded to four. They appeared in November 1826, December 1827, October 1828, and April 1830.[211]

208 Philip A. Bruce, *History of the University of Virginia*, II (New York: 1920), 27. See also pp. 24-26 on the difficulties connected with the appointments to this professorship. Horton does not mention this offer in his otherwise very complete biography of Kent.

209 Kent to Washington, Oct. 6, 1828, Kent Papers, Vol. V.

210 The cost of bringing out the first volume in sheets was $1076.27, "which was a very considerable venture considering his limited means." Kent, *Memoirs and Letters*, p. 193. William thought that the lecture "in which a view was taken of the progress and influence of the Supreme Court of the United States was really one of the most elegant things I have heard." Same to same, Jan. 20, 1825. In this letter, William tells his uncle that "Mr. Carter is very desirous of a copy for publication—but my advice is to refuse it, for, singular as it may seem, Pa's manner is certainly a great assistance to his writing, and for the world the reports of his zealous students will produce as much effect as a perusal of his lecture could do." William evidently changed his mind on this subject shortly thereafter. It is interesting to note that the outline of lectures that Chancellor Kent prepared in 1824 is much the same as the one which appeared in his *Commentaries*. Cf. the *Summary of Lectures appended to a Lecture, Introductory to a Course of Law Lectures in Columbia College*, delivered Feb. 2, 1824 (New York: 1824). Part II, lectures XI-XIX, were to be devoted to the Constitutional Jurisprudence of the United States. Part II, Lectures X-XIX, are on that subject in the *Commentaries*.

211 Kent, *Memoirs and Letters*, p. 195.

The *Commentaries on American Law* were immediately received with the highest commendations. Their author was admired in England and favorably known in France and Germany.[212] And with reason. His contribution to American jurisprudence was a great one.[213] He had no American model for his undertaking, and there is not even evidence that Blackstone served as a pattern. Dane's nine-volume *Digest,* the longest work on American law at the time, had only summarized statutes and decisions. Other works were more specialized. Kent set out to deal with jurisprudence as a comprehensive system. In so doing, he performed a great service for lawyers and judges at home and abroad. For example, Edward Everett, while abroad, often had recourse to the *Commentaries* to answer questions from English public men regarding the law of the American states.[214]

For the purposes of the present study, Part II of Volume I is of the greatest interest, as it contains a treatise on the constitutional jurisprudence of the American Union. This section was based on lectures actually delivered at Columbia, which Kent's son had described as " more elegantly written and [displaying] more acuteness of reasoning than any other of Papa's productions." [215]

It is the opinion of Professor Thomas Reed Powell that " if Chancellor Kent's judicial duties had required him to deal extensively with constitutional law, he would have attained in that field a place superior to that of Story and second only to that

212 Horton, *Kent,* p. 299. References to letters of Mittermeier of Heidelberg, June 15, 1841; Charles Sumner, Sept. 24, 1838; and Edward Everett, Oct. 31, 1845, all to Kent. Kent Papers, Vols. IX and X. The *Commentaries* were translated into German by Friedrich Bissing (Heidelberg: 1836), and into Spanish by J. Carlos Mexia (Mexico: 1878).

213 According to Harlan F. Stone, speaking at the Kent Centennial, the *Commentaries* " must be included in any list of five or six of the great law books of the English speaking world." *Columbia Alumni News,* XIV, 365.

214 Everett to Kent, Oct. 31, 1845, Kent Papers, Vol. X.

215 William Kent to Moss Kent, Jan. 7, 1825, *ibid.,* Vol. V.

of Marshall." [216] As it was, his contributions to this field from the bench were modest. In his *Commentaries,* however, he showed himself an able expositor of the constitutional law which had become established at the time he wrote. His paraphrase of the Supreme Court decisions is able, and Powell considers that Kent improved materially on Marshall's style. " One who today desires a brief review of the foundation stones of our constitutional jurisprudence can go nowhere else with such profit and pleasure as to this second part of the *Commentaries.*"[217]

In his presentation of constitutional law, Kent gave the court decisions as a practical factor in the government of the people. He emphasized the legislation upon which the decisions were based and the events which led up to the issue. The student is thus placed in a position to pass judgment on the wisdom with which the case was decided.[218]

Even during Kent's life-time, the primary significance of the *Commentaries* was apparent. As Duer said in his eulogy,

> It is the character of the Commentaries as a national work, and their masterly execution as such, that have stamped upon them a peculiar value. It is to these causes, that the extent of the influence which they rapidly acquired and now [1848] exert on the jurisprudence, not of a single State, but of all, must be ascribed. As a national work of admitted and controlling authority, they have a direct and powerful tendency to create and to preserve a uniformity in the laws and in the legislation of the respective States, and a necessary consequence of this assimilation of our laws, is to produce and per-

216 Thomas R. Powell, " Kent's Contributions to Constitutional Law," *Columbia Alumni News,* XIV, 372. See for discussion of People *v.* Croswell, involving freedom of the press, in which Kent laid some foundations for future constitutional law. On this occasion, he was forced to depart from English precedents. Powell also analyzes Kent's decision in Gibbons *v.* Ogden. *Ibid.,* p. 373.

217 *Loc. cit.*

218 *Loc. cit.*

petuate a unity in our national character. That unity is the firmest bond of the political compact that binds us together as a nation, and as such, is a constituent element and permanent source of our national prosperity and greatness.[219]

The former professor of law at Columbia, legally too old for the rigors of judicial life in 1823, was still active twenty years later. Kent saw five editions of his *Commentaries* through the presses, and had a sixth ready for publication at the time of his death.[220] His last years had been spent happily and quietly. Thanks to his *Commentaries,* his income was $5000 annually— double what he was getting when he left the bench.[221] He lived in an elegant house on fashionable Union Square and had the country home that he and his wife had dreamed of since they were young.[222]

In August 1841, Kent saw his son appointed to the Supreme Court of New York, in the seat that he himself had occupied many years before.[223] Later, in July 1846, he had the additional gratification of seeing this same son appointed Royall Professor of Law at Harvard when Professor Greenleaf vacated the chair in order to succeed Story as Dane Professor.[224]

Kent was extremely fortunate in the closing years of his life. His great-grandson thought that the last ten were his happiest. His finances were in good order; his family was with him; and he was still consulted by lawyers and jurists. His death, on December 12, 1847, was mourned by friends and admirers in England and Continental Europe as well as in the United States,

219 Duer, *Discourse on Kent,* p. 76. *Cf.* also, Frederick C. Hicks, " Kent's Commentaries," *Columbia Alumni News,* XIV, 370.

220 Horton, *Kent,* p. 325.

221 *Diary of Philip Hone, 1828-1851,* Allan Nevins, ed., II (New York: Dodd, Mead, 1927), 645-646.

222 Horton, *Kent,* pp. 312-315.

223 Kent, *Memoirs and Letters,* p. 262.

224 *Ibid.,* p. 271.

and all who knew him foresaw that his name would be immortal.[225]

### WILLIAM ALEXANDER DUER

William Alexander Duer, son of Hamilton's friend, Colonel William Duer, was born on September 8, 1780, at Rhinebeck, Dutchess County, New York. His family was already prominent in the life of the young republic.[226] At their home, such men as Hamilton and Morris gathered, and young William's earliest recollections were of the dramatic scenes surrounding the establishment of the new national government.[227]

In 1791, Duer was sent by his father to be educated in England.[228] Although the war was over, there was still some resentment among the English boys against their former fellow-subject. William was known as " the little rebel " and had to fight many battles for his country.[229] He returned to the United

---

225 *Diary of Philip Hone*, II, 828-831. A list of Kent's publications and notes on their location is in Franklin B. Dexter, *Biographical Sketches of the Graduates of Yale College*, IV (New York: 1907), 192-193. Edwin C. Kent presented the Chancellor's legal library to Columbia University in 1911, and it is now preserved in Kent Hall.

226 His maternal grandfather, William Alexander, who claimed to be Lord Stirling, had been a major-general of the Revolutionary Army, and his father was a member of the Continental Congress, Commissary-General for the Northern Department, and a member of the Committee of Public Safety. He was also one of the committee appointed to frame the first constitution of the state of New York. Duyckinck, *Cyclopedia of American Literature*, I, 382; William A. Duer, "William Alexander Duer, Fifth President of Columbia College," *Columbia University Quarterly*, IV (March 1902), 148. *Cf.* A. C. Flick, ed., *History of New York* (New York: New York Historical Society, 1933), 10 vols., *passim*.

227 The family had left their home in New York City after the battle of Long Island, but returned as soon as it was possible to do so. *Col. Univ. Q.*, IV, 147-150. *Cf.* Duer's *Reminiscences of an Old New Yorker*, address to the St. Nicholas Society, 1848 (New York: 1867), 102 pp.; and *New-York as It Was, During the Latter Part of the Last Century*, an address before the St. Nicholas Society, Dec. 1, 1848 (New York: 1849), 48 pp.

228 *Col. Univ. Q.*, IV, 150. The name of the public school he attended is not given.

229 *Loc. cit.*

States and soon was among those Columbia College freshmen who followed Dr. Peter Wilson to Erasmus Hall in Flatbush.[230]

In July 1796, when Duer was sixteen, his father sent him to Philadelphia to study law under Peter Stephen DuPonceau.[231] DuPonceau's ideas as to the ingredients of an adequate legal education are recorded in a letter to the senior Duer.

> . . . The mechanical part of the art of writing, the French language, and the practical part of the law, he will learn of course in my office. I have undertaken myself to improve his handwriting, and I hope you will soon be sensible of his improvement in this particular. But these are not objects to which I attach any great importance as they will follow of themselves in the situation in which you have placed him. But to form his mind and fit him for the stations which he may be one day called upon to fill, will be my principal duty. For this purpose I mean to cultivate his acquaintance with the ancient classics and put in his hands successively the best works of English and French literature. As the ground work of his professional studies, history, ethics, and metaphysics will be particularly attended to. I shall make him read the best authors on general jurisprudence and direct his attention particularly to the civil law, after which the study of our common law, already prepared by the daily practice of its forms, will be but child's play . . . . We have but few civilians in this country, which makes the acquirement more valuable to those who possess it. In short, my object will be not to turn your son out of my hands, a mere plodding attorney, creature of form and of routine, but to make of him a correct and enlightened jurist in the more enlarged sense of the word . . . .[232]

William's parents thought that a university diploma would be desirable, but DuPonceau disagreed. Said he,

230 *Loc. cit.* Wilson had resigned from Columbia because of an altercation in the faculty.

231 *Ibid.*, IV, 151; *Cyc. of Amer. Lit.*, I, 382.

232 *Col. Univ. Q.*, IV, 151-152. Letter dated July 18, 1796.

. . . these baubles are falling more and more into discredit and when a non-graduate distinguishes himself by his merit, Universities will fast enough force the learned title upon him, in which case it appears to me to be really honorable.[233]

Evidently, Duer was unable to withstand the rigors of a Du-Ponceau-ian education for very long, as he soon returned to New York to study in the office of Nathaniel Pendleton. During the quasi-war of 1798 with France, he was appointed a midshipman in the Navy, serving under Decatur. After two years of service, he resumed his law studies with Pendleton.[234]

In 1802, he was admitted to the bar, and shortly thereafter formed a business partnership with Edward Livingston, then United States district attorney and mayor of New York. After the latter left for New Orleans, Duer formed a professional partnership with his brother-in-law, Beverly Robinson. At about this time he began to write, contributing to the *Corrector,* a partisan weekly conducted by Dr. Peter Irving, in support of Burr. It appears, however, that this was a temporary affair, and that Duer did not break with Hamilton.[235] He then went to New Orleans where Livingston had established a law office, and studied Spanish civil law. He returned to New York in 1806 to marry Hannah Maria Denning, daughter of the prominent Whig merchant, William Denning.[236]

233 *Ibid.*, IV, 152. It is interesting to note that Duer was one of the two men who achieved the presidency of Columbia College without having a collegiate degree themselves.

234 *Cyc. of Amer. Lit.*, I, 382. According to the unsigned review of the second edition of Duer's *A Course of Lectures on the Constitutional Jurisprudence of the United States* (Boston, 1856), the elder Duer died a few years later, as yet not recovered from the results of the over-speculation which had led to his imprisonment during Washington's first administration. Mrs. Duer opened a girls' boarding school, and the two sons, William Alexander and John, entered the navy and army respectively, to meet the financial requirements of the family. *North American Review*, LXXXVI (April 1858), 464.

235 *Cyc. of Amer. Lit.*, I, 382.

236 *Col. Univ. Q.*, IV, 153.

Duer opened an office in Rhinebeck, his birthplace, and soon rose to an influential position in his community. He continued to write for Dr. Irving, who was now editing *The Morning Chronicle*.[237] From 1814 to 1829, he served in the state Assembly, representing first Dutchess County and then Albany County.[238] In 1823, following the adjustment of the courts under the new state constitution of 1821, Duer was appointed a judge of the supreme court for the third circuit, which office he held for about seven years.

In 1829, Duer undertook new duties as president of Columbia College. About two months before his election in December 1829, he had resigned from his judgeship in order to be free to accept the new appointment.[239]

Duer entered upon his collegiate duties on January 5, 1830. In addition to his experience as lawyer, legislator, and judge, he had evolved broad views on education. He took office when the financial situation of the college was discouraging, and had, therefore, to aid the trustees in their money-raising activities. Columbia was also threatened by the establishment of a rival institution, the University of the City of New York (the present New York University), which, it was feared, would further

237 *Cyc. of Amer. Lit.*, I, 382.

238 His legislative service was significant in various fields. As chairman of the Committee on Colleges and Academies, he succeeded in obtaining passage of a bill which provided a compulsory tax as the basis for common school income. Unsigned review of second edition of Duer's *Course of Lectures, North American Review,* LXXXVI, 465. In 1820, in recognition of his service to education, he was appointed a regent of Columbia College. *Col. Univ. Q.,* IV, 153. As chairman of another committee, he was the first to take ground against the validity of the exclusive grant to steam navigation on the rivers of the state to Livingston and Fulton, a position with which Kent was later to disagree. Later, he introduced a bill prohibiting lotteries, the provisions of which were incorporated in the Constitution of 1821. *North American Review, loc. cit. Cf.* pamphlets written at the time by Duer and Cadwallader Colden, and the reply of Duer. Also article, "Fitch's and Fulton's Steam Navigation," *Putnam's Monthly Magazine,* V (Jan. 1855), 103-105.

239 *Col. Univ. Q.,* IV, 153-154.

weaken its resources. Duer drastically reorganized the curriculum and system of professorships, and though the opening of
the new university in 1832 decreased the size of the freshman
class, Columbia recovered to have the largest enrollment in its
history to date in 1838.[240] Duer saw that an hour a day was
added to the time of instruction, took charge of the freshman
class in English composition, and delivered to the seniors a
course of lectures on the constitutional jurisprudence of the
United States.[241] With the publication of the *Outlines* of these
lectures in 1833, Duer became a commentator.

In constitutional interpretations, Duer placed himself somewhere between Kent and Rawle. In reality, he appears much
closer to the former than he is to the latter. The *Outlines of the
Constitutional Jurisprudence of the United States* were drawn
up following a resolution of the American Lyceum, which requested Duer to prepare a book that could serve as a " text book
for Lectures, and a class book to be used in Academies and
Common Schools." [242] Duer was evidently eager to obtain the
approbation of prominent persons, and to persuade universities
to adopt his book as a text. Letters from Marshall, Tocqueville,
Madison, and Edward Livingston, his former colleague, and by
this time the American minister to France, give evidence that
Duer sent complimentary copies of the book to these gentlemen.[243] An interesting sidelight is that Mr. Marshall's copy is

240 *Ibid.*, IV, 156-157.

241 *Cyc. of Amer. Lit.*, I, 383. James Kent's name was carried in the
Columbia catalogues from 1826 when he stopped lecturing until his death
in 1847, but no courses were delivered. Francis M. Burdick, "Legal Instruction at Columbia," *Col. Univ. Q.*, IV (March 1902), 126. On November
29, 1839, Simon Greenleaf, Royall Professor at Harvard, wrote to Charles
Sumner that Chancellor and Mrs. Kent had been in Cambridge recently,
and that "the New York school is defunct." Sumner Papers (MS. in
Harvard College Library).

242 Preface to the *Outlines*. Cf. Flick, ed., *History of New York*, IX,
82, on the New York Athenaeum.

243 See letters published in Duer's *A Course of Lectures on the Constitutional Jurisprudence of the United States.* (No. 160 of Harper's Family
Library series, New York: 1843, reprinted in 1868).

endorsed, in the Chief Justice's own handwriting, "Attention of Mr. Justice Story." [244]

A complimentary copy had been sent to Mr. Madison as an individual, and as head of the University of Virginia (a position which Duer thought he held). In his response, dated only September 1833, Madison informed Duer that he was merely the presiding member of the Board of Visitors. The institution was superintended by the Faculty, with a chairman annually appointed by the Visitors. The choice of text and class books was left to the professors, except in the law school, where the subject of government was specifically included. For that course, the Board of Visitors had prescribed as text authorities, the *Federalist,* the Virginia Resolutions of 1798 with the comment on them in 1799, and Washington's Farewell Address. Madison continued,

> The use, therefore, that will be made of any analogous publications will depend on the discretion of the Professor himself. His personal opinions, I believe, favor very strict rules of expounding the Constitution of the U. [*sic*] States. [245]

Madison said that he would be glad to receive the finished work, though he felt that his advanced age would prevent him from bestowing upon it all the attention he was sure it would deserve. He added,

> I can the less calculate the degree in which my views of the Constitution accord with or vary from yours, as I am so imperfectly acquainted with the authorities to which I infer yours are in the main conformable. [246]

Duer published his *Lectures on Constitutional Jurisprudence* in full in 1843, and revised it in 1856. There were few references

---

244 *Col. Univ. Q.,* IV, 155-156.

245 *Letters and Other Writings of James Madison,* published by order of Congress, IV (Philadelphia: 1865), 308-309. John A. G. Davis was professor of law at the time.

246 *Ibid.,* IV, 309.

in his original *Outlines*,[247] but his enlarged volume included citations of cases, laws, and law books, and was intended to be of use to the professional as well as to the general student of the Constitution.[248]

Duer remained as head of Columbia until May 1842, when ill health forced him to resign. While in office he gave his full attention to the affairs of the College, though the financial situation was one which could not be solved easily.[249] The relations between the president and students, alumni, and trustees seem to have been pleasant.[250] According to Evart A. Duyckinck, a member of the class of 1835, Duer's presidency was marked by his " high-toned and gentlemanly administration " of the affairs of the college. His courtesy, rather than severe discipline, secured for him the respect of the students,[251] and he proudly asserted his affection for them. In his address to the St. Nicholas Society, Duer said,

> The sons of my old friends, especially of those deceased, seem to have succeeded to their fathers in my affections. To many of them, and to others that I see before me, have I stood in the place of a parent; I have felt for them a parent's responsibility and solicitude, and I sometimes flatter myself that in return they feel for me almost the attachment of sons.[252]

After his retirement, Duer lived in Morristown, New Jersey. Restored health and leisure enabled him to write the life of his

247 Review of Duer's *Outlines of the Constitutional Jurisprudence of the United States, American Jurist*, XI (Jan. 1834), 235-236.

248 Duer, *Lectures* (2nd ed., 1856), Advertisement.

249 See chapter x on presidencies of Duer and Moore, *A History of Columbia University, 1754-1904* (New York: 1904), pp. 112-119. Allowance granted Duer ($1200 per year) small because of straitened finances. Also reference to hard times in Frederick Paul Keppel, *Columbia* (New York: 1914), p. 172.

250 *Col. Univ. Q.*, IV, 157.

251 *Cyc. of Amer. Lit.*, I, 383.

252 *Col. Univ. Q.*, IV, 157-158. Address also published separately, in full.

maternal grandfather, William Alexander, who claimed to be Lord Stirling. This biography was published as a volume of the *Collections of the New Jersey Historical Society*.[253] In addition, he made several addresses and revised his *Lectures*. His death occurred in New York on May 30, 1858.[254]

### DAVID HOFFMAN

David Hoffman, the only Marylander among the commentators, was Duer's junior by four years. The story of Hoffman's early life is not clear. We know that he was born on December 24, 1784, so late in the day that he always celebrated the twenty-fifth, thus giving holiday-minded biographers the opportunity to claim Christmas as his actual birth date.[255] He was the eleventh of twelve children of a family eminent for its literary accomplishments. Details of his education are not available, but he studied law, and soon rose to be one of the leading practitioners of Baltimore.[256]

In 1812, Hoffman was involved in two events of some significance. On June 20 of that year, an article opposing the declaration of war against England appeared in the *Federal Republican*. The people of Baltimore were so incensed that, on June 22, they destroyed the presses and drove the editors from town, thus silencing the paper. About a month later, a group which included the former editors met secretly in a private house. The paper was now published in Georgetown, and they had just distributed copies of it. When word leaked out of what was going on, a mob quickly assembled and proceeded to the house. After a violent demonstration, the military was sum-

---

253 *Life of William Alexander, Earl of Stirling; Major General in the Army of the United States, during the Revolution: with Selections from His Correspondence*, by his grandson... (New York: 1847). Vol. II of *N. J. Hist. Soc. Colls.*

254 *Col. Univ. Q.*, IV, 158.

255 Roberdeau Buchanan, *The Genealogy of the McKean Family of Pennsylvania* (Lancaster, Pa.: 1890), p. 143.

256 *Cyc. of Amer. Lit.*, II, 65.

moned, and twenty-four of the planners, Hoffman among them, were escorted to the jail for safekeeping. Later when many of these men were dragged from the jail and beaten violently by the infuriated mob, Hoffman was apparently left untouched, so he seems to have been a minor figure.[257] His connection with the incident would show, however, his Federalism (in a Democratic community) and his desire to uphold the freedom of the press.

Also in 1812, an attempt was made to organize a law school in the recently chartered University of Maryland. A law faculty of six was appointed, and one of them, Hoffman, assumed the task of planning the prospective curriculum.[258] The results were published in 1817 as *A Course of Legal Study,* and the volume was enthusiastically praised by the profession. Justice Story said it was " the most perfect system for the study of the law, which has ever been offered to the publick." [259] Hoffman organized his course around a group of thirteen general subjects, under each of which he prescribed certain readings.[260] Our pri-

257 J. Thomas Scharf, *The Chronicles of Baltimore; Being a Complete History of " Baltimore Town" and Baltimore City from the Earliest Period to the Present Time* (Baltimore: 1874), pp. 309-339. Data from report to the mayor, Edward Johnson, by the joint committee of the two branches of the City Council, and other documents.

258 Aumann, *Changing American Legal System,* p. 109.

259 Book review in *North American Review,* VI (Nov. 1817), 76. Reprinted in Joseph Story, *Miscellaneous Writings* (Boston: 1835), pp. 223-243. Story did not want his authorship revealed. *Cf.* his letter to Henry Wheaton, Nov. 13, 1817, regarding this article: " Show it to Mr. Hoffman, but without intimating that I had aught to do with it, for (without affecting secrecy) I shall not be *suspected* as the author of any thing in the Review." Story, *Life and Letters,* I, 309.

260 The subjects were, (1) moral and political philosophy; (2) the elementary and constitutional principles of the Municipal Law of England, including a study of (a) the Feudal Law, (b) the Institutes of the Municipal Law generally, and (c) the origin and progress of the Common Law; (3) the Law of Real Rights and Real Remedies; (4) the Law of Personal Rights and Personal Remedies; (5) the Law of Equity; (6) the Lex Mercatoria; (7) the Law of Crimes and Punishments; (8) the Law of Nations; (9) the Maritime and Admiralty Law; (10) the Civil or Roman Law;

mary concern is with his Section 11, " The Constitution and Laws of the United States of America." Hoffman had a rich background in both common and civil law, and he included many references to foreign works. His emphasis was on wide and systematic reading, but in addition, he sought to provide the basis for intelligent criticism.

Hoffman's academic career formally began when he was appointed professor of law in the University of Maryland in 1814, but he did not immediately begin to lecture. Part of the difficulties came from the competition of the large and successful private school conducted by Judge Walter Dorsey of the Court of Appeals.[261] In 1821, undismayed by the delay, Hoffman published a modification of his original plan of 1817, entitled *A Syllabus of a Course of Lectures on Law; Proposed to be Delivered in the University of Maryland; Addressed to the Students of Law in the United States.* The course was intended to occupy an hour a day for ten months of the year, and was to continue for two years.[262] It was designed to treat the more important topics in the law so that few difficulties would be left to the students in their private studies. Hoffman asked all students who proposed to enroll to write to him, so that he might be assured of a respectable class. Such enrollees would be informed when the class was to begin.[263]

Lectures were commenced in October 1822, and were better attended after the sudden death on August 1st, 1823, of Judge

---

(11) the Constitution and Laws of the United States of America; (12) the Constitution and Laws of the several states of the Union; and (13) political economy. There was a " particular syllabus " under every title of the general syllabus.

261 Hoffman, Letter to the Trustees of the University of Maryland, Nov. 20, 1836 (Baltimore: 1837), p. 3. Aumann, *Changing American Legal System*, p. 109, gives 1815 as the starting date.

262 Eugene Fauntleroy Cordell, *Historical Sketch of the University of Maryland School of Medicine (1807-1890), with an Introductory chapter, notices of the schools of Law, Arts and Sciences, and Theology*... (Baltimore: 1891), p. 49.

263 Hoffman, *Syllabus*, Prefatory note, p. xii.

Dorsey—he of the large and successful law school.[264] Hoffman lectured daily, according to plan, but the law department was not enthusiastically patronized.[265]

By the end of 1823, the financial troubles of the University forced its reorganization. The State stepped in, took over the property and ousted the faculty. Hoffman accepted an appointment under the new trustees and continued to lecture.[266] In 1826, the Legislature undertook to direct the application of the balance of the fund of $140,000 which had been authorized by the Lottery Acts. $14,200 went to the law school as a fair proportion of the whole amount. $5,000 were supposed to be paid to Hoffman for his law library, and the balance was invested with a view to the subsequent erection of necessary buildings. Meanwhile lectures were delivered in a rented hall.[267]

Hoffman claimed that he received no salary for four years, paid various debts of the University, and invested $20,000 of his own funds in the law school alone.[268] Perhaps because of this circumstance, he refused to deliver his law library and furniture to the trustees. He stopped lecturing in 1833, and in April of that year, proceedings were instituted against him by the trustees to recover the library and furniture.[269] Without delivering either, Hoffman gave bail and left for Europe. Even though a judgment was obtained against him, the claim still re-

---

264 Hoffman, Letter to the Trustees of the University of Maryland, Nov. 20, 1836, p. 3. Cordell, in *Historical Sketch of Maryland School of Medicine*, p. 49, says that Hoffman did not start to lecture until after Judge Dorsey's death.

265 Cordell, *loc. cit.*

266 Aumann, *Changing American Legal System*, p. 109.

267 Cordell, *Historical Sketch of Maryland School of Medicine*, pp. 49-50, note 2. From the *Joint Memorial of the Trustees of the University and Baltimore College, to the Legislature, 1830.* Hoffman claimed that the $5,000 were never paid to him. Letter to the Trustees, Nov. 20, 1836.

268 Hoffman, Letter to the Trustees, Nov. 20, 1836, p. 6.

269 Proceedings begun April 16, 1833, by action of trover in Baltimore County Court. Cordell, *Historical Sketch of Maryland School of Medicine*, p. 49.

mained " unsatisfied " when the University was restored to the regents in April 1839.[270]

Hoffman suffered severe financial set-backs as a result of his efforts to reform legal education. In 1821, speaking hopefully in the third person, he promised

> that his regular business at the bar *will not be interfered with in any degree,* nor the interest of his clients neglected. The nature of the studies connected with the present undertaking, is such as to advance him beyond any other plan in the knowledge necessary and proper to forensick business; and he has always looked to it as abundant compensation, should any accident defeat his proposed scheme of lecturing, that every hour expended in preparation for it, has disciplined him more strictly in the learning of his profession.[271]

But by 1826, he felt that he had lost about two-thirds of his practice, or at least $3,000.[272]

In 1829, Hoffman published his *Legal Outlines, Being the Substance of a Course of Lectures now Delivering in the University of Maryland* (Baltimore), which were in reality the full lectures on Title I of his *Syllabus.* He promised three volumes at the time, but only the one appeared. Previously, he had told Chancellor Kent that twenty volumes the size of Blackstone would be necessary to contain his lectures.[273]

In 1836, the *Course of Legal Study* appeared in a new and enlarged form, with a lengthy section entitled "Auxiliary Subjects." It was dedicated to Justice Story, who had praised the

---

270 *Loc. cit.*

271 Hoffman, *Syllabus,* preface, p. viii. Letter to the Trustees, Sept. 27, 1826, p. 34.

272 Hoffman said his practice had been worth $9,000, and fixed his losses at $3,000 because of the decline of business generally.

273 MS. note at end of Kent's copy of the *Course of Legal Study* (Baltimore: 1817), stating that Hoffman called " at my office in N. York, Dec. 13, 1823, and he told me that the fitting up of his Lectures upon his plan would require *20 Volumes* as large as those of Blackstone." Kent Hall Library, Columbia University.

first edition in the *North American Review*,[274] and whose personal friendship Hoffman enjoyed.[275] The bibliography was more complete, and the comments on legal writers more extensive. Hoffman provided for four distinct courses, by the simple expedient of indicating the importance of books listed, on a graduated scale. Students might finish a course in from less than three to six or seven years, depending on the intensity of their readings.[276] That the book was well received is attested by the following commendations of the first edition that it carried:

> This work is recommended in the strongest terms by CHIEF JUSTICE MARSHALL, Mr. Justice Story, Chancellor Kent, Judge Spencer, DeWitt Clinton, Professor Stearnes, Chief Justice Tilghman, Mr. Justice Washington, . . . the Hon. Daniel Webster, and by more than 200 eminent lawyers of this and other countries. It has been elaborately reviewed in the *North American Review,* the *Analectic Magazine,* and by many other periodicals. The British and Continental Reviews speak of it in the highest terms, and the entire edition was exhausted in eighteen months.[277]

274 *Vide supra,* p. 105, note 259.

275 See letter of Hoffman to Charles Sumner, Sept. 20, 1845, acknowledging the receipt of the latter's eulogy of Story: "... my regard and love for him [Story] were far beyond what is known—I have known him well nearly thirty years—part of the time more intimately than recently . . ." Sumner Papers.

276 Hoffman's degree designations bore the mark of originality. The graduated scale operated as follows: (1) For the "degree of Prolytae," all the books listed to be read, occupying about six or seven years; (2) For the "degree of Lytae," all works except those designated "E" to be read, requiring about four years; (3) For the "degree of Papinianistae," all works except those designated "E" and "e" to be read, requiring about three years; (4) For the special needs of those pursuing the profession in the interior and out of the maritime cities, all works marked "*." The students who read a little in the first and second titles might be termed "Dupondii," and were to be despised. Hoffman, *Course of Legal Study* I (2nd ed., 1836), 53.

277 Advertising sheet for 2nd ed., bound with Hoffman's *Introductory Lectures* (Baltimore: 1837). At end of volume. The *Course of Legal Study* was reprinted in 1846 in one volume.

The law professorship at the University of Maryland was discontinued soon after Hoffman stopped lecturing (1833). No attempt was made to revive it until 1869.[278] Hoffman published a volume of his Introductory Lectures in 1837, with this revealing prefatory note:

> This volume, together with the two editions of the author's *Course of Legal Study,* and his *Legal Outlines,* as also his *Moot Court Decisions* and Abridgment of *Lord Coke's Reports,* with notes . . . , will afford, as he hopes, sufficient evidence, were any needed, that *in breaking up* the law professorship, the Trustees have done the author no little injustice and themselves no great credit.[279]

Meanwhile, Hoffman had become a trans-Atlantic commuter.[280] He returned from his first trip to Europe in 1835, and in the fall of 1836, campaigned for William Henry Harrison. In both 1836 and 1840, he served as presidential elector-at-large from Maryland.[281] After another two-year trip to Europe, he moved to Philadelphia, where he was admitted to the bar, December 16, 1843.[282] In 1844, he attempted to start a private law school there, but gave it up in 1847 and returned to Europe.[283]

Hoffman failed in his attempt to reform American legal education single-handed. As Reed points out,

> The fundamental weakness of Hoffman's great design is revealed in his own introduction. American law was already ex-

278 Cordell, *Historical Sketch of Maryland School of Medicine,* pp. 49-50.

279 Advertisement to his *Introductory Lectures, and Syllabus of a Course of Lectures Delivered in the University of Maryland,* p. vi. The last two works were not published.

280 The reason for Hoffman's European trips is not given. Perhaps he was avoiding unpleasant demands from Maryland authorities.

281 Buchanan, *Genealogy of the McKean Family,* p. 143.

282 *Loc. cit.*

283 Aumann, *Changing American Legal System,* p. 109.

panding at such a rate that a systematic survey of the entire field became antiquated almost as soon as it was published.[284]

However, he had a wide influence on the course of American legal development. His *Legal Hints, Being a Condensation of the Leading Ideas as Relating to Professional Deportment* . . . (Philadelphia: 1846), anticipated many of the present canons of conduct of the American Bar Association.[285]

Hoffman's social standing was enhanced by his marriage in 1816 to Mary McKean, the beautiful granddaughter of Governor McKean of Pennsylvania.[286] Details are not available, but he apparently was active in civic affairs. At the 1816 session of the legislature, Hoffman and two others were appointed insolvency commissioners, to examine applicants and grant provisional relief.[287] Like Rawle, he was a member of the Board of Library Directors of Baltimore.[288] He was also one of the

284 Reed, *Training for the Public Profession of the Law*, p. 125.

285 *Cf.* Aumann, *Changing American Legal System*, p. 103, note 33. The *Legal Hints* were based upon "Resolutions in Regard to Professional Deportment" which originally appeared in the *Course of Legal Study*, II (Baltimore: 1836), 752-775. Compare, for example, Hoffman's Resolution No. III: "To all judges, when in court, I will ever be respectful: they are the Law's vicegerents [*sic*]; and whatever may be their character and deportment, the individual should be lost in the majesty of the office," with No. 1 of the *Canons of Professional Ethics...adopted by the American Bar Association* (as amended, Sept. 30, 1937): "It is the duty of the lawyer to maintain towards the Courts a respectful attitude, not for the sake of the temporary incumbent of the judicial office, but for the maintenance of its supreme importance..." Hoffman's standards were reprinted by James Ram in *A Treatise on Facts as Subjects of Inquiry by a Jury* (2nd Amer. ed., New York: 1870), as "Fifty Resolutions in Regard to Professional Deportment, by adherence to which the lawyer may reasonably hope to attain eminence in his profession," pp. 375-388.

286 Buchanan, *Genealogy of the McKean Family*, p. 143. See "Diary of Robert Gilmor," *Maryland Historical Magazine*, XVII (June 1922), *passim*, for references to social occasions when David Hoffman and/or his wife were present.

287 Scharf, *Chronicles of Baltimore*, p. 381.

288 "Diary of Robert Gilmor," *Md. Hist. Mag.*, XVII, 240. Note that Hoffman attended meeting held January 3, 1827.

original members of " The Protection Society of Maryland," a
group of leading citizens who believed that Negroes were often
unjustly deprived of their freedom. Their concern was with
freedmen and Negroes who would become free in the future.
They specifically pledged non-interference with slavery so long
as it was countenanced by Maryland law.[289]

That Hoffman was known to Madison is evidenced by two
letters included in the latter's *Works*. One acknowledged receipt
of a copy of one of Hoffman's lectures at the University of
Maryland,[290] and another was a letter of introduction given
Hoffman to present to the Baron de Humboldt in England.[291]

While in London on his third visit, Hoffman wrote a series
of able articles, explaining the political and social economy of
the United States government, which were published in *The
Times*.[292] He also wrote the work which he envisaged as his
*opus magnum,* a history of the world since the advent of Christianity, with emphasis on nations and peoples, entitled *Chronicles selected from the Originals of Cartaphilus, the Wandering
Jew*. The first two volumes were published in London in
1853.[293]

Hoffman returned to the United States in December of 1853
to arrange his private affairs, " which long absence from the
country had made a source of some solicitude." He was in New
York when he died suddenly of apoplexy, November 11,
1854.[294]

---

289 Constitution of the Society reproduced in the *Md. Hist. Mag.*, I,
358-362.

290 *Letters of Madison* (1865), IV, 223. Letter dated June 13, 1832.

291 *Ibid.*, IV, 292. Letter dated March 12, 1833.

292 *Cyc. of Amer. Lit.*, II, 66.

293 *Loc. cit.*

294 *Ibid.*, II, 67.

# CHAPTER IV
# THE NEW ENGLAND NATIONALISTS

NATHANIEL CHIPMAN, Nathan Dane, Joseph Story, and Timothy Walker—all may be considered members of the school of New England nationalists. Each served the nation well not only in the preparation of commentaries which helped to expound the law of the Constitution, but as a citizen. Chipman was instrumental in bringing Vermont into the Union; Dane made sure that the Harvard Law School would be a nationalizing agency, providing instruction in national law rather than concentrating on jurisdictional peculiarities; Story taught in that school and became one of the luminaries of the United States Supreme Court; and Walker spread the nationalist doctrine into the western country of Ohio. Chipman seems to have remained aloof from this group, perhaps because of his relative geographic isolation; but the lives of the other three were interconnected. As has been indicated, Dane stipulated that his chair of law at Harvard be occupied by Story, and Walker studied there under the Justice. George Ticknor Curtis, another of Story's students, wrote a two-volume constitutional history of the United States in which he followed the Story-Webster doctrine.[1] These volumes are not strictly a commentary, however,

1 George Ticknor Curtis (1812-1894) was born in Watertown, Massachusetts. He graduated from Harvard in 1832 and studied under Story in 1833. He completed his legal education in the office of his brother, Benjamin Robbins Curtis, who was later a Justice of the Supreme Court, and was admitted to the bar in 1836. He entered politics as a Whig and friend of Webster, serving in the Massachusetts House from 1840 to 1843, but his practice was so extensive that he declined re-election.

As one of Webster's literary executors, he wrote the *Life of Daniel Webster* (New York: 1869), 2 vols. In 1879, he wrote the biography which appeared in Volume I of *A Memoir of Benjamin Robbins Curtis, LL.D.*, edited by his son, Benjamin Robbins Curtis (Boston), 2 vols.

For our purposes, Curtis' main contribution is his *History of the Origin, Formation and Adoption of the Constitution of the United States* (1854-1858). This work is historical in approach and does not discuss any of the problems that arose after the Constitution was put into effect. It follows the

as they tell only of the formation of our government and do not discuss subsequent problems of constitutional interpretation.

### NATHANIEL CHIPMAN

In point of time, Chipman and Dane had priority. Both were born in 1752. Though Chipman outlived Dane by eight years, the active professional lives of both men ended several years before death.

Chipman's early life was spent in Salisbury, Connecticut. His father owned both a farm and a blacksmith shop, and Nathaniel was one of the brothers assigned to the farm.[2] The family devoted their evenings to reading—the only education Nathaniel had during his first twenty-one years. Then, after nine months of intensive study, he entered Yale College in 1774,[3] and went far beyond the regular curriculum with a self-imposed course of general reading and literary studies. His brother later described him as a " universal scholar." [4]

---

Federalist, Websterian school of interpretation. *Cf. infra*, chs. vi and vii, *passim*, for certain of the views expressed.

Curtis became a Democrat during the 'fifties. He was a moderate on the slavery question and as United States Commissioner, angered the abolitionists by facilitating the return of the slave, Thomas Sims, under the Act of 1850. He was a Unionist though a critic of the Administration during the Civil War. He died in 1894, survived by his wife, Louise A. Nyström, and five children. His first wife, Mary Oliver Story, had died in 1848, leaving two sons.

Sources on Curtis include volume I of *A Memoir of Benjamin Robbins Curtis, LL.D.*, as cited above; Obituary by " H.N.C.," *Harvard Graduates' Magazine*, II (June 1894), 572; and an article in the *New York Herald*, March 29, 1894, p. 16.

2 E. P. Walton, " Nathaniel Chipman," in Abby Maria Hemenway, ed., *Vermont Historical Gazetteer, A Magazine*, III (1877), 1154.

3 Daniel Chipman, *Life of the Honorable Nathaniel Chipman* (Boston: 1846), pp. 9-10; Dexter, *Biographical Sketches of the Graduates of Yale College*, III, 660. He continued his orderly habits at college, allotting regular time to languages, classical studies and general reading. His relaxation was in light reading. He so thoroughly enjoyed his work and arrangement of time that he recommended his method to younger students. Chipman, *Life*, pp. 10-11. However, it is recorded that the rigors of army life were required to restore his health.

4 *Ibid.*, p. 11; *Vt. Hist. Gaz.*, III, 1154.

Chipman left college in the spring of his senior year, with an ensign's commission in Col. Charles Webb's Second Connecticut Continental Line, but he was granted his degree in course.[5] Not much information has come down about his army life.[6] While in camp at Valley Forge in December 1777, he was promoted to a first lieutenancy.[7] He took part in the campaign of 1777 and the Battle of Monmouth in June 1778. While he was fighting under Washington in Pennsylvania, three of his brothers helped to defeat Burgoyne at Saratoga.[8] Nathaniel's military life influenced his later political convictions. As Honeywell puts it,

> His experiences with intrigue and insubordination, sharpened by the privations of Valley Forge, as he saw his great commander thwarted repeatedly through the weakness of the Congress and the jealousies of the states, made him a life-long Federalist.[9]

In October 1778, financial reasons forced Chipman to resign his commission—a possibility not now open to military men in wartime. His parents had moved to Tinmouth, Vermont, while he was in college, and the war had destroyed their property. He was thus left with only his inadequate salary as a subaltern, and was running deeper and deeper into debt.[10]

5 Dexter, *Biographical Sketches of Yale Graduates*, III, 660. In Alberto Lee Chipman, *Chipmans of America* (Poland, Me.: 1904), p. 51, it is recorded that on April 4, 1777, Nathaniel was made second lieutenant in the company commanded by Capt. David Parsons.

6 *Vt. Hist. Gaz.*, III, 1154-55. What is known is chiefly to be found in his letters.

7 Dexter, *Biographical Sketches of Yale Graduates*, III, 660.

8 Chipman, *Life*, pp. 5, 23, 35.

9 Honeywell, "Nathaniel Chipman," *N. Eng. Q.*, V, 559.

10 These details explained in a letter to his friend and classmate, Fitch, Oct. 3, 1778, and in his letter to Gen. Washington, resigning his commission, Oct. 10, 1778. Chipman, *Life*, pp. 28-30, 32-33.

Chipman had kept his Greek and Latin classics with him while in camp,[11] so was no stranger to books when he took up law in Salisbury. He completed his studies in four or five months and was admitted to the bar in the courts of Litchfield County, Connecticut, on March 20, 1779.[12] He went immediately to Tinmouth, and his admission to the bar there was the third in Vermont.[13]

The situation called for a pioneering temperament. The government of the " State of Vermont " had been in operation about a year. Its supreme court, which had been organized more recently, held its first session the previous December. At the time, as there were no authorized attorneys in the state, the parties involved in cases appeared personally. None of the five justices of the supreme court had been educated in the law. Chipman, surrounded by opportunities, soon built up an extensive practice, and his name appeared in nearly every case in the court dockets for the next ten years.[14] He served as State's Attorney from 1781 to 1785, and this position led to others.

On March 6, 1784, Chipman was appointed on a committee to revise the statutes of the state. In October the committee was enlarged and given the task of preparing a complete state code.[15] Chipman accepted the commission on condition that he have the use and finally the ownership of certain books from the confiscated library of Charles Phelps of Marlborough.[16] Phelps was pardoned in October 1784, but the law books were left with the

11 *Ibid.*, pp. 33-34.

12 *Ibid.*, p. 35; *Vt. Hist. Gaz.*, III, 1155.

13 *Vt. Hist. Gaz.*, III, 1155. His professional circuit embraced what are now the counties of Bennington, Rutland, Windham, and Windsor. Shortly after beginning his practice, he married Sarah Hill of Tinmouth, and together they reared seven children.

14 Charles L. Williams, compiler, *Statistics of the Rutland County Bar* ... (Brandon, Vt.: 1847), p. 13.

15 *Vt. Hist. Gaz.*, III, 1155.

16 Phelps, a Tory, had been educated in the law in Northampton, Massachusetts, and settled in Vermont in 1764. *Vt. Hist. Gaz.*, III, 1156.

committee. Walton concludes that the careful study of these books, and the detailed analysis of the statutes necessary in the preparation of the code, aided in preparing Chipman for the bench and raising him to it. During his brief period of legal study, he could have done no more than master the leading principles of the common law. His own library must have been small, and the books of his brother attorneys could not have provided much additional information.[17] The results of the work of the committee are apparently embodied in the code of laws adopted in February and March 1787.[18]

Meanwhile, from October 1784 to October 1786, Chipman served as one of the representatives of Tinmouth in the General Assembly.[19] Then, at the 1786 session of the legislature, he was elected assistant judge of the supreme court, the first lawyer to be so honored. At the end of the year he returned to practice at the bar. " Situated as he was on the bench, one of five judges, and he the only lawyer, it is believed that he did not at that time become very distinguished as a judge," [20]—an interesting commentary on the standards of the judicial profession at the time.

As for the Federal Constitution, Chipman favored it immediately. He was rewarded for his efforts in bringing Vermont into the Union [21] by an appointment by President Washington as judge of the United States District Court of Vermont, a lifetime post, but one which Chipman resigned two years later be-

17 *Ibid.*, III, 1155-56.

18 *Ibid.*, III, 1155.

19 The dates herein given for Chipman's service in the state legislature and as State's Attorney differ from those that appear in Chipman, *Chipmans of America*, p. 51.

20 Chipman, *Life*, p. 69.

21 *Vt. Hist. Gaz.*, III, 1156. Vermont was admitted on Feb. 18, 1791, the membership in the Union to date from March 4. For Chipman's correspondence with Hamilton regarding the desire of Vermont to join the Union and its attendant problems, see John C. Hamilton, ed., *The Works of Alexander Hamilton*, I (New York: 1850), 466-479.

cause he was "dissatisfied with the inactivity of its duties." [22]

Early in 1793, Chipman published a small volume entitled *Reports and Dissertations,* containing concise reports of twenty-five cases decided from 1789 to 1791 while he was Chief Justice of the Supreme Court of Vermont, with essays on the statute adopting the common law of England, the statute of offsets, negotiable notes, and the statute of conveyances. The reports were published, according to the Preface, to aid judges in recalling precedents. The opportunity to review earlier decisions would help them to determine what was right and wrong, and thus correct errors and establish principles of justice.[23]

More important in a study of commentaries is the small volume which Chipman published later in 1793—the *Sketches of the Principles of Government.* According to their author, the *Sketches* were a first attempt " to analyze the social nature of man, and from the relations, thence resulting, to derive the principles, which ought to be pursued in civil institutions." [24]

Chipman's work is unusual in many ways, particularly in that it set forth many theories that were just beginning to be advanced by contemporary thinkers—for instance, direct election of the President and judicial review of legislation. He endorsed

22 Williams, *Statistics of the Rutland County Bar,* p. 14. Daniel Chipman and F. B. Dexter agree that the reason was his anxiety for more active employment, since there was very little business before the court. (Dexter, *Biographical Sketches of Yale Graduates,* III, 661; Chipman, *Life,* p. 109.) But Chancellor Kent notes a factor which was probably of more importance —he could not afford the honor of the low salary ($800 per annum). (Note in Kent's handwriting on fly leaf of his copy of Chipman's *Sketches of the Principles of Government,* Kent Hall Library, Columbia University.) Chipman's pecuniary difficulties remained with him. His farm, to which he could not give due attention, was a drain on him, not a source of income. Daniel Chipman tells us that, "When he published his work on Government, he was compelled to ask assistance from his relatives." (Chipman, *Life,* p. 66.)

23 This volume is among the earliest of systematic court reports in the United States. It is now very rare. Later decisions of Chipman were reported by his brother, the first official court reporter of Vermont. See Daniel Chipman, *Reports* (1824).

24 Preface to the *Sketches,* dated at Rutland, June 25, 1793.

the theory of taxation which emphasizes ability to pay, and urged certainty rather than severity as the most important consideration in punishment of crime.

Believing man to be capable of unlimited improvement, Chipman advocated democratic education to promote the social and political order. Both Jefferson and Madison held the *Sketches* in high esteem, especially as their views on the improvement of society coincided closely with Chipman's.[25] In 1807, Jefferson recommended the volume along with certain European classics and the *Federalist* to the attention of young Americans.[26] He included it in a "Course of Legal Study" in 1814,[27] and in 1816, he urged its use as a text-book for William and Mary College.[28]

The *Sketches* covered a wide range of the philosophic problems involved in law and political science. Chipman's originality in this work is not marked, but, as Honeywell says, he showed himself

> a judicious critic, organizing the prevalent ideas of his time, and interpreting political institutions and tendencies in the light of his classical and legal training and conservative temperament . . . . Better than any other writer of his generation, he gives a judicious exposition of the principles of American republicanism.[29]

25 Honeywell in *N. Eng. Q.*, V, 570.

26 Letter to John Norvall, June 11, 1807, in *Writings of Jefferson*, XI (Library edition, Washington: 1903), 223.

27 Henry Barnard in *American Journal of Education*, XXVII (July 1877), 546.

28 Letter to J. C. Cabell, Feb. 2, 1816, *Early History of the University of Virginia* (Richmond: 1856), p. 53. Honeywell concludes that the book was widely read for those times, as many copies are still extant. He found a ms. letter from Chipman to Thomas and Andrews, Booksellers, Boston, dated Oct. 6, 1795, two years after publication, saying that he is sending to Boston 60 copies in sheets to be bound for sale. Letter at Massachusetts Historical Society. *N. Eng. Q.*, V, 571 note.

29 *Ibid.*, V, 583.

Shortly after the publication of the *Sketches,* Chipman was much embarrassed by the Democratic Society of Chittenden County, which quoted passages and reprinted them in their widely read *Proceedings,* making it appear that Chipman endorsed their activities. He hastened to write to Hamilton, whose esteem he valued highly, telling him that he had not sanctioned the use of his book. Chipman did not say that the democratic societies should be abolished, but he thought that improvements should be made in their methods.[30]

It is not easy to determine the sources of Chipman's political opinions. He had received the traditional classical training at Yale, and had evidently read and studied the political writings of his day, critically analyzing them in the light of American experience. He was not a party propagandist, but in his discussions of the Constitution, especially on such topics as the independent judiciary, there is a marked similarity to the reasoning of the *Federalist.*[31] There is also a noteworthy similarity between Chipman's work and that of James Wilson. Both were concerned with the philosophic basis of law, and both professed a belief that law, order, and justice rest ultimately on religious sanction. Wilson developed the subject somewhat differently, dividing law into God-made and man-made, while Chipman did not emphasize this distinction. They undoubtedly came to their conclusions independently, owing to the great distance between them.

Chipman was elected Chief Justice again in 1796, but resigned to serve as United States Senator from 1797 to 1802.[32] His senatorial term was unmarked by any dramatic actions. Although he made only one recorded speech, his votes show

30 Chipman to Hamilton, Jan. 9, 1794. Chipman, *Life,* p. 395.

31 Honeywell in *N. Eng. Q.,* V, 582.

32 The dates usually given for Chipman's service in the Senate are 1798 to 1804. However, he took his seat on Nov. 27, 1797 (*Annals of Congress,* 5th Cong., 2nd sess., p. 470), and no record of his attendance appears after the first session of the Seventh Congress (spring of 1802). Chipman was originally appointed to replace Isaac Tichenor, who was elected governor.

him to have been a staunch Federalist and supporter of the
Adams administration. In the first session he attended, he
backed the measures in preparation for a possible war with
France,[33] and served on a select committee considering " An
act providing arms for the militia throughout the United
States." [34] He voted for the Naturalization Act in its original
form, and opposed the amendment to decrease the period of
residence from fourteen to seven years.[35]

When the bill to define treason and to define and punish sedition came before the Senate, Chipman was on the committee to
which it was referred. No vote on the final passage of the act is
given, but on two previous occasions, he had signified his approval.[36]

The only full length speech recorded for Chipman was one
which he made after the Republicans became the dominant
party. He spoke against the resolution to change the judiciary
system (debated in 1802), and voted against the bill, too, but
on this occasion, he was on the losing side.[37]

When his term in the Senate ended, Chipman returned to the
practice of law, though he did not maintain an office. He restricted himself to only the most important cases. He represented Tinmouth in the legislature from 1806 to 1809, and in
1811. In March 1813, he was elected to the Council of Censors,
at the head of the list.[38]

33 No votes are recorded for Chipman between April 20 and May 21,
1798, when several measures came up for increasing the military. *Ibid.*,
pp. 544-559. Later, however, he voted for all such measures, including the
Act to declare void all treaties with the French Republic. *Ibid.*, pp. 587-
588, June 23, 25, 1798.

34 *Ibid.*, p. 582, June 18, 1798.

35 *Ibid.*, pp. 577-578, June 12, 1798.

36 *Ibid.*, p. 590, June 26, 1798; p. 597, July 3, 1798.

37 *Ibid.*, 7th Cong., 1st sess., pp. 122-132, 183, Jan. 19, 1802, Feb. 3, 1802.

38 Chipman, *Life*, p. 153; Walter Hill Crockett, *Vermont, The Green
Mountain State*, III (New York: 1921), p. 114. It was the duty of this body
of thirteen persons elected for a seven year term, to examine the constitution and to propose amendments. Chipman had long wished to see a Senate

In 1813, Chipman was again elected Chief Justice of the Vermont Supreme Court and held office for two years.[39] The most significant cases decided by the Supreme Court at this time were published in 1824 in Daniel Chipman's *Reports*.[40]

While he was serving his last term as Chief Justice, the Hartford Convention was called. Though an ardent Federalist, Chipman deemed the move a violation of constitutional principles.[41] When he heard that a proposition would be made in the Vermont legislature, then in session, to appoint delegates to the convention, he immediately went to Montpelier. His influence was an important factor in suppressing the measure, so that there were no official representatives from Vermont.[42]

---

established as a coordinate branch of the legislature; a board for the appointment of state officials, thus removing the power from the corrupting influence of the legislature; the appointment of judges of the Supreme Court during good behavior instead of for a single year; and the establishment of a court of chancery distinct from the courts of law. (Chipman, *Life*, p. 154.) *The Constitutionalist*, a pamphlet in support of the proposed amendments, using arguments that had earlier been propounded by James Wilson, was published anonymously in 1814. Daniel Chipman does not claim the honor of authorship for his brother, but it is assigned to him by E. P. Walton and other writers. (*Vt. Hist. Gaz.*, III, 1156.) The Republicans opposed the proposed amendments, and they were all defeated in a convention held at Montpelier, July 7-9, 1814. (Crockett, *Vermont*, III, 115.) The amendment establishing the bi-cameral system was finally adopted in 1836. (Chipman, *Life*, p. 192.)

39 *Ibid.*, p. 195, says October 1813–October 1815. Walton in *Vt. Hist. Gaz.*, III, 1156, says December 1813–December 1815, which had been the traditional terminal dates of state offices. Chipman was displaced, together with the associate judges, by a change of parties in the annual elections. *Loc. cit.*

40 Chipman, *Life*, p. 195; *cf.* Aumann, *Changing American Legal System*, p. 76, note 29.

41 Dane, on the other hand, held that the Convention was constitutional under Article I, Sec. 10 of the Constitution. Dane, 9 *General Abridgment*, 595-596.

42 Crockett, *Vermont*, III, 123; Henry Adams, *History of the United States in the Administrations of Jefferson and Madison*, VIII (New York: 1909), 227.

Chipman preceded Dane and Story in actively promoting the development of legal education in his state. In 1800, when Middlebury College was established by the legislature, both of the legally-minded Chipman brothers were named as trustees in the charter.[43] From 1806 to 1816, Daniel served as professor of law, and his successor from 1816 to 1843, was Nathaniel.[44] In 1817, the latter delivered a course of lectures which attracted considerable attention at the time, but were never published as a whole.[45] He retained the position nominally until his death, but gave no further lectures. Increasing deafness hampered him in his practice and his professorial duties, though his intellectual powers showed no decline.[46]

Chipman produced one of the early reactions to the tariff controversy of 1828-33. His "Observations on Mr. Calhoun's Exposé of his Nullification Doctrines" is a lengthy refutation of the South Carolinian's theories. This work remained in manuscript among his papers, but was said to have been published in the *Richmond Whig*.[47] Perhaps it was at this time that a contemporary remarked that the two states in the Union which had ideas were Vermont and South Carolina, and that Chipman and Calhoun "were the north pole and the south pole of the political sphere, leaders in the great controversy of the

43 Middlebury College, *Catalogue of the Officers and Students, 1800-1915* (Middlebury, Vt.: 1917), pp. xvii, xiii, xix. Nathaniel Chipman had received a LL.D. degree from Dartmouth in 1797.

44 *Ibid.*, p. xxxix.

45 Chipman, *Life*, p. 204. Lectures Nos. II-V reproduced in the Appendix as being of interest to general readers. President Samuel W. Boardman said in his Anniversary Address, July 1, 1900, that the two Chipmans "erected an ample building for a prospective law school, thus looking toward a university scheme, which, however, was never realized." *A Record of the Centennial Anniversary of Middlebury College* (Middlebury, Vt.: 1901), p. 65.

46 *Vt. Hist. Gaz.*, III, 1157; Chipman, *Life*, p. 208.

47 Chipman, *Life*, App. No. 6, pp. 293-382; Honeywell in *N. Eng. Q.*, V, 576.

rights of the people of *all* the States within the Union, vs. State rights." [48]

Meanwhile Chipman was also working on his *Principles of Government, a Treatise on Free Institutions* (Burlington, Vt.: 1833), a volume which he published when he was eighty-one years of age. Originally, he had intended merely to revise his earlier work, " as no treatise had appeared fully embracing the subject," but he found it " too limited in its plan, as well as deficient in arrangement."

> He, therefore, resolved to new-cast the whole, to enlarge the plan, to give it a more regular and scientific arrangement, and as far as he was capable, to make it an elementary treatise on that kind of government which has been adopted in these United States.[49]

The theories presented will be discussed in later chapters of this work.

The last years of Chipman's life were spent in a continuation of the wide studying that he had begun in his youth. The first mention of difficulty with his eyes, in spite of their hard usage, does not appear until a letter written in December 1842. It indicates that he had been bothered for some time, but that he was still able to write.[50] His health was remarkably good until his last illness, which struck him suddenly. Two days later, on February 15, 1843, he died, in the ninety-first year of his age.[51]

### NATHAN DANE

Chipman's contemporary, Nathan Dane (b. 1752), was one of twelve children of a prosperous farmer of Ipswich, Massachusetts. Until after he was twenty-one, he worked on the farm

---

48 William C. Bradley, quoted in *Vt. Hist. Gaz.*, III, 1159.

49 Chipman, *Principles of Government*, Preface.

50 Chipman, *Life*, p. 194. Letter to a friend, Dec. 20, 1842.

51 *Ibid.*, p. 215.

—as Chipman had done—thus gaining considerable physical strength.[52]

Unable to attend the regular town school, Dane prepared himself for Harvard by eight months of hard study. He graduated with a record of superior scholarship in 1778, and settled down to the double career of teaching school and studying law under Judge Wetmore of Salem, who was later to be Judge Story's father-in-law. In 1782 he began to practice law in Beverly, and almost at once attracted clients. Unlike many members of his profession, he did not encourage litigation, and frequently sent distraught clients home to sleep on their troubles before he would counsel them. He helped establish the habit in the Essex County bar, whereby the leading members got much of their income from cases never brought to trial.

Both Chipman and Dane were thus started on their careers in law before the United States began her history under the Constitution. And both men gave significant service in the formative period of the Confederation.

Shortly after he opened his law office in Beverly, Dane entered politics. He was elected to the legislature of Massachusetts, and was returned for four successive years. This was no mean honor, Beverly being distinguished then as the home of some of the wealthiest merchants and most influential men of the state. He could probably have stayed on in the legislature but in 1785 he was elected a delegate from Massachusetts to the Congress of the Confederation, and re-elected in 1786 and 1787.

In Congress, Dane is best known for his activities in connection with the Northwest Ordinance. It was not until the famous reply of Webster to Hayne in the debate over Foot's resolution in 1830 that the question of authorship was raised. At that

52 Peabody, *Harvard Graduates Whom I Have Known*, p. 12; E. M. Stone, *History of Beverly* (Boston: 1843), pp. 135-136. Unless otherwise indicated, these two volumes form the source for the early period of Dane's life. The article on Dane in Stone's volume is by the Rev. C. T. Thayer, and was originally published in the *American Jurist and Law Magazine* (July 1835). It is here republished with some additions by the author.

time Webster made a passing allusion to Dane as the author, only to have Senator Benton retort that the work was really that of Jefferson. As Dane was still living, Webster sent him a copy of his speech, and the reply which Dane wrote helps to clarify the matter.[53] Dane never claimed complete originality in drafting the Ordinance. He had drawn up the terms of the temporary organization of the Northwest Territory with a little help from Charles Pinckney.[54] In the Articles of Compact, the permanent part (for which the Ordinance is best known), Dane declared that he " furnished the provisions respecting impairing contracts, the Indian security, and some other smaller matters." Other portions of the Ordinance were taken " mainly from the constitution and laws of Massachusetts, as any one may see who knows what American law was in '87." [55] Dane gave full credit to Jefferson and Rufus King for their share in the clause prohibiting slavery. He had no idea that the provision would pass, so omitted it from the draft; but when he discovered that " the House was favorably disposed on this subject," he moved the article, " which was agreed to without opposition." [56]

Dane left Congress upon the dissolution of the Confederation, and has been accused of opposing the new Constitution as it was drafted.[57] The stand he took led the historian McMaster to call

[53] The letter in full appears in *Proceedings of the Massachusetts Historical Society*, X (Feb. 1869), 475–480. Ms. presented to the Society by George Ticknor Curtis.

[54] Pinckney did so little that he felt himself at liberty to condemn the Ordinance in debate. Dane 9 *General Abridgment*, App., p. 76, Note A.

[55] *Ibid.*, App., p. 74.

[56] Letter to Rufus King, excusing the Ordinance as the best they could do under the circumstances. Henry A. Chaney, " Nathan Dane," *The Green Bag*, III (Dec. 1891), 551–555. See note from George Ticknor Curtis to his publishers, containing copy of this excerpt from Dane's letter to King. Tipped into *History of the ... Constitution*, following Appendix in Vol. II, in copy owned by University of California. In the 1870's the theory developed that Manassah Cutler had had a great influence, despite the fact that no contemporary evidence appears. (*The Green Bag*, III, 555.) *Cf.* also Jay A. Barrett, *Evolution of the Ordinance of 1787* (New York and London: 1891).

[57] Article on Dane in *Dictionary of American Biography* by H. W. Howard Knott.

him " the most bitter and acrimonious anti-Federalist " in the Congress.[58] However, Dane opposed the activities of the Convention only because of his legal mind. He was always a Federalist in principle, voting for any measures designed to uphold national unity and supremacy. But he wanted to strengthen the national system by methods that were consistent with the existing organic law. The last clause of the Articles of Confederation stated specifically that the Articles could not be altered except by agreement of the Congress and later confirmation by all the state legislatures. Dane looked upon the proposed Philadelphia convention as a revolutionary movement, undertaken only in the interests of trade, and sought to prevent the Massachusetts legislature from sending delegates. Finally, after persistent effort, Dane succeeded in bringing the movement under the sanction of Congress. As chairman of the general committee on the subject, he reported to Congress that that body strongly recommended to the different legislatures that they send delegates. It does not appear that Dane was ever opposed to the Constitution itself, after it had been formulated. He voted for its submission to the people and for taking steps to put it into operation.[59]

Dane then returned to state politics, serving as state senator various times for five sessions between 1790 and 1798. He acted on four different commissions for the revision and publication of the laws and charters of the Commonwealth.[60]

The troubled years of the War of 1812 brought Nathan Dane to the fore again. During the embargo, he established and supported a society to give employment to men and families that

58 John Bach McMaster, *A History of the People of the United States*, I (New York: 1907), 399.

59 *Journals of the American Congress: From 1774 to 1788*, IV (Washington: 1823), 782, 827; *Journals of the Continental Congress, 1774-1789* (Washington: Govt. Printing Office, 1936), XXXII, 71-74; XXXIII, 543-544, 549. The foregoing analysis of Dane's reasoning and activities is taken from Chaney in *The Green Bag*, III, 549-551.

60 Peabody, *Harvard Graduates Whom I Have Known*, p. 17.

depended on the shipping interests.[61] But it is his participation in the Hartford Convention which has aroused the keenest interest and which is most worthy of comment. His attitude was almost directly opposed to Chipman's.

For many years, Dane had been a favorite of the " wise men " of Essex, those who were confident that conservative control in Massachusetts could be continued indefinitely, and that Union support was not needed.[62] Dane never cared to apologize for his share in the convention called by these " wise men," even when he was most strongly supporting the authority of the Federal Constitution. Professor Samuel Eliot Morison, who has made a thorough study of the convention in his biography of Harrison Gray Otis, has come to the conclusion that Otis and Governor Strong brought forward the convention project in October of 1814 in order to divert the popular attention from more radical propositions and thus prevent a physical conflict with the federal government. Dane and George Cabot accepted their election as delegates with the same end in view.

> The truth is that Otis and his friends were equally afraid of " refrigerating the popular zeal " and of permitting it to generate greater heat. By steering a middle course between inactivity on the one hand, and nullification or secession on the other, they hoped to force the government to recede on the militia question, to bring the war to an end, and to pose as the saviors of New England.[63]

In order to help keep the convention in conservative channels, Dane had emerged from the retirement into which he had been

61 Chaney in *The Green Bag*, III, 556.

62 Robert A. East, " The Massachusetts Conservatives in the Critical Period," in *The Era of the American Revolution,* Studies Inscribed to Evarts Boutell Greene, edited by Richard B. Morris (New York: Columbia University Press, 1939), p. 367.

63 Samuel Eliot Morison, *The Life and Letters of Harrison Gray Otis, Federalist, 1765-1848,* II (New York: 1913), 112.

forced by increasing deafness.[64] He served on two of the three major committees, apparently working with a small directing clique within the convention which was probably under the leadership of Otis.[65]

In his own analysis of the convention, Dane stated emphatically that there was no hostility to the Union felt by either the eastern states or their convention. The opposition was " to the then *administration of federal affairs*" which

> was misrepresented by some, and mistaken by others for op-
> position to the *Union*. In the then high excitement and party
> spirit, the administration and the Union were often con-
> founded by ignorance or design.[66]

Dane maintained a successful law practice for thirty years or more, retiring only when he lost his hearing. He held his last official position as a member of the Electoral College of 1812. In 1820, he was chosen to the Massachusetts Constitutional Convention, his fellow townspeople knowing that he could not attend the sessions, but feeling the value of his name.

Early in the 1780's, Dane had started work on his monumental *General Abridgment and Digest of American Law,* which appeared in eight volumes in 1823-24, with a supplementary volume in 1829.[67] It was designed on the general plan of Viner's English *Abridgment,* and was the first comprehensive compendium of law to be prepared and printed in this country. With all his experience in making, compiling, revising, and codifying laws during the formative period of American jurisprudence, both federal and state, Dane was undoubtedly one of

---

64 *Ibid.*, II, 131-132; Peabody, *Harvard Graduates Whom I Have Known,* pp. 18-19.

65 Morison, *Otis,* II, 144-145 and 145 note.

66 Dane, 9 *General Abridgment,* 594. Dane held that the convention was constitutional under Article I, Sec. 10 of the Constitution. *Ibid.*, pp. 595-596.

67 Story said in his review of Dane's *Abridgment,* " In this elaborate work are presented the matured fruits of nearly fifty years' study, meditation and research." *North American Review,* XXIII (July 1826), 1-41, at p. 39. Also in Story, *Miscellaneous Writings* (1835), pp. 321-343.

the best qualified men in the Union to undertake the work. Its emphasis is upon the American charters, constitutions, statutes, and adjudged cases, incorporated with such portions of English law as were recognized in the United States. Though it is not primarily a disquisition upon the theory of the American constitutional government, references to constitutional law and citations of cases are scattered throughout the work. The Appendix, written when the tariff controversy flared up, after the ninth volume was already in press, was inspired by Dane's fears over the tone of the South Carolina Exposition.

> It is the *State nullifying* doctrine, and *State separation,* which at present, almost exclusively, demand the serious attention of every friend of the union and of this nation. Not that these are grounds of much fear in themselves—but the danger to be feared is in our violent parties; and, especially, when the deep *sectional* interests of the East, of the South, or of the West, are, in heat, and passion, made to operate on high party principles . . . . But yesterday I saw it publicly proposed, in South Carolina, to separate from the union—make Charleston a free port, or lay impost duties five or ten per cent only; as measures promising fair to double her population and wealth in ten years. As if the other states, will quietly permit a small state to usurp *Judical* [sic] power, to decide acts of Congress are unconstitutional, to declare them void and to separate, and so to regulate her impost duties as to destroy the only revenue of the other states . . . . If South Carolina can do so, any other state can do so. I should not mention a case so pernicious and unlikely to be suffered did not two principles avowed even by the more moderate Col. Drayton lead to it—I mean the right to separate and holding the government by majorities a mere truism.[68]

This Appendix was praised by Story as being an essential part of the education of every constitutional lawyer,[69] and the entire

---

68 Dane, 9 *General Abridgment*, App., Preface, p. ii.

69 The Appendix is paged separately at the end of the volume, pp. 1-73. "The whole of that Appendix is worthy of the perusal of every constitutional lawyer, even though he may differ from some of the conclusions of the learned author." Story, *Commentaries on the Constitution*, sec. 214 note.

nine volumes proved to be highly useful to the legal profession until they became hopelessly outdated and were superseded.

A second work, which, if printed, would be as voluminous as the *Abridgment,* was begun in 1782. It is entitled *A Moral and Political Survey of America,* and consists of a series of essays on widely diverse subjects connected with America at large. Among the objectives of this work, as set forth in the Preface to the manuscript, the fourth is significant in connection with the chief benefaction of Dane's life. He hoped

> to do a little towards preserving in our country, a manly moral character, ' a more regulated liberty ', where this character and this wise union of law and liberty, are so very important, and where a vicious character and licentious liberty would soon destroy self government.[70]

Probably as he wrote his *Abridgment,* Dane evolved his idea of establishing an American parallel to the Oxford Vinerian Professorship, made illustrious by Blackstone. To Josiah Quincy, incoming president of Harvard, he offered $10,000 to found a Dane Chair of Law. Like Viner, he used the proceeds from the sale of his *Abridgment* to endow the professorship. He stipulated two conditions: that the first incumbent be the eminent Justice Story, and that everyone who filled the chair should publish some work on the law.[71] Later, when the success of the school was assured, he increased his gift to $15,000 and provided funds for the erection of Dane Hall.[72]

Dane's later years were spent in the solitude imposed upon him by his deafness. He maintained the severest simplicity in his personal habits. Always a student, he never spent less than

---

70 Stone, *History of Beverly,* pp. 140-141.

71 Viner's professorship gave the world Blackstone's *Commentaries.* Dane's poured forth a stream of treatises, including many of the best-known textbooks—all of Story's commentaries, and Greenleaf *on Evidence,* many by Theophilus Parsons, and Langdell's philosophical works.

72 Stone, *History of Beverly,* p. 139. See also Warren, *History of the Harvard Law School,* vol. I, ch. xx; and Reed, *Training for the Law,* pp. 142-144.

twelve and often fourteen hours a day in his library. He was sincerely religious, and never missed public worship, even though he never heard a word of the proceedings. On the Sabbath, he " rested " from his study of the law and American history, spending the time in his library in a critical study of the Scriptures in Hebrew and Greek and in sundry of the Christian Fathers in their original tongues. He avoided seeing people in his own house, and never was seen at the homes of others. His only public appearance in later life was his daily walk from his home to the post office, about half a mile away.

Late in 1834, Dane suffered an attack which paralyzed his body but did not affect his mind. Three months later, he died (February 1835). A few hours before the end, he gave directions for his funeral and then bade farewell to his friends.[73] Shortly thereafter, Justice Story wrote to Charles Sumner,

> I feel a melancholy at the Death of Mr. Dane, though his age forbade any hope of longer usefulness, or effort. He has gone to his grave full of honors as well as years; and I will, as the Professor of his choice, do what I may to perpetuate the knowledge of his Benefaction.[74]

### JOSEPH STORY

While Chipman and Dane were getting started on their careers in law, politics, and authorship, Joseph Story was growing to manhood. Joseph was born in Marblehead, Essex County, Massachusetts, on September 18, 1779, a few months after Chipman had begun to practice law in Vermont, and while Dane was teaching school and studying law in Salem.

---

[73] Stone, *History of Beverly*, pp. 148-149. Dane's wife, the former Mrs. Mary Brown, to whom he had been married for 55 years, survived him. They had no children of their own, but had educated various relatives or established them in business. Dane adopted his nephew, John Dane (Harvard, 1799), who became a Congressman from Maine. Chaney in *The Green Bag*, III, 558.

[74] Story to Sumner, dated at Washington, Feb. 22, 1835. Sumner Papers, Harvard College Library.

He was the son of Elisha Story and Mehitable Pedrick, and was the eldest child of his father's second marriage. His maternal grandfather was a wealthy merchant, who had Tory leanings during the Revolution, but who " never took any step except in favor of his countrymen." [75]   Joseph's father, an informally trained physician, served in the medical department of the Continental Army. He had been a member of the band of "Indians" of Boston Tea Party fame—an activity of which the whole family was proud.

As a child, Joseph took an interest in politics and the discussions of older men. His mother stimulated his love of study and ambition, often reminding him, " Now, Joe, I've sat up and tended you many a night when you were a child, and don't you dare not to be a great man." [76] His mother lived to watch the whole of his remarkable career, as he preceded her in death by two years.

Story's schooling began at Marblehead Academy where he was one of the earliest students. He withdrew late in 1794, and in January of 1795, entered Harvard. He had prepared in the requisite preliminary subjects in two months and in all the studies of the freshman class in the preceding semester in six additional weeks. In spite of this evident " cramming," it appears that Story had better opportunities for preparatory schooling than either Chipman or Dane. His four happy years at college, filled with the most intense kind of study, were climaxed by the honor. of graduating second in his class, outranked only by William Ellery Channing.

Story then entered the office of Mr. Samuel Sewall, at Marblehead, to study law. [77] At that time (1798), there were only three law schools connected with universities, and two

75 Story, *Life and Letters*, I, 2-3. This and succeeding information from an autobiographical letter.

76 *Ibid.*, I, 22.

77 *Ibid.*, I, 70. Sewall was a distinguished advocate at the Essex bar at the time, and a member of Congress. Later, he rose to the position of Chief Justice of the Supreme Court of Massachusetts.

private schools, in the United States. The university schools were at William and Mary in Virginia, the College of Philadelphia in Pennsylvania, and Columbia College, New York, and the private schools were the famous one of Judge Tapping Reeve at Litchfield and Peter Van Schaak's group at Kinderhook, New York.[78] Even had it been practicable for Story to attend such a school, it would probably not have entered his head. In the light of his own training, his later work in helping to establish the idea of a formal law school, and particularly the Harvard Law School, becomes even more interesting. His early tussles with the law were discouraging, and a letter to his friend, Samuel Fay, dated September 6, 1798, just after leaving Cambridge, is gloomy in the extreme.

> Conceive, my dear fellow, what is my situation, doomed to spend at least ten years, the best of my life, in the study of the law,—a profession whose general principles enlighten and enlarge, but whose minutiae contract and distract the mind. Ambition is truly the food of my existence, and for that alone life is desirable. Yet, hard lot! Those favorite studies, those peculiar pursuits by which I have fondly (however vainly) hoped to attain celebrity,[79] are ravished from me, and I must consent to be a *plodder* in order to be what the world calls a *man*. Yet it is the part of cowardice to shrink, and of imbecility to hesitate. I have determined, and will execute.[80]

But after intense application to Blackstone and then Coke on Littleton, the light began to break and he gained more pleasure from his studies. Nevertheless, he was lonesome and unhappy at Marblehead, particularly since Mr. Sewall's membership in Congress required that he be at the Capital for half of every year. Sewall was elevated to the Massachusetts Supreme Court in January 1801, and Story consequently moved to Salem to

78 Reed, *Training for the Law*, pp. 128-132, 423, 431; Warren, *History of the Harvard Law School*, I, 180-185; *Albany Law Journal*, XX (July 26, 1879), 72-73.

79 Story apparently desired a literary career while at Harvard.

80 Story, *Life and Letters*, I, 71.

continue his legal studies with Samuel Putnam, who also was destined to be raised to the same bench. In Salem, Story was not much happier than before; for two of his convictions were out of line with the majority in that town—his Harvard-acquired Unitarianism, which they regarded as atheism, and his leaning toward the Republicans, when almost all around him were staunch Federalists.[81]

Story was admitted to the Essex County bar in July 1801, and for lack of another place to go, he opened an office in Salem. As a member of a minority political group, clients did not immediately flock to him, but within three or four years he had built up a good practice and enjoyed an increasing reputation. In later years, when Story was known for his strong adherence to the tenets of the nationalist school,[82] he explained his youthful politics thus:

> I like as much to see a young man democratic, as an old man conservative. When we are old, we are cautious and slow of change, if we have benefited by experience. When we are young we hope too much, if we are generous and pure.[83]

Story gave rein to both a waxing and a waning ambition in 1804,[84] publishing his first legal work almost simultaneously

81 *Ibid.*, I, 57, 86. Story wrote that at the time, he scarcely remembered "more than four or five lawyers in the whole state who *dared* avow themselves Republicans." William Draper Lewis, ed., *Great American Lawyers*, III (Philadelphia: 1908), 132. William Schofield, Judge of the Superior Court of Massachusetts, who wrote the article on Story, used the material at the Essex Institute, but did not document his account.

82 According to one report which does not mention the effect of his removal to Cambridge in 1829, Story belonged to a social club of a dozen of his political friends for the last quarter-century of his life. The members of the group were Republicans of the variety backing John Quincy Adams. See Eulogy by "A Friend" [from the *Salem Register*, Sept. 1845?] in scrapbook of eulogies of Story prepared by Simon Greenleaf and presented to Harvard Law School, June 9, 1846. Now in Treasure Room at Langdell Hall.

83 Story, *Life and Letters*, I, 99.

84 Also in 1804, on Dec. 9, Story married Mary Lynde Oliver. She survived only a few months, passing away June 22, 1805. Story's grief was

with his didactic poem, "The Power of Solitude." [85] He later bought up and burned all available copies of the poem, but his *Selection of Pleadings in Civil Actions,* was favorably received by the profession, and for many years was the sole book of forms used in this country.[86]

At an early date, Story became active in efforts to increase the salaries of the justices of the Massachusetts Supreme Court. His main concern was apparently for Chief Justice Parsons whose salary was so low that he felt unable to stay on the bench. Story led the fight to raise the salaries from about $1200 for the Chief Justice and $500-$600 for the Associates, to $2500 and $2400 in 1806, and later to $3500 and $3000 where they remained for many years.[87]

Story's early attachment to the Republican party caused him to be held suspect for many years by the staunch Federalists of Massachusetts, especially Harrison Gray Otis and his followers.[88] Nevertheless, he commanded their respect. An excerpt from a letter from Otis to Robert Goodloe Harper of Boston, dated April 19, 1807, indicates at once Story's independence of thought and the good opinion which even his political opponents had of him.

---

made almost inconsolable by the death of his father two months later. On August 27, 1808, he married Sarah Waldo Wetmore, who survived him. *Ibid.,* I, 112, 113, 170.

85 The poem is rare now. Selections from it appear in *ibid.,* I, 109-112.

86 *Ibid.,* I, 112. According to a letter written by Richard H. Dana to W. W. Story, Story's first legal work was entitled *Precedents of Declarations* and was published anonymously. A copy had been presented to Dana's grandfather. Story had published four volumes on law before he joined the Supreme Court in 1811. Besides his *Pleadings in Civil Actions,* he edited *Chitty on Bills of Exchange and Promissory Notes* in 1809, edited *Abbott on Shipping* in 1810, and produced an American edition of *Lawes' Pleading in Assumpsit* in 1811. *Cf. Great American Lawyers,* III, 126.

87 *Selections from the Works of Joseph Story, LL.D., with a sketch of his life,* James Burns, publr. (Boston: 1839), pp. 19-22.

88 Josiah Quincy once expressed to Otis the idea that President Jackson could say to Story, after the death of Chief Justice Marshall, as Pharoah did to Joseph, "Thou shalt be ruler over my house." "Joseph, indeed! Why, yes, an excellent comparison," snorted Otis. "Pray, was anything said about his coat of many colors?" Morison, *Otis,* I, 220-221.

I shall in a few days give to a Mr Story from this place a line of introduction to you, at his particular request, and will thank you to pay him such attentions as may be consistent with your convenience and leisure. He is a young man of talents, who commenced Democrat a few years since and was much fondled by his party. He discovered however too much sentiment and honour to go *all lengths,* & acted on several occasions with a very salutary spirit of independence & in fact did so much *good,* that his party have denounced him, and a little attention from the right sort of people will be very useful to him & to us . . .[89]

After preliminary experience in the Massachusetts legislature (1805-1808),[90] Story was elected to the House of Representatives to fill the seat for the Salem district, vacated by the death of Jacob Crowninshield. He took his seat on December 20, 1808, and remained only a few weeks, but they were weeks filled with turmoil. He advocated an increase in the size of the navy, suggesting a fleet of fifty fast-sailing frigates. Other members of his party felt that any ships that we built would be sure prey for the British, even though Story assured them that the courage and skill " of the hardy sons of the ocean " would make it exceedingly difficult for Great Britain to get possession of our little navy. Since scarcely a Democrat from the West or South could be found to support him, the motion was quietly laid on the table, and the House proceeded to consider the augmentation of the land forces.[91]

89 *Ibid.*, I, 283. It should be noted, however, that Otis was biased in his attitude toward the relationship between the Federalists and " Democrats." The Republican Party had been slowly gaining in strength as the Federalists split over the embargo and non-intercourse measures of the Administration. In 1810, the Republicans carried the state elections. *Great American Lawyers*, III, 132-133.

90 Story again served in the Massachusetts legislature from 1810 until his appointment to the Supreme Court, presiding as Speaker for the last several months. *Ibid.*, III, 135.

91 Richard Hildreth, *The History of the United States of America*, VI (New York: 1871), 124-125. *Annals of Congress*, 10th Cong., 2nd sess., *passim*.

The second major issue with which Story was concerned during his brief stay in Congress was the embargo. According to Henry Adams, Story came to Congress determined to overthrow it, and there found Ezekiel Bacon, another Massachusetts member, equally determined.[92] These two managed to lead a party revolt, forcing repeal. Story claimed that

> The whole influence of the Administration was directly brought to bear upon Mr. Ezekiel Bacon and myself, to seduce us from what we considered a great duty to our country and especially to New England. We were scolded, privately consulted, and argued with, by the Administration and its friends . . .[93]

Jefferson never forgave Story for the repeal of the embargo, placing on him the entire blame for what he considered " a wound on our interests which can never be cured." Jefferson's description of the sequence of events is somewhat different from Story's:

> I ascribe all this to one pseudo-republican, Story. He came on (in place of Crowninshield, I believe) and staid only a few days; long enough, however, to get complete hold of Bacon, who, giving in to his representations, became panic-struck, and communicated his panic to his colleagues, and they to a majority of the sound members of Congress. They believed in the alternative of repeal or civil war, and produced the fatal measure of repeal.[94]

Story left Washington about January 20, 1809, thus taking no part in the public debate which began about ten days later,

92 Adams, *History of the United States during the Administrations of Jefferson and Madison*, IV, 432. On p. 358 of the same volume, however, Adams says that " Story took his seat Dec. 20, 1808, and instantly found himself in opposition to President Jefferson and the embargo," a wording which does not necessarily imply premeditation.

93 Story, *Life and Letters*, I, 187.

94 Jefferson to Gen. Dearborne, July 16, 1810, Thomas Jefferson, *Writings*, ed. by H. A. Washington, V (Washington: 1853), 529.

but he had obviously left his mark. He refused to be a candidate for re-election, as he was unwilling to sacrifice his own opinions for the sake of the party.[95] All indications point to the conclusion that Story was far more concerned with his independence as a political thinker than with adherence to any particular party. He thought of himself as a Republican for many years, but at the same time, he was always " a firm believer in the doctrines of General Washington and an admirer of his conduct, measures, and principles during his entire administration." [96] Story respected Hamilton and spoke of him as one of the greatest men of the age in which he lived.[97] Furthermore, it has been shown that he did not fear Jefferson's wrath in opposing the embargo. Hildreth has called him an " ultra-Federal war Democrat," which seems an accurate designation.[98]

Because, by a process of elimination, he apparently became the logical choice, President Madison appointed Story to the Supreme Court of the United States in November 1811, to fill the vacancy caused by the death of Mr. Justice William Cushing of Massachusetts.[99] Taking his seat at the February term,

95 Article on Story in *Dictionary of American Biography* by George Edward Woodbine.

96 *Great American Lawyers*, III, 136. In 1805, he wrote, "Convinced every day more and more of the purity of the republican cause, and believing it to be founded on the immutable rights of man, I can not and will not hesitate to make any sacrifice for its preservation." Story, *Life and Letters*, I, 106.

97 *Ibid.*, I, 195.

98 Hildreth, *History of the United States*, VI, 261. On Jan. 9, 1809, he wrote to Samuel Fay, "I am, from principle, a sincere lover of the Constitution of the United States, and should deplore, as the greatest possible calamity, the separation of the States." Story, *Life and Letters*, I, 182.

99 Beveridge, *Marshall*, IV, 106-110. There appears to be no basis for the sometimes expressed theory that Story, as a Republican, was expected to counter-balance Marshall. Jefferson had known since 1808 of Story's admiration for Marshall, and of his defection from orthodox Republicanism. *Cf. ibid.*, IV, 99-100. There is no mention of Story's appointment in Madison's letters.

1812, he was the youngest judge who ever sat in the court.[100] The post had already been offered to and turned down by Levi Lincoln, Alexander Wolcott, and John Quincy Adams. Story had been suggested by his old friend, Ezekiel Bacon, still a member of Congress, and his name had been supported "by Gen. Dearborn, Gen. Varnum, Dr. Hill, and the fathers of the Democratic party." [101]

Story had been greatly impressed with his new superior, Chief Justice Marshall, when they first met in 1808. The original attraction ripened into admiration and affection, and before long, Story and Marshall could be mentioned in one breath as spokesmen of a common interpretation of the law. Marshall's biographer, Beveridge, graphically describes the relationship between the two men.

> Where Marshall was leisurely, Story was eager. If the attainments of the Chief Justice were not profuse, those of his young associate were opulent. Marshall detested the labor of investigating legal authorities; Story delighted in it. The intellect of the older man was more massive and sure; but that of the youthful Justice was not far inferior in strength, or much less clear and direct in its operation. Marshall steadied Story while Story enriched Marshall. Each admired the other, and between them grew an affection like that of father and son.

100 The salary when Story accepted the position was $3500, only slightly more than half his professional income. But Story cared more for the opportunity "to pursue, what of all things I admire, juridical studies." His sincerity is proven by his refusal of William Pinkney's practice ($20,000 annually) in 1816. Aumann, *Changing American Legal System*, p. 170. *Cf.* Story, *Life and Letters*, I, 201.

101 *Great American Lawyers*, III, 123 *et seq.* See also article from the *Salem Register*, written by "A Friend," in scrapbook of Story eulogies prepared by Simon Greenleaf.

So perfectly did the qualities and attainments of these two men supplement one another that, in the work of building the American Nation, Marshall and Story may be considered one and the same person.[102]

The subject of Story's opinions while a member of the Supreme Court is not within the scope of the present study, although a summary of his work is of interest. William Schofield in his essay on Story in the *Great American Lawyers* series, has counted 286 cases in which Story wrote the opinion of the Supreme Court. 269 of these were the opinion of the court or a majority; three were concurring opinions, and fourteen, dissents. On questions of constitutional law, he wrote four dissenting opinions, that in Houston *v.* Moore [103] being during Marshall's lifetime. In Ogden *v.* Saunders,[104] Story and Duvall concurred with Marshall in his dissent. Schofield notes that Story and Marshall did not always agree, as Story wrote the opinion of the majority of the court in five cases in which Marshall dissented, and Marshall wrote the majority opinion in four of the cases to which Story dissented.[105] In addition to his work on the Supreme Court, Story conducted the Circuit Court for the First District, drew up the rules for the Circuit Court and for the courts of equity in the United States, and made recommendations to Pinkney, Webster, and others for improving the federal laws.[106]

102 Beveridge, *Marshall*, IV, 96. *Cf. ibid.*, pp. 99, 60, 61, for conclusions regarding Marshall's personality as dominating the court. As the same idea is phrased in *Great American Lawyers*, III, 147, Story " accepted naturally and without hesitation the large and liberal conception of the Constitution which is now firmly established by the decisions of the Supreme Court."

103 5 Wheat. 1 (1820).

104 12 Wheat. 213 (1827). This was the only case in which Marshall was in the minority on a question of constitutional law.

105 *Great American Lawyers*, III, 150-151. *Cf.* Beveridge, *Marshall*, IV, 60-61, for the opposite view: Even with a Republican majority on the Court, " Marshall continued to dominate it as fully as when its members were of his own political faith and views of government."

106 Story, *Life and Letters*, II, 372-373; 402-403.

Story's duties on the First Circuit, which included Massachusetts, New Hampshire, Rhode Island, and later, Maine, were very important.[107] Since this was the chief maritime district of the country, litigation had been increased by captures and forfeitures incident to the embargo and non-intercourse legislation and the War of 1812. Story's predecessor, the elderly Justice Cushing, had not been able to keep pace with business and a long list of causes had accumulated on the docket. Story began by eliminating 130 improperly appealed cases, thus decreasing the load materially.[108] He became deeply engrossed in the study of admiralty, inasmuch as so many of his cases involved this comparatively little known branch of the law. The Supreme Court sustained him in the assertion of admiralty jurisdiction by the federal courts, and in the years following his early opinion in DeLovio v. Boit (1815),[109] the admiralty jurisdiction of the Supreme Court was greatly extended.[110]

As a result of his duties on the First Circuit, Story had the opportunity to create almost from the beginning the American law of patents. When the embargo and non-intercourse acts cut off the usual commercial outlets, New England capital turned to domestic manufactures. One result of this development was that the value of the patented devices involved in manufacturing increased enormously. Arguments about them were carried to the courts, and it soon seemed to contemporaries that more

107 By law, Story held two terms in each state every year, and though he could lawfully leave the district judge in command, he was never absent except when ill. *Cf.* Anonymous "Biographical Notice of Mr. Justice Story," *American Review*, III (Jan. 1846), 68-82. The same author adds that Story had many patent cases owing to the peculiar character of the people in New England (p. 73). Story's decisions on the circuit are recorded in 13 volumes by Gallison, Mason, Charles Sumner, and his son, William W. Story.

108 *Great American Lawyers*, III, 147-148.

109 Story here decided that a contract of marine insurance, no matter where executed, was subject to the admiralty jurisdiction. 2 Gallison 398 (1815).

110 *Great American Lawyers*, III, 148-149.

questions on the law of patents were litigated in the First Circuit than in all the other states combined.[111]

Only rarely did Story break his rule of taking no public part in politics after his elevation to the Supreme Bench. He opposed slavery, and in December 1819, addressed a town meeting in Salem against the Missouri Compromise.[112] Later, his decision in Prigg v. Pennsylvania, while ostensibly upholding the federal fugitive slave law, actually left a loophole for states wishing to maintain the principle of the personal liberty laws, the form of which he was at pains to declare unconstitutional.[113]

His political conservatism was expressed in 1820, when he served as a member of the Convention called to revise the Constitution of Massachusetts.[114] As Kent was to do in New York

111 Simon Greenleaf, A Discourse Commemorative of the Life and Character of the Honorable Joseph Story, LL.D.... pronounced Sept. 18, 1845, at the request of the corporation of the University and the members of the Law School (Boston: 1845), p. 28. See also Story, Life and Letters, II, 584; and George S. Hillard, " Memoir of Joseph Story, LL.D.," reprinted from Proceedings of the Massachusetts Historical Society, 1867-68 (Boston: 1868), pp. 25-26.

112 Woodbine, in the Dictionary of American Biography, holds that Story was violently opposed to slavery. Rather, he preferred moderation, and had no use for abolitionists. On the subject of slavery, see Story, Life and Letters, I, ch. xi, and Story's opinion in U. S. v. La Jeune Eugenie, 2 Mason 409 (1822).

113 16 Pet. 539 (1842). State officials could not be forced to administer federal acts, and therefore, the state was not under obligation to participate in the reclamation of fugitives. See also Story, Life and Letters, II, ch. ix.

114 See Journal of Debates and Proceedings in the Convention of Delegates, Chosen to Revise the Constitution of Massachusetts (Boston: 1821; new ed., 1853). One of the best brief analyses of the Massachusetts Convention is in Claude Moore Fuess, Daniel Webster, I (Boston: Little, Brown and Co., 1930), 273-280. See also George Ticknor Curtis, Life of Daniel Webster, I (4th ed., New York: 1872), 178-190, esp. 184-186. Story complained in his autobiography, " I may say, that not a single speech of mine is given with any thing like fulness or accuracy [in the Journal], Mr. Webster, with great propriety and foresight, corrected all his own. I now regret that I did not undertake a similar labor ... " Story, Life and Letters, I, 388. Furthermore, Story said, " My principal labors were in the great Committee on the subject of the representation in the

in the following year, Story argued earnestly against the extension of the suffrage. Together with Adams and Webster, he supported the maintenance of the property qualification.[115]

When Joseph Story entered upon his duties as Dane Professor of Law at Harvard University in 1829, he was unconsciously inaugurating a new era in the history of American legal education. The Harvard Law School had been founded in 1817, but as was the situation with most such formal efforts at that time, it had not been entirely successful.[116] It was not until Nathan Dane's endowment was accepted that changes began to take place. The Corporation determined to reorganize the school at the time that the new professorship was begun, and this reorganization, coupled with Story's contributions to the school, spelled the difference between failure and success.

Story was at the peak of his intellectual powers when he was asked to accept the new professorship. He was already asso-

---

House, whose debates were necessarily private." *Ibid.*, I, 387. Thus, we have but one major speech recorded in full—that on the property qualification for voting. (*Cf.* note 115, following.)

115 The debate on the subject of retaining the property qualification in voting opened on December 13, 1820. John Adams' speech—his first in public debate since 1780, is recorded on pp. 134-135 (new ed., pp. 277-279) of the *Journal of the Convention.* Story's, which Fuess says he read from a carefully prepared manuscript, is on pp. 136-137 (new ed., pp. 283-295), and Webster's, which virtually concluded the discussion, was delivered on Dec. 15, and appears in the *Journal* on pp. 241-248 [*sic*—should read 141-148] (new ed., pp. 304-321). The resolution to abandon the property qualification lost by a vote of 164 to 247. *Ibid.*, p. 248 [*sic*—should read 148] (new ed., p. 322).

*Cf.* C. Edward Merriam, *A History of American Political Theories* (New York: 1918), pp. 187-189. Marshall, Monroe, Madison, Randolph, and Upshur were among the Virginians opposed to the manhood suffrage idea at the same time.

116 *Cf.* Warren, *History of the Harvard Law School,* I, chs. xv, xvii, xviii. Also various numbers of the *North American Review* contain information about the new school. See especially II (Nov. 1815), 135; III (May 1816), 11-27; V (July 1817), 289-291; VI (Nov. 1817), 146-147.

On contemporary law schools, see Warren, *History of the Harvard Law School,* I, 180-185; *Albany Law Journal,* XX (July 26, 1879), 72-73; and Reed, *Training for the Law,* pp. 128-132.

ciated with Harvard, having been appointed chairman of a committee of the Overseers in 1823. The duties of the committee
were to examine the condition of the college with reference to
needed reforms in instruction and administration.[117] At first,
Story did not think that he had time to be a professor, but when
Dane approached him the second time, he decided to accept.[118]
In his *Inaugural Discourse,* Story thus summarized his prospective tasks—

> The duties assigned to the Dane Professorship are, in the
> first instance, to deliver lectures upon the Law of Nature, the
> Law of Nations, Maritime and Commercial Law, Equity Law,
> and lastly, the Constitutional Law of the United States.[119]

A comprehensive teaching load! Another requirement of the
professorship not mentioned by Story at that time, was that his
lectures be published. It was in the fulfillment of this stipulation
that he wrote the series of commentaries that made his name so
notable in our legal literature.

Story had been trained in the common law, and it was therefore clear that he would teach it to his students. Furthermore,
he was widely versed in the philosophical background of the
law, and it was equally certain that the institution he directed
would be a professional school, " not a lawyer's office teaching
rules of thumb." [120]

117 Peabody, *Harvard Graduates Whom I Have Known,* pp. 48-49.
Peabody takes Story's appointment as marking the beginning of what was
called the " Salem regime," to which the college was indebted for a new
era of advancement and progress.

118 A good discussion of the negotiations preceding the establishment
of the Dane Chair of Law is in Warren, *History of the Harvard Law
School,* I, ch. xx. Story had declined the Royall Professorship when it
was offered to him in 1828. See letters to the Rev. John Brazer, Feb. 9
and Mar. 1, 1828, in Story, *Life and Letters,* I, 532-533.

119 Joseph Story, *A Discourse Pronounced upon the Inauguration of the
Author as Dane Professor of Law in Harvard University on August 25,
1829,* p. 41.

120 Aumann, *Changing American Legal System,* pp. 98-99.

When Story was named Dane Professor, the occupant of the other law chair, previously endowed by Isaac Royall, was James Hooker Ashmun, a brilliant young man who succumbed prematurely to tuberculosis. After his death, Story's co-worker was Simon Greenleaf, an eminent lawyer who perfectly supplemented Story's efforts.

> . . . Story quickened and stirred the minds of his hearers, awoke in them that love of the law, as a science, which he felt so strongly, and made them ready for the lectures by which Greenleaf satisfied that appetite for instruction which Story had awakened; and thus, what each did derived value and efficacy from what the other did.[121]

As the years passed, the strength of the Harvard Law School increased,[122] its enrollment doubled, trebled, and quadrupled, and its graduates went forth to carry its teachings far and wide.[123] Unlike many of the law school courses elsewhere, it was predominantly national in emphasis.[124] For students who

121 Eulogy of Greenleaf, entitled "Address to Students of Harvard Law School, by Professor Theophilus Parsons, delivered Oct. 20, 1853." In Warren, *History of the Harvard Law School*, I, 484. In Story's *Inaugural Discourse*, he indicated that his purpose was to do much as Parsons later noted that he had done. Since his duties were so varied, he felt that his professorship "must suggest matter for inquiry, rather than expound principles with copiousness. It must create rather than satisfy curiosity." *Inaugural Discourse*, p. 42.

122 Not everyone who attended the law lectures needed to be a member of the School. On Sept. 29, 1829, the Corporation voted to authorize the law faculty to admit such outsiders "upon the payment of such sum as the Faculty may see fit, not less in any case than $50." Warren, *History of the Harvard Law School*, I, 431.

123 Greenleaf's letters to Sumner refer constantly to the increasing enrollment, and there are frequent statements such as this in a letter of Oct. 31, 1838: "Our school has reached eighty-four and is attracting much attention." On Nov. 29, 1839, he wrote, "We had an unusual number of English visitors this year..." Sumner Papers, Harvard College Library.

124 This change came with the reorganization brought about by Dane and Story. Before this period the School had been local in character. C. C. Langdell, "The Harvard Law School, 1869-1894," *Harvard Graduates' Magazine*, II (June 1894), 490-491.

wished to master the details of local law in their own states, individual instruction was provided.[125] In fact, it was known that
Harvard gave a more complete course in the civil law practiced
in Louisiana than was given in Louisiana itself.[126] Thus the
school exercised a nationalizing influence which was to increase
in effectiveness as its enrollment grew, just at the time that
the divisive sectional forces were coming into greater prominence. Prospective lawyers from all over the Union, even including a few Southerners,[127] studied at Harvard, and there
were exposed to the interpretation of the Constitution as the
Supreme Law of the nation.

> [Story's] familiar bearing to the students invariably at-
> tached them to him. Many, who had come determined not to
> like him, and who had been brought up to consider his politi-
> cal views heretical, and his constitutional opinions unsound,
> ended by becoming his ardent advocates and admirers.[128]

When, in 1832, it became apparent that the rejuvenated law
school was growing steadily, Nathan Dane arranged to present
Harvard with a new building—Dane Law College.[129] This two-
story edifice was a decided improvement over the few rooms

125 " No public instruction is given in the local or peculiar municipal
jurisdiction of any particular State; but the students are assisted by the
Professors as occasion may require, in their private study of the law and
practice peculiar to their own States." Advertisement of the Harvard Law
School in *The Christian Review*, II (Nashville, Tenn.: Sept. 1845), no. 9.
In Harvard Archives.

126 " The Southrons increase among us; especially those from Louisiana,
who say they can study their own code better there than at home." Greenleaf to Sumner, Sept. 7, 1838. Sumner Papers.

127 Warren, *History of the Harvard Law School*, I, 505-506. Letter from
Story to College Treasurer, Sept. 24, 1836, regarding successful but ex-
pensive policy of advertising the law school throughout the United States.

128 Story, *Life and Letters*, II, 38.

129 See Warren, *History of the Harvard Law School*, I, 468-478, for
details of the arrangements between Dane and the Corporation.

that originally housed the school in old First College House.[130] A former student who had emigrated to the wilds of Cincinnati, thus expressed his joy upon hearing of the improvement:

> How high sounding you have become—Dane Law College! This produces a powerful sensation abroad—there is a potent charm in names and the word College conjures up images of awe, respect and distant admiration which were never destined to cluster around the plain unvarnished simplicity of the word, school, and the idea attached to it. Although as Mr. Quincy says,[131] " it was not necessary in order to preserve the name of Nathan Dane and transmit it with honor to posterity, that it should be associated with the great design and useful improvement ", yet I think Nathan has made assurance doubly sure by inscribing his name upon a monument which shall endure so long as the noblest of sciences shall continue to hold its place among the institution [sic] of man.[132]

As a teacher, Story was completely successful.[133] His reputation served to attract students to the school, so that from a total enrollment of twenty-four (all but two of whom were new) when he was appointed, there were 154 students listed in the catalogue at the time of his death.[134] Part of his attractiveness

130 Story, *Life and Letters*, II, 39. Dane Hall was dedicated Oct. 23, 1832. It housed the Harvard Law School until 1883, when the School moved to the new Austin Hall. Dane Hall, after being used for various other purposes, was destroyed by fire in 1918. Letter to the author from William Bentinck-Smith, editor of the *Harvard Alumni Bulletin*, April 3, 1951.

131 In his address at the dedication of the new building.

132 Uriah Tracy Howe (L. S. 1831-2) to Charles Sumner, Dec. 13, 1832. In Warren, *History of the Harvard Law School*, I, 478-479.

133 *Cf.* Story's reply to questions by T. Kennedy, Esq., Principal of the Dublin Law Institute, May 15, 1844, as to the "method of instruction and study best calculated to elevate the standard of legal knowledge, and facilitate acquirement by the student." Story, *Life and Letters*, II, 486-487.

134 *Harvard Graduates' Mag.*, II, 491. *Cf.* also *American Review*, III, 77, which claims that the increase was from less than 20 to more than 160. In the scrapbook of Story eulogies compiled by Greenleaf, there is mention of 180 students at the time of Story's death, but other evidence of enrollment would seem to make this figure an exaggeration.

was his own enthusiasm for what he was doing. He thoroughly enjoyed his classes, and delighted in keeping his students in touch with the cases brought before the Supreme Court. Richard H. Dana, who attended the Law School from 1837 to 1840, has given a graphic account:

> Do you remember the scene that was always enacted on his return from his winter session at Washington? The school was the first place he visited after his own fireside. His return, always looked for and known, filled the Library. His reception was that of a returned father. He shook all by the hand, even the most obscure and indifferent; and an hour or two was spent in the most exciting, instructive, and entertaining descriptions and anecdotes of the events of the term. Inquiries were put by students from different States, as to leading counsel or interesting causes from their section of the country, and he told us, as one would have described to a company of squires and pages, a tournament of monarchs and nobles on fields of cloth of gold;—how Webster spoke in this case, Legaré, or Clay, or Crittenden, General Jones, Choate, or Spencer, in that, with anecdotes of the cases and points, and all " the currents of the heady fight." [135]

Dana said that Judge Story " combined, in a remarkable manner . . . the two great faculties of creating enthusiasm in study, and establishing relations of confidence and affection with his pupils." [136] Someone else wrote effusively that " His

---

[135] Letter from Richard H. Dana to W. W. Story, May 3, 1851, Story, *Life and Letters*, II, 320-321. As a further sidelight, the following excerpt from a statement by Greenleaf on Story in the lecture-room is of interest: "As an instructor in jurisprudence, he never lost sight of his position as a judge, before whom the subjects of his lectures might again come under consideration. And while every topic of settled law was discussed in the lecture-room with his abundant learning and happy freedom, he carefully refrained from expressing an opinion upon open questions, and still more upon cases stated to him. Indeed, his sagacity in distinguishing between a real and a fictitious case was so well known, that in this way he was rarely approached." *Ibid.*, II, 602.

[136] *Ibid.*, II, 319.

mouth was a perennial spring, and from his lips there was a continuous gush of social eloquence that none but an opium eater could withstand." [137]

Story's efforts in behalf of the Harvard Law School were untiring. His gifts as a teacher helped greatly to bring about the transition from study in offices to study in formal schools of law.[138] His salary was moderate, thus keeping the expenses of the school as low as possible.[139] And when it became obvious that the school could not get along with the small number of books that it had on hand, he offered to sell his library to the Corporation at about half the replacement cost, in order that the students might use it.[140] By 1832, when it was moved to its new quarters in Dane Hall, the library boasted 3000 volumes.[141]

137 Eulogy by "A Friend" from the *Salem Register*, in scrapbook of Story eulogies prepared by Simon Greenleaf. The pastor of Story's church, William Newell, gave perhaps the most unusual tribute to Story's mind: "It might be compared to the lithe proboscis of the elephant in its union of delicacy, dexterity, and strength." *Discourse Occasioned by the Death of the Hon. Joseph Story, LL.D.* (Cambridge: 1845), p. 13.

138 *Great American Lawyers*, III, 170-171. Story was proudest of his title of Professor. He put it on the title pages of his books and only at the suggestion of his English publisher was he persuaded to add, "One of the Justices of the Supreme Court of the United States." Charles Sumner, "Tribute of Friendship: The Late Joseph Story," article from the *Boston Daily Advertiser*, Sept. 16, 1845, in *The Works of Charles Sumner*, I (Boston: 1875), 142.

139 "The annual salary received by my father from the College... during all his Professorial Life, was one thousand dollars, from which four hundred dollars were deducted for the annual rent of the house, belonging to the University, which he occupied in Cambridge, leaving a net salary of six hundred dollars." Story, *Life and Letters*, II, 41.

140 *Ibid.*, II, 39-41; Story to Quincy, Nov. 3, 1829, Dec. 9, 1829, and July 16, 1831, quoted in Warren, *History of the Harvard Law School*, I, 462-463, 464 note 2; 466 note 3. The first two letters pertain to the collection of Reports which Story had accumulated and the last to the remainder of the library which Story sold. The total cost to the Corporation was $3,612, and the value of the books was approximately double that amount. Story also persuaded Dane to give the school ten sets of his *Abridgment* (90 volumes). *Ibid.*, I, 464-465.

141 *Ibid.*, I, 477. Charles Sumner was appointed librarian in 1833.

As Story's lectures were primarily *extempore,* few written traces of them remain.[142] He used almost no notes, and could adapt his presentation to a chance remark, if he thought it advisable. He was often eloquent, particularly, we may assume, when expounding the Constitution. His son summarized one such lecture which he heard while a student at the school:

> It was the last lecture of the term, on the Constitution, and it was not probable that the whole class would ever again meet. As my father took his seat to commence the exercise, this fact seemed to strike his mind, and he began by alluding to it. Moved, as he proceeded, by the train of thought and feeling thus accidentally set in motion, he slid into a glowing discourse upon the principles and objects of the Constitution; the views of the great men of the Revolution, by whom it was drawn; the position of our country; the dangers to which it was exposed; and the duty of every citizen to see that the republic sustained no detriment. He spoke, as he went on, of the hopes for freedom with which America was freighted; of the anxious eyes that watched it in its progress; of the voices that called from land to land to inquire of its welfare; closing in an exhortation to the students to labor for the futherance [*sic*] of justice and free principles; to expand, deepen, and liberalize the law; to discard low and ambitious motives in the profession, and to seek in all their public acts to establish the foundations of right and truth.[143]

The three volumes of *Commentaries on the Constitution* were begun shortly after Story assumed his new role as professor.[144]

142 Story, *Life and Letters,* II, 488.

143 *Ibid.,* II, 488-489.

144 Story spent eighteen months on the actual preparation of this work, and references in the footnotes indicate that the text was completed by July 4, 1831, when John Quincy Adams gave his oration. See J. Q. Adams, *Memoirs,* VIII (Philadelphia: 1876), 387, which tell of Adams' presentation of a copy of his oration to Story on July 25, 1831. See also Warren, *History of the Harvard Law School,* I, 456. The three volumes were in press by late 1832. See letter from Story to Kent, Oct. 27, 1832. Story, *Life and Letters,* II, 109-110. In the same letter, Story tells Kent, " I have cited you freely, and used you frequently in the work."

He always considered correct constitutional interpretation extremely important, and in his *Inaugural Discourse,* had devoted considerable attention to constitutional law. His goal was to

> contribute to fix in the minds of American youth a more devout enthusiasm for the constitution of their country, a more sincere love of its principles, and a more firm determination to adhere to its actual provisions against the clamours of faction, and the restlessness of innovation . . . .[145]

The *Commentaries* constitute one of Story's chief claims to recognition as the intellectual leader of the nationalist school, even though he has been overshadowed by the more spectacular figures of Webster and Marshall in the popular mind.[146] Parrington has described the work as

> an unconscious testimony to the tenacious hold of the English Common Law on the legal mind of America, as well as to the rising spirit of Nationalism. It did much to strengthen both. It was a triumph of the lawyer over the historian and political philosopher, and it marks the beginning of the lawyer's custodianship of the fundamental law.[147]

Its failings we shall consider elsewhere. Its strength as the classical authority on the nationalist interpretation of the Constitution must not escape us here.

Story's ideas on the Constitution were published in four different forms which were intended to serve the needs of four distinct groups of readers. The original version, that of January 1833, appeared in three volumes. Most of it had already been delivered in lecture form to the students in the law school.[148]

145 Story, *Inaugural Discourse*, p. 55.

146 A month after the publication of the *Commentaries*, Webster delivered his speech in reply to Calhoun's exposition of the concurrent majority— "The Constitution Not a Compact between Sovereign States (*Works*, III [Boston: 1851], 449-505). A comparison of the two documents shows a close similarity between Story's ideas and their presentation by Webster. *Cf.* Parrington, *Main Currents in American Thought*, II, 311-312.

147 *Ibid.*, II, 303.

148 Warren, *History of the Harvard Law School*, I, 456.

It was dedicated to Chief Justice Marshall, who was then completing his thirty-second year on the Supreme Court. From its copious footnotes and extensive citations of precedents and arguments in the legal history of Continental Europe and England as well as the United States, it may be concluded that it was intended for members of the legal profession—even though Story himself placed it in the category of "elementary works." [149]

In April 1833, Story published an Abridged Edition, in which all the footnotes and the more technical references were omitted. On its title page, it bears the notation that it was meant "for the Use of Colleges and High Schools." [150]

> It presents in a compressed form the leading doctrines of that work [the original *Commentaries*], so far as they are necessary to a just understanding of the actual provisions of the constitution.[151]

This version was shortly translated into French.[152] The long version appeared in German in 1838.[153] A Spanish translation was made by the Argentinian lawyer, N. A. Calvo, and went through several editions.[154] It embodied the notes from the French edition of 1843, and as part of his annotations, Calvo

149 Preface to the first edition, I, v. The *Commentaries* have gone through five editions, as follows: 2nd ed., 1851, W. W. Story, ed.; 3rd rev. ed., 1858, Edmund H. Bennett, ed.; 4th ed., 1873, with notes and additions by Thomas M. Cooley; 5th ed., 1891, Melville M. Bigelow, ed., reprinted in 1905.

150 Joseph Story, *Commentaries on the Constitution of the United States,* ... *Abridged by the Author* (Boston and Cambridge: 1833). Story found time to prepare this abridgment "between the publication of the original work in the autumn, and the beginning of April, 1833." Story, *Life and Letters,* II, 129-130.

151 Advertisement to the Abridgment, p. vii.

152 Work done by Paul Odent, 1843.

153 Work done by Franz Josef von Buss. Published in Leipzig.

154 *Comentario sobre la Constitutión federal de los Estados-Unidos* ... (3rd rev. ed., Buenos Aires: 1881; 4th ed., 1888). 2 vols. The abridgment was published in Mexico City in 1879.

drew some interesting parallels between the Constitution of the United States and that of Argentina.

In 1834 appeared the brief *Constitutional Class Book*. Dedicated to the school-masters of the United States, it was designed for the use " of the higher classes in the common schools." [155] The volume was the outgrowth of an address on " The Science of Government as a Branch of Popular Education," which Story delivered in August 1834, before the American Institute of Instruction.[156]

Several years later, in January 1840, Story prepared another abridged work on the Constitution. He entitled it, *A Familiar Exposition of the Constitution of the United States: Containing a Brief Commentary on Every Clause, Explaining the True Nature, Reasons, and Objects Thereof; Designed for the Use of School Libraries and General Readers*. According to the statement in the Preface, it was intended not only for private reading, but for use " as a text book for the highest classes in our Common Schools and Academies." It was dedicated " to the people of the Commonwealth of Massachusetts . . . designed to aid the cause of education, and to promote and encourage the study of the Constitution of the United States, by her ingenuous youth." At the close of the volume, Story appended several documents which he considered vital in our constitutional history,[157] and a glossary of legal terms—of great assistance to the layman.

Story gives abundant evidence that he consulted many works in the preparation of his *Commentaries*. He says that he found his most valuable materials in

155 Story, *Constitutional Class Book: being a brief exposition of the Constitution of the United States* (Boston: 1834).

156 See Story, *Life and Letters*, II, 184-189, for the text of the address.

157 These include the Declaration of Rights by the Continental Congress, 1774; the Declaration of Independence; the Articles of Confederation; the Constitution of the United States; Washington's Farewell Address; the Definitive Treaty of Peace between the United States of America and his Britannic Majesty; and an Ordinance for the Government of the Territory of the United States, Northwest of the River Ohio. Pp. 271-337. The glossary is on pp. 339-349.

the Federalist, an incomparable commentary of three of the greatest statesmen of their age; and the extraordinary Judgments of Mr. Chief Justice Marshall upon constitutional law.[158]

Story did not have the benefit of the use of Madison's *Notes* on the Federal Convention, as they were not published until 1836. If they had been available to him, he might have modified some of his ideas regarding the arguments in the Convention, which play such a large part in the *Commentaries*. As it is, scholars have long searched for a reason why Story did not revise his constitutional commentaries in the light of the information to be found in Madison's invaluable records, as he revised several others.[159]

The opinion of Chief Justice Marshall on Story's full-length *Commentaries* is of particular interest against the background of growing sectional rivalries. He wrote,

I have finished reading your great work, and wish it could be read by every statesman, and every would-be statesman in the United States. It is a comprehensive and an accurate commentary on our constitution, formed in the spirit of the original text. In the South, we are so far gone in political metaphysics that I fear no demonstration can restore us to common sense. The word " State Rights," as expounded by the resolutions of ninety-eight, and the report of ninety-nine, construed by our legislature, has a charm against which all reasoning is vain. These resolutions, and that report, constitute the creed of every politician who hopes to rise in Virginia, and to question them, or even to adopt the construction given by their author is deemed political sacrilege. The solemn and interesting admonitions of your concluding re-

158 Preface to the first edition, p. v.

159 There is only one reference to the possibility of a second edition in Story's letters. See his letter to the Hon. John M. Berrien, Feb. 14, 1843, in which he says he is laying aside certain remarks of Berrien to use " if ever my book on the Constitution shall reach another edition." Story, *Life and Letters*, II, 433.

marks will not I fear avail as they ought to avail against this popular frenzy.[160]

In his *Commentaries on the Conflict of Laws* (Boston: 1834), Story touched on juridical concepts arising in the federal relations of the United States. The main body of the treatise concerns universal legal principles, including the laws of different nations on marriage, divorce, wills, successions, and judgments. According to his son, this work interested him most, even though the research involved was the most difficult. This effort " to evoke method from . . . chaos " was begun in April of 1833 and finished by the end of the year—a tribute to Story's untiring scholarship.[161] One of the earliest works in its field, it immediately attracted a large audience, and has long enjoyed an enviable reputation. Its early acceptance was noted by Story's son :

> To the Commentaries on the Conflict of Laws has been generally accorded the praise of being his best work. It is, indeed, more original in its plan and scope, more imposing in its array of learning, and more recondite and universal. Its European reputation above his other books, may, perhaps, be accounted for in measure, by the fact, that it is not limited in its subjects to the common law of England and America, but is cosmopolitan . . . .[162] Contrary to the usage of the English Bar, it was cited in their Courts, and spoken of in terms of high praise . . . .[163]

160 *Ibid.*, II, 655. See *ibid.*, II, 654-656 for other comments on the *Commentaries on the Constitution*. The collection of opinions there reproduced originally appeared in the advertising sheet of Messrs. Little and Brown, publishers.

161 *Ibid.*, II, 140, 142.

162 *Ibid.*, II, 572.

163 *Ibid.*, II, 161-162. The volume was immediately reprinted in England, and soon translated into French and German. *Loc. cit.* The second edition of the *Conflict of Laws* swelled to nearly double its original size, and was made so much more full and complete that, "compared with it, the first edition seems to be but a sketch." *Ibid.*, II, 344. This difference between the first and second editions is small in terms of pages. The 3rd edition,

In all, Story published nine commentaries during his sixteen years as occupant of the Dane Chair of Law.[164] All of them were valuable, many of them filling gaps in our legal literature, especially in equity jurisprudence. Equity had never been popular in the United States, but Kent on the bench and Story in his treatises, developed and expounded the subject in such a way as to facilitate its introduction.[165] And interestingly enough, Story's own works, together with Kent's *Commentaries*, were to be among the strongest forces working against codification, a movement which Story favored.[166] Codes proved to be unnecessary when the common law was available in convenient form. Dean Pound, in his critique of Story, has emphasized the point that what Story the judge failed in, Story the commenta-

----

however, was some 400 pages longer than either of the first two. Story himself revised, corrected, and enlarged the second edition of 1841, and his son prepared the 3rd of 1846, and the 4th of 1852. Later editions were the 5th, 1857, ed. by E. H. Bennett; the 6th, 1865, ed. by Isaac F. Redfield; the 7th, 1872, by Bennett; and the 8th, 1883, ed. by Melville M. Bigelow.

164 Story also wrote the following articles on legal subjects for the *Encyclopedia Americana*, edited by Francis Lieber between 1829 and 1831: Congress of United States, Contract, Courts of the United States, the American part of the article on Criminal Law, Capital Punishment, Domicil, Equity, the American part of the article on Jury, Law, Lien, Legislation and Codes, Natural Law, National Law, Prize, and Usury. *Cf. The Life and Letters of Francis Lieber*, ed. by Thomas Sergeant Perry (Boston: 1882), pp. 79-80. Evidence of Story's high opinion of Lieber's work on government (*The Manual of Political Ethics*) may be found in *ibid.*, pp. 118-119. See also Lieber Papers, Huntington Library, San Marino, California.

165 Roscoe Pound, "The Place of Judge Story in the Making of American Law," 48 *American Law Review* (Sept.-Oct. 1914), 695-696. Story seems to have understood the importance of equity in our system from the first, for he joined in a petition for the establishment of a court of chancery in Massachusetts at a time when this Commonwealth was persistently hostile to the whole system. *Ibid.*, p. 696.

166 Aumann, *Changing American Legal System*, pp. 124-125. *The North American Review* began publishing articles favoring codification as early as 1815, and continued for the next twenty years. Story is said to have contributed some of them, anonymously. In 1836, he headed a committee which reported favorably on codification of the criminal law in Massachusetts.

tor accomplished triumphantly—the preservation of the common law. Pound claims that the great nineteenth century text-book writers, especially Story and Kent, really saved this British heritage. At the crucial time, the common law was so presented as to make its reception easy. The energies of the judges could be turned from less rewarding pursuits to applying the common law principles in concrete cases.[167] The emphasis of Story's treatises on the civil law is on that part of the law where the Romans were at their best and where the common law was least developed.[168]

Even though Story produced commentaries on *Bailments* (1832), *Constitution* with an abridgment in the same year (1833), *Conflict of Laws* (1834), *Equity Jurisprudence* (1836), *Equity Pleadings* (1838), *Agency* (1839), *Partnership* (1841), *Bills of Exchange* (1843), and *Promissory Notes* (1845),[169] his " grand design " was not yet complete. His friend, Charles Sumner, has recorded that Story contemplated treatises on the law of Shipping, Insurance, Equity Practice, Admiralty, and the Law of Nations.[170]

Gradually, Story grew unhappier with his position on the Court,[171] and eager to devote his entire attention to the law school.[172] After Marshall's death, Story gave ten more years of

167 Pound in 48 *Amer. Law Rev.*, 692.

168 *Ibid.*, 692-694.

169 Each of these commentaries went through several editions.

170 *Great American Lawyers*, III, 178-179; Story, *Life and Letters*, II, 239. Another project which he had in mind was a work applying the rules of legal evidence to the events of the gospel narrative, in which the question of the divine origin of Christianity should be argued as before a jury in a court of justice. Although he claimed to be a loyal Unitarian, Story was convinced of the divine origin of Christianity. *Amer. Rev.*, III, 81.

171 Letter to Harriet Martineau, April 7, 1837—" I am the last of the old race of Judges. I stand their solitary representative, with a pained heart, and a subdued confidence." Story, *Life and Letters*, II, 277.

172 Letter to Chancellor Kent, June 10, 1845—" This is the last year I shall be a Judge of the Supreme Court, and in the early autumn my resignation will be given in. Henceforth, I shall devote the residue of my life and energies to the Law School exclusively." *Ibid.*, II, 538-539.

service. While the great Chief Justice lived, Story usually found himself among the majority, particularly on constitutional questions. However, Marshall's death in 1835 changed the situation. In the first place, Story, although the senior justice, and long considered Marshall's heir-apparent,[173] was passed over for Roger B. Taney.[174] Secondly, he found himself in the minority with increasing frequency. A third irritating incident—the publication of Justice Baldwin's *General View of the Constitution* in 1837—threatened to interrupt the agreeable personal relations among the judges because of its strictures upon Story's *Commentaries,* but Story took no notice of the work, consoling himself with the memory of Marshall's approval of all his conclusions.[175]

Story thought of resigning from the Court during the administration of Harrison, but decided against it when Tyler was suddenly elevated to the presidency.[176] It appears, however, that had not death intervened, he would have resigned in 1845 or 1846. On April 12, 1845, he wrote to his old supporter, Ezekiel Bacon, explaining his difficulties:

173 Marshall had long wanted Story as his successor, according to Sumner. "The Scholar, the Jurist, the Artist, the Philanthropist," Phi Beta Kappa Oration by Charles Sumner, Harvard College, Aug. 27, 1846. *Works of Sumner,* I, 261.

174 Many thought that Story ought to have succeeded as Chief Justice when Marshall died. A typical comment by a Story supporter is the following: "But unfortunately for the Republic, eminence and fitness are no longer the titles to office of distinction and trust. The scale of emolument and honor are now graduated according to the warmth of political friendship and partisan effort." Burns, publr., *Selections from the Works of Story,* p. 42 of sketch of Story's life. Jackson had already referred to Story as "the most dangerous man in America." Story, *Life and Letters,* II, 117, 119.

175 *Ibid.,* II, 273-274.

176 It was understood that Tyler had expressly avowed that in case of a vacancy in the Supreme Court, "no one should be appointed who was of the school of Story and Kent." Placing little reliance on Tyler, Story felt that his resignation would subject the court to the hazard of a party nomination. Story, *Life and Letters,* II, 523.

Although my personal position and intercourse with my brethren on the Bench has always been pleasant, yet I have been long convinced that the doctrines and opinions of the " old Court " were daily losing ground, and especially those on great constitutional questions. New men and new opinions have succeeded. The doctrines of the Constitution, so vital to the country, which in former times received the support of the whole Court, no longer maintain their ascendency. I am the last member now living, of the old Court, and I cannot consent to remain where I can no longer hope to see those doctrines recognized and enforced. For the future I must be in a dead minority of the Court, with the painful alternative of either expressing an open dissent from the opinions of the Court, or, by my silence, seeming to acquiesce in them. The former course would lead the public, as well as my brethren, to believe that I was determined, as far as I might, to diminish the just influence of the Court, and might subject me to the imputation of being, from motives of mortified ambition, or political hostility, earnest to excite popular prejudices against the Court. The latter course would subject me to the opposite imputation of having either abandoned my old principles, or of having, in sluggish indolence, ceased to care what doctrines prevailed. Either alternative is equally disagreeable to me, and utterly repugnant to my past habits of life, and to my present feelings. I am persuaded that by remaining on the Bench I could accomplish no good, either for myself or for my country.[177]

Less than five months later, on September 10, 1845, Story died. He worked steadily until very near the end, appearing in court only two days before his last illness to deliver an elaborate opinion upon a complicated case in equity; and another opinion, ready to be delivered, was found among his papers.[178]

177 *Ibid.*, II, 527-528. *Cf.* Newell, *Discourse Occasioned by the Death of Story*, p. 9.

178 Sumner, "Tribute of Friendship: The Late Joseph Story," *Works of Sumner*, I, 147-148. See Story, *Life and Letters*, II, 566-567, for a summary of Story's life work. Another side to Story's interests mentioned by "A Friend," is in a eulogy in the *Salem Register*: "Judge Story was

Story enjoyed a wider reputation in Europe than any other American jurist, and it was due to the excellence of his scholarship that American jurisprudence began to be recognized abroad. Some evidence is afforded by Lord Campbell's letter:

> I survey with increased astonishment, your extensive, minute, exact, and familiar knowledge of English legal writers in every department of the law. A similar testimony to your juridical learning, I make no doubt, would be offered by the lawyers of France and Germany, as well as of America, and we should all concur in placing you at the head of the jurists of the present age.[179]

Before Story's time, all of the influence had been exercised by Europe on America, and there had been no flow of legal thought in the other direction. Even before he began to publish his series of commentaries, Story was known by his decisions and through correspondence with Lord Stowell and other distinguished lawyers and judges in England. His reputation was established on the Continent by publication of his *Commentaries on the Constitution* and the *Conflict of Laws*.[180]

Jared Sparks, in England in 1840, wrote,

> As an American, and a friend of Judge Story, it gives me great pleasure to find how much his writings and judicial character are valued here. From what has been said to me by persons well informed, I doubt if there is a lawyer or Judge in England, whose authority is higher in the profes-

---

always an able financier, and from the incorporation of the Merchants Bank he was a Director, and for many years President; and under his advice, all those illegal and usurious practices then common were discarded and it became a model Bank. By his judicious management of his works and pecuniary affairs, he has left a larger fortune than any other lawyer in New England ever acquired from his profession, not withstanding he was most liberal in every public undertaking, and munificent in his benefactions to those friends to whom he was a father and a counsellor." In scrapbook of Story eulogies prepared by Simon Greenleaf.

179 Story, *Life and Letters*, II, 429.

180 *Great American Lawyers*, III, 177-178.

sion. A young and prominent member of Parliament told me that he asked a distinguished barrister to recommend to him a course of *equity studies*. The Barrister replied in two words, —" Read Story ".[181]

Much evidence of the wide circle of admirers who united in praising Story and his works could be cited, were it necessary. But Charles Sumner has expressed all of the tributes in brief compass. To him, Story was more than a lawyer, more than a judge. He was a jurist, a man for the ages.[182]

### TIMOTHY WALKER

In connection with Story's activities at the Harvard Law School, a brief word may be said about one of his students who was instrumental in spreading his teachings.

Timothy Walker was born December 1, 1802, the year that both Chipman and Dane reached their fiftieth birthdays, and at the time that Story was starting out to make his mark in Salem. His background was much like that of Dane, in that he was born on his father's farm in Wilmington, Massachusetts, and worked on it with scarcely any schooling until he reached the age of sixteen. Though hoping to attend Harvard himself, his sense of duty obliged him to send his brothers there before him-

---

181 Sparks to Sumner, London, Oct. 19, 1840. Sumner Papers, Harvard College Library. Story was often cited in Westminster Hall—an English tribute to a foreign jurist almost unprecedented, except for Kent. (*Cf. infra*, p. 90.) And the Chief Justice of England declared, with regard to a point on which Story differed from the Queen's Bench, that his opinion would "at least neutralize the effect of our [the English] decision, and induce any of our Courts to consider the question as an open one." (Letter of Lord Denman to Charles Sumner, Sept. 29, 1840, in Story, *Life and Letters*, II, 379.) The case Denman referred to was that of Peters *v.* Warren Ins. Co., 3 Sumner's Rep. 389 (1838), where Story dissented from the case of DeVaux *v.* Salvador, 4 Adolph. and Ellis 420 (1836). *Works of Sumner*, I, 269. "His authority was acknowledged in France and Germany, the classic lands of jurisprudence; nor is it too much to say, that at the moment of his death he enjoyed a renown such as had never before been achieved, during life, by any jurist of the Common Law." *Ibid.*, I, 269-270.

182 *Ibid.*, I, 271.

self. He taught at the Round Hill School, Northampton, in order to earn money for their education.[183]

Finally, in 1822, he entered Harvard, having prepared himself, and graduated in 1826, first in his class. For the next three years, he taught mathematics in the Round Hill School, meanwhile writing and attending the law lectures of Judge Samuel Howe. He entered Harvard Law School in 1829, the year that Story began his professorship, and studied with Story and Ashmun for one year.[184]

Attracted by a professional opening, Walker went to Cincinnati, Ohio, in August 1830, early enough to become one of the fathers of the city. His New England ancestry and particularly his recent proximity to Boston, gave him an easy entry to society and business. An elderly lawyer, reminiscing many years later, wrote that Walker "came here early . . . had the New England passport, married one of our rich girls, and was a success, in law as well as matter-o'-money." [185]

Walker was admitted to the bar in 1831, and began to practice. In 1833, in cooperation with Judge John C. Wright who had been a judge of the Supreme Court of Ohio and a member of Congress, and Edward King of New York, a former student at Litchfield, he organized a private law school. The students were few and at first the school had no power to grant degrees. However, it rapidly increased in prominence, and in 1835, it be-

183 Clara Longworth de Chambrun, *The Making of Nicholas Longworth* (New York: Ray Long and Richard R. Smith, Inc., 1933), p. 56. The Round Hill School was conducted by George Bancroft.

184 Obituary of Hon. Timothy Walker, *Monthly Law Reporter*, new series VIII (April 1856), 708-709.

185 A. G. W. Carter, *The Old Court House: Reminiscences and Anecdotes of the Courts and Bar of Cincinnati* (Cincinnati: 1880), p. 122. Walker married Ellen Page Wood, March 11, 1840, by whom he had three sons and two daughters. Chambrun, in *The Making of Nicholas Longworth*, pp. 63-66, however, dilates upon the fact that Ellen Wood was very poor, and that her poverty prevented her from responding to Walker's suit much earlier than she did. Chambrun also says that Walker was a widower at the time, but no clue has been found to the identify of his first wife.

came a part of Cincinnati College, founded in 1818.[186] Walker himself did most of the teaching in the early years, even as his practice increased. On November 4, 1838, he recorded in his journal,

> The Law School reopened on the fifteenth of last month with better prospects than ever; after all, my real vocation is to teach; I can do it better than anything else, but my practice is growing more and more interesting. We are concerned in all the most important cases in litigation and are often called upon for written opinions . . . .[187]

And for the entry of December 23rd, he wrote, "Business last year was worth at least ten thousand dollars and the law school is a third larger than ever before, regular attendance and fine young men, too." [188] Later, as the school's reputation improved, leading lawyers at the Cincinnati bar served as instructors, and Walker even entertained hopes of persuading Francis Lieber to join the faculty.[189]

By 1841, a loyal citizen of Cincinnati, in describing the attractions of his city, could write that the law school had been established for several years. "The student has great advantages in the pursuit of legal studies at Cincinnati; and when qualified, receives a regular degree of bachelor at law, from Cincinnati College." [190] A young man who worked in Walker's

186 Aumann, *Changing American Legal System*, pp. 116-117. See also Carrington T. Marshall, ed.-in-chief, *A History of the Courts and Lawyers of Ohio*, III (New York: American Historical Society, Inc., 1934), 665-667. Until 1867, it was known as the Law School of Cincinnati College. In 1896, it became a part of the University of Cincinnati.

187 Chambrun, *Making of Nicholas Longworth*, p. 62.

188 *Ibid.*, p. 63.

189 " I do not intend to give up the idea of having you among us some day. We must soon reorganize our college, and then, if not before, I trust we shall be able to offer you a sufficient inducement to come among us." Walker to Lieber, Sept. 30, 1846, Lieber Papers, Huntington Library, San Marino, California.

190 Charles Cist, *Cincinnati in 1841: Its Early Annals and Future Prospects* (Cincinnati: 1841), p. 119.

office as student and attorney clerk for three years and spent but one session in the law school, under the instruction of the moot courts, later wrote, "I learned more practical law than in all the time before." [191] If we assume that this comment was intended as a compliment, it bears out Walker's own feeling that his real vocation was teaching.

Walker's most important contribution to the law and his greatest achievement was his *Introduction to American Law,* published in 1837. It was dedicated to Story, the "Judge, Author and Teacher, . . . by one who has enjoyed the good fortune of being his pupil and friend." In the preface to this commentary, Walker stated that he had learned from experience that there were no adequate outlines of American law designed for the beginner.  It was therefore his purpose to provide an introductory work that would make the first studies of the law clearer.[192]

The various titles in the book were derived from his lectures in the law school. The book received immediate attention from the legal profession, particularly since there were no other single volume works on the same subject. Eleven editions were published, the last one appearing in 1905.

Walker served for a short time in 1842 as judge of the court of common pleas in Hamilton County, filling a vacancy. He then became editor of the *Western Law Journal,* which was published in ten volumes between 1843 and 1853. This magazine carried opinions of all courts, notices of new law books, biographical sketches of deceased members of the profession, etc. It was a private enterprise sponsored by the owner, Thomas L. Hamer, who wanted to create an organ of communication among western lawyers.[193]

191 Carter, *The Old Court House,* pp. 122-123.

192 Timothy Walker, *Introduction to American Law, Designed as a First Book for Students* (Philadelphia: 1837). Preface, p. v.

193 Marshall, *Courts and Lawyers of Ohio,* I, 293. Prospectus of the *Journal* in 1 *Western Law Journal* 1-2. For content, the editor had to rely on contributions. No anonymous articles would be published. The subscrip-

Walker was recognized as an able man, both in the law and out of it. He was in great demand as a public orator, and was known for his ability to speak on almost any topic, if he had time to prepare.[194] A contemporary has written that he

> was remarkable for the vigor and clearness of his mind, the absolute precision of his ideas, and his quickness and his conciseness. He was very able in cross-examination, and showed consummate tact in the management of a case. With masterly reasoning and simple eloquence, he was emphatically a strong man before both court and jury. He was a gentlemanly and high-toned advocate. He never did a discourteous or an unfair thing. He always acted on the rule that "no principle can justify us in doing, or our clients in requiring us to do for them, what we should blush to do for ourselves." [195]

Walker's death in 1856 was the result of a fall from his carriage in the preceding year.[196] Although his achievements were already noteworthy, he was a "might have been." He had served as a judge for one short period of time so successfully, that he might have attained greater opportunities for service had life been spared to him. Even so, he left his mark in Ohio, not only by the law school, his *Journal*, and his commentaries, but by concrete suggestions for improving Ohio law. He was instrumental in changing the laws having to do with crime and the status of married women. As early as 1835, he wrote an article on codification, and he was always interested in simplifying the rules of pleading and practice.[197]

---

tion price was $3.00 a year, and it is interesting to note that the remittance could be sent through the post office free of charge, as post masters were authorized to frank letters containing money for subscriptions to periodicals.

194 Carter, *The Old Court House*, p. 122. Proof of this ability may be found in the large number of addresses, many printed separately, that form the major part of his bibliography.

195 *Monthy Law Reporter*, n. s. VIII, 708-709.

196 Details are in Chambrun, *Making of Nicholas Longworth*, pp. 69-70.

197 Aumann, *Changing American Legal System*, p. 117.

The contribution which the New England nationalists made to the development of a regularized American legal system was a great one. Story's work was the best known during his lifetime, had by far the greatest influence, and remains the most widely recognized today. Dane's ponderous tomes have been out-dated. Walker's introductory work apparently is still in use by some beginning students. Chipman is now being resurrected as an advanced legal thinker, after his works have lain dormant for a century. Together, these four men produced more than thirty volumes on the law, not to mention revisions, speeches, reports, and arguments—truly a formidable addition to the nation's legal literature. We shall consider them again when we look into the uses and longevity of the commentaries at the conclusion of this study.

Remarkable as were their writings, the nationalists were not uncontested in their views. It is to their most intrepid opponents that we must now turn our attention.

# CHAPTER V
# THE STATES RIGHTS SCHOOL
# OF THE SOUTH

ALTHOUGH the strict interpretation of the Constitution was seized upon by various parts of the Union, depending upon the circumstances, the doctrine is most commonly associated with the states south of the Mason-Dixon Line. The main points in the theory were developed by a recognizable series of steps, the first two of which were the Virginia and Kentucky Resolutions of 1798-99, and St. George Tucker's edition of *Blackstone's Commentaries* with notes. At the time of the War of 1812, the South was one of the nationalistic areas of the country, leaving particularism to New England. Calhoun and his associates supported the Tariff of 1816, and the great South Carolinian himself was chairman of the Congressional committee which reported favorably on chartering the Second Bank of the United States. Another Southerner, Henry St. George Tucker, chairman of the Congressional Committee on Internal Improvements, in a committee report and in various speeches favored federal construction of roads and canals—an idea later to be anathema to the South. During this period, the only spokesman for the traditional idea of Jeffersonian Democracy was John Taylor of Caroline, who was never converted to nationalistic views, even temporarily. Another consistent particularist was Thomas Cooper [1] of South Carolina, " the school master of states rights,"

1 Thomas Cooper (1759-1840), famous for his various activities in politics, education, and law, published a pamphlet in 1826 containing an essay *On the Constitution of the United States and the Questions that Have Arisen Under It,* and another on *Propositions Respecting the Foundation of Civil Government.* The latter was originally prepared and read at Manchester in the winter of 1787, and was first published in the *Transactions of the Manchester Society,* III, 481 *et seq.* These essays, taken together, form a commentary of reasonable size, covering most of the points that agitated the commentators. But unlike the other works under consideration, they were planned for a course on political economy, rather than to meet the requirements of a law course. After preparing these lectures on " general

and a third was Abel Parker Upshur.[2] Because of the limita-

---

politics," Cooper felt that the decided tone which he had taken on disputed points rendered them improper for the classroom, so he published them to the world instead. (Columbia, S. C.: 1826). Preface to the first edition.

In the *Propositions*, Cooper was concerned with the assertion that government originated in the consent of the people. He placed great emphasis on the right of revolution and stressed the responsibility of the government to the people and the right of the latter to alter the government at will. In his essay *On the Constitution*, his emphasis shifted from the rights of man to the rights of the sovereign states. By way of safeguard, he advocated the strict interpretation of the Constitution, which he regarded as a bulwark against usurpation.

The pronounced opinions expressed in these works give Cooper rank among the pioneers in the formulation of the South Carolina states rights doctrine. Nor is this his only pioneering activity. He was interested in political economy, and was better acquainted with the literature of economics than most of his contemporaries. He had recommended that the subject be taught at the University of Virginia, and himself became the first academic lecturer on political economy in the South, perhaps in the entire country.

On Cooper, see Dumas Malone, *The Public Life of Thomas Cooper, 1783-1839* (New Haven: Yale University Press, 1926); *The South in the Building of the Nation*, XI (Richmond, Va.: 1909), 230-232; Lewis R. Harley, *Francis Lieber, His Life and Political Philosophy* (New York: 1899), pp. 67-69; and David Franklin Houston, *A Critical Study of Nullification in South Carolina* (New York: 1896), pp. 56-58, 138.

2 Abel Parker Upshur was born June 17, 1791, in Virginia. His father was a Federalist, who as a member of the Virginia legislature in 1809, voted against giving Jefferson a vote of thanks for his services to the country.

Young Upshur studied at the College of New Jersey (Princeton) until he was expelled in 1807 for participating in a student rebellion. He then studied at Yale, but did not graduate. He returned to Richmond and read law in the office of William Wirt, later opening his own practice in that city. He served in the Virginia House of Delegates in 1812-13 and again in 1825-27. At the state constitutional convention of 1829-30, he was among those who opposed democratic changes which would extend the suffrage.

Unlike his father, Abel Upshur was associated politically with the extreme states rights pro-slavery group. After fifteen years on the bench of the General Court of Virginia (1826-41), he was appointed Secretary of the Navy by President Tyler in 1841, and in 1843, succeeded Webster as Secretary of State. He advocated the annexation of Texas and was engaged in negotiations toward that end when he was killed in the explosion aboard the warship *Princeton*, Feb. 28, 1844.

Upshur's friends regarded his *Brief Enquiry into the True Nature and Character of Our Federal Government: Being a Review of Judge Story's*

tions of space, we shall devote our attention to the lives of John Taylor and the Judges Tucker, but the ideas of Cooper and Upshur will come up again in chapters vi and vii.

## ST. GEORGE TUCKER

The senior Southern commentator is St. George Tucker, who was born at Port Royal, Bermuda, July 10, 1752 (June 29, 1752, o.s.). His parents were Henry and Anne (Butterfield) Tucker, and Pocahontas was one of his ancestors.[3]

St. George reached Virginia in 1771, while still in his teens. He had begun to study law in Bermuda, in the office of a special pleader.[4] He attended William and Mary College for one year (1772), leaving to study law under George Wythe. In 1775, he obtained a license and began to practice in Williamsburg. Tucker's " urbanity, social disposition and literary attainments" were such that he was introduced into the best company

---

*Commentaries on the Constitution of the United States* (Petersburg: 1840), as a complete refutation of the nationalist theory of the Constitution. This volume was reprinted by the Northern Democrats in 1863 (Philadelphia) as a means of setting forth the political philosophy of the Confederacy.

For fuller accounts see the article on Upshur by Randolph G. Adams in S. F. Bemis, ed., *The American Secretaries of State and Their Diplomacy*, V (New York: 1928), 67-124; and that of William G. Bean in the *Dictionary of American Biography*.

3 St. George's brother, Henry, returned to England, while St. George and Thomas, another brother, came to the mainland of America. Thomas settled in South Carolina, and later became a friend of Washington and Jefferson. His friendship with the latter won for him an appointment as Treasurer of the United States, a post which he held from 1801 to 1828. John Randolph Tucker, " The Judges Tucker of the Court of Appeals of Virginia," *Virginia Law Register*, I (March 1896), 789. Prepared at the request of the *Virginia Law Register* and printed separately as *The Public Services of St. George Tucker and Henry St. George Tucker* [n. p.: 1896], in which form it is comparatively rare.

4 Daniel Call, " Biographical Sketch of the Judges of the Court of Appeals," 4 Call Rep. xlvi. (P. 628 in V-X Virginia Reports Annotated, Charlottesville: 1902). Call claimed that Tucker's decisions were more intricate than necessary, an indication that he never got over the bias which the rigid rules of eighteenth century special pleading gave him.

and most fashionable society at the capital [5]—a distinction which he retained.

Tucker favored the patriots during the Revolutionary War. When hostilities broke out, he went to Bermuda at the request of his father. While there, he and his associates located and captured a large quantity of military stores which were useful to Washington in the siege of Boston.[6]

After this exploit, Tucker returned to Virginia and settled down for a few years. On September 23, 1778, he married Frances (Bland) Randolph, the widow of John Randolph of Matoax. He thus became the stepfather of three boys, one of whom was the brilliant and eccentric John Randolph of Roanoke. After his marriage, he lived comfortably on his wife's inherited estate, Matoax, (except when disturbed by advancing British troops). His many noteworthy qualities brought him to the attention of the county authorities, who named him colonel of the militia, " to the satisfaction of everybody." [7] When North Carolina was invaded by Lord Cornwallis, Tucker assumed command of the Chesterfield militia, joined General Greene's army, and distinguished himself at the Battle of Guilford Courthouse. According to Daniel Call, this service " rendered him very popular with the militia, and was the source of his future appointments to office." [8]

5 S. S. P. Patteson, " The Supreme Court of Appeals of Virginia," Part I, *The Green Bag*, V (July 1893), 321.

6 Charles Washington Coleman, " The Southern Campaign, 1781," *Magazine of American History*, VII (July 1881), 37. At a later stage of the Revolutionary struggle, he served as secretary and aide-de-camp to Sir Thomas Nelson.

7 Call, 4 Call Rep. xlvi. (V-X Va. Rep. An., p. 627).

8 *Loc. cit.* See Coleman in *Mag. of Amer. Hist.*, VII, 36-47, for account of the battle. The leg wound Tucker received was apparently not so serious as asserted in the obituary that appeared in the *Gentleman's Magazine* (London: Nov. 1828), pp. 471-472. (A bayonet, driven through his knee pan, was supposed to have given him a stiff knee for life.) This same source quoted Thomas Tudor Tucker, who claimed to quote Washington, that " Mr. St. George Tucker's poem on liberty was equal to a reinforcement of 10,000 disciplined troops." The poem referred to may be a parody on Cornwallis' proclamation following this battle. See Coleman, *Mag. of Amer. Hist.*, VII, 45-46.

Like many of the Virginia soldiers, St. George Tucker combined the duties of a military man with his legal career and his domestic interests. His eldest son, Henry St. George, was born in December 1780, and was just a few months old when his father was off to help in the final defeat of Cornwallis.

After the peace, Tucker returned to practice in the county courts, soon advancing to the superior courts. As his reputation spread, he was " respected by all the court and bar," [9] and in 1786, though still in his early thirties, he was appointed, with James Madison and Edmund Randolph, delegate to the Annapolis Convention.[10] Later he supported the new Constitution, though he was worried about its effect upon the "scarecrow of the British debts." [11]

Tucker's life changed radically when Mrs. Tucker died in 1788, and he had to leave Matoax. He returned to Williamsburg, as the best place for the education of his children, and was soon involved in professional affairs.[12] He was made a member of the General Court, and was also appointed to revise the laws of the Old Dominion. In 1790, on the resignation of Chancellor

9 Call, 4 Call Rep. xlvi. (V-X Va. Rep. An., p. 627).

10 Sallie E. Marshall Hardy, " Some Virginia Lawyers of the Past and Present," *The Green Bag*, X (Feb. 1898), 58.

11 On June 29, 1788, Tucker wrote to his Randolph stepsons, " The recovery of the British debts can no longer be postponed, and there now seems to be a moral certainty that your patrimony will all go to satisfy the unjust debt from your papa to the Hanburys." Moncure Daniel Conway, *Omitted Chapters of History, Disclosed in the Life and Papers of Edmund Randolph* (New York and London: 1888), p. 106. *Cf.* also William Cabell Bruce, *John Randolph of Roanoke, 1773-1833*, I (New York and London: 1922), 103, and Hugh A. Garland, *The Life of John Randolph of Roanoke*, I (New York and Philadelphia: 1851), 62.

12 His stepchildren remained at Matoax, though he continued in close touch with them. See Bruce, *Randolph, passim*. See especially II, 267-272, for explanation of estrangement between Tucker and Randolph which began about 1805, and continued until some time before the latter's death. Randolph even took steps toward instituting legal proceedings against Tucker to recover part of the patrimony which he claimed had been embezzled. *Ibid.*, II, 641. *Cf.*, however, *ibid.*, II, 542.

George Wythe,[13] Tucker was appointed to his chair as professor of law at William and Mary College,[14] and began his career as a commentator.

As a professor, Tucker seems to have been highly successful, though he had a reputation for working his students very hard. In 1801, a neglected correspondent was told,

> I am desired by Cabell to inform you, that the employment which Judge Tucker's impetuous Lectures give him, is so great, that he has been obliged to neglect the correspondence of all his friends.[15]

13 Wythe was one of the most eminent of Virginia lawyers—a signer of the Declaration of Independence and teacher of both Jefferson and Marshall in legal science. The school of municipal law at William and Mary claimed to be the first of its kind in the United States. It was instituted in 1779 " for the study of the practice of the law in the courts and for the study of American constitutions." Lyon G. Tyler, *The Making of the Union* (Richmond, Va.: 1923), p. 10. The chair had a continuous existence from 1779 to 1861 "when the war occasioned a suspension." *Loc. cit.* Wythe had occupied the chair since its establishment. He wrote out his lectures but never published them. The manuscript was preserved at least as late as 1810, when it is mentioned by Judge Tyler in a letter to Jefferson. Lyon G. Tyler, *Letters and Times of the Tylers*, I (Richmond: 1884), 249. Tyler described the lectures as containing many original "thoughts on our constitutions and the necessary changes they have begotten [in Blackstone's *Commentaries*]." Cf. *William and Mary Quarterly*, IV (1), 265; VI (3), 183.

14 The *History of William and Mary College* (Richmond, Va.: 1874), p. 80, gives 1800 as the date of Tucker's appointment, and the *Dictionary of American Biography* has followed this statement. Bruce, in his *Randolph*, I, 67, gives 1788. These dates can be shown to be incorrect, however. The *William and Mary Quarterly*, XVIII (4), 220, presents a document showing Tucker's election by the Convocation of Visitors and Governors of William and Mary College on March 8, 1790, the salary to be £120 per annum; and a memorandum that Tucker took the oath of professor of law and police on that day. (Second mention of date reads March 8, 1700.) Furthermore, excerpts from the letters of John Coalter, later to be judge of the Supreme Court of Virginia, written between 1789 and 1794, refer to circumstances connected with both Wythe's and Tucker's professorships. Coalter was a tutor of Judge Tucker's family, but was unable to "live in" because the family was large and the house, small. Coalter attended the Judge's "instructive lectures" at William and Mary. *Ibid.*, VIII (1), 153-157.

15 J. S. Watson to David Watson, March 2, 1801. *Va. Mag. of Hist. and Biog.*, XXIX (April 1921), 165.

And in the same year, when Cabell found time to write, he told his friend that, " After the commencement of Mr. Tucker's lectures, the whole of his class withdrew from the speaking clubs and since that time have been totally cut off from that species of improvement." [16] Apparently, his students were a little in awe of his " hauteur or austerity," but his fairness was unquestioned,[17] and he was known to unbend occasionally. When Jefferson was elected, all Williamsburg, " the hotbed of the Republican party," [18] was joyful.

> Our enthusiasm spread, I believe thro the whole town . . . . As we passed down the street opposite Judge Tuckers [sic], the old fellow came out, overjoyed at the news as much as any of us, and insisted on our going in and taking a glass of wine with him.[19]

16 Joseph C. Cabell to David Watson, April 6, 1801. *Ibid.*, XXIX (July 1921), 278-279. Cabell added, " The Judge shortly before his departure gave us the plan of a law society and advised us to remain in Williamsburg till July for the purpose of assisting each other in the prosecution of our studies. But the plan although a very judicious one has not been attempted on account of its requiring a greater knowledge of the mode of judicial proceedings than we possess. Besides most of the chaps are taking their leave of the College." In April, Tucker's departure was occasioned by his circuit duties as judge of the district court. Cabell to Dr. William B. Hare, Jan. 4, 1801, *Wm. and Mary Q.*, VIII (4), 215.

17 Chapman Johnson to David Watson, May 18, 1800. *Va. Mag. of Hist. and Biog.*, XXIX (July 1921), 269-270. An exception to this statement may be found in the letter of Garrett Minor to David Watson, Dec. 20, 1797, in which a quarrel between Bishop Madison and the Visitors over the management of the college is discussed. Tucker and the Bishop " had never had any cordial regard for each other, but now it has transgressed the bounds of decency. On Tucker [sic] side I mean." Minor says that Tucker, " tho a man strictly honest, is too much warped by prejudice too much led astray by passion." *Ibid.*, XXX (July 1922), 233-234. Tucker's descendant, Charles W. Coleman, claims that Tucker and Madison were long and intimate friends. " St. Mémin Portraits, St. George Tucker," *Mag. of Amer. Hist.*, VII (Sept. 1881), 219.

18 *Wm. and Mary Q.*, IV (2), 107, note 2.

19 J. S. Watson to David Watson, March 2, 1801. *Va. Mag. of Hist. and Biog.*, XXIX (April 1921), 161. John Randolph, then in Congress, kept his stepfather posted by a series of brief notes on the voting between Burr and Jefferson. Bruce, *Randolph*, I, 168.

Tucker made his most lasting contribution to legal literature while he was serving as professor at William and Mary. He had been called to the position suddenly, and without adequate time to prepare his lectures. He therefore decided to use Blackstone's *Commentaries* as a text,

> and occasionally to offer remarks upon such passages as he might conceive required illustration, either because the law had been confirmed, or changed, or repealed, by some constitutional or legislative act of the Federal government, or of the Commonwealth of Virginia.[20]

And Tucker had a further reason for accepting this method— " the exalted opinion he held of the Commentaries as a model of methodical elegance and legal perspicuity." [21]

Using his lectures as the basis, Tucker determined to publish an annotated edition of Blackstone, adapted to American conditions. The publishers issued a *Prospectus* in 1797 to get the names of subscribers to the edition.[22]

When the volumes appeared in 1803, the promises of the *Prospectus* were fulfilled. There were fourteen to fifteen hundred notes, and of this number, " Those which refer to the constitution and laws of the *United States* are very numerous." [23] In addition, there are lengthy appendixes on subjects not fully

20 St. George Tucker, *Proposals for Publishing an American edition of Blackstone's Commentaries, with notes of reference to the Constitution and laws of the federal government of the United States, and of the commonwealth of Virginia: With an appendix to each volume, containing tracts upon such subjects as appeared necessary to form a systematic view of the laws of Virginia as a member of the Federal Union* (Philadelphia: 1797), p. ix. Tucker used Christian's edition of Blackstone. Advertisement to vol. I.

21 *Loc. cit.*

22 The entire set of five volumes "printed with a new type on superfine paper" and "bound in neat law binding" would go to press as soon as a "sufficient number of subscribers shall be obtained to make it prudent." Delivery was guaranteed within a year from that date, and the entire price of the set, payable on delivery, was to be $20.00. *Ibid.*, p. 3.

23 *Loc. cit.* Tucker's own interleaved copy of Blackstone's *Commentaries* with his manuscript notes is in the collection of William and Mary College.

covered by Blackstone, if they were touched upon at all. The most important of these is Appendix D, Volume I, entitled " View of the Constitution of the United States." [24] Here Tucker expounded in full his jealousy of centralism, and his firm belief in the reserved powers of the states as essential to the liberty of the citizen.[25]

Among Tucker's lectures at William and Mary were two which were published separately. The first was entitled *A Dissertation on Slavery: with a Proposal for the Gradual Abolition of It, in the State of Virginia.*[26] The details of the plan do not concern us, but Tucker's foresight must be mentioned. He considered the subject of the " first importance, not only to our moral character and domestic peace, but even to our political salvation." He thought his plan subject to fewer objections than others which had been submitted to the public,

> as it will be attended with a gradual change of condition in the blacks, and cannot possibly affect the interest either of *creditors,* or any other description of persons of the *present generation:* and posterity he makes no doubt will feel themselves relieved from a perilous and grievous burden by the timely adoption of a plan, whose operation may be felt by them, before they are borne down by a weight which threatens destruction to our happiness both public and private.[27]

The second pamphlet, an *Examination of the Question, " How Far the Common Law of England is the Law of the Federal Government of the United States,"* [28] may in some ways be

24 Tucker, *Blackstone's Commentaries,* I, Appendix, Note D, 140-377.

25 See *infra,* chs. vi-vii, for some of Tucker's views.

26 The work was first published in 1796 and was reprinted in 1861. It appears as Note H, Vol. II, App. 31-85, of Tucker, *Blackstone's Commentaries.* All of Vol. II is devoted to a consideration of the Rights of Persons, with which question that of slavery was immediately connected.

27 *Ibid.,* II, note " To the Reader." (P. 9 of separate edition of *Dissertation on Slavery.*)

28 (Richmond: no date). The copy in the manuscript collection at William and Mary College bears the name of John H. Cocke, with the date November 1800. Cocke was a student there at the time. Reprinted as Note E, I, App. 378-439, Tucker, *Blackstone's Commentaries.*

compared with DuPonceau's study of the same question several years later.[29] Tucker, however, was writing before the United States *v.* Hudson and Goodwin decision of the United States Supreme Court in 1812,[30] in which criminal jurisdiction on common law precedents was refused to the federal courts. Also, it is evident that Tucker was thinking of the common law in terms of its status in England as a *source* of power rather than the *instrument* through which power is exercised—a distinction which DuPonceau drew in 1824.[31]

Like Jefferson, who feared the far-reaching character of the common law, Tucker saw a danger in its acceptance by the federal government. Should such an eventuality occur, the federal courts would have *unlimited* jurisdiction, while the jurisdiction conferred by the Constitution is *limited*. To prevent the annihilation of the states, Tucker saw the necessity of maintaining common law jurisdiction within the states individually, as limited by their own constitutions and legislative acts.[32] On the federal level, its maxims and rules of proceedings could be applied when the statutes were silent on subjects over which the federal courts have been granted jurisdiction. ". . . it may govern and direct the course of proceeding in such cases, but *can not give jurisdiction in ANY CASE,* where jurisdiction is not expressly given by the constitution." [33] Tucker's fears were laid at rest when the Supreme Court handed down the self-denying decision mentioned above.[34]

29 See *infra*, ch. iii, pp. 75-76.

30 7 Cr. 32.

31 DuPonceau, *Jurisdiction of the Courts of the United States*, Preface.

32 Tucker, *Common Law*, p. 35; Tucker, *Blackstone's Commentaries*, I, App. 422-423.

33 Tucker, *Common Law*, p. 40; Tucker, *Blackstone's Commentaries*, I, App. 429-430. See *Common Law*, pp. 41-42 (*Commentaries*, I, App. 432-433), for summary of Tucker's findings on the subject—concerns mainly historical precedents on the use of the common law in colonial and state background.

34 *Cf.* Beveridge, *Marshall*, III, 28 note, for mention of Story's agitation over the fact that the Supreme Court could not apply the common law during the War of 1812.

After the publication of the *Commentaries* in 1803, Tucker remained at William and Mary only one more year. A student in the law school at that time wrote of his professor,

> He is a man of genuine cleverness and of the most exalted talents. I am more and more pleased with him every day. He pursues a course somewhat different from what he used to do; instead of lecturing, he puts his edition of Blackstone's Commentaries into our hands, allots a certain portion for us to read and examines us every day (except Friday, when we attend Mr. Madison's lectures on Natural Philosophy). In his examinations he is very minute and particular, I never underwent such strict ones before. He doesn't confine himself in his examinations to what is comprised in his late publication, but makes use of it as a text-book on which he comments largely . . . He is more luminous on the subject of law than any man I ever saw, and takes more pains to communicate instruction to his students. If I am attentive (and I think I shall be), I shall acquire more correct legal knowledge this winter than I did in twelve months while with James Brown.[35]

Tucker was appointed in 1803 to fill a vacancy in the Court of Appeals caused by the death of Edmund Pendleton.[36] This position constituted a promotion from the General Court, as the Court of Appeals had long been the Supreme Court of the state. For most of the rest of his life, Tucker served in a judicial capacity—on the Court of Appeals until 1811, and from 1813 until shortly before his death, as judge of the United States District Court for the eastern district of Virginia.[37]

St. George Tucker was a " State Rights partisan of the straitest sect," [38] and was "among Virginia's many exponents of the

---

35 William T. Barry to his brother, Jan. 30, 1804. Barry records that there were 50 students altogether, besides 12 or 13 law students enrolled at this time. *Wm. and Mary Q.*, XIII (2), 109. Among Tucker's more famous students, Thomas Hart Benton, U. S. Senator, 1821-1851, and Judge John Coalter of the Virginia Supreme Court of Appeals, may be mentioned. *Ibid.*, XII (2), 86; XVII (1), 4.

36 Call, 4 Call Rep. xlvi. (V-X Va. Rep. An., p. 627.)

37 *The Green Bag*, V, 321.

38 Bruce, *Randolph*, I, 99.

cause of localism." [39] An illustration of his views may be found at the time of the trial of Aaron Burr, shortly after his elevation to the bench. On this occasion, Tucker argued at length with John Marshall on a subject with which the ideas of both were to be connected more intimately later. The two jurists were attending a party in Richmond, when the question of Burr's plot to cause the secession of the Western States came up. " Judge Tucker, though a violent Democrat, seriously contended . . . with Judge Marshall . . . that any State in the Union is at any time competent to recede from the same, though Marshall strongly opposed this doctrine." [40]

In another instance, however, Tucker provided a highly significant precedent for one of the most far-reaching powers which the federal Supreme Court has claimed for itself—the doctrine of judicial review. Even before the appointment of John Marshall to the Chief Justiceship of the United States, cases had come up in Virginia regarding legislation under the state constitution of 1776. According to the most recent scholar on the subject, the original precedent was the Cases of the Judges of 1788—not really a case in the sense of A v. B—but two occasions taken by the judges of the Court of Appeals to pronounce acts of the legislature unconstitutional. The Remonstrance drawn up by the judges at this time was quoted by Tucker in his celebrated opinion in Kamper v. Hawkins.[41] In this case, Tucker held that the Constitution of 1776 was the sovereign act of the people of Virginia and was the supreme law of the land. Hence, every act of the legislature or any department of the government in conflict with it was absolutely null and void. Says Tucker's grandson,

39 Jesse T. Carpenter, *The South as a Conscious Minority, 1789-1861* (New York: New York University Press, 1930), p. 36.

40 William Harrison Safford, ed., *Blennerhassett Papers, Embodying the Private Journal of Harman Blennerhassett*... (Cincinnati: 1864, reprinted 1891), p. 425.

41 1 Va. Cas. 20 (1793). Margaret V. Nelson, " The Cases of the Judges, Fact or Fiction? " *Univ. of Va. Law Rev.*, XXXI (Dec. 1944), 243-255. See also, by the same author, *A Study of Judicial Review in Virginia, 1789-1928* (New York: Columbia University Press, 1947), *passim*.

. . . it is due to the memory of Judge Tucker to record that, as a disciple of Chancellor Wythe, he . . . heartily co-operated with the other Virginia judges in establishing this canon of constitutional law, which is the greatest American discovery in political science.[42]

The logical extension of Tucker's opinion in Kamper v. Hawkins was to the national field. In Marbury v. Madison, Marshall applied the same principle, only with regard to the Federal Constitution. Tucker, however, in supporting his concept of the Constitution as a compact between the states and the people thereof, did not interpret it in exactly the same way in which he did the Virginia state constitution.

Not much printed information is available on the remainder of St. George Tucker's life, and the manuscript sources are scattered. During most of these years he lived in Williamsburg,[43] where his home is still a point of interest to visitors. He kept records of all his opinions while on the bench in three large notebooks which have been preserved in his family. From a chance note in one of these volumes, his strained relations with Patrick Henry are glimpsed.[44] He evidently wrote more easily

42 *Va. Law Reg.*, I (Mar. 1896), 792-793. John Randolph Tucker mentions two other cases involving public questions in which his grandfather gave significant opinions—Woodson v. Randolph, 1 Va. Cas. 128 (1800), in which he dissented from a majority of the court, holding that "the power of Congress, though unlimited as to revenue, could not make rules of evidence with reference to a State contract sued upon in a state court," [quotation not in official records, but given by J. R. Tucker from his own sources] and Turpin v. Locket, 6 Call Rep. 113 (1804), in which he sustained the constitutionality of the act of 1802, by which the glebes of the Episcopal church were ordered to be applied to the poor of the parish wherein they lay.

43 *Cf.* Mary Haldane Coleman, *St. George Tucker, Citizen of No Mean City* (Richmond, Va.: The Dietz Press, 1938).

44 Henry St. George Tucker, "Patrick Henry and St. George Tucker," *University of Pennsylvania Law Review*, LXVII (Jan. 1919), 69-74. It seems that Henry, while governor during the Revolution, had been brusque with Tucker, who was presenting a report to him, not even asking his visitor to be seated. Later, Tucker had the opportunity to return the discourtesy, by not inviting Henry to sit on the bench at one time when he was in Tucker's court—a usual gesture to visiting dignitaries.

than he spoke. He wrote carefully, and it seems that on important political questions, he sought to influence the public through the press rather than by speech.[45]

Tucker's health was not good during many years of his life. Illness forced him to retire from the Court of Appeals in 1811, and again later, when he had served for some time as Judge of the United States District Court, he had to leave that bench. He died November 10, 1827, after a long and painful illness, at the home of Joseph C. Cabell, to which he had retired.[46]

Tucker's death was noticed as far away as England, where his fame as the " American Blackstone " had spread. The *Gentleman's Magazine* of London was over-enthusiastic on the length of time of Tucker's activities. According to its eulogy, Tucker had been judge of the province of Virginia for nearly fifty years (he was not the bench over thirty-six years), and had been known as the American Blackstone for the last thirty-five years (twenty-four, at the outside).[47]

As a person, Tucker was very attractive.

> The Judge was distinguished for his scholastic acquirements, his taste and wit, and was greatly endeared to the society of his friends by a warmhearted, impulsive nature which gave a peculiar strength to his attachments.[48]

On his death, Joseph C. Cabell referred to him as " that great and venerable man." [49]

45 J. R. Tucker in *Va. Law Reg.*, I, 794.

46 Cabell had married Mary Walker Carter, a daughter of Tucker's second wife, Lelia (Skipwith) Carter, whom he (Tucker) had married Oct. 8, 1791. *Wm. and Mary Q.*, VIII (3), 154. Coleman gives Nov. 10, 1828, as the date of Tucker's death, but this appears to be a misprint. " St. Mémin Portraits," *Mag. of Amer. Hist.*, VII, 220, 221. Nov. 10, 1827 is in *Va. Law Reg.*, I, 791.

47 *Gentleman's Magazine* (London: Nov. 1828), p. 472. The date of Tucker's death was here given as March [1828?].

48 Kennedy, *Memoirs of William Wirt*, I, 120.

49 Letter to Mrs. Gouverneur Morris, Sept. 6, 1831, University of Virginia Library, as cited in *ibid.*, I, 68.

Tucker did not live to witness the conflicts that were already looming when he died, but his viewpoint survived him and his arguments were utilized by countless others in the justification of the cherished rights of the states.

## JOHN TAYLOR

John Taylor of Caroline, a Virginia compatriot of Tucker's, was the son of James and Ann (Pollard) Taylor. He was born December 19, 1753, and was thus Tucker's junior by roughly a year and a half. John's father died when he was only three years old, and his uncle-in-law, Edmund Pendleton, undertook to rear him.[50]

Taylor was taught by private tutors at first, and later was enrolled in a private school which young James Madison also attended. From 1770 through 1771, Taylor studied at William and Mary College, but a graduation date does not appear.[51]

After he left William and Mary, Taylor read law in Pendleton's office, and began to practice in 1774. The philosophy of the Revolution affected him profoundly, and appears even in his last writings composed nearly half a century later. Unlike many of his contemporaries, Taylor did not change his ideas with the times, but remained consistent throughout his life.

At the first opportunity, Taylor joined the army, serving in Virginia in the Quartermaster Department in late 1775 and early 1776.[52] Then, promoted to Major, he went to the northern

50 The latest biography of Taylor is Henry H. Simms, *Life of John Taylor, the Story of a Brilliant Leader in the Early Virginia State Rights School* (Richmond, Va.: The William Byrd Press, 1932). See pp. 3-4 for Taylor's ancestry. Taylor was also Pendleton's first cousin, once removed. Unless otherwise indicated, this volume is the source of the biographical data.

51 The earlier biography of Taylor which Simms' work has, to some extent, replaced, is William E. Dodd, "John Taylor, of Caroline, Prophet of Secession," *John P. Branch Historical Papers of Randolph-Macon College,* II (June 1908), 214-252, followed by Taylor's letters, pp. 253-353. Dodd says that Taylor was graduated in 1770, but offers no documentary proof. (P. 214). Taylor is listed in the Catalogue of Alumni for 1770, *History of William and Mary College* (1874), p. 92.

52 According to Simms, *Life of Taylor,* p. 10, Taylor was especially active in providing horses for his regiment.

battlefields where he remained until 1779. He was much dis-
couraged with facilities and personnel. Though he seems to have
been a valuable officer, he saw little opportunity for advancement, and when he had the chance to resign in 1779, he did so.[53]

In 1781, when the British invaded Virginia, Taylor was a
member of the state legislature, where he helped draft war legislation. A Board of War was created and a bill was passed better
to regulate and discipline the militia. Taylor was commissioned
Lieutenant-Colonel in the militia in March 1781, and was given
command of the " First Legion." His new military activities are
not clear, but apparently his troops, collected from the various
counties around Caroline, were joined to Lafayette's command
and resisted the Hessian raids in Gloucester County during the
weeks before Yorktown.

At the time that he served in the legislature, his first experience in public life, state jealousies of each other and of a strong
central government were very pronounced. Taylor seems to have
opposed every measure tending to strengthen the powers of Congress, except for the authority of Congress over the extradition
of criminals. On this point, he was willing that the state executive should be required to hand over the fugitive.

Taylor was not a member of the Virginia Convention of
1788, nor did he care to be. He agreed with Patrick Henry,
George Mason, and Richard Henry Lee in their objections to
the Constitution, and opposed ratification without amendments
guarding individual and state rights. Although Virginia ratified
the Constitution unconditionally, the Convention commented
that powers not granted were, in their opinion, reserved to the
people of the United States, while those granted might be resumed by them, if " perverted to their injury or oppression."
This clause and later, the Tenth Amendment reserving the
residuary powers of government to the states, or to the people

---

53 Edmund Pendleton, *Sketch of the Life of Taylor*, as cited in *ibid.*,
p. 13. In 1799, Taylor was granted 5333⅓ acres of land in the Ohio
territory for his services as major in the Continental Army. *Ibid.*, p. 15.

thereof, were to be useful to Taylor and other Virginia states rights leaders in sustaining their constitutional arguments.[54]

Pendleton, in his *Sketch of Taylor,* gives an excellent summary of his nephew's early views of the Constitution:

> He had objections to the Federal Constitution, as who had not? But when ratified, he has ever considered it as fixing a rule of conduct to the whole society, governors and governed; and holds it to be a sacred duty in himself and every other citizen to watch over and guard it from violations by their several agents in the administration: being wisely hostile to the project of one general consolidated government for the whole United States, he has been particularly attentive to the strides of the Federal Government, which encroached upon the reserved rights of the state governments, and tended to their annihilation.[55]

John Taylor's career was strikingly different from that of either St. George Tucker or his son, whose biography we shall present subsequently. After the Revolution, he devoted himself to the law, and was well repaid for his advice—$10,000 a year, it is said. He invested much of his income in land, usually paying cash. In the eleven years from 1781 to 1792, he accumulated enough of a fortune to retire. From 1792 on, he lived as a member of the Southern aristocracy, though, like Jefferson, his ideas were democratic, and like Jefferson, too, he was genuinely interested in scientific farming. He had ample leisure to participate in government and in those other pursuits which would have been highly approved by Aristotle and his fellow Athenians who thought slavery a necessary basis for real democracy. As a member of the Virginia legislature (1779-1785, except

54 Simms, *Life of Taylor,* p. 48.

55 Quoted in *ibid.,* pp. 48-49. Dodd, in his *Taylor,* emphasizes Taylor's personal antipathy for Washington, whom he considered too conservative in his political views as well as in the management of military affairs during the Revolution. Dodd states that Taylor, using various assumed names, wrote several pamphlets opposing ratification, and describes the Constitution from the viewpoint of Taylor's associates, as "the hated instrument." *Branch Historical Papers,* II, 215-217.

for 1782),[56] Taylor also aided Jefferson in the last phases of his struggle for religious freedom in Virginia, and helped to establish a state land office.

As might be expected, Taylor opposed Hamilton's fiscal policies and the philosophy of government which underlay them.[57] He wrote critical pamphlets, and, as a United States Senator (1792-94), participated in the unsuccessful Congressional attempt of 1794 to break the power of the First Bank of the United States.[58] His influence in arousing the opposition of the planters was noted by Edmund Randolph when he made a trip through Virginia at the request of President Washington.[59] In one of his pamphlets, Taylor raised the question of what to do should the Constitution fail to limit the power of Congress, and suggested that the state legislatures might serve as a check. He did not say how, but he declared that they " have at least as good a right to judge of every infraction of the Constitution as Congress itself." [60] Before Taylor resigned from the Senate on November 15, 1794, he was asked by King of New York and Ellsworth of Connecticut to join with them in a " friendly

56 Simms comments that, " It was the day of giants in the State Assembly. Pendleton and Jefferson were both members of that body the first year of Taylor's membership, and he was associated during part of the period with Patrick Henry, Richard Henry Lee, John Marshall, Spencer Roane, Henry Tazewell, William Grayson, John Tyler, Wilson Cary Nicholas, Joseph Jones, an uncle of James Monroe, and John Breckenridge, future attorney general of the United States." *Life of Taylor*, p. 17.

57 *Cf.* Charles A. Beard, *Economic Origins of Jeffersonian Democracy* (New York: 1915), ch. xii, for analysis of Taylor's effort to give an economic basis to the localism of the South.

58 The titles of the pamphlets were, "A Definition of Parties, or the Political effects of the Paper System Considered," and "An Enquiry into the Principles and the Tendency of Certain Public Measures." Taylor generally wrote pamphlets because he did not believe that newspapers were proper channels to reach the public mind effectively. Simms, *Life of Taylor*, pp. 51-52.

59 Conway, *Omitted Chapters of History*, p. 152. Letter dated at Richmond, June 24, 1793.

60 " Enquiry into Principles," pp. 54-55, as quoted by Simms, *Life of Taylor*, p. 58.

scheme of disunion." Taylor, however, refused, thinking that the Union might be preserved if the interests of the sections could be reconciled.[61]

In 1795, Taylor returned to the state legislature. It was he who suggested to Jefferson the technique of resolutions as a method of combatting the Alien and Sedition Acts. In his letter of June 25, 1798, he recalled an idea already advanced in his "Enquiry into the Principles and Tendency of Certain Public Measures:"

> The right of the State governments to expound the constitution, might possibly be made the basis of a movement towards its amendment. If this is insufficient, the people in state conventions, are incontrovertibly the contracting parties, and possessing the infringing rights, may proceed by orderly steps to attain the object.[62]

Later, Jefferson claimed to have conferred with certain Republican leaders on the subject, but Professor Channing has demonstrated that his memory was faulty.[63] Apparently, Jefferson himself drafted the Kentucky Resolutions and had them transmitted by a third party to Breckenridge, who introduced them in the legislature. As soon as Kentucky had acted, Jefferson sent Madison a copy of the resolutions, and the latter

61 *Ibid.*, pp. 61-62. *Cf.* Gaillard Hunt, ed., *Disunion Sentiment in Congress in 1794. A Confidential Memorandum Hitherto Unpublished, Written by John Taylor of Caroline, Senator from Virginia, for James Madison* (Washington: 1905), 23 pp., including facsimile of the original memorandum.

62 Letters of John Taylor, *Branch Historical Papers*, II, 276. The entire letter appears on pp. 271-276.

63 *Cf.* Edward Channing, "Kentucky Resolutions of 1798," *American Historical Review*, XX (Jan. 1915), 333-336. W. E. Dodd evidently accepts the story as told by Jefferson in his letter to Breckenridge, Dec. 11, 1821 (*Works*, Federal ed., VIII [New York and London: 1904], 459-460), which Channing has disproven. In his "John Taylor, Prophet of Secession," Dodd suggests that Taylor might have been a member of Jefferson's conference group. *Branch Historical Papers*, II, 225-226. Simms says that Taylor and Jefferson took counsel together on the matter. *Life of Taylor*, p. 75.

drafted the Resolves which Taylor was selected to introduce into the Virginia legislature. In addition to his specific points against the objectionable acts, Taylor said, in opening the debate,

> A concentration of power in the hands of one individual tends to enslave others; a concentration in the hands of Congress tends to enslave the states. This oppression and concentration will bring revolution unless the states redress the balance.[64]

After this statement of his position, Taylor proceeded by deed and word to uphold his doctrines. He was active in the election of Jefferson to the presidency in 1800, helping to reform the electoral system of Virginia in order that Jefferson would be sure to receive the support of his home state. Taylor's duties in the state assembly ended in the same year and he was without public office until 1803, when he entered the United States Senate to complete another unfinished term.[65] At the time, the Twelfth Amendment, warmly supported by the Jeffersonian Republicans, was being debated, and Taylor helped to engineer it through the Senate. In this same session, he performed a few theoretical gymnastics to justify the Louisiana Purchase along the lines of strict construction.[66]

Taylor's strong endorsement of Jefferson's first administration was followed by censure of the second. Furthermore, he supported Monroe over Madison, whom Jefferson had selected as his successor. In this matter, he sided with John Randolph, leader of the Republican opposition, and Henry St. George

[64] *Resolutions of Virginia and Kentucky, penned by Madison and Jefferson, in relation to the Alien and Sedition Laws; and Debates in the House of Delegates of Virginia, in December, 1798, on the same, December 13, 1798*, pp. 6-8, as cited in Simms, *Life of Taylor*, pp. 76-77.

[65] Replacing Stephen T. Mason, deceased.

[66] Simms, *Life of Taylor*, pp. 110-111. In 1804, Taylor was a Jeffersonian elector. See *ibid.*, p. 111, for list of Jefferson's measures which Taylor approved in his articles, "A Defence of the Measures of the Administration of Thomas Jefferson." The articles were signed "Curtius."

Tucker.[67] The younger Tucker, a member of the Legislature, had participated in the caucus endorsing Monroe,[68] though his father, the Judge, supported Madison.[69]

Later in the same year (1808) both Taylor and young Tucker were part of an electoral ticket backing Monroe, who, they were convinced, was far better able to handle an impending war than was the philosophic Madison. They insisted that Monroe was highly regarded in France and England, was unbiased, and might possibly avert disaster. But Madison stood "committed by his writings and acts on every question between us and foreign nations," and the inevitable outcome of his election would be "*war,* or an *embargo* of indefinite duration." [70] When war came in 1812, Taylor accepted it, but was glad for a "barren, tho' an honorable peace." [71]

Taylor had been writing pamphlets and newspaper articles for many years before he began to publish books. His first volume was a collection of his articles on agriculture, and was entitled *Arator* (Columbia: 1813).[72]

The next year, he published the first of his long works on government, in which the ideas expressed earlier were brought together and expanded. His *Inquiry into the Principles and*

67 Bruce, *Randolph*, I, 293.

68 Held Jan. 21, 1808. Notice in the *Virginia Argus*, Jan. 26, 1808. Cited in Simms, *Life of Taylor*, p. 118.

69 Bruce, *Randolph*, II, 271. It is Bruce's opinion that this political difference was at the root of the rift that developed between Randolph and his stepfather, St. George Tucker.

70 *Virginia Gazette and General Advertiser*, Oct. 4, 1808, cited in Simms, *Life of Taylor*, p. 120.

71 Taylor to Monroe, May 26, 1815. Mass. Hist. Soc., *Proceedings*, XLII (May 1909), 333. The only aspect of the war that Taylor praised was Jackson's victory at New Orleans, after peace was signed.

72 The newspaper articles comprising this small volume had first appeared in 1803. The book was extremely popular; the sixth edition was published in 1818. Taylor was regarded as one of the greatest agricultural leaders of his day. *Cf.* Avery O. Craven, *Soil Exhaustion as a Factor in the Agricultural History of Virginia and Maryland, 1606-1860*, University of Illinois Studies (Urbana: University of Illinois, 1925), pp. 99-100.

*Policy of the Government of the United States* (Fredericksburg: 1814) is given a high place by Charles A. Beard, who
suggests that it comes nearer to immortality in political science
than any work since the *Federalist*.[73] The book had been begun
in 1794, but Taylor's self-confessed " wild, careless, and desul-
tory way " of writing [74] had postponed publication until ten
years after the date originally intended—1804. The volume had
been planned as a reply to John Adams' *Defence of the Constitutions of the United States of America* (1787-88) which Taylor
considered too aristocratic in tone. Taylor criticized Adams and
the authors of the *Federalist* for paying " too much respect to
political skeletons, constructed with fragments torn from mon-
archy, aristocracy and democracy . . . and too little to the
ethereal moral principles, alone able to bind governments to the
interest of nations." [75] The *Inquiry,* while an important part of
the literature of Jeffersonian Republicanism, is in the class of
peripheral commentaries. Taylor is more concerned with the
good and evil principles of the government of the United States
than with a systematic analysis of that government. Nevertheless, it will bear some examination.

Taylor organized his *Inquiry* in a different form than was
usual for political arguments against the bank, the tariff, and
the debt, which he claimed had created a feudal system in the
United States. These were the " Evil Moral Principles." The
" Good Moral Principles of the Government of the United
States " seem to include such a division of powers [76] as would

73 Charles A. Beard, " Time, Technology, and the Creative Spirit in
Political Science," *American Political Science Review,* XXI (Feb. 1927),
9. See also Beard's *Economic Origins of Jeffersonian Democracy,* ch. xii.

74 Taylor to Burr, Mar. 25, 1803. In M. L. Davis, *Memoirs of Burr,*
II (New York: 1837), 235.

75 Taylor, *Inquiry,* Note " To the Publick," p. v. Taylor explained that
his entire work had been written before Nov. 17, 1811, but the significance
of this particular date is not given. He had written his essays during twenty
years of leisure time, when he could spare it from his busy life, he said.

76 Taylor saw power as divided two ways—between the people and their
government and between the state and federal governments. Adams had
reference to the division among the three departments of the same government.

enable the people to retain their legal and political rights, and would " decrease power to that degree of temperature, which may make it a blessing and not a curse;" second, political equality; third, freedom of religion and of inquiry; fourth, popular sovereignty.[77]

Taylor traced all the evils of factional strife to the Hamiltonian financial system, whose laws enriched the few at the expense of the many. It was his contention that if everyone were really equal before the law, parties would end. He concluded by stating the mission of his volume:

> If, therefore, these essays should only prove, that it is the office of a republican government to protect, but not to bestow property, they may protract the period during which our government may remain the servant of the nation.[78]

Taylor sent the sections of the work to Adams as they came from the presses, but without explanation until the entire work had been forwarded. Adams wrote to Jefferson, upon receipt of the first section, " Aristocracy,"

> I gravely composed my risible muscles, and read it through. It is, from beginning to end, an attack upon me, by name, for the doctrines of aristocracy in my three volumes of *Defence,* &c. The conclusion of the whole is, that an aristocracy of bankpaper is as bad as the nobility of France or England. I most assuredly will not controvert this point, with this man. Who he is, I cannot conjecture. The Honorable John Taylor, of Virginia, of all men living or dead, first occurred to me.[79]

77 *Cf.* analysis by Benjamin F. Wright, Jr., " The Philosopher of Jeffersonian Democracy," *American Political Science Review,* XXII (Nov. 1928), 875-880.

78 Taylor, *Inquiry,* p. 656.

79 Adams to Jefferson, Sept. 15, 1813, John Adams, *Works,* ed. by Charles Francis Adams, X (Boston: 1856), 70. In a later letter to Jefferson, Mar. 14, 1814, Adams said that he had suspected the author by the time he had read three pages, as he had heard Taylor in the Senate, and knew his style well. *Ibid.,* X, 90.

Adams had paid no attention to the numerous criticisms of his work until Taylor wrote his *Inquiry*. Then, because of Taylor's " high rank, ample fortune, learned education, and powerful connections," Adams deemed it proper to offer " a few explanations and justifications of a book that has been misunderstood, misrepresented, and abused, more than any other, except the Bible, that I have ever read." [80] These justifications Adams enlarged upon in a series of thirty-two letters written over a five-year period. By the time of the thirtieth letter, he had reached only the twelfth page. Adams thought he should have as long to answer as Taylor took to write the criticism—twenty years.[81] He was finally compelled to cease his strictures upon Taylor's volume when his hand became so shaky that he could not hold a pen.[82]

Jefferson heartily approved of the *Inquiry,* found parts of it quite absorbing, and thought that Taylor had " completely pulverized " the artificial system of three orders that Adams had built up in the *Defence*.[83]

Many years later, Henry Adams, a descendant of the eminent John, was to write that Taylor's was " the voice of one crying in the wilderness." Admitting that the *Inquiry* was probably the only work of its time that could be said to represent a school of thought in politics, Adams contended that it "was probably never read,—or if read, certainly never understood,— north of Baltimore by any but curious and somewhat deep students, although to them it had value." [84]

80 Adams to Taylor, April 15, 1814, Adams, *Works*, VI, 447.

81 Same to Same, *ibid.*, VI, 514.

82 See *ibid.*, VI, 447-521, for collection of letters from Adams to Taylor.

83 Jefferson to Taylor, May 28, 1816. *Writings of Jefferson*, X (Ford ed., New York: 1899), 27-31. It should be noted that Jefferson had endorsed the *Defence* in 1787. See letter to Adams, Feb. 23, 1787, in *Works*, II (Washington ed., 1853), 128.

84 Adams, *History of the United States in the Administrations of Jefferson and Madison*, IX, 194-195. Adams thinks that Taylor realized " that his

At about the time that the *Inquiry* was published, Taylor was a member of the powerful political junto which controlled Virginia. Other members were Spencer Roane, President of the Court of Appeals (whom Jefferson had intended to appoint Chief Justice) ; Thomas Ritchie, editor of the influential Richmond *Enquirer,* and behind them all, Jefferson with his immense popularity and " unrivaled political sagacity." [85] Of these men, Taylor was " the bravest, most consistent, most unselfish, as well as one of the very ablest . . ." [86]

While Taylor thus participated in practical politics, he continued to write. His second major work on government appeared in 1820 under the title, *Construction Construed, and Constitutions Vindicated.* In contrast to the tardy *Inquiry* the new work was very timely, as it discussed Marshall's recent desion in McCulloch *v.* Maryland,[87] and the Missouri Compro-

---

disciples invariably deserted in practice the rules they praised in his teaching; but he continued to teach, and the further his scholars drifted from him the more publicly and profusely he wrote." Taylor's difficulty was his failure to recognize that the country had changed since 1787 when his *Inquiry* would have been acceptable. By 1814, the issues it dealt with were out of date. *Ibid.,* IX, 195-196.

85 Beveridge, *Marshall,* IV, 146. Beveridge summarizes the findings of a group of historians that the Virginia Republican machine was based on the county courts, which were the smallest political units. The justices of the peace who composed them were appointed by the governor. These justices, in turn, named the men to be sent to the state Legislature which appointed the governor and also chose the members of the Court of Appeals who held office for life. "A perfect circle of political action was thus formed, the permanent and controlling center of which was the Court of Appeals." *Ibid.,* IV, 146-147. Judge St. George Tucker's position on the Court of Appeals, and later, his son's, should be noted in this connection.

86 *Ibid.,* II, 397. This tribute is of all the more weight, coming, as it does, from Marshall's biographer.

87 4 Wheat. 316 (1819). Beveridge describes the issue in this case as really Nationalism *v.* Localism, and says that Taylor, Roane, and Ritchie were not prepared for Marshall's "bold and crushing blows" on their "fanatically cherished theory of Localism." *Marshall,* IV, 304, 309. See *ibid.,* IV, 335-339 for summary of *Construction Construed,* with special reference to McCulloch *v.* Maryland.

mise. Taylor kept his main argument—unlimited government is unjustified.[88]

Regarding the issue in McCulloch v. Maryland, Taylor pointed out that under the Constitution, the power to tax is concurrent. Therefore, he concluded that the states had the right to tax a branch of the Bank of the United States, since the Congress could tax state banks.[89] As to the Missouri Compromise, Taylor foresaw that the idea of a balance of power between the two great sections of the country would lead only to hostility and war.[90] He thus removed the issue from the direct problem of the extension of slavery and placed it on a political concept. The problems of slavery he thought could be solved only by a slow process of reformation. The Compromise itself he thought unconstitutional, as an invasion of the internal rights of the states.[91]

In 1822, Taylor published *Tyranny Unmasked,* an argument against protectionist policy.[92] This volume which appeared at the time that Hamilton's *Report on Manufactures* was being resurrected in Congressional debates, is considered by Professor Wright the first of its kind printed in the United States.[93]

88 Professor Wright points out the paragraph which he considers to be a thinly veiled foreshadowing of the Civil War: "There remains a right, anterior to every political power whatsoever, and alone sufficient to put the subject of slavery at rest; the natural right of self-defence...It is allowed on all hands, that danger to the slave-holding states lurks in their existing situation, however it has been produced; and it must be admitted, that the right of self-defence applies to that situation, of the necessity for which the parties exposed to the danger are the natural judges: Otherwise this right, the most sacred of all possessed by men, would be no right at all. I leave to the reader the application of these observations." P. 314, at end of section on "The Missouri Question."

89 Taylor, *Construction Construed,* pp. 92-93.

90 *Ibid.,* p. 291.

91 *Ibid.,* pp. 295-314.

92 *Cf.* Beveridge, *Marshall,* IV, 366-368, for summary of *Tyranny Unmasked,* with special reference to Marshall.

93 Wright in *Amer. Pol. Sci. Rev.,* XXII, 885.

Only a few years before, Jefferson and Madison had joined the American Society for the Encouragement of Domestic Manufactures, a protectionist organization, justifying this heresy by the requirements of post-war conditions.[94] Taylor would have nothing to do with this group, demonstrating again his adherence to his early convictions.[95]

John Taylor's most important work on the Constitution appeared in 1823. Its title, *New Views of the Constitution of the United States,* caused Justice Story great consternation. He is reported to have said,

> I once saw a book advertised, entitled, " New Views of the Constitution." I was startled! What right has a man to start *new* views upon it? Speculations upon our Government are dangerous, and should be discountenanced.[96]

And the contents would have disturbed the eminent Justice even more, had he taken occasion to dip into it. The volume was devoted almost entirely to the legal and historic justification of the states rights argument for a decentralized government in the United States. In this work, Taylor presented the clearest

94 See for example, *Niles Register*, XI (Jan. 25 and Feb. 15, 1817), 366-368, 401. Monroe was also elected to membership, but declined. The others expressed sympathy with the objects of the society. See also James Schouler, *History of the United States*, III (Rev. ed., New York: 1899), 42-43 and note.

95 In *Arator*, Taylor argued for bounties to agriculture to offset the bounties which Hamilton recommended for manufactures.

96 Quoted from one of Story's students who left memoranda of the Judge's views and expressions in an extra lecture. It was apparently delivered toward the close of his career. Story, *Life and Letters*, II, 506. See also newspaper article by "An Alumnus of the Dane Law School," in scrapbook of Story eulogies prepared by Simon Greenleaf. The remainder of the quotation does not sound quite so conservative, but indicates Story's recognition of the need for change, "in conformity to the demands of the times. I have been in public life forty years, and have seen the Union change much. You may think you are at last settled! But no! *our laws are written upon the sands of time, and the winds of popular opinion gradually efface them;* new layers are to be made, and your old writing renewed and changed."

statement of his opinions on the Constitution. Throughout, his fear of a judicial aristocracy and of other threats to the rights of the states dominated his thinking.

True to his convictions of forty years, Taylor began his discussion by establishing the Declaration of Independence as the basis of American Government. He had the records of the Federal Convention that were available at the time he wrote,[97] and used them to support his conclusion that the intention of the founders was to establish a *federal,* not a *national* form of government. Since the creation of the federal government had been the highest act of sovereignty of the states, they also had the right to repeat the proof of their sovereignty and annihilate what they had created.[98]

In case of controversy between the federal and state governments, Taylor contended that both should exercise a mutual right of control.[99] If a federal body such as the Supreme Court were to decide controversies of jurisdiction as between federal and state governments, that would make the former a judge in a case involving itself.[100] In his closing chapter on the relative merits of centralized and decentralized government, Taylor concluded that only in the latter form can despotism be avoided. " By dividing power between the federal and state governments, local partialities and oppressions, the common causes of revolution, are obliterated from our system." [101]

Beard has described Taylor as the " most trenchant and pertinent of all the Republican pamphleteers; and . . . perhaps, the most systematic thinker that his party produced within the two

97 The *Journal,* Yates' notes, and the account by Luther Martin. These were the same sources later used by Story. Madison's notes were not published until 1836.

98 Taylor, *New Views of the Constitution of the United States* (Washington: 1823), p. 37. Summary on pp. 176-177.

99 *Ibid.,* p. 147.

100 *Ibid.,* p. 121.

101 *Ibid.,* p. 238.

decades which followed the adoption of the Constitution." [102]
The significance of Taylor's writings as a whole has been well
summarized by Professor Wright:

> . . . it was a preliminary to the later and more bitter stages
> of the state rights and nullification controversies, as well as
> an early justification of secession. During the next three
> decades many southern writers drew from it the materials out
> of which they framed the arguments which served as the
> literary defence of southern sectionalism.[103]

Taylor was active until shortly before his death. He had been
elected to the Senate again in 1822 and, eager to help check the
progress of consolidation, held the position until he died, August 21, 1824.[104] Thomas Ritchie wrote the obituary for the
Richmond *Enquirer*:

> The death of John Taylor of Caroline is confirmed. The great
> lawyer—the profound politician—the friend of the Constitu-
> tion in its original purity—he who served as a member of the
> State Legislature in the dark days of '98 and '99—who for-
> merly shone as a member of the United States Senate, and
> who has been dotted anew with the confidence of Virginia in
> the same high capacity—he, who both by precept and example
> has scattered a flood of light over agriculture, the staple oc-
> cupation of this people, " the chosen people " of the land, has
> suddenly descended to the tomb, " full of years and full of
> honor "! Let Virginia weep over the ashes of the illustrious
> patriot.[105]

Taylor held an important place in the development of the
thought of the states rights school of the South. Jefferson,
Madison, and Monroe, the " Virginia dynasty," never published
formal statements of their political ideas. Taylor had urged

---

102 Beard, *Economic Origins of Jeffersonian Democracy*, p. 322.

103 Wright in *Amer. Pol. Sci. Rev.*, XXII, 886-887.

104 Simms, *Life of Taylor*, p. 201.

105 Aug. 27, 1824, as quoted in *ibid.*, p. 210.

Jefferson to write his memoirs, calling the nation back to true republican principles—a task, he thought, more important than the establishment of the University of Virginia.[106] But Jefferson preferred to leave the exposition of his theoretical system to his friend, giving it the sanction that " Colonel Taylor and myself have rarely, if ever, differed in any political principle of importance." [107] John Randolph had humorously deprecated Taylor's unfortunately diffuse literary style by asking Garnett, " For heaven's sake, get some worthy person . . . to do the second edition into *English*." [108] But he said, too, that Taylor's disinterested principles were the only bond of union among Republicans.[109] Though Taylor's works are little known now, they were influential in their time, and are today one of the best sources on the principles of Jefferson and his followers.

### HENRY ST. GEORGE TUCKER

At about the turn of the nineteenth century, a student of Judge Tucker's at the College of William and Mary wrote, "You ask who of the students are clever? Young H. Tucker and one Leigh from Chesterfield appear to be the cleverest." [110]

The " young H. Tucker " here referred to was the eldest son of the Judge, born December 29, 1780, just before his father went to help in the final defeat of Cornwallis. Henry grew up with his own brother, Nathaniel Beverley, and his three Randolph half-brothers as his closest companions. Like most good Virginians of the time, he attended William and Mary College, graduating in 1798. He immediately entered the law school and

106 Taylor to Jefferson, Feb. 25, 1821, Taylor MSS. in Archives of Maine Historical Society. Cited by Simms, *Life of Taylor*, p. 180.

107 Jefferson to Thomas Ritchie, Dec. 25, 1820. *Writings*, X (Ford ed., 1899), 170.

108 John Randolph to James M. Garnett, Feb. 14, 1814, with reference to the *Inquiry*. Garnett MSS. cited by Bruce, *Randolph*, II, 622.

109 *Ibid.*, II, 235.

110 J. Shelton Watson to David Watson, Nov. 4, 1799, *Va. Mag. of Hist. and Biog.*, XXIX (April 1921), 146.

took the formal training which his father gave, finishing in about 1801, and moving to western Virginia to begin his career.[111]

It was his father who suggested this change. During Judge Tucker's service on the General Court, he had been favorably impressed with the judges who lived in the west, and determined to send Henry to the Valley of Virginia at Winchester.[112] In 1802, the young law graduate set out with two horses and a Negro boy. His father promised to support him for the first three years of his career; after that he was on his own.

Henry's mentor in Winchester was the kindly Hugh Holmes, who first gave him fatherly advice and then, when he became Judge Holmes, gave him most of his practice.[113] Young Tucker's success was great. Even during his first three years, his accounts show that he asked his father for only $375.[114] His most important business was with litigation over the estates left by Lord Fairfax. He made a special study of the rents on the feudal grants, and later used his extensive knowledge in a chapter on the common law doctrine of rents in his commentaries on the laws of Virginia.[115]

In 1806, Tucker was married to Miss Ann Evelina Hunter, of Martinsburg, and together they reared a large family.[116] Later, like his father, he served as a soldier. In the War of 1812, he raised a company of horse and went to the defense of Baltimore and Washington.[117]

111 J. R. Tucker in *Va. Law Reg.*, I, 796-797.

112 *Ibid.*, I, 797-798.

113 *The Green Bag*, V, 322; *Va. Law Reg.*, I, 798.

114 *Va. Law Reg.*, I, 798.

115 *The Green Bag*, X, 59.

116 One of their sons, John Randolph Tucker, following the legal tradition of the family, wrote commentaries on the Constitution, was attorney-general in President Cleveland's cabinet, and President of the American Bar Association. *The Green Bag*, V, 321-322.

117 *Va. Law Reg.*, I, 798.

After preliminary experience in the Virginia House of Delegates in 1807, where he met many state leaders,[118] young Tucker entered the House of Representatives in December 1815, just in time to greet the Treaty of Ghent. In the heated arguments over the settlement of the war, Tucker upheld the authority of the legislative branch in putting a treaty into effect. Admitting that the President and the Senate were the constitutional agencies for the ratification of treaties, nevertheless the House of Representatives was not bound to make any grant dependent upon the legislative authority as a matter of course.

> If then the legislative power be vested in Congress, and if by this clause it be not taken away or subject to the control of the treaty-making power, I presume it remains unimpaired in the representatives of the nation. If so, their concurrence is not only essential to carry into effect a treaty touching upon legislative powers, but, in acting upon it, they must deliberate with the freedom of independent legislators.[119]

The House concurred with Tucker on this point, against the strong arguments of Pinkney, Calhoun, and others.[120]

Another question before the House was the recharter of the Bank of the United States, which Tucker favored. In his opinion, the constitutional question had been settled by precedent.[121] And Tucker supported another measure, later to be denounced by the South. After his re-election in 1817, he advocated in speeches and in the report of the Committee on Internal Improvements which he headed, that internal improvements should be extended at federal expense. His specific recommendation was that the Bank bonus and dividends be used, with the assent

118 *Loc. cit.*

119 *Annals of Congress*, 14th Cong., 1st sess., p. 560, Jan. 10, 1816.

120 *Cf.* debate in *ibid.*, pp. 522-674. Vote on p. 674.

121 *Va. Law Reg.*, I, 799. Tucker also favored specie payments as a fundamental principle of sound banking practice. *Annals of Congress*, 14th Cong., 1st sess., pp. 1385-1388, April 17, 1816.

of the states.[122] His resolution was debated for two weeks, but no decision was reached.[123]

These opinions of Henry Tucker were so un-Jeffersonian that his son thought it necessary to explain them.

> In reference to all these questions, which arose immediately after the war, there was a departure by many of the Jeffersonian school from the strict canons of construction which had been maintained by the Jeffersonian party in the early period of the Government; and Mr. Tucker was affected in the views which he then took by the general departure of the mass of his party from the ancient doctrines. That he acted with entire conscientiousness in this departure the writer has the most absolute assurance from his knowledge of his character and from the subsequent statements of his father.[124]

In 1819, Tucker was elected to the senate of Virginia where he served for four years. While in Congress, he had said that he disliked political life, but the fact that he could practice before the Court of Appeals while serving as state senator, probably encouraged him to accept the office.[125]

Tucker's first judicial position began in 1824, when he was elected Chancellor of the superior courts of chancery for the Winchester and Clarksburg districts, succeeding Chancellor Carr who was elevated to the Court of Appeals. During the

[122] *Ibid.*, 15th Cong., 1st sess., pp. 451-460. Dec. 15, 1817.

[123] Beveridge, *Marshall*, IV, 418, with ref. to *ibid.*, 1114-1250, 1268-1400, March 1818.

[124] *Va. Law Reg.*, I, 800. After the Census of 1820, Tucker, backed by his half-brother, John Randolph, suggested a 1:38,000 ratio for the new apportionment of Congressional representation. This would mean that Virginia would lose no representatives. The 1:40,000 ratio, which was finally accepted, meant that Virginia lost one of her Congressmen. Bruce, *Randolph*, I, 455, 458.

[125] *Loc. cit.* In 1825, both Tucker and Randolph were candidates for Congress. It is sometimes said that Tucker's withdrawal of his candidacy was responsible for Randolph's election, but it appears that Randolph would have been victorious, anyway. Bruce, *Randolph*, I, 505-506. *Cf. ibid.*, II, 512-515, for evidence of the high regard in which Randolph held Tucker.

seven years that he held this post, he also managed a private law school which he organized soon after assuming the chancellorship.

Chancellor Tucker's passion for work is illustrated by the following summary of a normal day, given by his son:

> He rose at four o'clock in the morning, wrote his notes for the press before breakfast, and after that devoted the remainder of the morning until court to the study of his cases. He went into court at mid-day, and heard arguments and decided cases. In the afternoon he lectured on his printed notes. At night he studied his court cases, and retired about ten o'clock, after relieving the mental pressure by social intercourse with family and friends, enjoying music and conversation. This routine he kept up the greater part of the year.[126]

Winchester was a provincial town, and at that time, not readily accessible. Nevertheless, Chancellor Tucker gathered large classes, numbering nearly fifty students in one year, from all parts of the state and the South. Among his students were three future judges, a governor, and a senator.[127]

The Court of Appeals was reorganized in 1831, following the adoption of the constitution of 1830. On nomination of the legislature, Tucker accepted the presidency of the Court, and filled it well. His reputation was such that his colleagues cheerfully received him as their presiding officer, even though he was the youngest of the four judges.

Shortly thereafter, Andrew Jackson asked Tucker to be attorney-general of the United States. Good Virginian that he was, Judge Tucker declined on the grounds that the honor of election to the Virginia Court of Appeals precluded acceptance of any federal office.[128] Had Tucker taken the position, he would probably have been involved in the fiery political issues sur-

---

126 *Va. Law Reg.*, I, 801.

127 *Loc. cit.*

128 *Ibid.*, I, 802.

rounding removal of the deposits from the Second Bank of the United States.

Tucker served the Court of Appeals for ten years, resigning in 1841. He was sixty, and though still vigorous, he preferred to give way to another. Unlike Chancellor Kent who was greatly irked that the New York constitution required his resignation at the same youthful age, Tucker took the step as a " preventive " measure. He feared that as he grew older, his ability to perform the duties of the court might be impaired, and that his " consciousness of growing infirmity might diminish with such infirmity." [129] Furthermore, he wished to accept another position which was offered to him at the same time. This was a professorship of law at the University of Virginia, a post which Chancellor Kent had declined, and which he himself had refused when it had been offered to him earlier.[130] On the previous occasion, Tucker had decided to remain at Winchester. The proposed salary was too small and besides, he felt unable to teach the sciences of politics and political economy. It is Philip A. Bruce's theory that by this Tucker probably meant, " in the strictest harmony with Jefferson's opinions on those subjects." [131] This is a plausible explanation in the light of Tucker's nationalistic views while in Congress.

Tucker finally accepted the invitation in 1841. By this time, his sons had reached college age and, wrote Tucker to a friend, " The expense of their tuition will be very heavy if I remain as I am, while they will be trivial if I remove to the University." [132] Furthermore, his duties on the Court of Appeals called

129 *Ibid.*, I, 802-803; Bruce, *University of Virginia*, II, 27-28.

130 Efforts to fill the law chair were made as early as 1823, before Central College was converted into the University. Francis Walker Gilmer declined it, made an unsuccessful effort to lure Kent away from Columbia, and then offered it to Tucker. William Wirt also declined the honor, and it was not until 1825 that an acceptance was secured from Lomax. MS. letter of Henry St. George Tucker to St. George Tucker, Mar. 21, 1824, in collection at Colonial Williamsburg; Bruce, *University of Virginia*, II, 26-32.

131 *Ibid.*, II, 28.

132 Tucker to Cocke, July 1841. *Ibid.*, III, 66.

him away from home and family eight months of the year. He preferred to live at home as a professor.[133]

Judge Tucker arrived at the University of Virginia in the midst of unfortunate circumstances. His predecessor in the law chair, Professor John A. G. Davis, had been murdered, and the reputation of the University was at a low ebb. In fact, this situation had been the primary consideration in offering Judge Tucker the position just at that juncture, for he was considered one of the few persons capable of handling it.[134]

The new professor was as successful as circumstances would permit. As might have been expected, Professor Davis' unfortunate end resulted in a decrease in the student body. The law school, however, retained an average of 25 per cent of the total enrollment during Tucker's incumbency, a larger proportion than after his resignation.[135] There were 165 students listed during Tucker's four years at the University, of whom 84, or about 51 per cent, won diplomas.[136]

Tucker divided the school of law into two classes. The curriculum of the juniors included subjects necessary to both vocational education and general culture; constitutional law was regarded as one of these. The senior class devoted its attention to the theory and practice of law as a profession.[137] The diploma

---

133 When the seventeen Tuckers and their servants arrived at Charlottesville, they had to find a house outside the precincts of the University, as none on the inside was nearly large enough. *Loc. cit.* In fact, Tucker had to make the privilege to live outside the University grounds a condition of his acceptance of the professorship.

134 *Va. Law Reg.*, I, 803. Nathaniel P. Howard had filled in as professor of law between Dec. 10, 1840, and July 3, 1841. Bruce, *University of Virginia*, II, 309-311; III, 65-66.

135 *Va. Law Reg.*, I, 804.

136 Bruce, *University of Virginia*, III, 46-47. John B. Minor succeeded Tucker. His methods of instruction were more thorough, and he used more severe examinations. Only 7 per cent of the enrollees graduated during his incumbency. Minor is considered by some students to be the greatest law teacher that Virginia has produced.

137 *Ibid.*, 45-46.

issued upon completion permitted the recipient to appear in the courts, by act of the General Assembly.[138]

According to Bruce,

> The political interpretations, during Tucker's incumbency, were marked by strict impartiality. Whilst he enforced, with all the weight of his great learning and high character, the necessity of maintaining the Union, on the one hand, and of preserving the rights of the States, on the other, he brought to the students' attention the ablest dissertations that presented the different sides,—often so antagonistic,—of the fundamental constitutional questions which had so long disturbed the country. With equal earnestness, he condemned that loose construction of the organic law which led to the invasion of the reserved rights of the States, and that rigid construction which found its reaction in principles which sought a remedy in disunion and convulsion, should that organic law appear to have been violated.[139]

It was in the preparation of textbooks for his classes that Tucker became a commentator. Years before, he had compiled a volume of *Notes on Blackstone* [140] for the use of his class in the Winchester Law School. These he now expanded into two volumes of *Commentaries on the Laws of Virginia,* in which he went into detail on the first three books of Blackstone's *Commentaries.*[141] For his class in constitutional law, he prepared *Lectures on Constitutional Law for the Use of the Law Class*

138 *Ibid.,* III, 46.

139 *Loc. cit.*

140 (Winchester, Va.: 1826). No reference to his father's work, except on p. 9, under Constitution, where nothing significant appears.

141 Published in 1831 and again in 1836-37. Prof. Davis had used Thomas' *Coke* as his text. J. R. Tucker says that the two-volume work was adopted as a text by the University of Virginia and was "the *vade mecum* of the bar of Virginia until the adoption of the Code of 1850, and the decisions of courts after the last edition, put it out of date. It was recognized by the bar of Virginia, and in many of the Southern States, as the most valuable text-book for students and lawyers then in existence." *Va. Law Reg.,* I, 807.

*at the University of Virginia* (Richmond: 1843), and *Lectures on Government* (Charlottesville: 1844).[142]

In these volumes, Tucker leaned more toward the states rights interpretation of the Constitution than Bruce has suggested in the quotation above. There are approving references to Upshur, whose work Tucker considered important, and as might be expected, strictures upon Story and his *Commentaries*. Apparently, these came even more frequently in the spoken lecture than in the written work. The copy of *Constitutional Law* at William and Mary College contains the pencilled notes of W. S. Hughes, one of Tucker's students at the University of Virginia. Among others are these: on page 40, line 29, " What does Justice Story think of the *fact* that the Congress had no power at all to enforce and none other than a simple power to recommend," (referring to the Congress of the Confederation). Again on page 128, note †, Hughes adds, " This resolution was soon expressly revoked. Judge Story cites as authority a revoked resolution." [143] And on page 130, " This statement is refuted by an overwhelming number of instances to the contrary." [144]

142 Nathaniel Beverley Tucker, Henry's brother, who was Professor of Law at William and Mary from 1834 to 1851, used the *Lectures on Constitutional Law* as a text, rather than write commentaries of his own. His interleaved, annotated copy is at the St. George Tucker house in Williamsburg.

143 Tucker quotes Story, *Commentaries*, sec. 355, note 3 [really note 1], in which Story says that " The very first resolution adopted by the convention (six states to two states) was that a national government be set up with a supreme legislative, judiciary and executive." And Story adds, "plainly showing, that it was a national government, not a compact, which they were about to establish..." Tucker's note † reads, " I earnestly protest against such strong inferences from a mere incipient proposition which was never carried out in its spirit or principles "—a somewhat milder statement than the one in Hughes' notes.

144 Tucker is here quoting Story's sec. 356: "And although many declarations of rights, many propositions of amendments, and many protestations of reserved powers are to be found accompanying the ratifications of the various conventions, sufficiently evincive of the extreme caution and jealousy of those bodies, and of the people at large, it is remarkable, that there is

In 1841 or 1842, Judge Tucker wrote about his students, " I am most happy in finding the greater part very diligent and attentive, and the whole very respectful, and indeed, devoted to me." [145] On the students' side, there are a few memoirs of Tucker as a teacher, including one written by a member of this " diligent and attentive " class:

> I regarded him [Tucker], as I still do, as an admirable teacher in all respects. The regard which I felt for him personally amounted to veneration, and I entertained the highest opinion of his ability and merits as a teacher of law. This opinion and these feelings have been in no degree changed in the time that has elapsed since I was a member of his class. He possessed the rare faculty of explaining in clear language the most abstruse subjects, and the affectionate respect with which he was regarded by each member of his class caused the relation between teacher and pupil to be as productive of good to the pupil as it was possible to make it. [146]

Judge Tucker was at the University of Virginia for only four years. [147] Nevertheless, he left his mark upon the institution. In 1842, he was influential in the introduction of the " honor system " in examinations, a progressive step which was soon

---

nowhere to be found the slightest allusion to the instrument, as a confederation or compact of states in their sovereign capacity, and no reservation of any right on the part of any state, to dissolve its connexion, or to abrogate its assent, or to suspend the operations of the constitution, as to itself."

145 Bruce, *University of Virginia*, III, 68. Bruce states that the entire class was enthusiastic over the elegance of Tucker's manners and that all were deeply attached to him. *Cf.* letter from John C. Rutherfoord, written in May 1844. Rutherfoord was later distinguished in political life. *Loc. cit.*

146 Judge William J. Robertson, formerly of the Court of Appeals, no date. This was evidently written many years later, perhaps at the request of John Randolph Tucker when he was preparing his article for the *Virginia Law Register*. *Va. Law Reg.*, I, 810.

147 Tucker went to the University in September 1841. On October 4 of the same year, his son tells us that he suffered a slight attack of paralysis from which he never recovered. Though not recognized at the time, it was the beginning of the end. *Ibid.*, I, 803.

copied by many other colleges and universities. He also played a significant part in the abolition of outmoded rules requiring the wearing of a uniform and early rising [148]—policies which must have made him quite popular with the students.

During most of his incumbency as professor of law, Judge Tucker was also chairman of the faculty, a post to which he was appointed by the Board of Visitors at the same meeting that he was elected to the professorship. This was an unusual honor for a new member of a collegiate faculty, and was a tribute to his reputation for judgment and discretion. He was reappointed in July 1842 and in July 1843, and would have continued in office indefinitely, but for the failure of his health.[149]

The Judge resigned from the University in 1845, primarily because of illness but partly because of the confusion caused by a prolonged riot at the University in the same year.[150] He was unable to carry out the last request, that he draft a report for consideration of the General Assembly regarding the establishment of a special court near the University to take cognizance of all serious disorders within the precincts.[151]

Judge Tucker retired to Winchester, his old home, where he died August 28, 1848. With his death, there passed one of the last of the moderate states rights advocates. In the ensuing years, the extreme doctrines of Calhoun and his followers, with which Tucker did not agree, came to full ascendency in the South. It is to the various ramifications of these theories and those of the nationalists with which they came into direct conflict, that we shall now turn our attention.

148 Bruce, *University of Virginia*, III, 53 *et seq.*; *Va. Law Reg.*, I, 803.

149 Bruce, *University of Virginia*, III, 67.

150 *Ibid.*, III, 111-118.

151 *Ibid.*, III, 118.

# PART III

### THE CONTENTS OF THE COMMENTARIES

# PART III
## INTRODUCTORY

It would be impossible, within a single volume, to present a complete analysis of all of the commentaries. As early as 1837, Justice Baldwin wrote, paraphrasing Lord Coke, that the glosses and commentaries on the Constitution and the common law, " *like the waves of the sea,* beat upon us in a constant flood, increasing in size with every foreign importation, or home production of books." [1] Furthermore, complained Baldwin, the commentaries " will not produce that certainty in the law, which is the *mother* and *nurse* of *quietness* and *repose* . . ." [2]

By way of a sampling, we shall approach the commentaries in two ways. First, we shall take two subjects on which the commentators expressed themselves—the location of sovereignty and the nature of the Union—and present their views. In the discussions of these subjects, the commentators showed themselves to be either nationalists or particularists. So far, no really successful middle-of-the-road attempt has been uncovered. Secondly, we shall examine one commentary, Story's, in its entirety, to see what subjects were included.

In this part of our study, we are concerned not with the rightness or wrongness of any one man's conception of the Union, but with the expositions of the nature of the Union as seen by many men. Whenever possible, the commentators have been allowed to speak for themselves, in order that their arguments may suffer as little as possible at the hands of a summarizer. Judgments based upon hindsight are avoided, and when descriptive adjectives are used, it is solely for the purpose of clarifying the opinion of the man whose ideas are under discussion at the moment.

1 Baldwin, *A General View of the Constitution*, p. 101.
2 *Loc. cit.*

# CHAPTER VI
# ON THE LOCATION OF SOVEREIGNTY

JEAN BODIN, a sixteenth century political philosopher, is usually given the praise (or blame) due to the founder of the doctrine of sovereignty.[1] Since his time, no age has been free from concern with this fascinating concept.[2] Bodin, in his *De Republica* (1576), defined sovereignty as the "highest power over citizens and subjects, unrestrained by laws." [3] In subsequent discussions, especially in those of Locke and Rousseau, sovereignty was connected with the age-old theory of the social contract as the basis of rights and duties, and in this form it came to the United States.[4] As time went on, the problem of the location of sovereignty became more and more elusive. To quote one of the earliest of the commentators,

> The fate of sovereignty has been similar to that of the Nile. Always magnificent, always interesting to mankind, it has become alternately their blessing and their curse. Its origin has often been attempted to be traced. The great and the wise have embarked in the undertaking; though seldom, it must be owned, with the spirit of just inquiry; or in the direction, which leads to important discovery. The source of sovereignty is still concealed beyond some impenetrable mystery; and,

1 James Wilson in his lecture on Law and Obligation, *Works* (Andrews ed.), I, 49-94, discusses ancient theories of sovereignty or law-giving power, but his citations seem to be concerned more with the relations between law-giver and governed than with what has come to be the modern theory of sovereignty. He termed it, the "doctrine of superiority" in that connection.

2 The most recent full-dress discussion of sovereignty has been with regard to the formation of the United Nations Organization.

3 Article on "Sovereignty" by Francis W. Coker, *Encyclopedia of Social Sciences*, Vol. XIV. *Cf.* article on Bodin by R. M. MacIver, *ibid.*, Vol. II.

4 Bodin's concern was to justify the centralized sovereignty of the state. Therefore, his ideas could not find many followers in the United States. He said, however, that sovereignty arises from human needs and does not emanate from God—a blow at the divine right of kings theory, prevalent in his day.

because it was concealed, philosophers and politicians, in this instance, gravely taught what, in the other, the poets had fondly fabled, that it must be something more than human: it was impiously asserted to be divine.[5]

## SECTION I

### THE OPINION OF THE NATIONALISTS

By the time that the United States was ready to embark upon a separate career of nationhood, the problem of the location of sovereignty was important for those who sought to justify theoretically the break from England. Among the commentators, James Wilson presents the best exposition of the thought of the Revolutionary and early Federal period. He begins his lectures on law by analyzing the " age-old search," and concludes that

> The dread and redoubtable sovereign, when traced to his ultimate and genuine source, has been found, as he ought to have been found, in the free and independent man.[6]

To the philosophers of the American Revolution, it was unnecessary to go further.[7] Generally, they agreed upon the social contract idea—first, that men came together in society, and second, that they formed a government. But at this time, they saw no need to take the third step of Puffendorf and Blackstone

5 Wilson, *Works* (Andrews ed.), I, 22.

6 *Loc. cit.*

7 Wilson disagreed with the British theory. He restated the reasoning which alleged that the Parliament of Great Britain could bind the American colonies as follows: "...there is and must be in every state a supreme, irresistible, absolute, uncontrolled authority in which the *jura summi imperii*, or the rights of sovereignty, reside;...this supreme power is, by the constitution of Great Britain, vested in the king, lords and commons:...therefore, the acts of the king, lords and commons, or in other words, acts of parliament, have by the British constitution, a binding force on the American colonies, they composing a part of the British empire." References to 4 Blackstone's *Commentaries* 48-51. Wilson used the fourth edition of Blackstone, which contained criticisms of the American colonists not appearing in the first edition. See 1 Hammond's *Blackstone*, note 36, p. 275. Wilson, *Works* (Andrews ed.), II, 506-507; I, 19 note.

and confer sovereignty on someone. Wilson thought that such action was derogatory from the general principles of legitimate sovereignty. As far as he was concerned, the sovereign people could act in any capacity—local, national, or international.[8]

Wilson agreed with Blackstone's proposition that in every state, there is and must be a " supreme, irresistible, absolute, uncontrolled authority, in which the rights of sovereignty reside." But he disagreed completely with Blackstone's corollary that this authority and these rights of sovereignty must reside in the legislature; because " sovereignty and legislature are convertible terms," and because " it is requisite to the very essence of a law that it be made by the supreme power." Wilson claimed that there was no authority in English law for this latter assertion.[9] ". . . sovereignty, dominion, and power are the parents, not the offspring of government." [10] Furthermore, sovereignty is capable of division and actually has been divided under the American system.[11]

This idea of the divisibility of sovereignty had emerged at the time of the Federal Convention, and was a distinctively American theory. Such a concept was in harmony with the idea of a government partly federal and partly national—a new type of government suited to American conditions. Thus, a new theory of sovereignty was justified. In the letter of the Constitutional Convention to Congress, it was expressly declared that " It is obviously impracticable in the federal government of these

8 Randolph G. Adams, *Political Ideas of the American Revolution* (Durham, N. C.: 1922), pp. 173-176. *Cf.* Wilson, *Works* (Andrews ed.), I, 166-167.

9 Wilson, *Works* (Andrews ed.), I, 160-163.

10 *Ibid.*, I, 165.

11 *Cf.* Ware *v.* Hylton, 3 Dall. 199 at 232 (1796), a Chase opinion: " . . . the several states retained all internal sovereignty; and . . . congress properly possessed the great rights of external sovereignty . . . " See also McCulloch *v.* Maryland, 4 Wheat. 316 (1819) ; and Worcester *v.* Georgia, 6 Pet. 515 at 591-592 (1832).

states, to secure all rights of independent sovereignty to each, and yet provide for the interest and safety of all." [12] The new Constitution was asserted to leave the states in possession of "certain exclusive and very important portions of sovereign power;" [13] they still held "all the rights of sovereignty which were not by that act exclusively delegated to the United States." [14] Though there were many sovereignties existing side by side, the real sovereignty rested not with the government, but with the people. Said Publius (Hamilton), "The ultimate authority, wherever the derivative may be found, resides in the people alone." [15] But the *Federalist* was careful not to specify who the people were, whether of the several states or of all the states taken collectively. This was a question left for future generations. [16]

In his significant opinion in Chisholm v. Georgia, [17] Wilson described the nature of sovereignty again. He saw that the problem of Georgia's amenability to the jurisdiction of the Supreme Court was dependent upon a more important question—"Do the people of the United States form a nation?" His conclusion that they did intend to form themselves into a nation, for national purposes, and had done so in the Constitution, [18] rested upon his assertion that sovereignty is vested in men in society. [19] He deplored the common tendency to notice the states rather than the people for which they exist. " A *state,* I cheerfully ad-

12 Letter signed by George Washington, President of the Convention, Sept. 17, 1787. *Journals of the American Congress,* IV (1823), 782.

13 *Federalist,* No. 9 (Hamilton).

14 *Ibid.,* No. 31; *cf.* No. 82 (both by Hamilton).

15 *Ibid.,* Nos. 33, 45, 82 (Hamilton, Madison, Hamilton).

16 Charles Edward Merriam, *History of American Political Theories,* p. 257. Ch. vii of this work, "Political Theory in Relation to the Nature of the Union," is an expansion of ch. ix, "Sovereignty and the American Union," in the same author's *History of the Theory of Sovereignty Since Rousseau* (New York: 1900).

17 2 Dall. 419 at 453-466 (1793).

18 2 Dall. 465.

19 2 Dall. 458.

mit, is the noblest work of man : but man himself, free and honest, is, I speak as to this world, the noblest work of GOD! " [20]
Once the people as a whole are admitted to be sovereign, the
individual states become subordinate to the national government and its courts.

Nathaniel Chipman, the only other Federalist among the
early commentators, avoided the whole issue, stating merely
that the government of the United States is founded on the
rights of man and derives all its energy from the sentiments of
the people.[21] In his revised edition of 1833, however, written
during the heat of the nullification controversy, a short chapter
is devoted to the subject in general, with an additional section
on a later page. Here, he accepts the ideas first expressed by
Wilson. External sovereignty is taken to mean simply national
independence, without any idea of supremacy.

> But when applied to the internal government of a state, it is
> made to signify a power somewhere vested, competent to
> regulate, control, and direct the will of the whole and of every
> subordinate member of the community. To this end, it is sup-
> posed to be absolute, unlimited, and incapable of being put
> under any control.[22]

Chipman makes no mention of Bodin's writings, but refers
to Puffendorf and Grotius who, he says, were " the first writers
of any note on the continent of Europe " to call in question the
divine right of sovereignty. Rather, they derived it from the
civil compact.[23] Both of these men, though differing from each
other and from former advocates of divine right in the mode of

20 2 Dall. 462-463.

21 Chipman, *Sketches of the Principles of Government*, p. 16.

22 Chipman, *Principles of Government*, p. 137.

23 *Ibid.*, p. 138. Chipman notes, however, that Puffendorf still adhered
to the doctrine of the divine right of kings. " ... he who affirms sovereignty
to result immediately from compact, doth not in the least detract from the
sacred character of civil government, or maintain that princes bear rule by
human right, and not by divine." Puffendorf, B. 7, Sec. 2. Quoted in
*ibid.*, p. 139.

the derivation of sovereignty, still agreed that it must be a unity —an abstract moral entity. Thanks to the tenacity of verbiage, many terms dating from the period of the belief in the divine right of kings and the abstractions of the Realists persisted, and influenced " the most eminent English writers," including Judge Blackstone. Chipman, upon a close examination of the British form of government, disagrees with Blackstone that sovereignty and legislature are convertible terms (the position which Wilson had also taken).[24] " We may then safely pronounce that this enormous, this omnipotent power of united sovereignty is not to be found in any single organ of the government, whether legislative, judicial, or executive." [25]

With regard to the United States, Chipman presents only a brief summary, leaving unanswered several of the problems with which other political philosophers struggled. The Constitution has entrusted different powers to different organs.

> Neither have the people, the original source of all power, retained to themselves the sovereignty, absolute and unlimited. It is retained under certain modifications and restrictions, agreeable to the constitution which they have submitted to observe. In this constitution there is no where lodged that united sovereignty, that supreme power, absolute, uncontrollable, arbitrary, and despotic, which it is declared, must, in all governments, reside somewhere, and is alike in all countries. If such be the necessary definition, our constitution has no provision of internal sovereignty; and yet experience has evinced that the powers of this government, so limited and controlled, are fully competent to the great end of all civil institutions, the permanent happiness of the people, and the prosperity of the state.[26]

24 1 Blackstone's *Commentaries* 46; Chipman, *Principles of Government*, pp. 140-141; Wilson, *Works* (Andrews ed.), I, 160-163. The same idea is embodied in Paley's *Moral Philosophy*, 2 part, 185, a book used by many of the commentators.

25 Chipman, *Principles of Government*, p. 144.

26 *Ibid.*, pp. 144-145a. Strange pagination due to later insertion of portion of work, mislaid at time of printing.

Chipman emphasizes this same point later and gives the pragmatic viewpoint more clearly than any of the pre-Civil War commentators. Referring to the claims of certain persons that each state retains " the sovereign right to judge for itself of all the acts of the general government, and to interpose its authority to suspend and annul all the acts of that government which it shall judge to be unconstitutional," [27] Chipman presents the following point:

> Still it is of little consequence what character the several states sustained under the confederation, or at the time of establishing the general government, but what character they now sustain in respect to that government, in what relation they have been placed by an authority which all must allow to be competent, the sovereign people of each state.[28]

" The opinion formerly entertained," he adds, " that the sovereignty of a state was a sort of indivisible escence [sic], a power absolute, uncontrolled and uncontrollable, has been corrected in modern times. Experience has proved that it is capable of division . . ." [29]

Chipman is unique in his reliance upon present actuality in supporting his contention. The other commentators weakened their arguments by trying to establish the fact that the states either were or were not sovereign during the critical years 1775-1787. Chipman alone recognized that this was not important. Rather, the significant relationships within the Union depended upon what had happened since then.[30]

27 *Ibid.,* p. 271.

28 *Ibid.,* pp. 271-272.

29 *Ibid.,* p. 273.

30 Chipman's position is very interesting. In his reliance on present fact, he is ahead of his time, but his adherence to the contractual theory of the origin of the Union shows him to be a member of the earlier generation. The organic theory set forth by the new school, led by Francis Lieber, repudiated the contract idea, but agreed with the pragmatic evidence of the existence of a national government. Lieber, in his *Political Ethics* (2 vols., Boston: 1838-39) is acclaimed as the first political writer in America to expound the idea of sovereignty clearly and to distinguish between the

Chancellor Kent did not show much interest in the problem of sovereignty in the section on the Constitution in his *Commentaries on American Law*, [31] possibly because he wrote before the tariff difficulties of 1828-33 became acute. He says vaguely that the government of the United States " is clothed with the principal attributes of political sovereignty," [32] and refers to the Articles of Confederation as the first attempt " to define with precision . . . the nature of our compact, the powers of Congress, and the residuary sovereignty of the states." [33] In the same section, Kent explains that

> The great and incurable defect of all former federal governments . . . is, that they were sovereignties over sovereigns, and legislations, not for private individuals, but for communities in their political capacity. The only coercion for disobedience was physical force, instead of the decree and the pacific aim of the civil magistrate.[34]

The only other significant reference to the idea of sovereignty is in his discussion of the Senate, the organization of which is " grounded on the idea of sovereignty in the states." [35] He implies that the states were sovereign at the time of the writing of

nation and the people. For a discussion of Lieber's theories, see Harley, *Francis Lieber, passim.* " Lieber was strongly influenced by the rising spirit of nationalism in Germany and by the German philosophy of the organic and personal nature of the state as a crystallization of national spirit." He glorified the nation as a real existence behind and above the Constitution, as the "actual entity to which supreme power was attributed," and it was his theory which was eventually adopted by the Union. Raymond G. Gettell, *History of American Political Thought* (New York and London: Century Co., 1928), pp. 309-310.

31 Vol. I, Part II, Lectures X-XIX, inclusive. For the purposes of this study, only this part is taken into consideration (with the exception of one reference to Lecture XX). Kent's discussion of sovereignty over property in Vol. II and his judicial decisions are omitted.

32 Kent, *Commentaries*, 1st ed., I, 189; (2nd and succeeding eds., I, 201).

33 *Ibid.*, I, 196 (I, 210).

34 *Ibid.*, I, 203 (I, 217). *Cf.* also I, 199 (I, 213).

35 *Ibid.*, I, 211 (I, 225).

the Articles of Confederation, since only independent communities could dictate their own terms before entering into a social contract. Furthermore,

> On the principle of consolidation of the states, this organization [the Senate] would have been inadmissible, for in that case, each state would have been merged in one single and entire government . . . The election of the senate by the state legislatures, is also a recognition of their separate and independent existence . . .[36]

It is interesting to note that Kent made no changes on these points in any of the five revisions which he personally prepared. No specific mention of the South Carolina difficulties has been located in either the text or the footnotes, even though Kent was well aware of the situation.[37]

Like Kent, Nathan Dane says little on the nature of sovereignty in the main body of his multi-volume work, but in the Appendix to the ninth volume, he writes explicitly and at length. He points out that the word sovereignty had been used so frequently since the time that the old Confederation was formed that one would expect to find it in all our public documents.

> How surprised must [one] be, on examination, to find it is not in that Declaration [of Independence] ; nor in the Constitution of the United States; nor in 22 of the state constitutions, now existing—that this word, *sovereignty,* as so applied, was in a subordinate sense, first used in the articles of confederation, entered on the Journals of Congress, Nov. 15th, 1777; so, then first made public; that from these articles it was in the year 1780, adopted, in a *subordinate* sense, into the Constitution of Massachusetts—and from that, in 1792, was copied into the Constitution of New Hampshire. This is the last time we find it *constitutionally* used.[38]

36 *Loc. cit.* (Typographical errors in 1st ed. corrected in 2nd.)

37 See letters exchanged by Webster and Kent, Oct. 29 and 31, 1832. Kent, *Memoirs and Letters,* pp. 208-210.

38 Dane, 9 *General Abridgment,* App., p. 10, sec. 2.

Dane asserts that the terms sovereign states, state sovereignties, state rights, rights of states, etc., were " only *popular,* not *constitutional* expressions "—that they grew very popular in " party times; especially in the contests between the more zealous supporters of the General Government and the more zealous supporters of the State Governments." [39]

Unlike Chipman, Dane was greatly concerned with proving historically that the states were subordinate to the general government, even during the Revolution. According to his theory, the people, in their original sovereign capacity, acting on revolutionary principles, instituted the general government and the state governments in subordination thereto, the crucial date being July 4, 1776.

> These *State* Governments have been, by the people of each State, instituted under, and expressly, or impliedly, in subordination to the General Government, which is expressly recognized by all, to [be] supreme law; and as the power of the whole, is, in the nature of things, superior to the power of a part, other things being equal, the power of a State, a part, is inferior to the power of all the States.[40]

In a later section, however, he takes a slightly different tack, admitting that " in one sense, the states existed before the constitution, but not in the most important sense. We must follow power, not form "—and the general government exercised the power by popular consent.[41]

Dane wrote his ninth volume and Appendix at a time when he was greatly concerned over the condition of national affairs. He explained his remarks on the nature of the Union and the problem of sovereignty as being brought forth by " some very recent proceedings, as published in *Virginia, South Carolina,* and *Georgia,* respecting *State rights* and *State sovereignty,*

39 *Loc. cit.*

40 *Ibid.*, p. 11, sec. 2. *Cf.* sec. 8, pp. 18-19, in which Dane criticizes Rowan's contention that Delaware is as sovereign as Russia.

41 *Ibid.*, p. 35, sec. 26. This statement is similar to Chipman's reasoning.

[which] demand the serious attention of every man in the United States." [42] Guessing that the activities of his home state, Massachusetts, might be subject to criticism because of the Hartford Convention, Dane hastened to her defense. On that occasion, he says, the opposition of New England " to the then *administration of federal affairs* was misrepresented by some, and mistaken by others for opposition to the *Union*." [43]

Dane objects to the idea of indivisible sovereignty, then being elaborated in the South, as possible only among a secluded people. In our system, he finds that we " give and distribute, almost *ad infinitum delegated* power or what is vaguely called sovereignty." [44] Part of it

> is placed by the people in their original, sovereign capacity, in their government, which is divided and placed, part in Congress, part in the Executive, and part in the Judiciary; and each of these portions is further distributed, exactly as is directed in the Federal Constitution. So a vast portion of it is placed in the State Governments by the people of each State, and divided in their original, sovereign capacity, among their state agents, as above, and as directed in their State constitution.[45]

In opposition to the developing Southern doctrine, Dane says, " It is only a visionary, metaphysical sort of reasoning, that makes a *state in a union of states,* under and subordinate to it, as sovereign as the whole union." [46]

During the period that we have just been considering, the basic contention between the Union and the states as to which held the sovereign power had been quieted by a constant reference to the people as an authority over both. But Professor Merriam has pointed out that,

42 *Ibid.*, p. 588.

43 *Ibid.*, p. 594.

44 *Ibid.*, App., p. 19, sec. 8.

45 *Loc. cit.*

46 *Ibid.*, p. 31, sec. 18.

When the contest between nationalism and particularism entered the acute state, . . . this doctrine became less easy to maintain. The difficulty long concealed behind the complicated governmental machinery and the ambiguous term " people " became evident, the compromise doctrine was rejected by both North and South, and the battle fought out between the sovereignty of the states and that of the Union.[47]

It was Joseph Story who made the clearest distinction between the two major uses of the term " sovereignty " in such a way as to avoid the difficulties inherent in the idea of a double supremacy. To his mind, confusion of the various applications of the term (broad and narrow, external and internal, etc.) often led to " very mischievous and unfounded conclusions."

> By " sovereignty " in its largest sense is meant, supreme, absolute, uncontrollable power, the *jus summi imperii*,[48] the absolute right to govern . . . A state, which possesses this absolute power, without any dependence upon any foreign power or state, is in the largest sense a sovereign state.[49] And it is wholly immaterial, what is the form of the government, or by whose hands this absolute authority is exercised.[50]

In addition to this extremely broad usage, Story sees sovereignty often used in a far more limited sense. Thus, it designates " such political powers, as in the actual organization of the particular state or nation are to be exclusively exercised by certain public functionaries, without the control of any superior authority." [51] Viewing the subject in this light, Story finds himself in agreement with Blackstone's statement that " sovereignty and legislature are, indeed, convertible terms "—a point

47 Merriam, *American Political Theories*, pp. 261-262.

48 Ref. to 1 *Black. Comm.* 49; 2 Dall. 471 *per* Jay, C. J.

49 Ref. to 2 Dall. 456, 457, *per* Wilson, J.

50 Story, *Commentaries*, sec. 207.

51 *Loc. cit.*

on which both Chipman and Wilson took issue with the Sage.[52]
Says Story,

> The sovereignty of a nation or state, considered with reference
> to its association, as a body politic, may be absolute and un-
> controllable in all respects, except the limitations, which it
> chooses to impose upon itself.[53] But the sovereignty of the
> government, organized within the state, may be of a very
> limited nature. It may extend to few, or to many objects. It
> may be unlimited, as to some; it may be restrained, as to
> others. To the extent of the power given, the government may
> be sovereign, and its acts may be deemed the sovereign acts
> of the state. Nay the state, by which we mean the people
> composing the state, may divide its sovereign powers among
> various functionaries, and each in the limited sense would be
> sovereign in respect to the powers, confided to each; and
> dependent in all other cases.[54] Strictly speaking, in our re-
> publican forms of government, the absolute sovereignty of the
> nation is in the people of the nation; and the residuary sov-
> ereignty of each state, not granted to any of its public func-
> tionaries, is in the people of the state.[55]

As used in this latter sense, sovereignty may easily be divided
in theory as it has been in practice, between the states and the
Union. But as the " absolute right to govern," it still remains
in its original unity. Sovereignty in the limited sense is divided;
in the broader sense it remains one.[56]

Though Story does not point the contrast between internal
and external sovereignty so clearly as does Chipman, he recognized this distinction. In fact, the preceding discussion fits into
Chipman's " internal " category. Externally, if a nation " has

---

52 Ref. to 1 *Black. Comm.* 46; " See also 1 Tucker's *Bl. Comm.*, App.
note A, a commentary on this clause of the author's text."

53 Ref. to 2 Dall. 433; Iredell, J.; *Id.*, 455, 456, Wilson, J.

54 Ref. to 3 Dall. 93, Iredell, J.; 2 Dall. 455, 457, Wilson, J.

55 Story, *Commentaries*, sec. 208; ref. to 2 Dall. 471, 472, Jay, C. J.,
and John Quincy Adams' Fourth of July oration, 1831.

56 *Cf.* Merriam, *American Political Theories*, pp. 262-263.

the sole power of governing itself and is not dependent upon any foreign state, it is called a *sovereign state . . .*" [57]

In the application of his theories, Story follows much the same line of approach that Dane used, and cites Dane as his authority. He begins his analysis of the problem with the statement that ". . . antecedent to the Declaration of Independence, none of the colonies were, or pretended to be sovereign states, in the sense in which the term ' sovereign ' is sometimes applied to states." [58] Like Dane, Story finds the Declaration of Independence to be the work of the

> whole *people* of the united colonies, by the instrumentality of their representatives . . .[59] It was an act not competent to the state governments, or any of them, as organized under their charters to adopt . . . It was an act of original, inherent sovereignty by the people themselves, resulting from their right to change the form of government, and to institute a new government, whenever necessary for their safety and happiness.[60]

Like Dane, Story depends primarily upon history to support his arguments. In spite of vehement disagreement from many states rights advocates, he asserts as an historical truth,

> that before the declaration of independence these colonies were not, in any absolute sense, sovereign states; that that event did not find them or make them such; but that at the moment of their separation they were under the dominion of a superior controlling national government, whose powers were vested in and exercised by the general congress with the consent of the people of all the states.[61]

57 Story, *Commentaries*, sec. 209.

58 *Ibid.*, sec. 207, citing Dane, 9 *Gen. Abridgment*, App., sec. 2, p. 10; sec. 3, p. 12; sec. 5, p. 16.

59 Ref. to Dane, 9 *Gen. Abr.*, App., secs. 12, 13, pp. 23-24.

60 Story, *Commentaries*, sec. 211.

61 *Ibid.*, sec. 214. Story quotes C. C. Pinckney, a South Carolina nationalist, who in the debates in his state legislature on the calling of a ratifying

To Story, the most significant proof of the constitutionality of the acts of the Continental Congress was the fact that " they emanated from the representatives of the people, and were acquiesced in by the people." [62]

William Alexander Duer attempted to cover in much shorter compass all of the material that Story needed three volumes to elaborate, and, as is expected, his section on sovereignty is far briefer. But it was written while the same problems were facing the nation, and it is none the less definite.

The government of the Union is held to be " emphatically and truly a Government of the people." [63] The people, organized in their respective sovereignties, which had already established the state governments,

> united with each other in forming a paramount Sovereignty, and establishing a Supreme Government; for which purpose

---

convention, said much the same thing. See *ibid.*, sec. 212, citing *Debates in South Carolina*, 1788, printed by A. E. Miller, Charleston, 1831, pp. 43, 44; also more conveniently found in Elliot's *Debates*, IV, 301-302. Along the same line, Story also gives extended quotations from John Quincy Adams' Fourth of July oration of 1831. This oration was published after the original preparation of the *Commentaries*, and therefore finds place only in the footnotes. See notes to secs. 208 and 212. Another expression of Union sentiment which Story approved so heartily that he inserted it at the last minute, was President Jackson's Proclamation to South Carolina. Incidentally, N. Beverley Tucker, a rabid states rights enthusiast, puts forth the suspicion that "the Judge had something to do in working the fingers, that held the pen, on that occasion." *A Series of Lectures on the Science of Government* (Philadelphia: 1845), p. 428.

[62] Story, *Commentaries*, sec. 217. DuPonceau in his *Brief View of the Constitution* touches sovereignty so lightly that the points may best be included in a footnote. He agrees that the Declaration of Independence made the colonies "free, sovereign, and independent" states, but makes the reservation that a union subsisted between them at the time of the Declaration. The exact effect of this union, he does not enlarge upon (p. 5), but the implication that it had an effect in altering the absolute sovereignty of the states is clear.

[63] Duer, *Outlines of Constitutional Jurisprudence*, sec. 865, p. 217. Duer's *Outlines* were intended for younger students, but since they were later elaborated upon in his *Lectures*, the doctrines expounded will be noted here.

each yielded a portion of its individual Sovereignty, and modified its State Constitution, by rendering it subordinate to the Federal power.[64]

The people, in delegating power to the state governments granted directly; they did not erect an independent Sovereignty which could do more than form such a league as the Confederation.

> . . . and when it was proposed to change that league into an effective Government, operating directly on the People as individuals, it became necessary to derive its powers directly from the people themselves.[65]

These doctrines were discussed more fully in the *Lectures on Constitutional Jurisprudence,* published ten years later. Herein Duer still finds ultimate sovereignty in the people. His statement is that if the people of the United States had never before acquired a common character, they assumed it when they ratified the Constitution in conventions.

> The assent of the States in their sovereign capacities is implied, if not expressed, in calling their conventions, and thus submitting the new scheme of government to the people. But the people of each state were at perfect liberty to accept or reject it, and their act was final. The Constitution required not the affirmance of the state governments, nor could it be negatived by their act; but, when ratified by the people, it became of perfect obligation, and bound the states.[66]

The sovereign powers within each state established the state governments, and then " united with each other in forming a paramount sovereignty, and establishing a supreme government." [67] In order to form such a government, each of the sov-

64 *Ibid.,* sec. 863, pp. 216-217.

65 *Ibid.,* sec. 864, p. 217.

66 Duer, *Lectures,* p. 323 (1st ed.) ; p. 409 (2nd ed.). The subject is not listed in the index to the first edition. Capitalization and punctuation follow the first edition.

67 *Ibid.,* p. 324 (1st ed.) ; p. 409 (2nd ed.).

ereign powers within the states surrendered a portion of its individual sovereignty and "modified its state constitution, by rendering it subordinate to the Federal power." They had full power for this act. Contrary to the prevalent opinion in the South, the legitimacy of the federal government might have been questioned much more "had it been erected by the states to operate upon the individual citizens of the several states." The powers delegated to the state governments were to be exercised by themselves; they therefore could not erect a distinct and independent sovereignty to which they could pass these powers. The state governments could form a Confederation, or league, but when

> "in order to form *a more perfect union*," and change that league into an effective government, clothed with high sovereign powers for national objects, and acting directly on the people as individuals, the necessity of referring it to the people themselves, and deriving its powers immediately from them, was universally felt and acknowledged . . .[68]

Midway between Duer's two contributions to constitutional theory, Timothy Walker published his *Introduction to American Law* (1837). Since his work was introductory to law as a whole, the treatment of sovereignty is quite brief. Walker shows the influence of the nationalists in his discussion. He says that supreme power and sovereignty are equivalent terms, and asserts that they belong originally "*to the people in mass.*" [69] Therefore, in the first instance, it is probable that arrangements would be made for exercising it personally—i.e., as in a simple democracy. As the people became more numerous and diffused, the principle of representation would need to be adopted. The representatives to whom authority was delegated would be the servants of their constituents. To obviate the necessity for special instructions to the representatives for each separate occasion, a set of general and permanent instructions is prepared.

68 *Loc. cit.* (1st ed.) ; pp. 409-410 (2nd ed.).

69 Walker, *American Law*, sec. 14.

The people as a whole constitute the highest earthly authority. What they create, they alone can dissolve.[70]

Following the majority of the commentators, Walker sees sovereignty as divided between the states and the national government, with the states retaining a qualified sovereignty over internal objects.[71]

George Ticknor Curtis, writing in the last decade before the Civil War, did not add much to the nationalist theory of sovereignty. He states a point upon which all agreed—that the American Revolution settled " that all sovereignty resides originally in the people; that they derive no rights by way of grant from any other source . . ." But the final point which he claims was settled by the Revolution does not seem entirely clear, namely, " that no powers or privileges can exist in any portion of the people as distinct from the whole." And the later statement of the major problem to be solved by the Constitutional Convention does not elucidate the matter—" so to parcel out those portions of original sovereignty, which the people of the States might be willing to withdraw from their State institutions, as to constitute an efficient federal republic, which yet would not control and absorb the powers that might be reserved." [72]

The idea of " withdrawing " powers from the state governments, Curtis repeats more than once, thus giving his interpretation of sovereignty a slightly different slant from the one to be found in Story's *Commentaries.* Curtis envisages the people, the original sovereigns, as depositing the power of the community with the state governments, in the first instance. The states then proceeded to exercise their sovereignty.

> As the States had conferred certain powers upon the Confederation, so it was equally competent to them to enlarge

70 *Ibid.*, sec. 15.

71 *Ibid.*, sec. 65. See *infra*, ch. vii, for a slightly fuller discussion of Walker's theories.

72 Curtis, *Constitutional History*, I, 379.

and add to those powers . . . But the people of the States, and not their governments, held the supreme, absolute, and uncontrollable power. They had created, and they could modify or destroy; they could withdraw the powers conferred upon one class of agents, and bestow them upon another class.[73]

Curtis finds no difficulty in the problem of a double authority over each of the citizens as a result of this withdrawal and re-vesting of sovereignty by the people. Clear definition only was required, to prevent confusion regarding the duties of the individual to the two classes of governmental agents.[74]

In the name of the people of the United States, the framers of the Constitution brought into action a national authority on certain subjects. The organs of the general government thus created are the agents of the will of a collective people, and thus are not concerned with the separate will of the people of each state.[75] Political sovereignty implies supremacy, and as there were to be two supreme powers in the same country, acting upon the same individuals, one must be superior to the other.

But there is nothing in the nature of political sovereignty to prevent its powers from being distributed among different agents for different purposes . . . It was the purpose of the framers of the Constitution of the United States to provide a paramount rule, that would determine the occasions on which the authority of a State should cease to be supreme, leaving that of the United States unobstructed.[76]

Beyond these few points, there is little discussion of the nature of sovereignty. Curtis took his story chronologically only

73 *Ibid.*, II, 28-29.

74 *Ibid.*, II, 38-39.

75 *Ibid.*, II, 381. And he adds, " That the will of the whole should not be defeated by the will of a part, was the purpose of the supremacy assigned to the Constitution of the United States; and that the rights and liberties of each part, not subject to the will of the whole, should not be invaded, was the purpose of the careful enumeration of the objects to which that supremacy was to extend." *Loc. cit.*

76 *Ibid.*, II, 377-378.

through the adoption of the Constitution, and thus omitted the important issues which came up later to challenge the document and the relationships between the Union and the states therein established.

## Section II

### SOUTHERN IDEAS OF SOVEREIGNTY

To the Southerners, sovereignty was one of the most momentous subjects on the political horizon. Shortly after the beginning of the federal period, certain Southern theorists, jurists, and legislators began expressing their opposition to the Northern contentions on the location of sovereignty in the people of the United States as a whole. The concern was not so much with the idea itself, as with the implications connected with it. The fundamental concern of the South was with its ultimate position in the Union, a position that would be threatened by acceptance of the Northern interpretation of sovereignty.

It seems clear, as Parrington has said, that the root of the Southern philosophy lay in its " frank bias towards the Physiocratic agrarianism that was so congenial to the needs and temper of a plantation society." The political aspect of this agrarianism followed the French rather than the English school, and the economic leaned towards Quesnay and DuPont de Nemours rather than Adam Smith.[77]

The Southern political writers were not all of the same stamp. In fact, at least two distinct intellectual tendencies may be noted, both linked with the political and economic situation. The more idealistic of the two was the school of Virginians, led by Jefferson and Taylor, who stressed equalitarianism in their arguments for states rights. The South Carolina school, headed by Calhoun with some pioneering by Cooper, emphasized economic realism in its contention for recognition of the rights of the states.[78] By the time that Calhoun came to leadership, the

77 Parrington, *Main Currents in American Thought*, II, 3.

78 Parrington recognizes three facets to the problem, the third represented by the West. *Ibid.*, II, 3-4.

evil effects of soil exhaustion and the resultant westward movement (to mention only two of the major economic problems)
had been at work long enough to produce a static or even declining population in the old seaboard states. Meanwhile, thanks
to immigration and a freer system of enterprise, the North was
growing in population and hence in representation. Calhoun's
defensive attitude betrays the reaction of a minority group to
the threats of domination by a hostile majority.

As the statesmen of the South watched the organization and
growth of the new federal government, they saw it leaning
more and more pronouncedly in the direction indicated by
Hamilton and his followers. The fact of control of the federal
executive by Virginians was outweighed by the power of the
nationalists in the Supreme Court. Increasingly, the reliance in
Southern theory came to be upon the assertion of the importance of the states as opposed to the central government. History was cited to prove the seniority of the states and therefore
their continuing superiority over the more recent federal government. And sovereignty, signifying ultimate authority, assumed great significance in the Southern argument. According
to particularist reasoning, once the sovereignty of the states, or,
more correctly, the people of the states, could be established, the
federal government would be relegated to its inferior position
and the threats to the states would be abolished. At first, the
South acquiesced in the vague revolutionary concept of the ultimate authority of the people and the implied divisibility of sovereignty among various agents. But under the leadership of
Taylor and later more emphatically of Calhoun, when threats
to the Southern way of life became menacing, the essential unity
of sovereignty was asserted in an attempt to enhance the waning authority of the states and to reduce that which the federal
government was arrogating to itself.

This transition in thought, linked with the increasing economic difficulties of the South and its declining political power,
may be noted in an examination of the commentaries. As early
as 1803, St. George Tucker stated firmly that the colonies be-

came sovereign and independent at the time of the Revolution—
with no subordination implied. While the ultimate sovereignty
resided in the people, the government was vested in their agents
or servants, and the latter were the ones who apparently exercised the sovereignty.[79] The federal government, created after
the states and subject to them, has an authority rather distantly
removed from the seat of sovereignty.

All powers delegated to the federal government are positive,
and whatever is not enumerated is retained (by the states or
the people). ". . . sovereign states cannot be deprived of any
of their rights by implication; nor in any manner whatever but
by their own voluntary consent, or by submission to a con-
queror." [80]

At the time that each state became a member of the federal
republic, it had an uncontrolled jurisdiction over all cases of
municipal law. The few cases in which the federal government
was granted similar authority are definite and enumerated,

> and are all carved out of the sovereign authority, and former
> exclusive, and uncontrollable jurisdiction of the *states* respec-
> tively: they ought therefore to receive the strictest construc-
> tion. Otherwise the gradual and sometimes imperceptible
> usurpations of power, will end in the total disregard of all its
> intended limitations.[81]

Where sovereignty is thus vested in the people, government
becomes a subordinate power—the mere creature of the people's
will.[82] This idea, however, refers primarily to the federal government, not to that of the states. According to Tucker's way
of thinking, the governments of the states seem to enjoy a somewhat exalted position with relation to their federal counterpart.
The Federal Constitution was thus ratified *twice* in each state—
once by the state legislatures insofar as they could under the

79 Tucker, 1 *Blackstone's Commentaries*, App., pp. 150-154.

80 *Ibid.*, App., p. 143. Tucker says that this is a "maxim of political law."

81 *Ibid.*, App., pp. 152-153.

82 *Ibid.*, App., p. 155.

state constitutions, and then by the people of each state, " in their sovereign character and capacity."

> . . . the assent of the people was indispensably necessary to the validity of the compact, by which the rights of the people might be diminished, or submitted to a new jurisdiction, or in any manner affected.[83]

After analyzing the retained sovereignty of the states under the Articles of Confederation, and the assurances in the *Federalist* that the new Constitution did not imply a complete subordination of all the states,[84] Tucker says, in summary,

> The federal government then, appears to be the organ through which the united republics communicate with foreign nations, and with each other. Their submission to it's [*sic*] operation is voluntary: it's councils, it's engagements, it's authority are theirs, modified and united. It's sovereignty is an emanation from theirs, not a flame by which they have been consumed, nor a vortex in which they are swallowed up. Each is still a perfect state, still sovereign, still independent, and still capable, should the occasion require, to resume the exercise of it's functions, as such, in the most unlimited extent.[85]

Tucker's position as senior writer of the states rights school makes certain of his dicta particularly interesting. As indicated above, he reserved for the states the right of resuming their sovereignty " when the occasion requires . . . (and far be that period removed when it shall happen )." In the meantime, the sovereign rights of the states in the enumerated instances are " wholly suspended, or discontinued . . . nor can that suspension ever be removed, so long as the present constitution remains unchanged, but by the dissolution of the bonds of union." [86]

83 *Ibid.*, App., pp. 169-170.

84 *Ibid.*, App., p. 176. Ref. to *Federalist*, I, 196, 197, 199, 200.

85 *Ibid.*, App., p. 187.

86 *Loc. cit.* In the light of this statement, Tucker probably would not have sanctioned the idea of state nullification and secession as it was elab-

The theories about sovereignty of John Taylor of Caroline first found expression in the Kentucky Resolutions, the idea for which he seems to have given to Jefferson.[87] Although each of his works on government contains a discussion of sovereignty, he considers the doctrine dangerous, likely to be double-edged. The word itself has crept into our political dialect possibly because " mankind prefer mystery to knowledge; and . . . governments love obscurity better than specification." [88] Perhaps this very mystery was the cause of the lengthy effort to clarify the issue. At any rate, Taylor parts company with the Founding Fathers and the nationalists who claimed that sovereignty could be divided, *ad infinitum,* if necessary, and substitutes the doctrine of indivisibility of sovereignty. He recognizes that two sovereignties or supremacies over the same subject have often appeared in history, citing the familiar example of the Holy Roman Empire. But unlike Aquinas and his successors who saw nothing incongruous in the dual allegiance to Pope and Emperor (dubious as the analogy may be), Taylor sees only usurpation in the division of what is essentially a unit:

> . . . the king, the parliament, the emperors and the popes, in exercising it, were all usurpers; and hence an allotment or division of the powers of sovereignty by our governments among ourselves, would also be an usurpation.[89]

Taylor apparently reverts to his philosophical predecessors of several centuries before in saying that the term should not be

---

orated by Calhoun. Tucker does not discuss the Virginia and Kentucky Resolutions, but he is known to have supported them. J. R. Tucker in *Va. Law Reg.,* I, 795. A short section on the Alien Acts appears in the Appendix on pp. 256-257 in connection with the power of Congress over naturalization, but the emphasis is on the distinction between naturalization, over which Congress has control, and denization, over which the states retained control.

87 Taylor to Jefferson, June 25, 1798, " Letters of John Taylor," *John P. Branch Historical Papers of Randolph-Macon College,* II, 276. The entire letter appears on pp. 271-276. *Cf. supra,* pp. 186-187.

88 Taylor, *Construction Construed,* p. 25.

89 *Ibid.,* p. 27.

used to describe things temporal, as it was essentially an attribute of God.[90] (Wilson had regarded this idea as " impious.") But if we must use terms " taken from the deity to adorn the brows of men," we must use them with their proper meaning. Sovereignty is admittedly found among us, " either in congress or in the people; but I deny that it can exist in both."

> Chastened down to the signification of a natural right in nations to institute and limit their own governments, it only embraces the principle by which alone social liberty can be established; extended to the idea of a power in governments to regulate conscience or to distribute property at its pleasure, it includes the principle by which social liberty is destroyed.[91]

Taylor, in *Construction Construed,* approves of the omission of the term in the documents prepared by the Founding Fathers because of evil association in English history between sovereign power and tyranny.[92]

Following from these premises is the proposition that if sovereignty and despotism are synonymous, the sovereignty of the people may also be a despotism. Taylor says, however, that if societies are instituted by consent, the despotism is converted into free will and becomes the opposite of despotism. If the majority institutes the society, then the prime consideration is as to whether this is preferable to sovereignty (or despotism) in one person or in a minority.

> In theory, it is probable that much fewer causes will exist, which would induce the majority of a nation to invade the rights of a minority, than such as solicit one or a few to invade the rights of the nation or of some of its parts. In fact, the first have been extremely rare and evanescent; the latter, continual and lasting.[93]

90 *Ibid.,* p. 26.
91 *Ibid.,* p. 27.
92 *Ibid.,* pp. 25, 33-34.
93 *Ibid.,* p. 34.

It should be noted here that Taylor's spiritual successor, Calhoun, took a stand almost diametrically opposed to Taylor's in elaborating the theory of the Concurrent Majority.[94]

According to Taylor's view, sovereignty is an attribute of the natural right of self-government and applies exclusively to the people [95]—hence the appellation, " popular sovereignty." [96] If the government had created the people, that is, organized them into a nation, the government would be sovereign. Since our nation had created the government, it is clear to Taylor that no sovereignty can possibly be found in the latter.[97] In the *Inquiry into the Principles of Government* (1814), popular sovereignty is treated as one of the good moral principles of government, but the distinction between good and bad principles disappears in later works.

The same problem appears in Taylor's *New Views of the Constitution* (1823). Again, there is a separate section (the thirteenth) devoted to sovereignty, but the emphasis is different. It is now made the equivalent of the term " state powers," and its essence is taken to be " A will to enact, and a power to execute . . . Take away either, and it expires. The state governments and the federal government, are the monuments by which state sovereignty, attended with these attributes, is demonstrated." [98]

Changing his mode of attack Taylor presents a new idea which he marshals all the other theories to support:

94 *Cf.* also the following from Tucker, 1 *Blackstone's Commentaries*, App., pp. 168-169: " The right of the majority to bind the minority, results from a due regard to the peace of society..." Unanimous consent cannot be expected, and " if the will of the majority is not permitted to prevail in questions where the whole society is interested, that of the minority necessarily must. The society therefore, in such a case, would be under the influence of a minority of its members, which, generally speaking, can on no principle be justified."

95 Taylor, *Construction Construed*, p. 33.

96 Not to be confused with the specialized way in which Stephen Douglas used the term in the 1850's.

97 Taylor, *Construction Construed*, p. 35.

98 Taylor, *New Views of the Constitution*, p. 171.

> There are many states in America, but no state of America, nor any people of an American state . . . The word America is used to designate the quarter of the globe in which the recited states were established, and not to designate a nation of Americans . . .[99]

> By these political individual entities, called states, the constitution was framed; by these individual entities it was ratified; and by these entities in [sic] can only be altered. It was made by them and for them, and not by or for a nation of Americans.[100]

According to this interpretation, a separate sovereignty in each state or in the people of each state was necessary if they were to have the right to convey or retain powers. If they could do both, " it could only be in virtue of state sovereignty . . . But a delegation of limited powers, being an act of sovereignty, could not be a renunciation of the sovereignty attached to the powers not delegated." [101]

> A power to resume the limited delegation, was the strongest expression of sovereignty, and rejects the idea, that the delegated authority may positively or constructively subject the sovereign power to its own will; that no sovereignty may destroy an actual sovereignty. By this power of amendment, the states may re-establish the confederation of 1777, and thus unquestionably revive their separate sovereignties said to be extinct; because they are positively asserted by that confederation. If it is not absurd, it is yet a new idea, that a dead sovereignty contains an inherent power to revive itself whenever it pleases.[102]

99 *Ibid.*, p. 172.

100 *Ibid.*, p. 173.

101 *Loc. cit.*

102 *Ibid.*, pp. 173-174. *Cf.* point made by Eugene Tenbroeck Mudge, *Social Philosophy of John Taylor* (New York: Columbia University Press, 1939), p. 36, that Taylor considered sovereignty as indestructible. It is always present in some form. *Cf.* also idea of N. Beverley Tucker, *A Series of Lectures on the Science of Government*, p. 386, that a dormant sovereignty in the people is revived if the constitution or government of a state

It is by such contentions as this last that Taylor more than justified his title, *New Views of the Constitution!*

Taylor disagrees with most other authorities in his contention that state legislatures and conventions are equivalent state organs, both equally competent to express the will of the state sovereignties. St. George Tucker had asserted that conventions had to be called to perform such deeds as the delegation of part of the sovereignty of the people to the federal government, because the people alone could assent to a diminution of their rights or a submission to a new jurisdiction.[103] Taylor, on the other hand, gives a practical reason for not having the respective legislatures ratify the Federal Constitution: ". . . it was apprehended that a considerable transfer of powers from the state governments to a federal government, might produce an opposition from men in the exercise of these powers . . ." [104]

Further proof of state sovereignty is to be found in the mechanism for ratification. The Constitution provided that the new government should go into operation as soon as the fundamental document was accepted by nine of the thirteen states to which it was submitted. Had the four others ultimately refused, they would not have constituted a portion of an American nation, even though they were states of America. Their " right of refusal resulted from their acknowledged sovereignty and independence . . . By acknowledging the sovereignty of the refusing, it [the Constitution] admits the sovereignty of the concurring states. Assent or dissent, was equally an evidence of it." [105]

Taylor introduces the idea of " state nations," entities whose existence was proven by the establishment of the state governments. In elaborating this theory he points out that

---

is abolished. " But take away the constitution of the United States, and no such august object is disclosed. The people of the United States vanish."

103 Tucker, 1 *Blackstone's Commentaries*, App., pp. 169-170.

104 Taylor, *New Views of the Constitution*, pp. 174-175.

105 *Ibid.*, p. 175.

The constitution of the United States was only obligatory upon the ratifying states, because each state comprised a sovereign people, and no people existed, invested with a sovereignty over the thirteen states. . . . A majority of a state legislature or convention dictates to a minority, because it exercises the sovereignty of an associated people over individuals. If state nations had not existed, they could not have exercised this authority over minorities, and therefore it is necessary to admit their existence in order to bestow validity upon the federal constitution.[106]

Taylor holds that the states exercised the highest act of sovereignty in the creation of the federal government, and that they might, if they pleased, repeat the proof of their sovereignty by annihilating it. The Union possessed no innate sovereignty, as did the states; it was not self-contained; it was totally subordinate to the sovereignties by which it was formed.[107]

It may not be entirely appropriate to include William Rawle with the advocates of states rights. As has been pointed out, his ideas seem to be transitional between those of the North and those of the South. In some ways, he agreed with the nationalists, but the theories for which he is best known cause him to find place here. To Rawle, each state became a part of the federal body " with an express reservation . . . of its freedom, sovereignty and independence . . ." [108] The act of forming the Constitution was not simple—

It was to be the act of many independent states, though in a greater degree the act of the people set in motion by those states; it was to be the act of the people of each state, and not of the people at large.[109]

106 *Ibid.*, pp. 8-9. *Cf.* pp. 171-172. The name of the United States implies separate sovereignties. If a consolidated nation had been intended by the founders, it should have been given a consolidated name, such as Fredonia.

107 *Ibid.*, p. 37.

108 Rawle, *A View of the Constitution*, p. 21 (2nd ed., p. 26).

109 *Ibid.*, p. 13 (2nd ed., p. 18).

Unlike Taylor, Rawle does not regard the states in the character of nations. This latter term he reserves to the United States as a whole. But though the states " not possessing that absolute independence, cannot with full propriety be so designated . . . a name is of little importance if the substance is retained." [110] The fact that Virginia and Pennsylvania are not known abroad as nations does not affect their power at home as states.

> In this relation every state must be viewed as entirely sovereign in all points not transferred by the people who compose it to the government of the Union: and every exposition that may be given to the constitution, inconsistent with this principle, must be unsound. The supremacy of the Union in all those points that are thus transferred, and the sovereignty of the state in all those which are not transferred, must therefore be considered as two co-ordinate qualities, enabling us to decide on the true mode of giving a construction to the constitution.[111]

Important as Rawle evidently considers the states to be, he later refers to the Union as " an association of the people of republics," [112] and he further holds that " the secession of a state from the Union depends on the will of the people of such state. The people alone . . . hold the power to alter their constitution." [113] Rawle's doctrine of the legality of secession will be discussed further in the next chapter.

Thomas Cooper's position is typical of the states rights school with regard to sovereignty, and contains no unusual variations. He argues that the Confederation of 1777 and the Convention of 1787 [114] both " consisted of delegates or representatives, *not*

110 *Ibid.*, p. 27 (["be retained"] 2nd ed., p. 31).

111 *Loc. cit.*

112 *Ibid.*, p. 288 (2nd ed., p. 295).

113 *Ibid.*, p. 295 (2nd ed., p. 302).

114 Cooper defines a Confederation as "a meeting of delegates from several sovereign and independent states, for the purpose of devising the best

*from the People of the United States,* but from the several and respective states in their capacity of States; free, sovereign and independent of each other, as of all the rest of the world." The people of the respective states could have chosen to send representatives from the whole People of the United States, had they so desired. The "notion that the *People* framed the Constitution, has been urged from the time of General Hamilton to the present time, to keep out of view the agency of separate, sovereign and independent states . . ." [115] After a survey of the revolutionary period, Cooper concludes,

> that the Constitution of the United States was an instrument conveying specific, expressed, and limited powers, and those only: that the government was a federal government; a creature of the several independent states that consented to it: and that so far from being sovereign, independent, and uncontroulable [*sic*], it was originally created, is now kept in force, and may be altered, limited, controuled, or annulled, at the will of the several independent states or sovereignties who united to give it existence.[116]

Justice Baldwin adhered to no party, and his opinions so varied between strict and liberal construction that it was hard to predict exactly what he would do in a given case. This phenomenon may be explained by his own statement that he agreed with neither side, but held to a third interpretation of the Con-

---

means of ensuring their common defence, and promoting their general welfare in all cases, where their common interest as united and confederated Sovereign States, may require." The terms are expressed in a written Constitution. A Convention "consists of delegates chosen by the people for the purpose of devising that form of government, which is the best calculated in their opinion to provide for and secure the common defence, and promote the general welfare." In the instances used in the text above, Cooper says that the "appellations [are] practically synonimous [*sic*]." Essay *On the Constitution of the United States,* pp. 20-21, 22.

115 *Ibid.,* pp. 22-23.

116 *Ibid.,* p. 24.

stitution.[117] Upon close examination, however, it would appear that this third interpretation comes closer to agreement with the states rights interests than with those who favored a national government. Baldwin holds that the people were supreme, but that their supremacy was vested in their character as members of states.[118]

Beyond this point, it is difficult to follow his argument. A large part of his text consists of quotations from various Supreme Court decisions, often strung together without connecting clauses. Apparently, Baldwin agrees with the concept of divisibility of sovereignty, a doctrine enunciated in McCulloch v. Maryland.[119] He does not seem to approve of the doctrine of majority rule among the states, but is concerned with the retained powers of the states *as units*.

> This is the essence of supreme and sovereign power, which testifies that the ultimate absolute sovereignty, is in " the several states," and the people thereof; who can do by inherent right and power, any thing in relation to the constitution, or change of government, except depriving the smallest state of *its equal suffrage in the senate:* not in the United States, or

117 Baldwin, *General View of the Constitution*, p. 37. The members of the third class, "of which there is yet a small remnant, ... were willing to take the constitution with its amendments, as it is, and to expound it by the accepted rules of interpretation; whatever might be the result on the powers granted, restricted, excepted, or reserved; if it was the meaning and intention of the supreme law of the land, it was their rule of action." Members of the first two classes (liberal and strict constructionists) "endeavor to find by construction, a lever by which to give it a power, stronger in one case, and weaker in the other; while the third would leave it at the precise point where the first moving power had fixed it; believing, that it ought to remain stationary, till the amending power should turn it forward or backward from its original position." "Those who use it as a lever, by which to press the screw [political power] more severely on the powers of the several states, must trace the power which first propelled it to some source of sovereignty, absolute and unlimited, in matters of government; else it cannot restrict the states." *Loc. cit.*

118 *Ibid.*, pp. 12-13, 24.

119 4 Wheat. 316 at 410 (1819).

the people thereof, as one nation, or one people, who in their unity of character or power, can do nothing either by inherent right, *or by representation,* as a majority.[120]

In common with the particularists, Baldwin is interested in the status of the colonies at the time of the Declaration of Independence. It is his contention that " from the moment that the authority of Great Britain ceased to operate, that of each colony became absolute and sovereign; and no government could exist thereout, which could prescribe laws within it." [121] Furthermore, each state was " a single unconnected sovereign power " in adopting the Constitution.[122]

Baldwin sets forth yet another theory about sovereignty which seems unique. He holds that if the Constitution were taken as a grant of the people of each state (the original sovereigns), their grant conveyed power in proportion to their supremacy before making the grant. ". . . the more absolute the sovereignty is, which grants the power, the greater will be the strength of the grant and the security from violation." [123]

By way of conclusion, Baldwin sets forth certain extracts in which are found " the antagonist propositions to those which I have endeavored to establish." These are in " an able and learned commentary on the constitution, published in 1833 "— namely, that of Judge Story.[124] The system used calls for great attention on the part of Baldwin's reader, as Story's statements are strung together, without intervening comment. It is up to

120 Baldwin, *General View of the Constitution,* p. 24.

121 *Ibid.,* p. 72, quotes from McIlvaine *v.* Cox, 4 Cr. 209 at 212 (1808), as follows: " *the several states* which composed this Union, so far at least as regarded their municipal regulations, became entitled, from the time when they declared themselves independent, to all the *rights and powers of sovereign states...*" Italics Baldwin's.

122 *Ibid.,* p. 83.

123 *Ibid.,* p. 101.

124 *Ibid.,* pp. 108-111. On pp. 111-112, there is also an extract from one of Chief Justice Jay's opinions in 1793. ". . . it will show the coincidence of views entertained and declared by him in 1793 and those of the learned commentator forty years afterwards." *Ibid.,* p. 111.

the reader to remember what Baldwin's disagreement was and where it may be found in the main body of his work—a sizable intellectual feat, considering the lack of organization.

The most elaborate refutation of Story's views was undertaken by Abel Parker Upshur, one of the leading members of the states rights school of Virginia, and published in 1840. Upshur used only the Abridgment of Story's *Commentaries* (although he knew that a longer edition was in existence), and constantly criticizes the Judge for failure to cite his authorities.[125] In the early part of his work, Upshur's chief objection to Story is the way in which he repeatedly referred to the inhabitants of the United States as " one people." [126] Using Story's same approach, the historical, he disproves to his satisfaction all of the proofs which Story offered to indicate *de facto* the *de jure* supremacy in the old Continental Congresses. Upshur's conclusion is that " the boasted ' sovereignty ' of the Federal Government was merely nominal, and owed its entire efficiency to the co-operation and aid of the State governments." [127]

Upshur nowhere analyzes the nature of sovereignty. He apparently accepts the term as fully understood by his readers, and proceeds to a consideration of its transition from the British government to the American. He admits that sovereignty over the colonies was in the British crown,

> but that sovereignty was not *jointly over all,* but *separately over each,* and might have been abandoned as to some, and retained as to others. The declaration of independence broke this connexion . . . What then became of the sovereignty?

125 For example, on p. 33 of the *True Nature of the Constitution,* the following sentences appear: " There is in this passage great want of accuracy, and perhaps some want of candor. The author, as usual, neglects to cite the judicial decision...etc." If Upshur had consulted the three-volume work, he might have been disturbed by a plethora of references!

126 *Ibid.,* at least once on each page from 10 to 19; less frequently thereafter. (Paging of the 1840 edition followed, as the 1863 edition was prepared after Upshur's death.)

127 *Ibid.,* pp. 32-33.

. . . It could not be in *abeyance;* the moment it was lost by the British crown it must have vested somewhere else. Doubtless it vested in the states themselves. But, as they were separate and distinct as colonies, the sovereignty over one could not vest, either in whole or in part, in any other. Each took to itself that sovereignty which applied *to* itself, and for which alone it had contended with the British crown, to wit, the sovereignty *over* itself. Thus each colony became a free and sovereign State.[128]

The crux of Upshur's argument, as of all the other supporters of the rights of the states, is his contention that the states, if once sovereign, did not cease to be so when they entered the Union. And if the states were once sovereign, they must therefore still be sovereign. Under the Confederation, the states reserved " their *entire* sovereignty, their *entire* freedom, and their *entire* independence . . . for these are not partible." [129] Thus, Upshur would clarify his attitude on the preamble to the Constitution, " without any violence to the rules of fair construction," by changing the order to read, " We, the people of the States united." [130]

As to the location of sovereignty, Upshur begins by agreeing with most of the American political theorists, North and South, and then by taking a distinctly states rights position:

. . . sovereignty does not reside in any government whatever, neither State nor federal. Government is regarded merely as the agent of those who create it, and subject in all respects to their will. In the States, the sovereign power is in the people of the States respectively; and the sovereign power of the United States would, for the same reason, be in " the people of the United States," if there were any such people, known as a single nation, and the framers of the federal government. We have already seen, however, that there are no

128 *Ibid.,* p. 45.

129 *Ibid.,* p. 47.

130 *Ibid.,* p. 61. There is no evidence that Upshur used Madison's *Notes* though they had been published by the time he wrote.

such people, in a strict political sense, and that no such people had any agency in the formation of our Constitution, but that it was formed by *the States,* emphatically as such. It would be absurd, according to all principles received and acknowledged among us, to say that the sovereign power is in one party, and the power which creates the government is in another. The true sovereignty of the United States, therefore, is in the States, and not in the people of the United States, nor in the federal government. That government is but the agent through whom a portion of this sovereign power is exerted; possessing no sovereignty itself, and exerting no power, except such only as its constituents have conferred on it.[131]

According to Upshur's reasoning, the sovereign states have a right to determine, in the last resort, any question which arises between them, the creators, and the creature—the federal government.[132] This principle of state interposition is "not to be found *within* the Constitution but exists independent of it."[133] Upshur naturally disagrees with Story who said that the interposition idea was "forced . . . into the language of that instrument." The right of nullification is an incident of the sovereignty of the states, which the Constitution has not taken away.[134] It was never pretended that the right was so justified; rather, it is extra- or supra-constitutional. The next step in this chain of reasoning, secession, springs from the theory of the Constitution as a compact between sovereign states and will be discussed in the next chapter.

Both of St. George Tucker's sons were concerned with constitutional interpretation, and both taught law. Henry St. George Tucker, who was trained in his father's classes at William and Mary College and accepted his teachings, was milder and more influential than his brother, whom we shall discuss

131 *Ibid.,* p. 93.
132 *Ibid.,* p. 131.
133 *Loc. cit.*
134 *Ibid.,* p. 69.

later. Since the subject matter of Henry Tucker's *Lectures on Government* (1844) was designed to precede the material in his volume on *Constitutional Law* (1843), we shall examine it first. In Lecture III, " Of Sovereignty and of the Constitution or Form of Government," Tucker rewords and accepts Blackstone's definition of law :

> . . . law is a rule of action prescribed by a competent power commanding what is right and prohibiting what is wrong. And the power which thus makes the law must be the supreme power in the state . . . since if there be a power actually superior to that which declares the law, it is no law to that superior.[135]

The principle of the sovereignty of the people lies at the foundation of all our American institutions. For example, the Virginia Bill of Rights declares that all power is vested in the people and is derived from them. Thus government is but the agent of the society or people. The instrument by which government is called into existence is the constitution of the state. The constitution itself is not an act of government, but of the people, and thus can only be altered by the people.[136]

Tucker admires the federative system of the American government, in part because it prevents centralization over too great a geographical area. Furthermore, the individual interests of the citizens are under the control of the states " which form the barrier between the homestead of the citizen and the action of the general government." The state governments have

> no temptations to invade the rights of the people, and no inducements to seize upon the limited sovereignty of the states, since that sovereignty is shorn of all its principal attractions, by the powers which are transferred to the general government.[137]

135 Tucker, *Lectures on Government*, p. 35.

136 *Ibid.*, pp. 47, 36-37.

137 *Ibid.*, p. 163.

The second volume which Tucker prepared for his classes at the University of Virginia, the *Lectures on Constitutional Law,* draws heavily on Upshur for the greater part of the material and hence is primarily a refutation of the nationalistic arguments in Story's *Commentaries.*[138] (The notable exception with regard to the doctrine of nullification, will be discussed in the next chapter.) There is a passing mention that Story, who was once thought to be of the states rights party, was no longer of that group.[139]

Following Upshur, Tucker contends that Story was mistaken as to the real condition and relation of the colonies. The inhabitants were bound together by the king, but when independence from England was proclaimed, the binding was cut, and the states became separate political entities.[140] Story was judged correct in saying that the sovereignty passed from the Crown of Great Britain to the people of this country, but this transfer meant that " *Each* of the thirteen revolting colonies . . . , in throwing off the authority of Great Britain became itself a sovereign." The sovereignty did not pass to the people as a whole, because they had never constituted one whole. " The *whole* continent was not *our* country. Virginia was *our* country, and the government of Virginia passed of course to the people of Virginia . . ."[141]

> In strictness, according to the theory of our government, the *people* are the sovereign. And they have delegated a part of their power to the general government, and part to the state governments, and each exercise the respective portions of sovereignty allotted to them. Each may in this sense be said to be sovereign, though the sovereignty in fact still re-

138 The various direct citations of Story's *Commentaries* by Tucker indicate that he used the full length version, unlike Upshur, who used only the Abridgment.

139 Tucker, *Lectures on Constitutional Law,* p. 9.

140 *Ibid.,* p. 44.

141 *Ibid.,* p. 51.

sides in the people. In what people? The people of each state, distinct from the other states, and the people of *each* state accordingly delegates the power. For as there is no people of the United States, considered aggregately, the sovereignty must be in the people of *each state*.[142]

Story had claimed that the Declaration of Independence was the united act of all, and that none of the colonies had pretended to be sovereign before its promulgation. Tucker points out that the voting on the Declaration was by states, not by individuals, thus making America free, but composed of separate communities.[143] Furthermore, the legislature of Virginia declared her independence in June 1776, and she was therefore free and separate before July 4.[144]

Tucker belittles the revolutionary congress which Story makes important as the original and sovereign union.

> It was the creature of those who were *de facto* sovereign; and all its powers were not only derivative, but derivative from bodies politic, or societies of people distinct and separate, in the assumed character of sovereign, during the convulsions of the time. Notwithstanding the existence, also, of the congress, the state exercised every attribute of sovereignty.[145]

Story had admitted that the powers of Congress were assumed in most instances and only acquiesced in by the tacit consent of the states. " Can this exercise of the powers of government by *sufferance*," asks Tucker, " constitute sovereignty or supreme controlling power?" The acts of Congress were really the acts of the states themselves, through their own servants, their delegates. The Congress, then, was the servant, not the master of the states. " Who ever dreamed that the sovereignty

142 *Ibid.*, p. 95.

143 *Ibid.*, pp. 89-92.

144 *Ibid.*, p. 88.

145 *Ibid.*, p. 45.

of the states was swallowed up in their *confederacy? That* sovereignty is essential to *its existence.*" [146]

The fact that the states agreed to submit to the decision of the majority in Congress was unimportant. For practical reasons, the states should act in concert. In fact, " the idea of coalescing between political bodies implies sovereignty in each, and admits they were not coalesced before." [147]

In ratifying the Constitution, " each convention represented its own state only, and assented to [it] . . . in the *name* and *behalf* of *the people thereof.*" [148] The people of the states had to act separately, because they were still a part of the Confederation, under which the states were sovereign. [149] Viewing the subject legalistically, Tucker concludes that " as there is no people of the United States, considered aggregately, the sovereignty must be in the people *of each state.*" [150] Since a union of people must act as one, no union of states could be one people, " for while they continue states, each acts for itself, and that entire unity of action is wanting, which, alone, constitutes oneness." [151]

N. Beverley Tucker's *Lectures on the Science of Government* (1845) emphasizes more extreme interpretations. He agrees that sovereignty is located in the people of the states. [152] The term, " people of the United States," as used in the Federal Constitution is " a mere noun of multitude." [153] As sovereignty

146 *Ibid.,* p. 53.

147 *Ibid.,* pp. 53-54 and note *h.* Tucker then quotes Upshur's "much more satisfactory refutation of the heretical notion of the *oneness* of the colonies and of the states anterior to the declaration of independence," p. 55 *et seq.*

148 *Ibid.,* p. 155.

149 *Ibid.,* p. 154.

150 *Ibid.,* p. 95.

151 *Ibid.,* p. 15.

152 N. B. Tucker, *Lectures on Government,* pp. 375, 382. He says that the term "people" refers to the body politic. (P. 382) Lecture XIX is on Sovereignty, pp. 372-396.

153 *Ibid.,* p. 385.

rests in people and not in government, we do not owe allegiance to governments—even to that " which, Colossus-like, bestrides the continent . . ." [154] He agrees with most Southerners that sovereignty is not divided. *" There can be but one Supreme. There is no god but God."* [155]

N. B. Tucker shares with Taylor the idea that a dormant sovereignty may be revived. If the Constitution of Virginia were abolished, the people and the commonwealth would remain (case of actual sovereignty). But if the Constitution of the United States were abolished, the people of the United States would vanish, leaving twenty-six separate states (case of imaginary sovereignty). [156] The only reason that the people of Virginia must obey federal officers is that Virginia commanded them to do so. The state acts through both its own officials and those of the federal government, *" surrendering* nothing of its sovereignty to either, but *delegating* an authority to exercise some of the functions of sovereignty to *one* set, some to the *other."* [157]

These statements seem to give a fair summary of the states rights position on sovereignty. But while the Southerners could conclude from the history of the Revolutionary period that the American people were a mythical concept, and that the states were still superior to the federal government, the Northerners could not overlook the *fact* that an American people had since come into existence. Although the nationalist commentators did not make full use of the implications in their argument by pointing out the significance of the changed situation, they still held the stronger of the two positions, and their supporters were later to prove their strength by trial at arms.

154 *Ibid.,* p. 380.
155 *Ibid.,* p. 388.
156 *Ibid.,* p. 386.
157 *Ibid.,* pp. 387-389.

# CHAPTER VII
## COMPACT THEORY *vs.* SUPREME LAW THEORY

THE compact theory of government and of the Constitution, specifically, was connected with the idea of sovereignty, and like sovereignty, was interpreted variously. In practice, the two subjects were usually treated together, but have been separated here for clarity. The conflict turned on the source of the authority for forming the Constitution, the nature of the instrument created, the difference between the state and federal constitutions, and the perpetuity of the obligation.

There is no hard and fast rule which makes all nationalists supporters of the supreme law theory, and all advocates of the rights of the states devotees of the compact theory. Some of the nationalists viewed the Constitution as a compact, but none the less binding, and at least one of the ardent Southerners repudiated the compact idea altogether, but still upheld the sovereignty of the individual states. Part of the disagreement lay in whether or not the contract had been executed at the time that the Constitution was ratified and had existed since then as law. The opposing argument held that the Constitution was not the result of the compact, but was the compact itself, and therefore was subject to the continuing approval of the contracting parties, i.e., the states.

Furthermore, a change was going on in the idea of the nature of a compact, which was reflected in the writings under consideration. Some of the commentators adhered to the older idea that a compact was absolutely binding. Others gave evidence of accepting the nineteenth century distinction between law as binding, and a compact as resting upon the consent of the parties involved and hence subject to dissolution.[1]

1 The able article of Andrew C. McLaughlin, " Social Compact and Constitutional Construction," *American Historical Review*, V (April 1900), 467-490, analyzes this subject at length for the pre-Civil War period.

The idea of the Constitution as a contract or compact was the American expression of the old social contract theory. This well-known doctrine presumes that men once existed in a state of nature; that they eventually came together to form a government to satisfy their mutual needs; and that the resultant agreement, which substituted civil rights for natural rights, was a social contract. This document (if, indeed, it assumed that form) was based upon the consent of the people whom it bound, and it was valid only so long as they continued to approve its operation. If the contract was between a ruler and his subjects, it was valid so long as the ruler fulfilled the terms of the contract. If the ruler violated these terms, the society returned to the state of nature.

There were certain political thinkers who held that this theory applied to the Constitution of the United States, but there were others who claimed that the statement of the Constitution itself that it was the " supreme law of the land," was conclusive. The distinction, then, between a compact and a law is a significant one for our purposes, and we shall welcome any light which the commentators may throw on the subject.

## SECTION I

### THE EARLY NATIONALISTS

James Wilson (1790) is explicit in his definition of the significance of the new document:

---

McLaughlin also considers a point which we have mentioned only briefly in chapter vi—the substitution of the organic theory of the Union for the compact theory. He concludes that " the important fact is not so much that men thought the Constitution a social compact as that they thought of society and the state in general as artificial and based on intellectual consent." (P. 478 note) Early discussions of the subject showed much confusion in thinking. Thus, " One side declared that the Constitution was a compact and therefore not binding; and the other declared that the Constitution was a compact and therefore was binding." (P. 486) For our purposes, McLaughlin's treatment of Wilson is most pertinent. Story receives only a single, uncomplimentary footnote. (P. 487 note)

A different approach to much the same material is given in Benjamin F. Wright, Jr., *American Interpretations of Natural Law* (Cambridge: Harvard University Press, 1931). See esp. chs. viii and ix on systematic studies of politics and constitutional interpretation.

By the term constitution, I mean that supreme law, made or ratified by those in whom the sovereign power of the state resides, which prescribes the manner, according to which the state wills that the government should be instituted and administered. From this constitution the government derives its power; by this constitution the power of government must be directed and controlled; of this constitution no alteration can be made by the government; because such an alteration would destroy the foundation of its own authority.[2]

Again, he states with regard to the federal instrument: " The constitution is the supreme law of the land: to that supreme law every other power must be inferior and subordinate." [3] As has been indicated previously, Wilson finds the sovereign power, and therefore, the constitution-making power, in the people.

. . . in our governments, the supreme, absolute, and uncontrollable power remains in the people. As our constitutions are superior to our legislatures, so the people are superior to our constitutions.[4]

At the time that Wilson wrote, the new federal government was very young, and many of the problems which were to trouble political theorists later had not yet been raised. Thus, his ideas about the perpetuity of the federal obligation are connected with his concept of sovereignty as being vested in the people as a whole, and with the recently asserted right of revolution. The " citizens at large . . . always retain the right of abolishing, altering, or amending their constitution, at whatever time, and in whatever manner, they shall deem it expedient." [5] In Chisholm *v.* Georgia, Wilson takes the position that the Con-

2 Wilson, *Works* (Andrews ed.), I, 374-375.

3 *Ibid.*, I, 416.

4 *Ibid.*, I, 543.

5 *Ibid.*, I, 14-15.

stitution is a bond of national unity, not a federal league, dissoluble at the pleasure of any party to it.[6]

It should be noted that Wilson maintained a highly consistent position on the nature of the Constitution as the supreme law. He had differed with Blackstone on the definition of law as a command from the supreme power of the state,[7] holding that the consent of the people to whom it applied was the essential element. Thus, the Constitution, as law, depended upon the consent of the sovereign people who framed it for its validity.[8]

As in the case of sovereignty, Nathaniel Chipman avoids an expression of opinion on the exact nature of the Constitution in the first edition of his *Sketches of the Principles of Government* (1793). He uses general terms:

> This constitution, as a *unique* in federal politics, originated in an actual, deliberate agreement between the states, and was ratified by the free consent of the people of each state, by their Representatives, chosen for that purpose.[9]

He holds that the Federal Constitution was founded on the same principles as the constitutions of the several states of the Union, as nearly as the relative situations would admit.[10]

In his revised edition (1833), Chipman expands upon the subject. He adheres to the eighteenth century interpretation of compact as a binding agreement, and he sees " the people acting in the capacity of their primary sovereignty " as the " real and efficient parties." [11] He fits the Constitution of the United States

6 2 Dall. 419 (1793). *Cf.* Thomas M. Cooley, *Constitutional History of the United States as Seen in the Development of American Law* (New York: 1889), pp. 46-49.

7 Wilson, *Works* (Andrews ed.), I, 159.

8 McLaughlin shows that Wilson and the other Founding Fathers thought in terms of the compact theory. Though he denied that the Constitution was a compact, Wilson admitted that it was founded on prior consent— an essential part of the theory. *Amer. Hist. Rev.*, V, 478.

9 Chipman, *Sketches of the Principles of Government*, p. 247.

10 *Ibid.*, p. 277.

11 Chipman, *Principles of Government*, p. 270.

into his discussion of the civil or social compact, and describes the adhesion of the people to it as " a voluntary, a moral act, sufficient to bind the party." [12] Furthermore, in the United States, a compact cannot be affected by any delinquency or violation of stipulations, however the delinquent functionary may be affected.[13]

In contrasting the Confederation (which he recognizes as a league of sovereign states) with the government under the Constitution, Chipman presents the following summary:

> . . . the constitution of the United States was ratified by the people of each state in concurrence with the people of all the states, and thus it became a mutual compact between all, binding upon all, and upon their respective state governments. The people were, in fact, the original and only efficient parties in the character, and the manner described, and the state governments became their authorized agents so far as they were empowered by their several state constitutions and the constitution of the United States. The governments of the several states, by which we are to understand the functionaries of those governments, were not authorized, they were not competent to ratify the compact, to establish the national government proposed.[14]

12 *Ibid.*, p. 125.

13 *Ibid.*, p. 129.

14 *Ibid.*, pp. 266-267. Chipman adds the following footnote: " I find that it has lately been asserted by an authority, from whom I would dissent with reluctance, and certainly, not without great consideration, that the constitution is not in strictness of language, a compact, but is acknowledged to be founded on compact, meaning nothing more by compact, than assent... [This authority is Nathan Dane.] Now if the constitution be founded on compact, of whatever nature it may be, it will amount to the same thing, to consider the states as parties to that compact; and if the states cannot be parties to the constitution because it is not a compact, neither can the people, nor can there be any parties at all for the same reason.... The constitution of the state, has for centuries been denominated by all political writers and publicists, ... a compact and by way of distinction, the civil compact. I have always considered the constitution of the United States as a compact, to which the people of the United States were the only efficient parties . . . [The word ' ratify '] from its solemn use, ... strikes the mind with more force, and seems to give a higher sanction to the compact, than the common words of agreement." *Ibid.*, pp. 267-268 note.

Chipman sees no incongruity in the subjection of the people to the supreme power of the government. In forming the Constitution they had exercised their sovereign power. The government they had thus instituted they declared to be supreme, so that they no longer acted in their sovereign capacity, " but as individuals in society subordinate to that government by their own solemn agreement and consent." [15] Meanwhile, their sovereign power remained dormant until again called into action on the same subject—namely, " the constitution, on the occasions only, and in the manner which they shall have prescribed." [16]

The authority of the Constitution was perpetual, except

> in cases of violent oppression, where all constitutional remedies have been tried, and have become hopeless, a people in that situation, are discharged and freed from all the obligations of the constitution, however solemnly ratified, and are thrown back upon the law of nature . . . which authorizes, and enjoins as a duty, resistance to oppression, under the guidance of reason and prudence.[17]

With regard to the relationship between the national and state governments, Chipman concludes that the latter is subordinate to the former, but only " within the limits of the powers delegated to that government, and to the end for which they were delegated." [18] The constitutions of the states are creatures of the parts, while the Constitution of the Union is the creature of the whole.

15 *Ibid.*, p. 286.

16 *Loc. cit.* N. Beverley Tucker had a similar idea on dormant sovereignties. *Cf. infra*, p. 238, note 102.

17 Chipman, *Principles of Government*, p. 284.

18 *Ibid.*, p. 287. Chipman adds, " Could I find a term in our language less offensive to state pride, than the word subordination, thus qualified, to express the relation in which the constitution has placed the states in respect to the general government, I would readily adopt it; but I can find no other word that will so correctly express that relation, and I conceive it a matter of the first consequence that we should form a correct opinion upon that subject."

. . . each people have the power over the creature they have made, and the right to place it in such relation to the creature made by the whole, as they please, and in such degree of subordination as they may conceive to be most conducive to their interest, and to the common interest of the whole. Indeed, if we reject this reasoning, we must of necessity resort to the exploded doctrine of the divine right of sovereignty. Nothing short of that can establish the authority of any government.[19]

Chancellor Kent does not consider at length the arguments on the Constitution as a compact.[20] He seems to regard a constitution as above the law, in that it is " the act of the people, speaking in their original character, and defining the permanent conditions of the social alliance." Here, he foreshadows Story, who was more explicit in the exposition of this idea.[21]

In his discussion favoring judicial review by the federal courts, Kent stresses the fact that

the United States are one nation and one people, as to all cases and powers given by the constitution . . . [The] Supreme Court of the nation must have power to revise the decisions of local tribunals on questions which affect the nation, or the most important ends of the government might be defeated, and we should be no longer one nation for any efficient purpose. The doctrine would go to destroy the great fundamental principles on which the fabric of the union stands.[22]

This power in the judiciary is necessary to uphold the action of the people of the United States who declared the Constitution

19 *Loc. cit.*

20 Kent refers to the Articles of Confederation as a compact, but he does not draw a contrast with the Constitution. *Commentaries*, I, 198 (2nd and succeeding eds., I, 212).

21 *Ibid.*, I, 421 (I, 449). Beginning with the third edition (1836), Kent cites Story's *Commentaries*. In a footnote (I, 242) he says, "...I agree entirely with that learned commentator, that we are to look to the instrument itself, 'as a constitution of government ordained and established by the people of the United States.'" Ref. to Story, I, 382-442 [secs. 397-456], *re* rules of interpretation of the Constitution.

22 Kent, *Commentaries*, I, 308-309 (I, 329-330).

to be the supreme law of the land, and as such, entitled to universal and implicit obedience.[23] It is also through the medium of the Supreme Court that the degree of subordination under which the state governments are constitutionally placed can be ascertained.[24]

> The general government, though limited as to its objects, was supreme with respect to those objects. It was supreme in all cases in which it was empowered to act . . . The sovereignty of the states was limited, or surrendered, in many cases where there was no other power conferred on congress than a constructive power to maintain the principles established in the constitution.[25]

## Section II

### EARLY PARTICULARIST DOCTRINE

Directly opposed to the nationalists who seemed to argue more forcibly as time went on that " whatever is, is right," the states rights school of the South presented a doctrine which was more carefully elaborated by each succeeding commentator. The first, St. George Tucker, summarized his position at the beginning of the " View of the Constitution of the United States," appended to his edition of *Blackstone's Commentaries* (1803):

> The constitution of the United States of America, . . . is an original, written, federal, and social compact, freely, voluntarily, and solemnly entered into by the several states of North-America, and ratified by the people thereof, respectively; whereby the several states, and the people thereof,

23 *Ibid.*, I, 293-294 (I, 313-314).

24 *Loc. cit.* " If the courts of the union could not correct the judgments of the state courts, inflicting penalties under state laws, upon individuals executing the laws of the union, each member of the confederacy would possess a *veto* on the will of the whole. No government ought to be so defective in its organization, as not to contain within itself the means of securing the execution of its own laws." *Ibid.*, I, 307 (I, 328).

25 *Ibid.*, I, 306 (I, 328). (Punctuation of first edition followed.) Paraphrase of Marshall in Cohens *v.* Virginia, 6 Wheat. 264 (1821).

respectively, have bound themselves to each other, and to the federal government of the United States; and by which the federal government is bound to the several states, and to every citizen of the United States.[26]

Herewith follow thirty-two pages describing in full the nature of the Constitution as a compact.[27] Only a few of the major points presented may be considered here.

As members of the federal compact, " several sovereign and independent states may unite themselves together by a perpetual confederacy, without each ceasing to be a perfect state." [28] Furthermore, the states are necessary to the existence of the federal government, thus establishing an important point as to the continuing nature of the compact.[29]

In admitting that the Constitution also partook of the nature of a social compact, Tucker draws an interesting distinction:

> A federal compact, alliance, or treaty, is an act of the state, or body politic, and not of an individual; on the contrary, the social contract is understood to mean the act of individuals, about to create, and establish, a state, or body politic, among themselves.[30]

The provisions which appeared to be of the latter variety excited " a considerable alarm . . . in the minds of many, who considered the constitution as in some danger of establishing a na-

26 Tucker, 1 *Blackstone's Commentaries*, App., p. 140.

27 Tucker describes the Constitution under the following heads: 1. It is a compact; 2. It is a federal compact; 3. It is also, to a certain extent, a social compact; 4. It is an original compact; 5. It is a written contract; 6. It is a compact freely, voluntarily, and solemnly entered into by the several states, and ratified by the people thereof, respectively; 7. It is a compact by which the several states and the people thereof, respectively, have bound themselves to each other, and to the federal government; 8. Lastly, It is a compact by which the federal government is bound to the several states, and to every citizen of the United States. *Ibid.*, App., pp. 141-173.

28 *Ibid.*, App., p. 141.

29 *Ibid.*, App., pp. 141-142.

30 *Ibid.*, App., p. 145.

tional, or consolidated government, upon the ruins of the old federal republic." And here Tucker quotes at length from the numbers of the *Federalist* which showed the Constitution to be partly federal and partly national—a section designed by Publius to calm those who sought to preserve the rights of the states.[31]

Tucker claims that the Constitution is an original compact because the Revolution made the states severally independent and sovereign. Any possible political contact between the colonies during the period of British supremacy had been ended by the Revolution, and therefore the states could create only such new ties as they wished. The history of the formation of the Constitution and its ratification by conventions in the several states shows that that document has " all the features of an original compact . . ."[32]

Another argument characteristic of the states rights school is introduced here. Since the Constitution is an " instrument by which *power is created* on the one hand, and *obedience exacted* on the other,"

> . . . it is to be construed strictly, in all cases where the antecedent rights of a *state* may be drawn in question; as a social compact it ought likewise to receive the same strict construction, wherever the right of personal liberty, of personal security, or of private property may become the subject of dispute . . .[33]

Tucker sees two checks on the power of the federal government to meet two types of possible usurpations. Where an individual is affected, the remedy is by recourse to the judiciary.

31 *Ibid.*, App., pp. 145-149.

32 *Ibid.*, App., pp. 150-151.

33 *Ibid.*, p. 151. " . . . because every person whose liberty or property was thereby rendered subject to the new government, was antecedently a member of a civil society to whose regulations he had submitted himself, and under whose authority and protection he still remains, in all cases not expressly submitted to the new government."

" Where it may affect a state, the state legislature, whose rights will be invaded by every such act, will be ready to mark the innovation and sound the alarm to the people." [34]

According to Tucker, the acceptance of the Constitution was an act of the body politic of each state *and* of the people thereof respectively, in their sovereign character and capacity. The body politic was

> competent to bind itself so far as the constitution of the state permitted; but not having power to bind the people, in cases beyond their constitutional authority, the assent of the people was indispensably necessary to the validity of the compact, by which the rights of the people might be diminished or submitted to a new jurisdiction, or in any manner affected.[35]

Thus, the government established when the Constitution was ratified bound all the members of the United States together. The bodies politic of the several states, and each citizen thereof, bound themselves to each other, and to the federal government for the due observance of the Constitution.[36]

As the creature of the compact (since it could not be a party to a compact made anterior to its existence), the federal government was bound to its creators, the several states and their citizens.

> Having no existence but under the constitution, nor any rights but such as that instrument confers; and those very rights being in fact duties; it can possess no legitimate power, but such as is absolutely necessary for the performance of a duty,

34 *Ibid.*, App., p. 153. Reference here is to the *Federalist*, II, 74. There is ample opportunity for Tucker to have cited the Virginia and Kentucky Resolutions in this connection. We know that his notes were written by 1797, and it seems that he did not revise them to include such interesting developments, even though his volumes did not appear until 1803. See also *ibid.*, App., p. 151, *re* strict construction.

35 *Ibid.*, App., pp. 169-170. Tucker's son, N. Beverley Tucker, thought that the people and the body politic of a state were the same thing. They created the state government. *Lectures on the Science of Government*, p. 382.

36 Tucker, I *Blackstone's Commentaries*, App., p. 170.

prescribed and enjoined by the constitution. Its duties, then, become the exact measure of its powers; and wherever it exerts a power for any other perpose [*sic*], than the performance of a duty prescribed by the constitution, it transgresses its proper limits and violates the public trust.[37]

Even with this introduction, Tucker nowhere discusses the possibility of secession from the Union. Rather he proclaims the government a " confederate republic, composed of several independent, and sovereign democratic states . . ." [38] The perpetuity of the obligation depends upon posterity, whose ancestors have no right to bind those yet unborn. Since " government derives its just authority from the consent of the governed," posterity gives its consent to the government under the Constitution by not repealing that instrument.

Until, therefore, the people of the United States, whether the present, or any future generation, shall think it necessary to alter, or revoke the present constitution of the United States, it must be received, respected, and obeyed among us, as the great and unequivocal declaration of the will of the people, and the supreme law of the land.[39]

John Taylor of Caroline, whose works came first in time after that of St. George Tucker, took an unusual stand from the viewpoint of the states rights advocates, and one which remained unique. However, his attitude has the merit of being more realistic than that of his fellows. In his works, the theory of the social contract is introduced only to be repudiated. As will be noted, Joseph Story also disagreed with the theory, but beyond this, he and Taylor had little in common.

Taylor regards the theory of the social contract as " a purely hypothetical controversy and of small consequence for the development of his main theme, which is a constant attack on the

37 *Loc. cit.*

38 *Ibid.*, App., p. 171.

39 *Ibid.*, App., p. 173.

growing power of aristocratic minorities." [40] In fact, he attaches only slightly more significance to this theory than he does to the discarded idea of the divine right of kings. Part of his discussion of the subject is to be found in his *Inquiry into the Principles and Policy of the Government of the United States* (1814). According to his way of thinking, liberty in the United States exists not by social contract but by natural right, the result of military victory over England. Since it takes two to make a contract, it is impossible to find a party strong enough to bargain on equal terms with a sovereign people: " No contractor, with the right of self government, can exist." [41] Self government is a natural right and when the government of the Union was established all restraints upon its exercise were swept away. These restraints included " the whole herd of fictitious compacts between the people and the government, or between the states, or the states and the Union." [42] Since the will of the people of each state is unlimited, no state could have been forced to join the Union against its will, and any state may withdraw from the Union whenever it desires. Neither the federal government nor all state governments together can force a single state to act against its will.[43]

The argument in *Construction Construed and Constitutions Vindicated* (1820) is somewhat different. In this volume, Taylor is concerned with the McCulloch *v.* Maryland decision, and is therefore discussing the question of who has the right to construe the Constitution. He begins his chapter on " The Union " by saying that it really does not matter whether " the associated inhabitants of each state or the unassociated inhabitants of all the states " formed the Constitution.[44]

40 Mudge, *Social Philosophy of Taylor*, p. 55.

41 Taylor, *Inquiry*, p. 424.

42 *Ibid.*, p. 425.

43 *Cf.* summary of Taylor's reasoning in Mudge, *Social Philosophy of Taylor*, p. 59.

44 Taylor, *Construction Construed*, p. 39.

A man, having two titles, may distinguish himself by which he pleases, in making a contract; and whichever he uses, he remains himself. So the people having two titles or capacities, one arising from an existing association, the other from the natural right of self-government, may enter into a compact under either, but are themselves still; and their acts are equally obligatory, whichever they may select. Politicians may therefore indulge their taste in deducing the constitution of the union from either, but whichever they may fancy, no sound ground will thence result for their differing in the construction of it.[45]

After thus successfully establishing the insignificance of the whole question, Taylor proceeds with great minuteness to prove the importance of the states as entities in the federal Union.[46] He cites various clauses in the Constitution which emphasize this separate character, among them the phrase, " more perfect union." The intention here is to improve on the Articles of Confederation under which each of the state governments had the right to destroy the existing relationship. The substitution of the authority of the people of the United States for that of the governments of the states united was " not with an intention of excluding from the new union the idea of a compact between the states, but of placing that compact upon better ground, than that upon which it previously rested." [47]

The term " union " has never been applied to describe a government, established by the consent of individuals; nor do any of our state constitutions use it in that sense. They speak of individuals " uniting " to form a government, not to form a union; and I do not recollect that a single compact

45 *Loc. cit.*

46 On pp. 40-42, *ibid.*, he cites sections from most of the state constitutions of the uses of the words " state " and " government." " The terms ' state and government ' far from being synonimous [*sic*] are used to convey different ideas; and the latter is never recognised as possessing any species of sovereignty." P. 42.

47 *Ibid.*, p. 43.

between individuals for the establishment of a government, has ever been called a union; though a multitude of cases exist, in which that name has been given to agreements between independent states.[48]

After thus demolishing the existence of the Union as such, Taylor then considers the manner in which the people exercised their authority in the formation of the federal government. Referring to the " new doctrine . . . that the government of the union is responsible to the sovereignty of the people residing throughout the union, and not to the sovereignty of the people residing in each state," he says,

> Now as an effective sovereignty of the people can only result from their having constituted themselves into a civil society, and the first people having never done so, an acknowledgment of a sovereignty which does not exist, only annuls that which does; and escapes altogether from any species of loyalty to this superior authority.[49]

If a tacit social compact were to be admitted between the federal government and the people individually of the states, all the specifications of the division of powers between the federal and state governments would be abolished. ". . . as it is unwritten, the government of the union might construe it as was most convenient to itself, as all governments have done, which have condescended to acknowledge implied obligations only." [50]

The major idea in Taylor's work—that of the supremacy of the states, and of the Federal Constitution as having been given powers infinitely more limited than those originally bestowed on the state governments [51]—is carried further in his analysis of where the power to construe the instrument lies.

48 *Loc. cit.*
49 *Ibid.*, p. 45.
50 *Ibid.*, p. 46.
51 *Loc. cit.*

If the states made the union, they demonstrate, that the same consent, necessary to create, is necessary to construe. Wherever the creating consent resided, there we are directed to look for the construing consent. It would be a much grosser violation of their principles, for no party to a treaty to usurp an exclusive right of construing it, than for one party to do so. As neither the executive, legislative nor judicial departments of the state or federal governments have ever consented to the union, no one of these departments can have an exclusive right of construing it.[52]

At best, these federal departments (notably the judiciary in this book) have a mutual right of construction.

In his last volume, *New Views of the Constitution of the United States* (1823), Taylor is still concerned about the overweening powers of the judiciary, the existence of which made " inviolable sovereign state jurisdiction " an impossibility.[53] He also continues to support ideas which are different even from those of most of his compatriots. In the first place, he holds that there is no difference between the states and the people, as the states include all the people and the people all the states.[54] (The inhabitants of the District of Columbia and the territories are ignored.) The federal and state legislatures are coordinate, coequal, and independent, neither being controllable by the other.[55] Thus, the constitutions of the states and the federal government are of equal weight. And furthermore,

If the proposition, that unconstitutional laws are not the supreme law of the land, is true, its converse, that constitutional laws are the supreme law of the land, must be also true; and of course the constitutional laws of the states are equally supreme with those of the federal government.[56]

52 *Ibid.*, pp. 49-50.

53 Taylor, *New Views of the Constitution*, pp. 115-116. He finds Madison's argument in the *Federalist* on this subject confusing rather than convincing.

54 *Ibid.*, p. 94.

55 *Ibid.*, p. 81.

56 *Ibid.*, p. 78.

As to the nature of the Constitution, Taylor considers it

> an instrument for uniting any nine of specified states, and
> not for constituting a government for a consolidated nation.
> Its provisions are so many recognitions of its federal charac-
> ter. If the word implies sovereignty or supremacy, it also
> conveys these attributes to the government of each state, and
> destroys the sovereignty of the people.[57]

Taylor injects an interesting, and, it would appear, a valid
criticism of the nationalist strictures upon the states rights
school. He says that the disciples of a consolidated national
form of government use the word " union " in the same way in
which the word " infidelity " is used by the members of one
creed against those of another, not for the sake of finding truth,
but to hide " error, ambition, avarice, or pride."

> It vociferates, " Your faith is not my faith, and therefore you
> are an infidel." Thus the consolidating says to the federal
> doctrine, " Your union is not my union, and therefore you
> mean to destroy the union; " using the general enmity against
> its subversion, as religious politicians use the word in-
> fidelity." [58]

Taylor directs the love of his followers to the federal form of
government, if " our love " is for " a compact of the states." [59]

Throughout all his books, Taylor evinces his opposition to a
consolidated national government, and assumes that it is the
goal of the Northern nationalists. If the plan proposed in the
convention had succeeded, " it could not have oblitered [*sic*]
the local interests established by nature; and these would have
remained as a pledge for a revolution." [60]

57 *Ibid.*, p. 223.

58 *Ibid.*, pp. 235-236.

59 *Loc. cit.*

60 *Ibid.*, p. 247.

Even under the limitations of the constitution, local prejudices and partialities have been disclosed in Congress, and
these occurrences have excited local resentments. A supreme
power in the federal government over state rights, would
accumulate local aggressions and dissatisfactions, until they
would be insurmountable by laws and judgments, and be only
conquerable by an irresistible mercenary army. A national
government, though established by popular consent, could only
be sustained in this mode; established by construction, the
reservation of state rights would leave no other mode for en-
forcing its supremacy.[61]

The state governments intervene between the federal government and the people, and were designed to provide a better security against the effects of a concentrated power than the king
between the lords and commons.[62]

If this idea of intervention be considered as the negative approach, Taylor also presents a positive discussion, though it is
very brief. The Constitution availed itself of pre-existing political sovereignties and certain powerful qualities of human nature in securing its own enforcement. The agencies were not
" the penalties of power, but . . . the sympathies of a common
interest." Accordingly, federal powers were assigned to a " federal sympathy," and local powers to a " local sympathy." To
find the line between them, we have only to consider upon which
sympathy the measure proposed will operate.[63] Following this
reasoning, Taylor concludes that " our union, founded in the
division of powers between the state and federal governments
and annexing genunine [sic] sympathy to each department, is
the strongest government hitherto discovered for securing all
the benefits which have induced mankind to construct political
societies." [64]

61 *Ibid.*, pp. 247-248.
62 *Ibid.*, p. 243.
63 *Ibid.*, p. 265.
64 *Ibid.*, p. 285.

But all is not always sweetness and light. Taylor indicates with great accuracy the dangers implicit in the different geographical interests of the country. The opposition had been noted by Madison in the Federal Convention, as North *v.* South.[65] Since that time, the West had been added to the complex of local interests. Should any one of these sections gain complete national supremacy, " a dissolution of the union will result." And here, Taylor introduces another of his " new views." To prevent the calamity of the breakup of the Union, Taylor points out that our political system is composed of two unions, one of local state interests and the other of common federal interests.

> The reservation of powers to one, was a prohibition to the other, intended to avoid geographical collisions; and the expressed prohibitions upon the states were intended, not to take away the local rights reserved, nor to give to the federal government a power to exercise geographical partialities, but to prevent the states from assuming the regulation of the common interests intrusted to the care of a federal government. The two unions were respectively allotted to the care of governments which could feel and understand them, and made independent of each other to prevent geographical combinations of some states in Congress from making local laws for others.[66]

The rule that three-fourths of the states could subject the others to their control, completed the protection of the whole against local interests. In later days, Calhoun was to deny that the system thus " happily contrived " had actually avoided the dangers inherent in the differences between the three geographical sections.[67] Taylor sees the maintenance of states rights as the key-

65 *Ibid.*, p. 248. Ref. to Yates' Notes, p. 190.

66 *Ibid.*, p. 249.

67 *Ibid.*, pp. 262-263: " To prevent local interests from going to war with each other, they are incarcerated within the lines of a state, and if they should be let loose through the avenue of Congress, and the postern of the supreme court, the soundest security for the union of the states and

note to the continued peace of the Union. A national supremacy would "either produce a mass of fragments as materials for some new form of government, or require the almighty power of despotism to enforce its fraudulent awards." [68]

The commentator who first unequivocally asserted the right of secession was William Rawle, who was not advocating extreme state sovereignty but who had evidently reached the conclusion by legalistic reasoning.

Rawle defines a constitution as "the principles on which a government is formed and conducted." [69] It thus need not be a written instrument, but the men who come together in a republic to formulate the terms agree that the constitution "shall be the supreme rule of obligation among them." [70] In the case of the United States, where each citizen is under two such documents, the Federal Constitution is the superior. To form the Federal Constitution, the people of the states united with each other, but without destroying their previous organization.[71]

> Two governments of concurrent right and power cannot exist in one society. Superiority must, therefore, be conferred on the general government, or its formation, instead of promoting domestic tranquillity, would produce perpetual discord and disorder.[72]

Rawle does not view the Constitution itself as a compact.[73]

---

the liberty of the people, will be lost. Local interests, instead of being confined within the boundary of each state, will go to war with each other in Congress, the causes of their hostility, intended to be removed by the union, will be revived, victories will be gained and defeats suffered, and both will generate new battles..."

68 *Ibid.*, p. 263.

69 Rawle, *A View of the Constitution*, p. 5 (2nd ed., p. 2).

70 *Loc. cit.*, and p. 11 (2nd ed., pp. 9, 15).

71 *Ibid.*, pp. 25-26 (2nd ed., p. 29).

72 *Ibid.*, p. 26 (2nd ed., p. 30). *Cf.* p. 194 (2nd ed., p. 205), *re* supreme law clause.

73 The following definition of a contract does not make that term applicable to the Federal Constitution either. (Several of the states rights

Rather, it is the result of a compact.

> The instantaneous result on our political character, from the declaration of independence, was to convert allegiance from compulsion into compact, and while it still remained due to the sovereign, to see that sovereign only in the whole community.[74]

This compact, created among the citizens by the Declaration of Independence, was understood by them " not to be of a temporary nature, and in the power of the individual at pleasure to dissolve." [75] By this compact, the individual gave his allegiance to the new nation in return for protection from it. The compact was thus the basis for the formation of the new government.[76]

> So far as related to the new rights and duties, springing from the new political association, the same tacit compact which is acknowledged to exist in all society, necessarily accompanied this. Nothing short of express negation could exclude it.[77]

Furthermore, the obligation was mutual and perpetual, binding posterity as well as those who first entered into the compact.[78]

---

supporters regarded the terms contract and compact as interchangeable.) By the word contract, Rawle describes executed and executory agreements, " but it does not comprehend the political relations of a government and its citizens; civil institutions which must be liable to change with circumstances, and to be modified by ordinary legislation, those which deeply concern the public, and which to preserve good government, the public judgment must control." *Ibid.*, pp. 131-132 (2nd ed., p. 137), with ref. to 6 Cr. 87 at 136 and 4 Wheat. 518 at 627.

74 *Ibid.*, p. 85 (2nd ed., p. 90).

75 *Ibid.*, pp. 86-87 (2nd ed., p. 92).

76 *Ibid.*, p. 87. See p. 251 for similar idea—" When the period arrives for the formation of positive laws, which is after the formation of the original compact..." (2nd ed., pp. 92, 260).

77 *Ibid.*, p. 253 (2nd ed., p. 261).

78 *Ibid.*, p. 87 (2nd ed., p. 92). " No one can suppose that the parent intended, that while he was a permanent member of the state, his children should not partake of the same rights, enjoy the same liberty, and be protected by the same government."

The compact, so far as relates to the state, of course extends to the individual and to all his descendants, and therefore, as the child is entitled to the benefit of being recognised as a citizen, the state is entitled in its turn, to view the child as under its allegiance.[79]

The greatest interest in Rawle's *View of the Constitution* is in connection with his doctrine of secession. Up to the last chapter, there is no indication that such a possibility exists. His emphasis is on the beauties of the constitutional government and its perpetuity. In the last chapter, he concludes by " adverting to the principles of its cohesion, and to the provisions it contains for its own duration and extension." [80] Rawle sees the Union as " an association of the people of republics." Its life is therefore dependent upon the preservation of these republics. The people have compacted with each other as to the form of government (republican) and the Union can enforce the terms of the compact.[81]

> Yet it is not to be understood, that its interposition would be justifiable, if the people of a state should determine to retire from the union, whether they adopted another or retained the same form of government, or if they should, with the express intention of seceding, expunge the representative system from their code, and thereby incapacitate themselves from concurring according to the mode now prescribed, in the choice of certain public officers of the United States.
>
> . . . It depends on the state itself to retain or abolish the principle of representation, because it depends on itself whether it will continue a member of the Union. To deny this right would be inconsistent with the principle on which all our political systems are founded, which is, that the people have in all cases, a right to determine how they will be governed.[82]

79 *Ibid.*, p. 88 (2nd ed., p. 93).

80 *Ibid.*, p. 288 (2nd ed., p. 295).

81 *Loc. cit.* Ref. to Constitution, Art. IV, sec. 4.

82 *Ibid.*, p. 289 (2nd ed., p. 296).

In the event of the dissolution of the society to which they were due, the reciprocal allegiance and protection mentioned above, would necessarily cease, and the citizen would no longer be bound by the compact.[83]

So long as the states remain members of the Union, they must retain the character of representative republics.[84] But " if the majority of the people of a state deliberately and peaceably resolve to relinquish the republican form of government, they cease to be members of the Union." [85] Action on the part of a mere minority calls for the force of the Union to guarantee the republican form of government to the loyal majority—provided that the state authorities request such interference. " Otherwise the self-government of the state might be encroached upon at the pleasure of the Union." [86]

Secession, to be lawful, depends upon the people of each state, as they only have the power to alter their constitution. Such action is not within the competence of the state legislatures, who hold only delegated authority.[87] Secession may be conditional for a limited period, but when decided upon, the act should be " deliberate, clear and unequivocal." [88] From the standpoint of the Union, no proportion of states is constitutionally required to maintain it. Therefore, " Secessions may reduce the number to the smallest integer admitting combination."

> . . . a state cannot be compelled by other states to withdraw from the Union, and therefore, if two or more determine to remain united, although all the others desert them, nothing can be discovered in the constitution to prevent it.[89]

83 *Ibid.*, p. 290 (2nd ed., p. 297).

84 *Loc. cit.*

85 *Ibid.*, p. 292 (2nd ed., p. 299).

86 *Loc. cit.*

87 *Ibid.*, p. 295 (2nd ed., p. 302). If the legislatures could declare a state seceded, such a provision must be in the state constitutions. None had it at the time, "and it would perhaps be impolitic to confide it to them." *Loc. cit.*

88 *Ibid.*, p. 296 (2nd ed., p. 302).

89 *Ibid.*, p. 299 (2nd ed., p. 305).

Rawle also considers the consequences to the seceding state of the " loss of the aid and countenance of the Union." It should be expected to pay its share of the national debt upon withdrawal, as it would be removing a part of the national revenue. As a foreign state, differences would be likely to develop that might even lead to war.[90]

In spite of his objective consideration of a subject on which no nationalist wasted so much as a page of space (except in refutation), Rawle emphasizes his devotion to the Union and his abhorrence of the idea of dissolution.

> . . . we unite the interests of those who coldly calculate advantages with those who glow with what is little short of filial affection; and we must resist the attempt of its own citizens to destroy it, with the same feelings that we should avert the dagger of the parricide.[91]

These strong words, together with selected quotations from Washington's Farewell Address, " speak a persuasive language to every reflecting and virtuous mind, and exhibit the continuance of the union as a primary object of patriotic desire." [92]

Rawle has been mentioned as a transitional commentator. Some of his ideas thus were in agreement, while others were in conflict with both nationalists and particularists. Certain of these similarities and differences will appear as we consider the orthodox nationalist positions of Dane and Story.

## SECTION III

### THE ORTHODOX NATIONALISTS

Nathan Dane devoted the bulk of the Appendix to the ninth volume of his *General Abridgment and Digest of American Law* (1829) to an analysis of the nature of the Constitution. He was

---

90 *Loc. cit.* (2nd ed., p. 306).

91 *Ibid.*, p. 301 (2nd ed., p. 307).

92 *Ibid.*, p. 303 (2nd ed., p. 310). Thomas Cooper does not discuss the compact theory of government in his essay *On the Constitution*. For his ideas on sovereignty, see *infra*, pp. 241-242 and note.

untiring in his efforts to prove that the federal government was not a compact, a term which he seems to consider the root of all evil. He finds the primary proof of his contention in the fact that the word was not used in federal documents.[93]

Dane takes the extreme nationalist position, in one sense, in that he considers that the states were always subordinate to the general government. They became independent by virtue of the declaration of the independence of *all* the states, and ever since then had occupied a lower position.[94] At the time of the formation of the Federal Constitution, they functioned merely as convenient units for the purposes of voting.[95] The state constitutions were not designed as compacts,[96] and therefore the Federal Constitution partakes of no such character either.

> A little reflection evinces, that there is no foundation for the idea of a compact, which ever requires a capacity to contract, and the contractor to be remembered as long as the contract remains in force. Therefore, applying the word compact to a constitution, only misleads . . . The *ratification* alone gave it validity, and this was all done by *individual* voters, voting in 13 places by majorities, minorities individually opposing, absent persons and voters submitting, as far as any of them were legally able to submit . . . I repeat, the ratification alone was of any importance, and that was by *individual* citizens, voting in their natural sovereignty.[97]

In the formation of the Constitution, the people of the United States acted as one people. " As *one people,* they could not form two parties, so could not form a compact—and as the people of *separate* states, they could not act as one people." The people, as one, have never had an agent to contract for them internally, or make them a party to a federative compact. " Then, a com-

93 Dane, 9 *General Abridgment,* App., p. 33, sec. 24.

94 *Ibid.,* pp. 23-24, sec. 13.

95 *Ibid.,* pp. 22-23, sec. 12.

96 *Ibid.,* p. 24, sec. 13; pp. 25-26, sec. 14.

97 *Ibid.,* pp. 37-38, sec. 28.

pact between a state, or all the states, and the General Government, is out of the question." [98]

Dane disagrees with those who contended that the expression "between the states" implied that the arrangement was a compact. To his mind, the word "establish" was of greater significance and emphatically referred to a constitution.[99] He followed Wilson's reasoning that law is based upon consent, but he apparently does not mean continuing consent. "The enactment of a statute begins in consent; but when enacted, it binds of itself, and the consent and votes which made it are forgotten." [100] So with the Constitution of the United States—as soon as it was established, it alone was looked to and the consent and votes were no longer regarded.[101] In fact, the agreement is only to *make* a constitution in a manner understood. When it is made, "the agreement has answered its purpose, and is at an end." [102]

Most of the commentators agreed that the people, in establishing the federal government, took some of the sovereignty delegated to the states and re-delegated it to the federal government. Dane reversed this order, holding that the first and most important powers were vested in the general government

> by the whole American people, . . . in their original sovereign capacity, leaving in the people of each state, only a *residuum,* out of which to delegate state, legislative, executive,

98 *Ibid.*, p. 42, sec. 32.

99 *Ibid.*, p. 43, sec. 33. Dane gave as an example, thirteen hypothetical counties in a state ratifying a state constitution. The use of the word "between" would not make the state constitution a compact between just nine counties needed for ratification. "This catching at the word between, is of a piece with the other compact, and appears like catching at straws." *Loc. cit.*

100 According to McLaughlin, this admission of Dane's would mean that he accepted the basic premise of the compact theory, whether he recognized it or not. *Amer. Hist. Rev.*, V, 470, 488.

101 Dane, 9 *General Abridgment*, App., p. 26, sec. 14.

102 *Ibid.*, p. 32, sec. 22.

and judicial powers, to be exercised as *delegated* powers under state constitutions, vested *de novo*, expressly, at the respective times of adopting them . . .[103]

Dane is careful to explain that the American system is unique in politics. One major difficulty comes with the misapplication of old names to our system. The government " is neither a *federative compact* nor a *confederacy*, a consolidation nor a *central* government . . . The whole American system is *sui generis.*" [104] This explains the omission in the Constitution of so many words that later troubled the commentators—sovereignty, federation, and compact, for example.

The possibility of a break-up of the Union was a frightening one to Dane. He believed that " each state is an essential permanent member of the union," [105] and he saw that peaceable nullification of Congressional acts was a delusion. After the experience of the New England states, with which Dane was very familiar, he was willing to assert that it was " totally impracticable for a state, *peaceably,* to nullify or to suspend an act of Congress, within itself, while it remains a member of the Union." It was further " impracticable for it to cease to be a member and to separate, but on *revolutionary* principles, and by exerting superior force." [106] " Whatever South Carolina may think, she is driving to *separation* to secession." [107] " Secession, not assented to, draws the sword." [108]

103 *Ibid.*, p. 32, sec. 21. The people of Massachusetts expressly said that they were acting on such *residuum* in forming their constitution " nor could the people of any state act otherwise." This idea fits into the organic theory of the government.

104 *Ibid.*, p. 44, sec. 34; p. 33, sec. 23. Dane blamed the corrupting influence of Plato, which operated particularly on Jefferson. " Plato's school, never in the Old or New World, however captivating, produced an accurate, close-thinking lawyer." *Ibid.*, pp. 44-45, sec. 35.

105 *Ibid.*, p. 45, sec. 37.

106 *Ibid.*, p. 70, sec. 59.

107 *Ibid.*, p. 71, sec. 59.

108 *Ibid.*, p. 72, sec. 60.

Generally speaking, this is Dane's clinching argument:

> Those who have supported the constitution as it is supreme law, and a rule of conduct, have had the advantage, and they, generally, have supported this [the Supreme] court. Those who have viewed the constitution as a *compact,* have laboured under some disadvantages, and they have been most opposed to this court. Their ideas of their compact have been various and fluctuating, and confused; hence, they have had no rally-ing point as the supporters have, and who have had by far the most able guides in an arduous, judicial controversy.[109]

The influence of Dane's thinking on the nature of the Constitution is clearly seen in Judge Story's interpretation of the same subject. In his discussion of sovereignty, Story had given the reasoning behind his contention that the states were subordinate to the general government, even at the time of the Declaration of Independence. (The colonies did not act for themselves in becoming independent; the states which had formed " incipient governments for themselves " before the general declaration had done so following the recommendations of congress.) [110]

Most of Story's lengthy chapter on the nature of the Constitution is devoted to an analysis of what that document is *not* rather than to what it *is*. Story presents *in extenso* the arguments set forth by Tucker in the Appendix to his edition of *Blackstone's Commentaries,* together with a complete refutation, and then proceeds to a consideration of the ultimate results of the acceptance of such doctrines. He often uses Tucker's own words, " as representing, in a general sense, the opinions of a large body of statesmen and jurists in different parts of

109 *Ibid.,* p. 55, sec. 44.

110 Story, *Commentaries on the Constitution* (1833), sec. 210 *et seq.* Note to sec. 214: " This whole subject is very amply discussed by Mr. Dane in his Appendix to the 9th volume of his Abridgment of the Laws; and many of his views coincide with those stated in the text. The whole of that Appendix is worthy of the perusal of every constitutional lawyer, even though he might differ from some of the conclusions of the learned author."

the Union, avowed and acted upon in former times; and recently revived under circumstances, which have given them increased importance, if not a perilous influence." [111]

According to Story, the Constitution is a CONSTITUTION of government, as it purports on its face to be. All other appellations and definitions are to be rejected " especially as they may mislead us into false constructions and glosses, and can have no tendency to instruct us in its real objects." [112] The term " constitution " is used in contradistinction to the term " confederation," and is defined as

> a permanent form of government, where the powers, once given, are irrevocable, and cannot be resumed or withdrawn at pleasure. Whether formed by a single people, or by different societies of people, in their political capacity, a constitution, though originating in consent, becomes, when ratified, obligatory, as a fundamental ordinance or law. [113]

Furthermore, the language of the Constitution itself—that the *people* do *ordain* and *establish,* not contract and stipulate with each other—Story regards as conclusive. [114]

One other positive statement of what the Constitution is, Story bases upon the supreme law clause: The term law, from

111 *Ibid.,* sec. 319. Tucker's reasoning appears in secs. 310-318. As a footnote, Story adds that " Many traces of these opinions will be found in the public debates in the state legislatures and in congress at different periods. In the resolutions of Mr. Taylor, in the Virginia legislature of 1798, it was resolved, 'that this assembly doth explicitly and peremptorily declare, that it views the powers of the federal government as resulting from the compact, *to which the states are parties'*." According to Story, the word *"alone"* originally appeared after states, but was struck out when, in debate, the position that the people were also (or even exclusively) parties, was taken.

112 *Ibid.,* sec. 372.

113 *Ibid.,* sec. 352. Though he does not cite Tucker in this instance, Story sees that gentleman's " confederated republic" as " not less an irrevokable form of government, than the constitution of a state formed and ratified by the aggregate of the several counties of the state." Ref. to the *Federalist,* Nos. 9, 15, 16, 33, 39.

114 *Ibid.,* sec. 352; also sec. 338.

the very nature of political institutions, includes supremacy.[115]

> A constitution is in fact a fundamental law or basis of gov-
> ernment, and falls strictly within the definition of law, as
> given by Mr. Justice Blackstone. It is a rule of action, pre-
> scribed by the supreme power in a state, regulating the rights
> and duties of the whole community.  It is a *rule,* as contra-
> distinguished from a temporary or sudden order; permanent,
> uniform, and universal. It is also called a rule, to distinguish
> it from a compact, or agreement; for a compact . . . is a
> promise proceeding from us; law is a command directed to us.
> The language of a compact is, I will, or will not do this; that
> of a law is, Thou shalt, or shalt not do it . . . It is a rule
> prescribed; that is, it is laid down, promulgated, and estab-
> lished. It is prescribed by the supreme power in a state, that
> is, among us, by the people, or a majority of them in their
> original sovereign capacity. Like the ordinary municipal laws,
> it may be founded upon our consent, or that of our representa-
> tives; but it derives its ultimate obligatory force, as a *law,*
> and not as a compact.[116]

Story's opposition to the idea of the Constitution as a compact comes, not so much from a dislike for the word itself, as
from a consideration of the deductions derived from the theory
as a whole. If the Constitution is a compact between the states,
it would operate as a " mere treaty, or convention between
them, and [would have] an obligatory force upon each state no
longer, than suits its pleasure, or its consent continues." Each
state could judge for itself regarding the obligations of the instrument, and need not be bound by the interpretation of the
federal government or by that of any other state. Each state

> retains the power to withdraw from the confederacy and to
> dissolve the connexion, when such shall be its choice; and

115 *Ibid.,* sec. 340. Ref. to the *Federalist,* Nos. 33 and 15.

116 *Ibid.,* sec. 339. Story quotes this distinction from Blackstone: " In
compacts we ourselves determine and promise, what shall be done, before
we are obliged to do it. In laws, we are obliged to act without ourselves
determining, or promising any thing at all." 1 Black. Comm. 45. See also
*ibid.,* 38, 44.

may suspend the operations of the federal government, and nullify its acts within its own territorial limits, whenever, in its own opinion, the exigency of the case may require.[117]

Carried to the logical conclusion (to which Tucker does not go), these documents reduce the government to a mere confederacy during pleasure and present " the extraordinary spectacle of a nation existing only at the will of each of its constituent parts." [118]

Thus Story deems it of the highest importance to undermine the compact argument, and his main discussion of the nature of the Constitution assumes the negative character of an analysis of why the Constitution is *not* a compact.[119]

Story agrees with Blackstone that the theory of an original contract upon the first formation of society is a visionary notion.[120] He also accepts Blackstone's analysis of this hypothetical contract and uses it to justify the otherwise heterodox statements by certain eminent jurists that the Constitution is a compact. According to Blackstone, the contract meant

> that the whole should protect all its parts, and that every part should pay obedience to the will of the whole; or, in other words, that the community should guard the rights of each individual member; and that in return for this protection each individual should submit to the laws of the community.[121]

117 *Ibid.*, sec. 321.

118 *Loc. cit.*

119 McLaughlin considers Story to be inconsistent on this point, as sometimes he talks in terms of the compact theory, and sometimes not. *Amer. Hist. Rev.*, V, 487 note.

120 Story, *Commentaries*, sec. 326.

121 1 *Blackstone's Commentaries*, 47; Story, *Commentaries*, sec. 326. Chief Justice Jay in Chisholm *v.* Georgia, 2 Dall. 419 at 471, had said, " Every state constitution is a compact made by and between the citizens of a state, to govern themselves in a certain manner; and the constitution of the United States is likewise a compact made by the people of the United States, to govern themselves, as to general objects, in a certain manner."

In general, however, Story disapproves of the social contract theory as requiring too many limitations and qualifications. Many persons bound by the contract have no voice in the determination of its terms, and the majority only of the actual voters have the deciding voice.[122]

Arguing from the exact terminology of the Constitution, Story contends that the document would have been declared to be articles of compact, if such had been the intention of the framers. " The only places, where the terms, *confederation* or *compact,* are found in the constitution, apply to subjects of an entirely different nature, and manifestly in contradistinction to *constitution.*" (Art. I, sec. 10 and Art. VI) In Amendment No. X, it is declared that " the powers not *delegated* by the constitution, nor prohibited by it to the states, are reserved to the states respectively, or to the people." Says Story, " A contract can in no just sense be called a delegation of powers." [123]

With regard to the perpetuity of the Constitution, Story recalls the arguments of its supporters who elaborated upon it " as a permanent form of government, as a fundamental law, as a supreme rule, which no state was at liberty to disregard, suspend, or annul." [124] In fact, these were some of the strongest reasons advanced for replacing the Articles of Confederation. Here, Story disagrees with William Rawle: [125]

122 Story, *Commentaries,* sec. 327. Harold J. Laski, in discussing the social contract theory in his article for the *Encyclopedia of Social Sciences,* Vol. XIV, says that the idea of a contract as the basis of rights and duties in the state is almost as old as political philosophy itself. "Indeed it may be said that not until the time of Justice Story (*Commentaries on the Constitution of the United States* ... , sec. 327) did it cease to play an important part in American political theory." Laski evidently finds this section 327 far more decisive than it appears to this student. Sec. 328 seems a stronger statement, stressing the importance of the will of the majority rather than the assent of the whole people.

123 Story, *Commentaries,* sec. 353.

124 *Ibid.,* sec. 359.

125 Ref. to Rawle *On the Constitution,* ch. 32 [sic—should read ch. 31], pp. 295, 296, 297, 302, App. no. 1, 305 (2nd ed., pp. 302, 303, 304, 308, 309, 142).

It is a matter of surprise . . . that a learned commentator should have admitted the right of any state, or of the people of any state, without the consent of the rest, to secede from the Union at its own pleasure. The people of the United States have a right to abolish, or alter the constitution of the United States; but that the people of a single state have such a right, is a proposition requiring some reasoning beyond the suggestion, that it is implied in the principles, on which our political systems are founded.[126]

This section, and a footnote comment that " it is certain, that a right of the minority to withdraw from the government, and to overthrow its powers, has no foundation in any just reasoning," [127] are virtually the only references to secession. Evidently, Story considered that if he could properly demolish the compact theory, nullification and secession would no longer rear their ugly heads.

Story does not regard the states as parties to the Constitution. It is irrelevant to the subject that the Constitution was framed by delegates chosen by the states, and submitted by the legislatures thereof to the people of the states for ratification, and that the states are necessary agents to give effect to some of its provisions.[128]

No state, as such, that is the body politic, as it was actually organized, had any power to establish a contract for the establishment of any new government over the people thereof, or to delegate the powers of government in whole, or in part to any other sovereignty. The state governments were framed by the people to administer the state constitutions . . . and not to transfer the administration thereof to any other persons, or sovereignty . . . The people, and the people only, in their original sovereign capacity, had a right to change their form of government, to enter into a compact, and to transfer any sovereignty to the national government.[129]

126 Story, *Commentaries,* sec. 359.

127 *Ibid.,* sec. 332 note.

128 *Ibid.,* sec. 362.

129 *Loc. cit.*

The states, in their political capacity, were not called upon by the Congress to ratify the Constitution, and their approval was not deemed essential to give validity to it.

The only way in which Story can admit the notion of a compact is in the same sense in which Dane admitted it. The government might originate in the voluntary compact or consent of the people of the several states. After the government is made (i.e., the Constitution), the agreement is at an end; it becomes an executed contract, or a fundamental law.[130] Story found Tucker's theory that the federal government, as the creature of the compact, must be bound to it by its creators, the several states of the Union and the citizens thereof, " a doctrine far more involved, and extraordinary, and incomprehensible, than any part of the preceding." [131] How can the federal government as the result of the Constitution, be a party to the compact to which it owes its existence? Even if such a phenomenon could take place, when did the general government signify its assent to become a party? [132]

Such metaphysical complexities were useless, according to Story. In departing from the words of the Constitution to sustain the compact theory, Story claims that its proponents " serve no better purpose, than to confuse the mind in relation to a subject otherwise clear." [133] In fact, he finds it hard to explain why these ideas should have been so extensively adopted and so zealously propagated. He finds them objectionable in every way;

> first, because they are not justified by the language of the constitution; secondly, because they have a tendency to impair,

130 *Ibid.*, sec. 365.

131 *Ibid.*, sec. 367. Ref. to 1 Tucker's *Blackstone*, App., pp. 169-170. It would seem to this student that Story misinterpreted Tucker's meaning. Tucker considered the federal government to be the creature of the compact (i. e., the Constitution). Story evidently regarded the government and the Constitution as convertible terms, while Tucker did not.

132 *Ibid.*, sec. 368.

133 *Ibid.*, sec. 365.

and indeed to destroy, its express powers and objects; and thirdly, because they involve consequences, which, at the will of a single state, may overthrow the constitution itself.[134]

## SECTION IV

### THE RESPONSE OF THE PARTICULARISTS

That such problems did not trouble the followers of Tucker is apparent in the commentaries to which we may now turn our attention. Abel Parker Upshur had written with the specific object of refuting Story, and his arguments were approved by Judge Tucker's two sons.

Throughout his work,[135] Upshur is concerned with disproving Story's basic point—" the doctrine, that the Constitution of the United States is a government of ' the people of the United States,' as contradistinguished from the people of the several States; or, in other words, that it is a consolidated, and not a federative system." [136] He therefore submits opposing arguments to Story's assertion that the people of the United States were one in any sense prior to the Revolution. Such unity as might be found stemmed from the relation between the colonies of the mother country, and was not the result of the relation between the colonies themselves.[137] If the people of the colonies were not one in this early period, Upshur contends that the Declaration of Independence, an act of all, did not unite them.[138]

Upshur admits that the power and authority of the federal government is superior to that of the states within its constitutional sphere, but he assigns a different reason for the submission of each citizen to this superiority—it is because ". . . *his*

134 *Ibid.*, sec. 369.

135 *A Brief Enquiry into the Nature and Character of Our Federal Government* (1840).

136 *Ibid.*, p. 14.

137 *Ibid.*, p. 11 *et seq.*

138 *Ibid.*, p. 39.

*own State, by the act of ratifying the Constitution, has com-
manded him to do so.*" [139]

With regard to the authority to construe the Constitution,
the umpire is admitted to be the United States Supreme Court,
which has full jurisdiction in " certain cases involving the rights
of individual citizens," and in " certain others affecting those
of the individual States." [140]

> But there are many cases involving the question of federal
> power which are not cognizable before the federal courts;
> and, of course, as to these, we must look out for some other
> umpire. It is precisely in this case that the question, who are
> the parties to the constitution, becomes all important and con-
> trolling. If the States are parties as sovereign States, then it
> follows, as a necessary consequence, that each of them has the
> right which belongs to every sovereignty, to construe its own
> contracts and agreements, and to decide upon its own rights
> and powers.[141]

Story's contention that the Constitution is not a compact because it does not say it is, is thrown out by Upshur. " He
[Story] himself knows, as a *judge,* that a deed, or other instrument, receives its distinctive character, not from the *name*
which the parties may choose to give to it, but from its *legal
effect and operation.* The same rule applies to constitutions." [142]
In this connection there appears the difference in definition of
a compact that has been noted above. To Story, the terms compact and supreme law were mutually exclusive. To Upshur, on
the other hand, it was entirely possible so to frame a compact,
that no party to it would have a right to " repeal or abrogate
or suspend it,"—thus making the terms almost synonymous.[143]

139 *Ibid.,* p. 63. The same idea is expressed by N. Beverley Tucker in
his *Lectures on the Science of Government,* p. 387.

140 Upshur, *Brief Enquiry, loc. cit.*

141 *Ibid.,* p. 64.

142 *Ibid.,* p. 65.

143 *Ibid.,* pp. 66, 67. *Cf.* the following: " For myself, I am unable to
discover why States, absolutely sovereign, may not create for themselves,

Upshur finds that the proponents of the states rights doctrine have been much misunderstood.[144] Though they view the Constitution as a compact, they do not use the term to imply that it is the less binding. The Constitution is a compact *" because it was made by sovereign States, and because that is the only mode in which sovereign States treat with one another."* Thus, whether the government be federative or consolidated, it is still a compact, or the result of a compact; it could not be made in any other way.[145]

> The Nullifier contends only for the right of a State to *prevent the Constitution from being violated by the general government,* and not for the right either to repeal, abrogate or suspend it. The Seceder asserts only that a State is competent to withdraw from the Union whenever it pleases; but does not assert that in so doing it can repeal, or abrogate or suspend the Constitution, as to the other States. Secession would, indeed, utterly destroy the compact as to the seceding party; but would not necessarily affect its obligation to the rest.[146]

Under the subject of the interpretation of the Constitution, Upshur further enlarges upon his primary thesis that the states, as sovereign and independent, have the sole right to judge of the compacts and agreements to which they are parties. Should they surrender this right, they impair their sovereignty. " The Constitution of the United States is but the agreement which each State has made, with each and all the other States, and is not distinguishable, . . . from any other agreement between sovereign States." [147]

---

by compact, a common government, with powers as extensive and supreme as any sovereign people can confer on a government established by themselves." *Ibid.*, p. 79.

144 *Ibid.*, pp. 68-69.

145 *Ibid.*, p. 71. Note that Upshur says that the government may be *either* a compact or the result of a compact. Other writers generally made it one or the other; the nationalists would have admitted the latter possibility. See also pp. 92-93.

146 *Ibid.*, p. 66.

147 *Ibid.*, p. 85. *Cf.* pp. 93-94.

Like Tucker, who said that the federal government was not a party to the compact between the states, but was nevertheless bound by the act of its creators, Upshur asserts that

> The Federal government is the creature of the States. It is not a party to the Constitution, but the result of it—the creation of that agreement which was made by the States as parties. It is a mere agent, entrusted with limited powers for certain specified objects; which powers and objects are enumerated in the Constitution. Shall the agent be permitted to judge of the extent of his own powers, without reference to his constituent? [148]

Since the federal government as a whole cannot judge of its powers, how much worse it is that a single department (i.e., the judiciary) can have the authority! " This is an absurdity as pernicious as it is gross and palpable." [149] Upshur is willing to concede to the court all the jurisdiction and authority which properly belong to it, but " we cannot safely or wisely repose in it the vast trust of ascertaining, defining or limiting the sovereign powers of the States." [150]

Near the close of his critique, Upshur says, " Whatever the *theory* of our Constitution, its *practice* of late years, has made it a consolidated government; the government of an irresponsible majority." [151] William Rawle, writing several years previously, had made the opposite observation: ". . . time has proved that . . . the state sovereignties are, in all respects not voluntarily ceded to the United States, as vigorous as ever." [152]

148 *Ibid.*, p. 85.

149 *Ibid.*, pp. 85-86.

150 *Ibid.*, pp. 91-92.

151 *Ibid.*, p. 128.

152 Rawle, *View of the Constitution*, p. 243. Rawle retained this point in his second edition (1829), p. 252, and Upshur himself said that he wrote his treatise in 1837. No indication has been found that Rawle changed his opinions on this subject, even after the events of 1832-33. He lived until 1836.

It will be remembered that the nullification controversy and Jackson's decisive action had occurred during the interim between the publication of these two commentaries. Nevertheless, it is probable that time would not have changed the authors' views, and that each man saw what he was looking for in the developments of the period.

Henry St. George Tucker disagreed with Story on the nature of the Constitution, but his position is not so extreme as that taken by Upshur. The younger Judge Tucker agrees that government must be founded upon express compact, otherwise "there can have been *no express* transfer from society (or the people who constitute it) of that sovereignty which confessedly was originally vested in it." [153] He thinks that Story's assumptions (which he quotes at length) are not warranted by the history of the formation of the Constitution. Furthermore, he disapproves of Story's reliance on Dane, "whose notions I deem as unsound as they are novel." [154]

In answer to Story's rhetorical question (*Commentaries*, sec. 350), "In what light . . . is the constitution of the United States to be regarded?" Tucker says,

> As a compact between the states, whereby they have ordained and established the constitution for the United States of America. The people of the thirteen distinct and separate political bodies or communities constituting states, agreed together in a general convention of delegates from them sever-

153 Tucker, *Lectures on Government* (1844), p. 41.

154 This comment refers to Story's citation of Dane, in disagreeing with St. George Tucker's analysis of the Federal Constitution as an original compact. Tucker, *Lectures on Constitutional Law* (1843), p. 117, with ref. to Story, *Commentaries*, sec. 314, and to Dane, 9 *Gen. Abridgment*, App., sec. 2, p. 10. Says Tucker, Jr., " Such absurdities scarcely admit of a grave and calm refutation." Again, Tucker dismisses Dane (on the right of the people of a single state to abolish or alter the Constitution of the United States, 9 *Gen. Abridgment*, App., secs. 59, 60, pp. 69, 71), with the words, " We scarcely need to express our total dissent to the views of Mr. Dane, presented in this passage. We do not recognize him as *authority*, and still less do we defer to his very unsatisfactory reasoning." Tucker, *Lectures on Constitutional Law*, p. 132.

ally and respectively, to ordain and establish the constitution as a form of government for the United States. The constitution may therefore be looked upon rather as the *result* of the *agreement,* than as the agreement itself. The *agreement* of the states is in the preamble, " We the people of the United States, do ordain and establish this constitution for the United States of America." [155]

Tucker's primary contentions may be summarized as follows :

1. The formation of the Constitution was in origin, progress, and ratification, the act of the free and sovereign states, and not of the American people as one people.

2. If the sovereignty of the states is admitted, the Constitution could not have been adopted without their consent.

3. If it be the act of the states, it is a compact.[156]

Admitting that the states are parties to the constitutional compact, the question arises as to the right of the states to interfere in federal legislation. Here, Tucker begins to steer his middle course, saying that the true point is " not as to the existence of the *right* to interfere, but as to the extent of the interference only." [157] He explains that the states rights party was split over this issue at one time, " though there may be reason to hope that the advocates of some of the extravagant positions attributed by judge Story to all the party, are no longer urgent in pressing these questionable pretensions." [158]

155 *Ibid.,* p. 124 note.

156 *Ibid.,* p. 149. Here Tucker agrees with Story, at least in part. He quotes Story (*Commentaries,* p. 330 [sec. 362]), to the effect that "the states never, in fact, did in their *political capacity* (*as contradistinguished from the people* THEREOF), ratify the constitution." (Italics Tucker's.) And Tucker clarifies this statement: " That is to say, the *legislatures* did not, though he admits the *people thereof* (that is, of each state) did. And this is all we contend for: believing that the ratification by the people of each state, in their conventions, was an act of separate state sovereignty, which made the constitution a compact between states, and not a national or consolidated government." (P. 135 note).

157 *Ibid.,* p. 191.

158 *Loc. cit.*

Tucker does not agree with Story that the doctrine of nullification naturally follows from the premise that the Constitution is a compact between the states, as this theory was set forth in the Virginia Resolutions of 1798. The Virginia legislature had expressly voted down the extreme wording as it was originally proposed by John Taylor, and had never officially supported nullification as a remedy for any difficulties.[159] Tucker describes the doctrine as " the mere figment of the brain of politicians teeming with new conceptions generated by the heat of party feuds." [160]

Judge Tucker disagrees with Upshur [161] and Taylor that the judiciary is the great enemy of the sovereign states, and points out the error of the states in assuming that the Constitution did not appoint an umpire in the judiciary.[162] In his argument that there is no constitutional right of a state to resist an act approved by Congress and pronounced valid by the judiciary,[163] Tucker notes,

> I occupy an isthmus that divides two great contending parties in the nation. I have endeavored to maintain a middle course between dangerous extremes. On the one hand is nullification, and upon the other centralization; the rocks of Scylla and the engulfing whirlpool of Charybdis.[164]

The only method of resistance to federal legislation approved by Congress and the courts must be by revolution, and secession is revolution.[165]

159 *Ibid.*, p. 192. The bulk of Lectures VII and VIII, pp. 189-242, is a refutation of the doctrine of nullification.

160 *Ibid.*, p. 197.

161 *Cf. ibid.*, pp. 201, 209.

162 *Ibid.*, pp. 194, 201.

163 *Ibid.*, p. 209 note.

164 *Ibid.*, p. 210.

165 *Ibid.*, p. 209 note.

N. Beverley Tucker thinks that the social contract in written form is in the constitution of Virginia, adopted June 29, 1776; [166] the Federal Constitution is a federal compact.[167] The authority of the federal government over the people of Virginia rests solely on Virginia's command in her ratification, to obey. This ratification had stated " that the powers granted under the constitution, being derived from the people of the United States, may be resumed by them, whensoever the same shall be perverted to their injury or oppression." Tucker then asks,

> Is the sovereign right of the people to annihilate the work of their hands, to recall the powers they have granted, to abolish the government they have established, the less sacred, the less unquestionable, because the exercise of the right might be attended with greater difficulty in the latter case than in the former? [168]

He foresaw the Civil War with remarkable acuity. He hints at it in his *Lectures*,[169] and developed the theme at length in his novel, *The Partisan Leader,* written in 1846, but published with the date of 1856. (Actually, it was very timely in 1856.)

N. B. Tucker agrees with Upshur in his historical analysis of the priority of Virginia as an independent, sovereign state. After lengthy quotations from the first part of Upshur's review of Story's *Commentaries,* Tucker makes the important admission that the root of the matter is in Story's first point—

> the *one-ness* of the United States. If Judge Story is right in this, he is right throughout; and, if constrained to concede this one point, we would hardly think it worthwhile to dispute any of the rest . . .[170]

166 Tucker, *Lectures on the Science of Government* (1845), pp. 373, 377.

167 *Ibid.*, p. 457.

168 *Ibid.*, p. 381.

169 *Ibid.*, pp. 457-458.

170 *Ibid.*, pp. 446-447.

Although the commentators whose views have thus far been presented made the most significant statement of the opposing sectional views, there are a few others who cannot be neglected.

## SECTION V

### SOME ADDITIONAL VIEWPOINTS

William Alexander Duer, Chancellor Kent's successor at Columbia, prepared his first volume on constitutional jurisprudence in 1833. In his preface, Duer explains that he does not agree with Kent's restricted views of the supremacy of the government of the United States, or with Rawle in his idea that the obligation of the Federal Constitution could be terminated by a state. Upon both of these points, he " has maintained . . . principles more favourable, . . . to the power and stability of the National government " than those of either of the two gentlemen referred to.[171]

Duer defines a constitution, in its legal and political sense, as the " fundamental principles on which a government is formed." [172] Duer considered himself a nationalist, but like Chipman, he regarded the Constitution as a compact. The relation between the federal and state governments is thus given:

> By the terms of the compact, the States, as members of the Union, are no longer regarded in their sovereign and corporate capacities, as they surrendered such portions of their sovereignties as were requisite for the purposes of National Government; retaining, however, their previous organization and the exclusive control of their local concerns.[173]

Also,

> From the nature of the case, the National and State Governments cannot be coequal; for two governments, of entirely concurrent right and authority, cannot exist in the society.

171 Duer, *Outlines of Constitutional Jurisprudence* (1833), pp. xi-xii.

172 *Ibid.*, p. 25, sec. 1.

173 *Ibid.*, p. 33, sec. 41. See also Preface, p. xv, and p. 188, secs. 739, 740.

Superiority was therefore conferred on the General Government, as the Government of the whole nation, over the State governments, or the Government of its several parts.

The Constitution, in the name of the whole People, accordingly declares its own supremacy, and that of the Laws made in pursuance thereto, and of Treaties . . .[174]

The contracting parties are evidently the citizens of the respective States, who on " becoming parties to the federal compact," expressly declared their natural, political, and civil rights " to belong to them as citizens of the Union." [175] In a later section, it is asserted that the Government is " formed from the union of the people of . . . separate and independent States, as well as of those States themselves, into one nation, organized under a written compact of government . . ." [176] In voting on the Constitution, the people assembled in their respective states as a matter of necessity. Under the Confederation, no authority existed for calling a general convention of the people of the United States, and even if such authority had existed, " it would not have been a proper mode of assembling the People on an occasion in which they were in effect, to pass on virtual amendments of their State Constitutions." [177] The Constitution was " adopted by the people themselves and not by the State Governments; and it derives its binding force solely from the act of the People in their State Conventions." [178] But this is not all—

This Government extends over the Union, as one National community or body politic; composed, not only of the people of the States, but to a certain degree of the States themselves, for the purpose of investing the States, as well as the People, with one National character.[179]

174 *Ibid.*, p. 115, secs. 409-411. This wording is almost identical with Rawle's on the same subject.

175 *Ibid.*, p. 32, sec. 37.

176 *Ibid.*, pp. 80-81, sec. 263. The terms used in this sentence borrow from both states rights supporters and nationalists.

177 *Ibid.*, p. 216, sec. 859.

178 *Ibid.*, p. 216, sec. 860. See also p. 219, sec. 869(3).

179 *Ibid.*, p. 219, sec. 869(4).

And the people of the Union, for all purposes of the Constitution, are one people as of the time they ratified the Constitution. They owe local allegiance to the states in which they reside, but paramount allegiance to the national government.[180]

Duer follows Rawle very closely in the propositions just stated. But when it comes to the analysis of the clause guaranteeing a republican government to the states, their opinions differ. Duer holds that the federal government can intervene in "unconstitutional violence" within a state only when the violence is directed against the state constitution itself,

> and in that manner accidentally and indirectly affects the Government of the Union; for, when the violence is immediately directed against the Federal authority, the National Government is invested with power to repress it, independently of any requisition of the State.[181]

Rawle, it may be remembered, insisted that the federal government could not intervene without specific request of the state.

Duer's basic disagreement with Rawle is on the subject of secession. Rawle had accepted the idea as entirely consonant with the right of the people to determine how they should be governed.[182] To Duer and many of the others, however, secession was a revolutionary act. The Union was intended to be perpetual, and no state can dissolve the relation subsisting between the federal government and the individuals under its authority.[183] The final result of Duer's examination of the principles, organization, and powers of the United States government is

> That no State authority has power to dissolve the relations existing between the Government of the United States and the People of the several States; and consequently, that no

180 *Ibid.*, p. 219, sec. 869(5) ; p. 216, sec. 861.

181 *Ibid.*, p. 189, sec. 745.

182 Rawle, *View of the Constitution*, p. 289 (2nd ed., p. 296).

183 Duer, *Outlines*, pp. 218, 217; secs. 868, 867.

State has a right to secede from the Union, except under such circumstances as would justify a Revolution in the Government; and that an attempt by any State to abrogate or annul an act of the National Legislature, is a direct usurpation of the powers of the General Government, an infringement on the rights of all the other States, and a plain violation of the paramount obligation of its members, to support and obey the Constitution of the United States.[184]

In the more complete volume of *Lectures on Constitutional Jurisprudence* (1843), Duer takes much the same stand which he took in his *Outlines*. He enlarges somewhat on the idea of the Constitution as a contract, describing this type of agreement as that found best suited by Americans to the formation of a political community.[185] In fact, he regards the Federal Constitution as " the first practical example of a ' SOCIAL CONTRACT '." [186]

Nullification as a principle receives no specific attention in the *Outlines,* but in the *Lectures,* it is described as a " monstrous claim," which even " pretended to reconcile " itself with the amendment reserving undelegated powers to the states and the people.[187] Duer treats the heresy as dead after Jackson's proclamation.[188] The Union is perpetual; secession could come only as a concomitant of revolution.[189] No state can undo what the people have done, nor absolve its citizens from their obligations to obey the laws of the Union. Not even a convention of the

184 *Ibid.,* p. 220, sec. 869(9). *Cf. Lectures on Constitutional Jurisprudence,* pp. 329-330 (2nd ed., pp. 418-419).

185 Duer, *Lectures,* p. 43 (2nd ed., p. 28).

186 *Ibid.,* p. 46 (2nd ed., p. 31). *Cf.* Story, *Commentaries,* sec. 327, where he asserts that the idea does not fit American experience. *Cf.* also Laski's statement in note 122, *supra.*

187 *Ibid.,* p. 326. Expanded upon in 2nd ed., pp. 411-415, with reference to Madison's " Memorandum on Nullification."

188 *Loc. cit.* (2nd ed., p. 415). Duer notes that this paper was known to be written by his former associate, Edward Livingston, then Secretary of State.

189 *Ibid.,* pp. 329-330 (2nd ed., p. 418).

people of the state could dissolve their allegiance to the United States, "unless they respectively possess the constitutional power of settling for themselves the construction of this supreme law in all doubtful cases." [190]

Peter Stephen DuPonceau in his *Brief View of the Constitution* (1834), attempts to steer a middle course between the strict and liberal interpretations of the Constitution, advocating that it be construed "*fairly* and *honestly,* always keeping in view the objects for which it was made." [191] In practice, this fair and honest interpretation is found to be on the side of the national government, more often than not. DuPonceau agrees with Rawle that there was no danger that the Union would degenerate into a consolidated government, and crush the independence of the states. Rather, there was more danger of the dissolution of the Union. The organization of the general government and the powers reserved by the states to themselves

> are not only sufficient to secure the independent existence of the latter, but recent events have shown that they are even possessed of the means to make themselves formidable to those who might attempt to encroach upon their constitutional rights. What has been done by a single state, when nothing more than a doubtful local interest was in question, shows what might be done by a combination of states, if more serious disturbances should take place.[192]

DuPonceau traces the cause of most of the disorders threatening the perpetuity of the Union to violent party spirit. ". . . the political, like the natural body, is not immortal, and it will sink at last, if efficient means are not taken to prevent the recurrence of those disorders, which gradually weaken it, and must at last operate its dissolution." [193]

190 *Ibid.,* pp. 330-331 (2nd ed., p. 419).

191 DuPonceau, *Brief View of the Constitution,* p. xxi.

192 *Ibid.,* p. xxii.

193 *Ibid.,* p. xvi.

After this word of prophecy, DuPonceau touches upon the relations between the national government and the states. He finds that the Union and the states are mutually dependent. In fact, the state authorities constitute an auxiliary system for the administration of the details of government.[194] The Constitution is a compact by which a national government was formed. Its title points out the difference between it and the Confederation that existed before. It was designed to deprive the states of no more of their sovereignty and independence than was necessary to insure the permanence of the Union and its welfare and safety.[195] He takes the term, "We, the People of the United States," as

> excluding the idea of a mere confederation of independent communities, by making the people at large a party to this compact, and binding not only each state, but every individual to each other, and to the government of their creation.[196]

DuPonceau recognizes strong federal features, but he feels that upon the whole, the national character is predominant.[197]

Unlike other commentators writing in the period immediately following the nullification agitation of 1828-33, DuPonceau makes no comment about whether or not a state should secede from the Union, or of its own authority declare an act of Congress null and void. Says he, regarding this omission, " I feared lest the shade of Washington should frown upon me." [198]

---

194 *Ibid.*, pp. xxii-xxiii. *Cf.* p. 38 *re* the court system: "This *auxiliary system* is calculated not only to promote harmony between the general and the state governments, but also to prevent the consolidation of the Union; for were the state authorities to refuse their assistance, congress would be compelled to fill the land with their inferior officers and magistrates, which could not be long tolerated by the people; and a dissolution of the Union might be the fatal consequences."

195 *Ibid.*, pp. 14, 47.

196 *Ibid.*, pp. 14-15.

197 *Ibid.*, p. 14.

198 *Ibid.*, p. xxi. Washington's Farewell Address in Appendix.

Justice Baldwin, as has been noted in preceding chapters, regarded himself as taking a middle ground between the two schools of thought, as did DuPonceau. Unlike the latter, who tended to agree with the nationalists, Baldwin held many tenets in common with the particularists. He begins his *General View of the Constitution* (1837), in terms which would be approved by any nationalist, accepting the Constitution as " a law, paramount in authority over the people of the several states," and supreme in its very nature. The effect of this situation is that " the constitution, the creature, prescribes rules to its creator," and further restricts the actions of the states within specified limits.[199] In essence, the Constitution is a grant by the people of the several states.[200] But its operation " must, of necessity, be like that of a treaty of cession, by a foreign state to the United States." [201] " The constitution is a cession of jurisdiction only, made by the people of a state . . ."

> It was a cession, by nine states, of so much of their separate power as was necessary for federal purposes, to the body politic, called the United States, the " American Confederacy," " Republic," or " Empire; " as a term of designation, including states and territories. The constitution was the charter of this federal corporation, as those of the different states were the charters of their state corporations of government; each with power to legislate according to the terms of their respective charters, subject only to that charter which had been made supreme for its designated purposes.[202]

Beyond these points, Baldwin's position is not clear. If, however, his prefatory note is indicative of that which follows in detail, a summary of his ideas is this:

> By taking it [the Constitution] as the grant of the people of the several states, I find an easy solution of all questions aris-

199 Baldwin, *General View of the Constitution*, p. 12.

200 *Ibid.*, pp. 29 *et seq.*, 61.

201 *Ibid.*, p. 83.

202 *Ibid.*, p. 84.

ing under it; whereas, in taking it as the grant of the people of the United States in the aggregate, I am wholly unable to make its various provisions consistent with each other, or to find any safe rule of interpreting them separately.[203]

Timothy Walker, who wrote during the same year that Baldwin did (1837), develops the idea of a constitution from the simple democracy in which the sovereign people of the community exercise their power personally, to a representative democracy. The Constitution is a set of general and permanent instructions for these representatives in order that they will be sure to be the servants, not the masters of their constituents.

In other words, a constitution is a written expression of the sovereign will of the people, in relation to the form and powers of government. Proceeding from the people in their supreme capacity, as the highest earthly power, it could be transcended or abrogated by them only; while to their representatives, it would be a supreme and inviolable law.[204]

With these general propositions as a basis, Walker proceeds to a consideration of the Constitution of the United States. Reasoning like the nationalists, he concludes that " the states have ceased to be *supreme* or *sovereign,* in the strict sense of these words, since there is a power above them." [205] By virtue of the powers vested in the federal government, " the states have ceased to be sovereign in relation to all national objects, but retain a qualified or partial sovereignty, extending to all internal objects." [206]

---

203 *Ibid.,* p. 1. Baldwin adds, " In a matter of such importance as this, I cannot *assume* a proposition on which all my opinions depend, but must establish it by all the authority that can be brought to support it, against opposing opinions of great weight, and which are those most commonly received."

204 Walker, *American Law,* sec. 15.

205 *Ibid.,* sec. 65.

206 *Loc. cit.* Any doubt on this matter was removed by the Tenth Amendment.

According to Walker, the sovereign will of the people thus operated in the formation of the Constitution of the United States. ". . . the federal government is not the creature of the state governments; but emanates from, and expresses the sovereign will of all, the people of the United States, in their original and aggregate capacity." [207]

To Walker, as to Story, the supremacy of the Constitution is asserted in unequivocal language in the supreme law clause.

> It would be difficult to devise language stronger than this. The latter part may almost be considered supererogation; for the subordination of the state governments would have followed as a necessary consequence from the supremacy of the federal government.[208]

From this premise, Walker discerns four gradations of authority: first, the Federal Constitution which is paramount over all; second, treaties and acts of Congress; third, state constitutions; and fourth, acts of state legislatures.

> With respect to these four degrees of subordination, the invariable rule is, that in case of conflict, the lower must yield to the higher; each degree being subordinate to those which go before, and superior to those which come after. Thus, in order to be valid, treaties and acts of Congress must conform to the federal constitution; state constitutions must conform to the federal constitution, treaties and acts of Congress; and the acts of state legislatures must conform to all these, and to their particular state constitution. This idea of subordination among laws, springs from the very nature of written constitutions, limiting delegated power; and our federal organization only renders it somewhat more complicated.[209]

With regard to the interpretation of the Constitution, Walker again considers that document to be absolutely explicit. " In

207 *Ibid.,* sec. 60.

208 *Ibid.,* sec. 63.

209 *Loc. cit.*

order to preserve the subordination thus declared, the *judiciary* is empowered to decide, in the last resort, when either government has transcended its constitutional limits, and to declare such proceeding void." [210] The doctrine of nullification by any one of the states of federal acts which it considered unconstitutional, made it appear that the Constitution had not been sufficiently explicit. However, Walker thinks that the language of the Constitution is so clear that " of course nothing is left to be exercised by any other tribunal." [211]

Another point on which Walker is especially emphatic is that " the States cannot at pleasure secede from the Union."

> This is no where expressly declared in the Federal constitution, but it results necessarily from the fact that the obligations it creates are without reservation as to time. The Union was no doubt intended to be perpetual. The preamble declares one of the objects to be " to secure the blessings of liberty to ourselves and our *posterity*." [212]

Furthermore, if a state could withdraw at pleasure, the Union would not be a " more perfect Union " as the preamble declares. Walker does not deny the ultimate right of revolution by which one or more states might effectually secede.

> But they could not do it in virtue of any right reserved under the constitution, unless they amounted to three-fourths of the states. Then they might amend, and of course destroy the constitution. But in no constitutional way can a minority separate themselves from the Union . . . So long . . . as a

210 *Ibid.*, sec. 64.

211 *Loc. cit.* Walker held a high opinion of the function of judicial review: " One cannot easily conceive of a more sublime exercise of power, than that by which a few men, through the mere force of reason, without soldiers, and without tumult, pomp, or parade, but calmly, noiselessly, and fearlessly, proceed to set aside the acts of either government, because repugnant to the constitution."

212 *Ibid.*, sec. 67.

majority of the people of the United States are contented with the existing government, the minority must acquiesce.[213]

As George Ticknor Curtis' primary concern was with the history of the formation of the Constitution, his points as to its nature are derived from the debates in the Convention. His interpretation of the nature of the Constitution is in the section discussing the method of ratification.

> . . . the design of the committee [of the whole] was to substitute the authority of the people of the States in the place of that of the State legislatures, for a three-fold purpose. First, it was deemed desirable to resort to the supreme authority of the people, in order to give the new system a higher sanction than could be given to it by the State governments. Secondly, it was thought expedient to get rid of the doctrine often asserted under the Confederation, that the Union was a mere compact or treaty between independent States, and that therefore a breach of its articles by any one State absolved the rest from its obligations. In the third place, it was intended, by this mode of ratification, to enable the people of a less number of the States than the whole to form a new Union, if all should not be willing to adopt the new system.[214]

The intention to subordinate the states to the new federal government was clearly indicated in the establishment of a judicial department with powers co-extensive with the legislative. Of itself, this establishment of the judiciary " evinces an intention to clothe that government with powers that could be executed peacefully, and without the necessity of putting down the

---

213 *Loc. cit.* The copy of the first edition of Walker's book owned by the Law School at the University of California contains the pencilled notes of W. K. Hough. His signature and the date 1858 appear on the title page, and on the dedication page is the signature of A. M. Hough, Jefferson City, Mo. After the last quotation given above, the following note appears: "Absurd. Constitutions were made to protect minorities. When the majority pervert the govt. [*sic*] for despotic purposes, the minority may justifiably resort to Revolution."

214 Curtis, *History of the Constitution of the United States* (1858), II, 85.

organized opposition of subordinate communities." [215] The functions of the federal judiciary further evolved as, under the Constitution, it went into operation over state laws—one part of this evolution. Curtis makes the interesting point that "the indirect effect of judicial action on the laws of the States after they had been passed, was far preferable to a direct interference with those laws while in the process of enactment." Authority over all questions involving national peace and harmony had given ample power in this instance. [216]

Curtis devotes a chapter to the subject of the national supremacy. He finds proof of the intention of the framers in several places in the Constitution. The preamble itself was changed from including the names of all thirteen of the states, to " We, the people of the United States, etc." Additional proofs are the supreme position of the national executive, legislative, and judiciary departments; the supreme law of the land clause; the provision that all officials of the state and national governments must take an oath upholding the Constitution; and the method prescribed for ratification of the document. [217]

Admitting that the powers of sovereignty are divided, and that the states possess supremacy over certain subjects, Curtis gives the purpose of the framers of the Constitution as to provide a " paramount rule, that would determine the occasions on which the authority of a State should cease to be supreme, leaving that of the United States unobstructed."

> Certain conditions were made necessary to the operation of this rule. The State law must conflict with some provision of the Constitution of the United States, or with a law of the United States enacted in pursuance of the constitutional authority of Congress, or with a treaty duly made by the authority of the Union. The operation of this rule constitutes the supremacy of the national government. It was supposed that,

215 *Ibid.*, II, 63, 65. *Cf.* Walker's views, *supra*, p. 304 and note 211.

216 *Ibid.*, II, 67.

217 *Ibid.*, II, ch. xii, esp. pp. 372-374.

by a careful enumeration of the objects to which the national authority was to extend, there would be no uncertainty as to the occasions on which the rule was to apply; and as all other objects were to remain exclusively subject to the authority of the States within their respective territorial limits, the operation of the rule was carefully limited to those occasions.[218]

It may be noted that Curtis shows a marked similarity to Walker in his discussion of this subject as he also does in his emphasis on the importance of the arrangement that every conflict between the authority of the federal and state governments is made a judicial question and handled peacefully. " This peculiar device has enabled the government of the United States to act successfully and safely." [219] And here Curtis differs with the Southern idea of state nullification, but by implication only:

> Without it [the device of the judiciary], each State must have been left to determine for itself the boundaries between its own powers and those of the Union; and thus there might have been as many different determinations on the same question as the number of the States.[220]

Again by indirection, Curtis explains that the success of the Constitution is to be measured primarily by " the practical efficiency with which the powers of the Union have operated, and the general readiness to acquiesce in the limitations given to those powers by the department in which their construction is vested." This acquiescence has steadily increased,

> and it has now come to be well understood, that there is no alternative to take the place of a ready submission to the national will, as expressed by or under the Constitution interpreted by the proper national organ, excepting a resort to methods that lie wholly without the Constitution, and that would completely subvert the principles on which it was founded.[221]

218 *Ibid.*, II, 378-379.

219 *Ibid.*, II, 379.

220 *Loc. cit.*

221 *Ibid.*, II, 380.

Within two years after Curtis wrote these words, one section of the country had ended its " submission to the national will," and his fears of extra-constitutional measures had come true.

The differences in the theories presented in the last two chapters have not always been clear cut, and it is apparent that the commentators did not all agree on the meanings of the words which they used. The framers thought of the Constitution in terms of the compact theory, but two major changes soon took place. First, the idea of the compact itself evolved from the binding arrangement of the eighteenth century, to a temporary agreement in the nineteenth, subject to the continuing approval of both parties. Second, the organic theory was emerging which held that the state was not an artificial being, created by consent among men, but was a superior entity within itself. This idea has not been discussed in the text because it was not clear until after the Civil War.

However, it should be noted that the particularists used the terms of this theory when they argued that the separate states could never form a union: the end of agreement is only an agreement. Thus, if the states were proved independent and sovereign before the Constitution, they would forever remain so, and were free to secede from the Union at any time. On the other hand, the nationalists looked below the surface and saw that the states individually could never have gained nor kept their independence, thus making the Union anterior idealogically to the states. Neither side seemed to recognize at the time that they were using the ideas of a new theory, utterly foreign to the framers of the Constitution, while adhering to the terminology of an old one.[222] A war was fought, more thinkers analyzed the problem, and several more books were written before it became apparent that some very basic changes had taken place in the nature of the Union, making the old ideas inadequate as explanations of the realities that men saw about them.

222 *Cf.* McLaughlin in *Amer. Hist. Rev.*, V, 467-490, for an able discussion of this transition in thought. He points out that it was only by means of the organic theory of the Union that the nationalists were able to meet the particularists on their own ground, and it is this theory which has almost universal acceptance in the twentieth century.

# CHAPTER VIII

## STORY'S *COMMENTARIES ON THE CONSTITUTION*

### SECTION I

IN the last two chapters, we have examined the commentaries with the object of giving the reader some indication of the viewpoints expressed in them on two of the major subjects of controversy. Now, we may proceed to analyze one of the commentaries in its entirety. No problem is involved in the selection of Story as the subject of this study. His work was the most comprehensive, probably the most widely read and discussed by Southerners and Northerners alike, and still occupies a central position in the pre-Civil War studies of this nature. To avoid a purely technical discussion of the points presented, the emphasis will be upon Story's basic theory of nationalism as it appears in his *Commentaries*.

In the exposition of the Constitution, Story divided his work into three sections. The first contains a sketch of the charters, constitutional history, and ante-revolutionary jurisprudence of the colonies. The second embraces the constitutional history of the states during the Revolution, and the rise, progress, decline, and fall of the Confederation. The third is

> the history of the rise and adoption of the Constitution; and a full exposition of all its provisions, with the reasons, on which they were respectively founded, the objections, by which they were respectively assailed, and such illustrations drawn from contemporaneous documents, and the subsequent operations of the government, as may best enable the reader to estimate for himself the true value of each.[1]

1 Preliminary chapter, I, 1-2. These three categories appear as three separate books in both the full-length and abridged versions, both of which will be cited hereafter. The *Class Book* and *Familiar Exposition* contain the divisions implicitly, though no explicit segregations into books occur between the chapters.

## Book I.   History of the Colonies

In recounting the history of the colonies, Story asserts that though they had a common origin, owed a common allegiance, and were inhabited by British subjects, they had no direct political connection with each other. Occasionally, they made efforts to associate for common purposes of defense, but " these confederacies were of a casual and temporary nature, and were allowed as an indulgence, rather than as a right." [2] Efforts toward the establishment of some general superintending government over them all failed because of their own differences of opinion as well as the opposition of the Crown.[3] However, they were fellow subjects, and for many purposes, one people.[4] Thus, these early efforts " prepared their minds for the gradual reconciliation of their local interests, and for the gradual developement [sic] of the principles, upon which a union ought to rest . . ." [5]

## Book II.   History of the Revolution

The second book is primarily concerned with refuting the particularist argument that the states were sovereign at the time that they joined together to fight the Revolution.[6] These points have been presented in full in the two preceding chapters of this section and need not be reiterated here. The only significant quotation which we may add is one in which Story comes close to the pragmatic school of thought. He says,

> . . . as soon as congress assumed powers and passed measures, which were in their nature national, to that extent the

2 Story, *Commentaries*, sec. 177; Abr., sec. 90.

3 *Loc. cit.*

4 *Ibid.*, sec. 178; Abr., sec. 91. *Cf. infra*, chs. vi and vii, for disagreement by the Southerners.

5 *Ibid.*, sec. 177; Abr., sec. 90.

6 This statement is particularly true of the full-length version and the Abridgment. The argument is not presented in the *Class Book* or in the *Familiar Exposition*, in which the account is historical rather than argumentative, the conclusions being given without the reasoning which led to them.

people, from whose acquiescence and consent they took effect, must be considered as agreeing to form a nation.[7]

These first two books were perhaps more open to criticism than the latter part of the *Commentaries*. Story came to his task with his mind made up as to the relative positions of the states and the federal government in the American Union. He used history as a tool to implement his conclusions. As has been noted, Upshur and the two Tucker brothers questioned his accuracy shortly after he wrote, and we shall have occasion to mention the post-Civil War treatise of Alexander Stephens who made another careful attempt to undermine Story's entire structure by hitting at the flaws in the historical statement.[8]

*Book III.   Constitution of the United States*

A rather lengthy section devoted to the nature of the Constitution and its interpretation precedes the actual clause by clause analysis in the full-length version of the *Commentaries*. Here Story calls attention to the serious differences of opinion between those who favor the superior power of the Union and those who favor the states.[9] In the circumstances, he suggests that the wonder was not the argument over the Constitution, but its adoption by a majority of the states.[10] Looking again at our history, he concludes that it may be that

> there will forever continue to be a strong line of division between those, who adhere to the state governments, and those,

7 Story, *Commentaries*, sec. 213; *cf.* Abr., sec. 111.

8 For example, Story was criticized for regarding the colonists as "one people" before the Revolution. *Commentaries*, sec. 178; Abr., sec. 91. Upshur contends (*True Nature of Our Federal Government*, pp. 10-14) that such unity as they had, they derived from their common relation to the British crown, not as the result of any agreement among themselves. Therefore, they broke up into separate entities when the connecting bond of the crown was removed. Recent historians generally agree upon the existence of great differences among the various colonies, and emphasize the divisive factors that had to be overcome before they could act together effectively.

9 Story, *Commentaries*, sec. 285.

10 *Ibid.*, sec. 287.

who adhere to the national government, in respect to principles and policy.[11]

Using the appeal of ambition, Story charges, rather unfairly, that those who support the state governments are likely to be in search of personal popularity, or seeking to advance local interests. Such men have " no eager desire for a wide spread fame, or no acquirements to justify it." [12]

> On the other hand, if the votaries of the national government are fewer in number, they are likely to enlist in its favour men of ardent ambition, comprehensive views, and powerful genius.[13]

The glowing description of the admirable factors that go to make up the Union as against the petty interests of the states, was well calculated to leave the reader with little inclination to absent himself from the national councils.

Certain general objections to the Constitution are presented, each followed by the answer as given by the friends of the instrument. The first of these attacked the entire scheme for establishing a government over individuals rather than a confederation of states.[14] The counter-argument asserts the indispensable necessity of the form of government proposed, and demonstrates " the utter imbecility of a mere confederation, without powers acting directly upon individuals." However, it is noted that there were limits on the powers of the national government and that a large mass of sovereignty was retained by the states. Thus, the Constitution was neither federal nor national, but a mixture of both.[15]

11 *Ibid.*, sec. 289.

12 *Loc. cit.*

13 *Ibid.*, sec. 290.

14 *Ibid.*, sec. 293; Abr., sec. 140.

15 *Ibid.*, sec. 294; Abr., sec. 141. Ref. to the *Federalist*, No. 39, and 1 Tucker's *Blackstone's Commentaries*, App., 145, 146.

The second objection had to do with the nature and extent of the powers of the Constitution, and in this, Story notes that the opponents were unable to agree as to the exact nature of the danger.[16] While one group might think a term of office was too long, another thought its danger lay in its shortness.

The third type of objection was on the score of deficiencies and omissions, and mainly demanded a bill of rights. Many of these protests found their way into the amendments. Story observes that the chief opposition to the amendments when they reached the state legislatures came from the very party that had raised the objections in the first place. " The friends of the constitution generally supported them upon the ground of a large public policy, to quiet jealousies, and to disarm resentments." [17] With regard to the argument for a Bill of Rights, Story agrees with the *Federalist* [18] that the Constitution had one, even without the first ten amendments.

> It was emphatically found in those clauses, which respected political rights, the guaranty of republican forms of government, the trial of crimes by jury, the definition of treason, the prohibition against bills of attainder and *ex post facto* laws and titles of nobility, the trial by impeachment, and the writ of *habeas corpus*.[19]

As for the objections, Story submits that time has

> assuaged the fears, and disproved the prophesies of the opponents of the constitution . . . The states still flourish under it with a salutary and invigorating energy; and its power of direct action upon the people has hitherto proved a common blessing, giving dignity and spirit to the government, adequate to the exigencies of war, and preserving us from domestic

16 Story, *Commentaries*, secs. 296-297; Abr., secs. 142-143.

17 *Ibid.*, secs. 300-303; Abr., secs. 144-147.

18 Ref. to *Federalist*, No. 84 (Hamilton).

19 Story, *Commentaries*, sec. 304.

dissensions, and unreasonable burthens [*sic*] in times of peace.[20]

Following Marshall, Story points out that one of the fundamental rules in the exposition of every instrument is, " so to construe its terms, if possible, as not to make them the source of their own destruction, or to make them utterly void, and nugatory." [21] In other words, if any implications are to be made beyond the terms of a constitution of government, they should be implications to preserve and not to destroy it.[22]

With regard to the interpretation of the Constitution in cases of controversy, Story believes that there is no doubt that the power to construe belongs to the judiciary. The only point on which there might conceivably be disagreement is whether the decision of the judiciary is conclusive and binding on the states and the people of the states.[23] To support his argument that the judiciary does so bind, Story asserts that the judicial power of the United States is conclusive in all cases to which its authority extends. Furthermore, if each state could decide for itself on the interpretation of the Constitution, " there would be at no time in the United States the same constitution in operation over the whole people." [24] Article IV of the Constitution provides that full faith and credit shall be given in each state to the judicial proceedings of every other state. Since no like provision is made with regard to the judgments of the federal courts, Story concludes that they are " plainly supposed to be of paramount and absolute obligation throughout all the states." [25]

Story's second argument in favor of the supremacy of the federal judiciary is, that

20 *Ibid.*, sec. 295. Story's next subject, the refutation of the compact theory, has already been discussed in ch. vii, *infra*.

21 *Ibid.*, sec. 369.

22 *Loc. cit.*

23 *Ibid.*, sec. 376; Abr., sec. 166. Refs. to Dane's Appendix, sec. 42, pp. 49-50; sec. 44, pp. 52-53; 1 Wilson's *Lectures*, 461-463.

24 Story, *Commentaries*, sec. 380.

25 *Ibid.*, sec. 378.

as the judicial power extends to all cases arising under the constitution, and that constitution is declared to be the supreme law, that supremacy would naturally be construed to extend, not only over the citizens, but over the states . . . The people of any state cannot, then, by any alteration of their state constitution, destroy, or impair that supremacy.[26]

If it should happen that the judiciary should make a wrong decision, Congress might be required to interpose, or in the last resort, the states would have to amend the Constitution, to redress the grievance.[27]

Finally, Story contends that the Constitution has been in operation forty years, and that during this period, the Supreme Court has constantly used its power of interpreting the Constitution, the laws and treaties of the Union, and state constitutions and laws insofar as they affect the Constitution.

> Their decisions upon these grave questions have never been repudiated, or impaired by congress. No state has ever deliberately or forcibly resisted the execution of the judgments founded upon them; and the highest state tribunals have, with scarcely a single exception, acquiesced in, and, in most instances, assisted in executing them.[28]

It is clear that Story considers these facts as his trump card. He says further,

> . . . it may be asserted with entire confidence, that for forty years three fourths of all the states composing the Union have expressly assented to, or silently approved, this construction of the constitution, and have resisted every effort to restrict, or alter it.[29]

26 *Ibid.*, sec. 383; Abr., sec. 169. Ref. to *Federalist*, No. 33.

27 *Ibid.*, sec. 384; Abr., sec. 170.

28 *Ibid.*, sec. 391; Abr., sec. 175. This is one of the generalizations which memories of Worcester *v.* Georgia, etc., cause one to question. (Punctuation throughout follows full-length version.)

29 *Loc. cit.*

Justice Story sets forth a list of nineteen rules for interpreting the Constitution. Those most important for our purposes are the following: The Constitution " is to be construed as a *frame* or *fundamental law* of government, established by the PEOPLE of the United States, according to their own free pleasure and sovereign will." [30] The state and federal constitutions should not be construed alone, but with reference to each other, as each belongs to the same system of government, and each is essential to the existence and due preservation of the power and obligations of the other.[31]

The interpretation of the language and powers, if it is to be reasonable, should keep in view the purposes for which the powers were conferred. In case there are two meanings for a given word, the one strict, the other more liberal,

> that should be adopted, which is most consonant with the apparent objects and intent of the constitution; that, which will give it efficacy and force as a *government* . . .[32]

Story contends that to be reasonable, all notions of subjecting the Constitution to a strict interpretation should be thrown aside.[33] Where the power is granted in general terms, the power is to be construed as co-extensive with the terms, unless some clear restriction upon it is given in the text.[34] Every power given to Congress is by the Constitution necessarily supreme. If, by wording or implication, it is apparently intended to be exclusive, the effect is the same as if the states were expressly forbidden to exercise it.[35]

Following his lengthy introduction, Story proceeds to an analysis of the Constitution, clause by clause. He gives in con-

30 *Ibid.*, sec. 409; Abr., sec. 186.

31 *Ibid.*, sec. 416; Abr., sec. 187.

32 *Ibid.*, sec. 419; Abr., sec. 188.

33 *Ibid.*, sec. 423.

34 *Ibid.*, sec. 424; Abr., sec. 191.

35 *Ibid.*, sec. 437; Abr., sec. 200.

nection with each, the debates on it in the Federal Convention, arguments from other commentators or general writers against it, and then a strong defense of the provision as he understands its statement in the Constitution. He includes subsequent court decisions, and any general philosophical considerations on points of policy or law which may occur to him.

In his treatment of the Preamble, Story discusses each of the purposes for the formation of the national union separately. He takes up the economic interests of each of the major groups of states, concluding after an examination of all of them, that the " peculiar interests of some of the states, . . . would, upon a separation, be wholly sacrificed, or become the source of immeasurable calamities." [36] It is only by the maintenance of the " more perfect Union " that their interests are properly secured. Granting that justice lies at the basis of a free government, and demonstrating from our history that injustice was done to our own people and to foreigners under the states before the ratification of the Constitution,[37] a view of our subsequent history indicates to Story that justice had been achieved with union. Story thinks common defense provisions necessary because they pointed the way toward preserving peace.[38] The national government filled a vital function in providing a unity of operations, the absence of which rendered the individual efforts of the states divided, " inert and inadequate." [39]

The clause stating that the promotion of the general welfare is a major concern of the new government, excites interest, inasmuch as the same provision appears in all state constitutions. In answer to the normal question as to why this repetition occurred, Story replies that the states, separately, would not possess the means to guarantee the general welfare. For instance, a unification of commerce is invaluable to the welfare of

36 *Ibid.*, sec. 477; Abr., sec. 231.

37 *Ibid.*, sec. 482 *et seq.*; Abr., sec. 236 *et seq.*

38 *Ibid.*, sec. 494; Abr., sec. 246.

39 *Ibid.*, sec. 495; Abr., sec. 247. Ref. to *Federalist*, Nos. 24, 25.

the people, but the jealousies of the individual states would prevent its achievement. Furthermore, even if the states did possess the means, they would not have the power to carry the appropriate measures into operation.[40] With respect to the national government, Story feels that

> Generally speaking, it will be better administered; because it will command higher talents, more extensive experience, more practical knowledge, and more various information of the wants of the whole community, than can belong to smaller societies.[41]

The aims of the state and national governments again run parallel with regard to the clause securing the blessings of liberty to ourselves and our posterity. According to Story, the question is whether the states " of themselves furnish a complete and satisfactory security." [42] Calling attention to his earlier arguments, he reiterates that the states cannot furnish this security, and devotes the remainder of the chapter to refuting the claim that the national government would destroy the states.[43] He points out that while the states can exist—legally and theoretically, at least—without the national government, the national government cannot exist without the states. The election of important national officials is directly dependent upon the states. Furthermore, according to Story's way of reasoning, the powers of the general government must necessarily be employed primarily in external affairs, such as war, peace, negotiations with foreign powers, and foreign commerce. He says that the national government can touch little of the internal life of the nation, its powers being restricted to commerce, intercourse, and other relations between the states, and certain powers of taxation. The states, on the other hand, manage all matters

40 *Ibid.*, secs. 496-505; Abr., secs. 248-253.

41 *Ibid.*, sec. 505; Abr., sec. 253.

42 *Ibid.*, sec. 507; Abr., sec. 255.

43 *Ibid.*, sec. 508 *et seq.*; Abr., sec. 256 *et seq.*

which closely touch the lives of the people.[44] Again, Story uses history to clinch his argument:

> Hitherto our experience has demonstrated the entire safety of the states, under the benign operations of the constitution. Each of the states has grown in power, in vigour of operation, in commanding influence, in wealth, revenue, population, commerce, agriculture, and general efficiency.[45]

As in an earlier connection, the argument for nationalism in the section on the legislative branch may, in part, be described as psychological. By exalting the position of the men who sit in national councils and passing off state politicians with a light touch, Story rather deftly draws the sympathies of his readers toward the more important tasks of the national government.[46]

Story thinks it entirely proper that members of Congress should receive their compensation from the national treasury rather than from the state which they represent. " The labour is for the benefit of the nation, and it should properly be remunerated by the nation." [47] Had the compensation been left for the state legislatures to establish, " the general government would have become dependent upon the governments of the states; and the latter could almost, at their pleasure, have dissolved it." [48]

In analyzing the powers of Congress, Story gives the greatest attention to the taxing power. His argument is that if " there is to be a real, effective national government," the power of taxation must be " co-extensive with its powers, wants, and duties." [49] Story admits that the members of the Federal Convention intended the Constitution to be the " frame of a na-

44 *Ibid.*, secs. 510-512; Abr., secs. 258-260.

45 *Ibid.*, sec. 514; Abr., sec. 261.

46 *Ibid.*, Book III, chs. viii-xi, *passim*. Abr., same.

47 *Ibid.*, sec. 854; Abr., sec. 433.

48 *Loc. cit.* Ref. to 2 *Elliot's Debates*, 279.

49 *Ibid.*, sec. 930; Abr., sec. 467.

tional government, of special and enumerated powers, and not of general and unlimited powers." [50] Thus, the general and unlimited interpretation of the taxation clause must be rejected, and that which makes the latter part a qualification on the former must be accepted. The clause, so interpreted, would read,

> The congress shall have power to lay and collect taxes, duties, imposts, and excises, *in order* to pay the debts, and to provide for the common defence and general welfare of the United States.[51]

However, after a lengthy consideration of the arguments on the exact meaning of this clause, Story concludes that "the power to lay taxes is not by the constitution confined to purposes of revenue." He states that it was never limited to such purposes by Congress, and the constant interpretation of the Constitution by the functionaries of the government has been that it was not constitutionally so limited.[52]

The lack of the commerce power, Story agrees, was one of the leading defects of the Confederation. "It is a power vital to the prosperity of the Union; and without it the government would scarcely deserve the name of a national government; and would soon sink into discredit and imbecility." [53] He contends that without the power to control commerce between the states, the power to regulate foreign commerce would be incomplete and ineffectual.[54] In answer to the question of whether or not the regulation of commerce is exclusive with the national government or concurrent with the states, as is the case with the taxation power, Story calls attention to the decisions of the Supreme Court that the power is general and unlimited in its

50 *Ibid.*, sec. 906.

51 *Ibid.*, sec. 905; Abr., sec. 464.

52 *Ibid.*, sec. 970.

53 *Ibid.*, sec. 1053; Abr., sec. 507.

54 *Ibid.*, sec. 1062; Abr., sec. 515.

terms, and thus leaves no residuum.[55] Although the police powers of the states have a connection with commerce,

> These powers are entirely distinct in their nature from that to regulate commerce; and though the same means may be resorted to, for the purpose of carrying each of these powers into effect, this by no just reasoning furnishes any ground to assert, that they are identical.[56]

The war power vested in Congress seems to Story to be one that no one could deny who believed that the national government " ought to have any powers whatsoever, either for offence or defence, for the common good, or for the common protection." [57] He feels that to be of any value, the power must be unlimited, inasmuch as national exigencies could not be foreseen.

> The power must be co-extensive with all possible combinations of circumstances, and under the direction of the councils entrusted with the common defence. To deny this would be to deny the means, and yet require the end.[58]

55 *Ibid.*, sec. 1063; Abr., sec. 516.

56 *Ibid.*, sec. 1066; Abr., sec. 519. Story adds, citing Gibbons *v.* Ogden, 9 Wheat. 1 at 203-209, that among the police powers are "inspection laws, health laws, laws regulating turnpikes, roads, and ferries, all of which, when exercised by a state, are legitimate, arising from the general powers belonging to it, unless so far as they conflict with the powers delegated to congress. They are not so much regulations of commerce, as of police; and may truly be said to belong, if at all to commerce, to that which is purely internal. The pilotage laws of the states may fall under the same description. But they have been adopted by congress, and without question are controllable by it." Referring to Kent's discussion of Gibbons *v.* Ogden, in which he (Kent, as chief justice of the Supreme Court of Errors and Appeals, New York) had been reversed by Marshall, Story says that this doctrine on the power of Congress in the regulation of commerce "has not been of late seriously controverted; and it seems to have the cheerful acquiescence of the learned tribunals of a particular state, one of whose acts brought it first under judicial examination." Ref. to 1 Kent's *Commentaries*, Lect. 19, p. 404 *et seq.*, 1st ed. (2nd ed., p. 432 *et seq.*). Story, *Commentaries*, secs. 1066-1067; Abr., sec. 516.

57 *Ibid.*, sec. 1164; Abr., sec. 568.

58 *Ibid.*, sec. 1178; Abr., sec. 577.

As to dangers from an undue exercise of the war power, Story considers them imaginary.

> It can never be exerted, but by the representatives of the people of the states; and it must be safe there, or there can be no safety at all in any republican form of government.[59]

No difficulty resulted from the authority of the executive, as the legislative branch controlled the granting of supplies.[60] Furthermore, " The power of the president . . . might well be deemed safe; since he could not, of himself, declare war, raise armies, or call forth the militia, or appropriate money for the purpose; for these powers all belonged to congress." [61]

The " necessary and proper " clause had aroused the wrath of those who favored state power, so Story is careful to point out its true significance.

> The plain import of the clause is, that congress shall have all the incidental and instrumental powers, necessary and proper to carry into execution all the express powers. It neither enlarges any power specifically granted; nor is it a grant of any new power to congress. But it is merely a declaration for the removal of all uncertainty, that the means of carrying into execution those, otherwise granted, are included in the grant.[62]

When the question of the constitutionality of a given power arises, the Constitution must be consulted. " If it be not *expressed,* the next inquiry must be, whether it is properly an incident to an express power, and necessary to its execution. If it

59 *Ibid.*, sec. 1182. Ref. to the *Federalist,* Nos. 23, 26, 28.

60 *Ibid.*, sec. 1184, with ref. to the *Federalist,* No. 26. *Cf.* Story's additional contention that the army " may be disbanded at the pleasure of the legislature, and it would be absolutely impossible for any president, against the will of the nation, to keep up a standing army in *terrorem populi.*" *Loc. cit.*

61 *Ibid.*, sec. 1486. Ref. to 3 *Elliot's Debates,* 103. Story did not live to witness Lincoln's actions early in the Civil War.

62 *Ibid.*, sec. 1238; Abr., sec. 603.

be, then it may be exercised by congress. If not, congress cannot exercise it." [63]

The fact that "necessary" is to be construed in a broad instead of a strict sense is evident from the inclusion of the word "proper" immediately following it.[64] Furthermore, the clause is included among the powers of congress, and not among the checks on those powers. By affirming the use of all necessary and proper means to effectuate the other powers, it thus becomes an *express* power where it would otherwise have been merely *implied*. If the framers had intended to make this clause anything but an enlargement of the national power, they would have done so, as they knew "that the national government would be more endangered in its adoption by its supposed strength, than by its weakness." [65]

Story rather enjoys the fact that the "most remarkable powers, which have been exercised by the government, as auxiliary and implied powers," and which "go to the utmost verge of liberal construction"—the embargo of 1807, the purchase of Louisiana in 1803 and subsequent admission to the Union, and the later purchase of Florida—were proposed, supported, and carried by strict constructionists. These measures "were justified at the time, and can be now justified, only upon the doctrines of those, who support a liberal construction of the constitution." [66] Story then points up this moral on the interpretation of constitutions:

[63] *Loc. cit.* In sec. 1240; Abr., sec. 605, Story refers to Hamilton's argument on the constitutionality of the Bank, "that every power, vested in a government, is in its nature sovereign, and includes, by force of the term, a right to employ all the means requisite, and fairly applicable to the attainment of the end of such power; unless they are excepted in the constitution, or are immoral, or are contrary to the essential objects of political society." Ref. to 1 *Hamilton's Works*, 112.

[64] Story, *Commentaries*, sec. 1248; Abr., sec. 613.

[65] *Ibid.*, sec. 1249; Abr., sec. 613.

[66] *Ibid.*, sec. 1277; Abr., sec. 640.

The mere [*sic*] recent acquisition of Florida, which has been universally approved, or acquiesced in by all the states, can be maintained only on the same principles; and furnishes a striking illustration of the truth, that constitutions of government require a liberal construction to effect their objects, and that a narrow interpretation of their powers, however it may suit the views of speculative philosophers or the accidental interests of political parties, is incompatible with the permanent interests of the state, and subversive of the great ends of all government, the safety and independence of the people.[67]

From Story's analysis, it would appear that there were fewer controversies over the powers of the executive branch than there had been on those of the legislative. Much of the difficulty concerned details of selection and length of term. The executive is eminently a national power, inasmuch as the President and Vice President are elected by the entire nation.

Story takes it for granted that there ought to be a national executive department, and proceeds from there. He also assumes that strength is necessary, for " A feeble executive is but another phrase for a bad execution; and a government ill executed, whatever may be its theory, must, in practice, be a bad government." [68] In the American system, the limitations on the executive are such that the danger is not that he will become an absolute dictator, " but, that he may be overwhelmed by the combined operations of popular influence and legislative power." [69]

The great duty of the executive department is to see that the laws under the Constitution are executed. If it fails, the government will be " worthless for offence, or defence; for the redress of grievances, or the protection of rights; for the happiness, or good order, or safety of the people." [70]

67 *Ibid.*, sec. 1283.

68 *Ibid.*, sec. 1411; Abr., sec. 723. Much of the argument following is concerned with establishing the superiority of a single over a plural executive.

69 *Ibid.*, sec. 1433.

70 *Ibid.*, sec. 1558; Abr., sec. 810.

Story considers a judiciary with powers co-extensive with the legislative branch, necessary to the existence of the Union.[71]

> The laws and treaties, and even the constitution, of the United States, would become a dead letter without it. Indeed, in a complicated government, like ours, where there is an assemblage of republics, combined under a common head, the necessity of some controlling judicial power, to ascertain and enforce the powers of the Union, is, if possible, still more striking. The laws of the whole would otherwise be in continual danger of being contravened by the laws of the parts. The national government would be reduced to a servile dependence upon the states . . .[72]

According to Story, it would be utterly impossible to have any uniform administration or interpretation of the laws and powers of the Union without some superintending judiciary establishment. This would be true even if there were no danger of collision between the laws of the Union and those of the states.[73]

Another advantage in the federal judiciary is in the provisions for its jurisdiction in controversies involving states.

> Nothing can conduce more to general harmony and confidence among all the states, than a consciousness, that controversies are not exclusively to be decided by the state tribunals; but may, at the election of the party, be brought before the national tribunals.[74]

Borrowing the language from his own decision in Martin v. Hunter's Lessee [75] as later sustained in Cohens v. Virginia, [76] Story points out that it was an historical fact that the extension of the appellate power of the Supreme Court to state courts was

71 *Ibid.*, sec. 1568; Abr., sec. 818.

72 *Ibid.*, sec. 1569; Abr., sec. 819.

73 *Loc. cit.*

74 *Ibid.*, sec. 1685; Abr., sec. 883.

75 1 Wheaton 304 at 322-362 (1816).

76 6 Wheaton 264 at 413-423 (1821).

accepted before the adoption of the Constitution; that this appellate jurisdiction had been sustained in a great variety of cases, brought from some of the most important states of the Union; and that " no state tribunal has ever breathed a judicial doubt on the subject, or declined to obey the mandate of the supreme court until the present occasion." [77]

Story subscribes to Marshall's theory of judicial review. The clause asserting the supremacy of those national laws which are made in pursuance of the Constitution, " only declares a truth, which flows immediately and necessarily from the institution of a national government." [78]

> From this supremacy of the constitution and laws and treaties of the United States, within their constitutional scope, arises the duty of courts of justice to declare any unconstitutional law passed by congress or by a state legislature void. So, in like manner, the same duty arises, whenever any other department of the national or state governments exceeds its constitutional functions . . . . [The] right of all courts, state as well as national, to declare unconstitutional laws void, seems settled beyond the reach of judicial controversy.[79]

In his " Concluding Remarks," Justice Story calls attention to the agitated condition of the Union and the threats of dissolution, the existence of which may have been a determining factor in his writing of the *Commentaries on the Constitution*. He notes that the South already had more representatives than the North,[80] but that the South still felt that the interests of other parts of the Union were better protected. The West was

[77] Story, *Commentaries*, sec. 1741; Abr., sec. 911. The " present occasion " refers to the case of Martin *v.* Hunter's Lessee. The Abridgment does not show that this section is quoted, and hence refers to "a late occasion."

[78] *Ibid.*, sec. 1831; Abr., sec. 965. Ref. to the *Federalist*, No. 33, Gibbons *v.* Ogden (9 Wheaton 1 at 210, 211), McCulloch *v.* Maryland (4 Wheaton 316 at 405, 406).

[79] Story, *Commentaries*, sec. 1836; Abr., sec. 967. The Abridgment reads, " . . . the right of courts . . . is now settled . . . "

[80] " twenty-five, beyond its due proportion . . . "

beginning to sense its growing power, and the Atlantic states were learning "that the sceptre must one day depart from them." If in these circumstances, the Union should break up, Story saw that it would be impossible ever to form a new constitution, embracing the whole territory. Rather must the nation disintegrate into " several nations or confederacies, rivals in power and interest, too proud to brook injury, and too close to make retaliation distant or ineffectual." [81]

Story affirms that " The national constitution is our last, and our only security. United we stand; divided we fall." [82] He addresses his final appeal to the people, from whom the Constitution had come and by whom it must be sustained. His hope for the *Commentaries* was hardly a modest one. He desired that they would " inspire the rising generation [with] a more ardent love of their country, an unquenchable thirst for liberty, and a profound reverence for the constitution and the Union . . ." [83]

## Section II

With this brief statement of Story's doctrines on the Constitution, it may be useful to consider the evidence provided by the *Commentaries* on Story's philosophy of constitutional law.

In contrast to the static approach of the compact school, Story adopted the organic, or evolutionary theory of the Constitution.[84] As was noted in chapters vi and vii above, Story apparently did not understand the implications of this approach as fully as did Chipman and Lieber in his own time, or as his successors have developed it more recently. Story hints rather than definitely states that for the purposes of the nation, the situation as it existed in 1832 was of more significance than it was

81 Story, *Commentaries*, sec. 1906; Abr., sec. 1015.

82 *Loc. cit.*

83 *Ibid.*, sec. 1907; Abr., sec. 1016.

84 McLaughlin in *Amer. Hist. Rev.*, V, 487 note, does not agree that Story accepted the organic view, as he sometimes spoke in terms of the compact theory. However, Laski in the *Encyclopedia of Social Sciences*, " Social Contract," thinks that Story was one of the first major writers to break with the compact theory.

in 1776 or 1787. Under the evolutionary approach, it was possible to concede the entire states rights argument and then to say that the situation had changed by 1830.

Webster came closer to this idea, and Lincoln stated clearly what was implicit in Story's reasoning. Even if there had been no American people in 1776, they had since come into existence, and a present actuality was more significant in Lincoln's eyes than an historical one. For part of his argument, Lincoln could depend upon Story, whose stress on *de facto* power touched the pragmatic approach. The Constitution is what works. If it does not work out in practice, it can not exist *de jure* any more than it can *de facto*. In the application of this doctrine to the exigencies of the Civil War, Lincoln went a step further. He considered that his oath to preserve the Constitution meant that he should use every means to preserve the nation.

> Was it possible to lose the nation and yet preserve the Constitution [which is its organic law]? . . . I felt that measures otherwise unconstitutional might become lawful by becoming indispensable to the preservation of the Constitution through the preservation of the nation.[85]

Historically considered, much fault can be and has been found with Story's treatise. He came to his work with his mind already made up, and perhaps, closed:

> I was and always have been a lover, a devoted lover, of the constitution of the United States, and a friend to the union of the states. I never wished to bring the government to a mere confederacy of states; but to preserve the power of the general government given by all the states, in full exercise and sovereignty for the protection and preservation of all the states.[86]

85 Lincoln to A. G. Hodges, Apr. 4, 1864. J. G. Nicolay and John Hay, eds., *Abraham Lincoln, Complete Works*, II (New York: 1894), 508.

86 Story, *Life and Letters*, I, 128. *Cf.* Hermann Eduard von Holst, *The Constitutional and Political History of the United States*, I (Chicago: 1877), 66-67: "The Constitution has found many learned and intelligent commentators; but they have all considered its excellence to be an undoubted and universally admitted fact. What should have been only the result of their investigation, they made the premises of their arguments."

With these definite views as a basis, he proceeded to a study of the antecedents of the Constitution. Small wonder that he found precedents for union in the mid-seventeenth century, repeated until the culminating events of 1787-89. As Parrington has said, " With its pronounced bias, *The Commentaries* must be regarded as a partisan document, which like *The Federalist* has grown in authoritativeness with the triumph of its party principles." [87]

If Story had been willing to concede to the particularists that the states had been independent and sovereign at the time of the Revolution, but that their existence within the Federal Union had materially changed the situation (a *non sequitur* to the Southerners), he could have avoided much of the controversy that he entered by including his vulnerable historical section. Such, however, was not the method of argument in politics at the time. Some of the replies to Story's points have been included in the earlier chapters of this section, and after the Civil War, in his *Constitutional View of the War between the States*,[88] Alexander Stephens made another attempt to refute him.[89] Apparently, Story's legalism was such that he could not agree with those nationalists (Chipman and Duer, for example) who held that the Constitution was a binding compact. Story had advanced to the more prevalent nineteenth century idea that a compact was terminable. Like Kent, Story tended to give natural law an historical content, thus shifting the theoretical basis of positive law from natural law to history. He thus moved from dependence upon reason to dependence upon experience [90]—and made a bid for membership in the pragmatic school of legal philosophers.

---

87 Parrington, *Main Currents in American Thought*, II, 302.

88 Alexander Stephens, *A Constitutional View of the Late War between the States* (Philadelphia, 1868). 2 vols.

89 Parrington, *Main Currents in American Thought*, II, 302. Parrington says that Stephens " quite demolished Story's feeble attempt at an historical justification of the anti-compact theory."

90 Aumann, *Changing American Legal System*, p. 129.

Regardless of twentieth century criticisms, Story's *Commentaries on the Constitution* will probably retain their rank with Marshall's opinions and the *Federalist* as the classic interpretations of the Constitution and Union as settled by the Civil War. Certain it is that the work was received enthusiastically when it was published.[91] Said Edward Everett,

> We rejoice in its appearance;—in its appearance at this crisis. Earnestly do we desire, that it may perform the salutary office of aiding to win back the judgments of our Southern brethren to the sound doctrines of 1789. It seems impossible to us to resist the conviction, that the theories, which have been recently broached, carry us back to the rude and abortive confederacies and plans of confederacies of other days.[92]

Everett saw the *Commentaries* as a " scientific and systematic exposition of an entire framework of government," and thought that its effects would be hard to resist. The danger lay in the fact that " Temper is up and men hate each other for their logic." [93]

In direct contrast to Parrington's criticism of Story's obvious bias, a contemporary reviewer wrote,

> The author evidently most scrupulously endeavors to present in their full force and most advantageous light the doctrines to which he does not himself apparently assent.[94]

91 The *American Monthly Review* stated that during the first year the *Commentaries* "had an extensive sale, and has already gained the favorable regard of the public." IV (Dec. 1833), 501.

92 [Edward Everett], " Story's Constitutional Law," *North American Review*, XXXVIII (Jan. 1834), 84. Everett thought that the doctrine of nullification was well named, as it would mean that the experience of two centuries went for nothing and the " sole and express object for framing the Constitution is set at naught." *Loc. cit.*

93 *Ibid.*, XXXVIII, 66.

94 Anon., " Story's Commentaries—Vols. II and III," *American Jurist and Law Magazine*, X (July 1833), 124. The work was " the more instructive and the more interesting because it is practical as well as philosophical and speculative." *Ibid.*, X, 119.

Another author regarded Story as best qualified to write the *Commentaries,* not only because of his habits of severe study, his accurate investigation of written instruments and his long official experience, but also because of his powerful and penetrating mind. His work was particularly timely, coming " when many of the questions he has discussed have an interest from the movements which they lately excited in the South." [95]

An American critic said the work was " to our Constitution, all that Blackstone's Commentaries were to the English Constitution," [96] while an Englishman asserted that Story " should be attentively read by all who are desirous of acquiring a correct view of the original constitution of our American colonies." [97]

Perhaps the best conclusion to this chapter is the question raised by Edward Everett, and, we may judge, expressing the views of his fellow nationalists whose cause was ultimately to triumph : " now we have the book, How we did without it ? " [98]

95 Anon., Review of Story's *Commentaries on the Constitution, American Quarterly Review,* XIV (Dec. 1833), 329. The same sentiments are expressed in the *American Jurist and Law Magazine,* IX (Jan. 1833), 230-232. See also the full-length reviews in *ibid.,* IX (April 1833), 241-288; X (July 1833), 119-147.

96 *American Monthly Review,* IV, 500.

97 Anon., "The Late Mr. Justice Story," *The Law Review, and Quarterly Journal of British and Foreign Jurisprudence,* III (London: May 1846), 375.

98 *North American Review,* XXXVIII, 63.

# PART IV

## THE USES OF THE COMMENTARIES

# PART IV
# INTRODUCTORY

IN this, the concluding part of our study, it will be our purpose to examine briefly the uses and longevity of the commentaries. The conclusions reached must be regarded as tentative, as they are based on evidence which is fragmentary at best.

Kent, Story, and Wheaton [1] head the list of authors of American legal classics prepared by Professor Frederick C. Hicks. These three men may be compared with Glanville, Bracton, Littleton, Coke, and Blackstone in the annals of English law. Since Wheaton, who was primarily interested in international law, has not come within our field of study, we may begin with Kent and Story in our inquiry into the significance of the commentaries. These two men were responsible for laying the foundations of legal literature in this country and for gaining European recognition of American legal development. Their works were used most extensively in the training of lawyers, and their fame has best withstood the ravages of time.

1 Henry Wheaton, Supreme Court reporter, 1816-1827, and author of various works, including the *Elements of International Law* (1836). Prof. A. C. McLaughlin would add the name of Marshall to these three, leading the others in the order given above. *Cambridge History of American Literature*, II (New York: Macmillan, 1933), 71. Dean Pound omits Wheaton from the list, retaining the other three. "The Place of Judge Story in the Making of American Law," *American Law Review*, XLVIII (Sept.-Oct. 1914), 678.

# CHAPTER IX
## USES OF THE COMMENTARIES
### Section I

FROM the available evidence, it would appear that before 1860, the first volume of Kent's *Commentaries* was more widely used for collegiate instruction than any other single study on the Constitution,[1] with the possible exception of Rawle. In fact, in some instances, as, for example, at West Point, Kent superseded Rawle as the official text almost immediately after its publication.[2] Upon his acceptance of the Dane professorship at Harvard, Story specified that in addition to copies of Blackstone, " some copies of *Kent's Commentaries,* say a half dozen," were indispensable to the students.[3]

> Into how many other hands than those of college youths the *Commentaries* must have come cannot be answered with certainty; but if one considers how rapidly the work went through its several editions, if he accepts the contemporary opinion that no American work had ever earned so much money, the conclusion . . . is inescapable. Kent had become the favorite preceptor of the legal profession.[4]

1 *Cf.* Horton, *Kent,* p. 302. Philip Lindsley, President of the University of Nashville, wrote asking that the first volume be edited separately for academic use. Letter of Jan. 14, 1833, Kent Papers, Vol. VII. Kent had already decided to do this, " and thus the volume which contained his exposition of the constitutional law of the American Union passed into the hands of boys at college and became a textbook at the University of Nashville, at West Point, at Harvard and at the author's Alma Mater in New Haven." Horton, *loc. cit.* Little and Company to Kent, Apr. 12, 1838, with appended note in Kent Papers, Vol. IX.

2 Douglas Southall Freeman, *R. E. Lee, A Biography,* I (New York and London: Charles Scribner's Sons, 1934), 78-79. In 1828, Kent was appointed to the Board of Visitors to West Point. In connection with his duties, he attended an examination in constitutional law. Later he wrote, "[The cadets] appeared to be masters of the first volume of my Commentaries." Kent Journal, Apr. 23, June 3, 1828, as cited in Horton, *Kent,* p. 303.

3 Warren, *History of the Harvard Law School,* I, 432.

4 Horton, *Kent,* pp. 303-304, with refs. to Philip Hone, *Diary,* II, 645-646, and letter of Kent to Story, April 18, 1844, Story Papers.

Another significant proof of the popularity of Kent's work may be found in the number of condensations, guides, and simplifications that were prepared for beginning students.[5] This honor, if such it be, seems to have been extended to none of the other commentators, with the exception of Walker, whose single volume was also condensed.[6] Story prepared his own abridgments, with the hope of presenting his ideas to all types of readers. Story himself passed over his books and court opinions and considered his work in the Harvard Law School as the most significant of his life. He wrote to Sumner in 1836,

> If I do not live otherwise to posterity, I shall at all events live in my children in the law. While that endures I am content to be known through my pupils.[7]

At Harvard, where the building of the law library was a constant care of Story and his associates, we find some of the commentaries included in the course bibliographies. In the report of 1832-33, Kent's *Commentaries* were listed with Blackstone as the two basic works which must be read, even if the student took just the accelerated two-year course. In the " Parallel Course, designed chiefly for private reading," Hoffman's *Legal Outlines* found a place. Select titles in Dane's *Abridgment* are given for the collateral readings in various courses. Under " Consti-

5 Examples: Asa Kinne, *The Most Important Parts of Kent's Commentaries, Reduced to Questions and Answers* (New York: 1st ed., 1838; 2nd ed., 1840) ; J. Eastman Johnson, *An Analytical Abridgment of Kent's Commentaries on American Law*, with a full series of questions for examination, adapted both to the Analysis and to the original commentaries (New York: 1839) ; John Fine, *Lectures on Law, Prepared Principally from Kent, by a lawyer, for the use of his sons* (Albany and New York: 1852) ; Frederick S. Dickson, *An Analysis of Kent's Commentaries* (Philadelphia: 1875) ; Reuben M. Benjamin, *Questions on Kent's Commentaries, with References to Illinois Statutes and Decisions, where the law of the state differs from that laid down in the text* (Chicago: 1880).

6 Reuben M. Benjamin, *Student's Guide to Elementary Law consisting of Questions on Walker's American Law and Blackstone's Commentaries, with references to Illinois Statutes and Decisions, where the law of the state differs from that laid down in the text* (Chicago: 1879).

7 Feb. 10, 1836. In Sumner Papers, Harvard College Library.

tutional Law," the required texts were the American Constitutions and Story's *Commentaries on the Constitution* (also required in the two-year course). Along with the *Federalist* and select cases and speeches, Rawle *on the Constitution* was listed in the parallel course.[8] In 1845, Rawle was still used in this latter course and Lieber's *Political Ethics* and Sergeant's *Constitutional Law* had been added.[9]

Middlebury College retained Kent as the text during the entire pre-Civil War period,[10] and Dartmouth adopted Rawle for its students.[11]

The most heated controversy over the use of a commentary for class instruction arose in connection with Rawle's *View of the Constitution*. Records show that this volume was the text in a course on constitutional law at West Point in 1825-26. On the assumption that the same book was used in later years, an impressive case has been built up. Jefferson Davis, Robert E. Lee, and other leaders are supposed to have obtained their views on secession from Rawle, or at least had their Southern opinions confirmed by the official text of the national military academy. Douglas Southall Freeman, who examined all the possible leads for his biography of Robert E. Lee, finds " no first-hand evidence that he [Lee] was instructed in Rawle, or that he ever read the book." Freeman quotes a letter in which Lee is mentioned as saying that Rawle was a textbook during his cadet-

8 List in President's Eighth Annual Report, Harvard Archives. Other records in the archives show that Rawle was used throughout the Story-Ashmun period.

9 *Course of Legal Studies*, Sept. 6, 1845. Harvard Archives. On June 10, 1845, Story invited Kent to a dinner celebrating the enlargement of the law school, so he could see the school " where your Commentaries constitute one of the leading works of instruction, every year." Story, *Life and Letters*, II, 538.

10 Middlebury College, *Catalogue of Officers and Students*. Annual editions in college library were consulted through 1859.

11 *Cf. infra*, p. 63. Anna Haddow, in her *Political Science in American Colleges and Universities* (New York and London: D. Appleton-Century Co., 1939), esp. ch. xi, gives further examples of schools and colleges which used the commentaries as texts.

ship at West Point, but there is no direct affirmation that Lee was in the class which studied it; rather, he seems to have been instructed in Kent.[12]

Jefferson Davis stated that at the time he was a cadet at West Point, he was taught Kent's *Commentaries,* though previous classes had studied Rawle. There is some evidence of Davis' familiarity with Rawle, however, and " it is probable that if he had been brought to trial after the War between the States he would have sought to vindicate the constitutionality of secession by reference to the use of Rawle at West Point." [13] It is not known if constitutional law was a regular course at West Point at this time, but records show that on a later occasion when the course was taught, Kent was used as the text, as he had been in 1827-28. Kent continued in use for many years and was the text during Lee's superintendency of the military academy.[14]

12 Freeman, *Lee,* I, 78-79. *Cf.* Robert Bingham, *Sectional Misunderstandings* which was originally published in the *North American Review,* 179 (Sept. 1904), 357-370, and was republished as a pamphlet (Asheville, N. C.: no date). Horton cites evidence from Kent's Journal that Kent singled out Lee as one of the most proficient students of his *Commentaries. Kent,* p. 303, note 144. *Cf.* also Col. Edgar S. Dudley, " Was ' Secession ' Taught at West Point? What the Records Show," *Century Magazine,* 78 (Aug. 1909), 629-635.

13 Freeman, *Lee,* I, 78, citing Bingham, *Sectional Misunderstandings,* p. 4, quoting the Rev. L. W. Bacon. Freeman finds the conclusive evidence that Rawle was used in 1825-26 in four references in Heintzelman's MS. Diary, Feb. 21, 23, March 27, and June 7, 1826. *Ibid.,* I, 78 note. See also Address of the Hon. R. T. Bennett, May 22, 1894, " Morale of the Confederate," *Southern Historical Society Papers,* XXII (1894), 83. According to Elisabeth Cutting, *Jefferson Davis, Political Soldier* (New York: Dodd, Mead and Co., 1930), p. 21, Calhoun ordered the use of Rawle at West Point during his last year in office as Secretary of War. Allen Tate in *Jefferson Davis: His Rise and Fall* (New York: Minton, Balch and Co., 1929), p. 64, says that constitutional law was taught as a part of a course in " Rhetoric and Moral Philosophy." Tate points out that Davis was inclined to make Rawle's doctrine a more important influence on his later life than it was. At any rate, Davis did better with this course than with any other while at the Academy. *Loc. cit.*

14 Freeman, *Lee,* I, 79 and 347 note, citing Lee to E. W. Morgan, Oct. 30, 1854, *Letter Book of the Superintendent of West Point* (MS.), p. 146.

We have not attempted, in this chapter, to repeat the names of all the commentators and list the places where their works were used. Some of this information is included with their biographies. But since most of the works mentioned, with the exception of Rawle, have been by Northerners, expounding the nationalist interpretation of the Constitution, it might be well to recall that the Tuckers prepared most of the works that were used south of the Mason and Dixon line. Two of the main intellectual centers, William and Mary College and the University of Virginia, used St. George Tucker's edition of Blackstone's *Commentaries* at first, and then Henry St. George Tucker's *Lectures on Constitutional Law* as a text. N. Beverley Tucker at William and Mary considered his *Lectures on the Science of Government* as introductory to his brother's more specialized work. Upshur's critique of Story's *Commentaries* was also required reading, along with the *Federalist* and the Virginia and Kentucky Resolutions of '98 and '99.

In addition to all of the rather advanced analyses of the nature of the Constitution and the Union, many attempts were made to present the ideas in simplified form for younger minds.[15] Such efforts were almost entirely restricted to Northern writers. Perhaps one explanation may be in the fact that the school system was more fully developed in the North. Tutors were still used in the wealthy families of the South, and thus less attention, logically, would be paid to formal textbooks. At least one Southerner, N. Beverley Tucker, was bothered by the discrepancy. He observed that while all the political changes of the mid-nineteenth century were taking place,

> the book-makers of the north were busy in preparing works for propagating, through the minds of the rising generation,

---

In Ex. Docs, 26th Cong., 2nd sess., I, 152, Doc. 2, there is a protest by the minority of the board of visitors of 1840 against the use of Kent's *Commentaries* and Bayard's *Exposition* as teaching latitudinarian doctrines. *Re* Bayard, *cf. infra*, Bibliography.

15 Many of these textbooks are listed in the first part of the Bibliography, marked with an asterisk.

and especially through the legal profession, principles of constitutional law suited to the views of centralism.[16]

It was apparently quite difficult for a conscientious Southerner to find a book on the Constitution that he considered suitable for his children to read.

The significance of the textbooks of the first half of the nineteenth century in the training of lawyers has been mentioned many times. Their availability, largely through the efforts of St. George Tucker, Story, and Kent, facilitated the teaching of the common law to aspirants to the legal profession. While the texts were in use, they and their authors were far better known than they are today.

In general, it would appear that the demise of the commentaries as textbooks came with the introduction of the case method in the academic study of the law.[17] Thus, in the new era, the opinions of Kent the judge and the chancellor are preferred "to the mellifluous passages of Kent the commentator."[18] In this fundamental change in the character of legal education may be seen one of the most important explanations of the decline of the commentators in public knowledge.

## Section II

Aside from the textbook uses of the commentaries, there is evidence that they were used by lawyers in the preparation of their cases. Daniel Call, writing in 1828, said regarding

16 Tucker, *Lectures on the Science of Government*, p. 426. He cites as an example a Northern school-book, "intended for the use of young gentlemen of the ripe age of ten years, in which they are taught by rote, that 'Congress has power to provide for the common defence and general welfare.'" This disputed point is included with such facts as, "the chief magistrate of the United States is called the president." Tucker found this in a Peter Parley book. He says that he has heard that others were using this *nom de guerre* of Mr. Goodrich and hopes "that this political fraud was the work of one of these knaves." *Loc. cit.*, note.

17 Hicks, *Men and Books Famous in the Law*, introd. by Harlan F. Stone, p. 10. *Cf.* Warren, *History of the Harvard Law School*, II, ch. xliii.

18 Hicks, *Men and Books Famous in the Law*, introd. p. 11.

Tucker's *Blackstone,* that the volumes " are necessary to every student and practitioner of the law in Virginia." [19] And Kent was told by Sumner in 1835, " Your admirable *Commentaries* have now become the manual of the practitioner, as they have since their first publication been the institute of the student." [20]

Story's *Commentaries on the Constitution* are regarded by Aumann as having had a great influence on the bench and bar for two generations. For a long time, this work continued to be the only authoritative and extensive treatise on the Constitution, and after passing through various editions, it was given " new life and utility by Thomas McIntyre Cooley when he prepared the fourth edition with copious annotations." [21]

> It would be difficult to overestimate the importance of such volumes in the days when the critical case system was not used by beginners, when texts were comparatively few, and when practising attorneys and judges were not provided with long series of reports, in days also when the layman was interested in problems concerning the nature of the Union and the powers of government.[22]

Many of the commentaries were significantly used in the Supreme Court of the United States. No rule prevented the citation of textbooks on law, as was the situation in England. Before long, the text writers were recognized as authorities in both argument of counsel and opinions from the bench. Ordinarily, the commentators were cited in conjunction with regular legal precedents, but occasionally they were considered strong enough to stand alone in the support of an argument.

19 4 Call Rep. xlvi. One of the works which eventually superseded St. George Tucker's volumes was the *Commentaries on the Laws of Virginia,* prepared by his son, Henry St. George Tucker. *Cf. infra,* ch. v.

20 As quoted by F. C. Hicks, " Kent's Commentaries," *Columbia Alumni News,* XIV, 370.

21 Aumann, *Changing American Legal System,* p. 129.

22 A. C. McLaughlin in *Cambridge History of American Literature,* II, 76.

A survey of the citations of recognized authorities in constitutional cases before the Civil War indicates what might be expected—that both justices and counsel relied heavily on English precedents, both court decisions and legal commentaries. Men who were well versed in Latin, French, etc., referred to continental authors, such as Grotius, Puffendorf, and Bynkershoek.

As the years went on, the number of American precedents cited increased in proportion to those of English and other foreign origin, but the latter never completely disappeared. The commentaries were mentioned infrequently at first, but increased in popularity and achieved their greatest recognition in the 1840's.[23]

In general, the commentaries were cited with approbation, but occasionally the opposite was true. For example, in the case of Gibbons v. Ogden, Emmet, arguing for the respondent, says that Tucker stated the matter regarding commerce " very imperfectly." [24] Again, Henderson, arguing for the defendant in

---

[23] The table of 527 constitutional cases upon which the conclusions here stated are based was compiled from three sources: 1) the list of cases under the heading, " Constitutional Law " in the Index of each of the first 65 volumes of the *United States Reports*; 2) the table of cases in A. C. McLaughlin, *A Constitutional History of the United States* (New York and London: Appleton-Century Co., 1935) ; and 3) the table of cases in the 1938 edition of the *Constitution Annotated* (Washington, D. C.: Govt. Printing Office).

References to citations of the commentaries are noted only if made contemporaneously with the case, in argument of counsel, or by one of the justices. Thus, no record appears in this study if the commentaries are cited by Brightly in his notes to the *United States Reports*, written in 1888, or other later editors. Examples of this type of omission: Ref. to Baldwin's *Constitutional Views*, 29-42, in Chisholm v. Georgia, 2 Dall. 419 at 470 (1793), and to Rawle 30, Sergeant 305, 1 Kent 257, in Hylton v. United States, 3 Dall. 171 at 171 (1796).

It was found that 12 of the commentaries included in this study were noticed in the printed records of the Supreme Court. It is probable that the commentaries were occasionally used without citation. No attempt has been made to check any instances of this use, as the present concern is with the times when the commentators received credit for their work.

[24] 9 Wheat. 1 at 119 (1824), citing 1 Tuck. *Bl. Com.*, Part I, App. D, exact page not given.

Stacy *v.* Thrasher, disagrees with Story, who, in the *Conflict of Laws,* writes that the states are foreign to each other to the degree that creditors do not have the same rights in all states.[25] And more or less as a climax, Justice Daniel, in his opinion in the License Cases, asserts that

> in matters involving the meaning and integrity of the constitution, I never can consent that the text of that instrument shall be overlaid and smothered by the glosses of essay writers, lecturers, and commentators . . . I must interpret exclusively as that conscience [his own] shall dictate.[26]

The first commentary, the *Federalist,* was early recognized as an important gloss upon the Constitution. The *Federalist* was first used as an authority in a Supreme Court case in Penhallow *v.* Doane, when Attorney-General Bradford and Counsellor Ingersoll called upon it to bolster their argument that wherever an alliance is not corporate but confederate, the sovereignty resides in each state.[27] Justice Chase was the first member of the bench to notice the *Federalist.* He did so in Calder *v.* Bull, with regard to *ex post facto* laws. Chase stated that he agreed with Blackstone, and that in turn, Blackstone's opinion

> is confirmed by his successor, Mr. Wooddeson; and by the author of the *Federalist,* who I esteem superior to both, for his extensive and accurate knowledge of the true principles of government.[28]

Following in the footsteps of his predecessors, John Marshall accepted the *Federalist* as an authoritative statement of what the Founding Fathers really meant. Thus, the official recognition of this work was greater than that given any other commentary. It was found that the *Federalist* was cited a total of 147 times by number in the cases under investigation. Also,

25 6 How. 44 at 57 (1848), citing Story, *Conflict of Laws,* sec. 522.

26 5 How. 504 at 612 (1847).

27 3 Dall. 54 at 67 (1795). No number cited.

28 3 Dall. 386 at 391 (1798). No number cited.

there were 21 other references to " certain numbers " or " several numbers," or just to *" The Federalist "* without any number at all. Of the 85 Letters, 38 were cited specifically, the most popular being No. 32 on Taxation, Nos. 42 and 43 which give a general view of the powers conferred by the Constitution, Nos. 80 and 82 on the Judiciary, and No. 44 on restrictions on the authority of the several states.[29]

The *Federalist* was cited ten times in majority opinions of the court, and the cases were significant ones—by Marshall in McCulloch *v.* Maryland [30] and Cohens *v.* Virginia; [31] by Thompson in Ogden *v.* Saunders; [32] by Marshall in Weston *v.* City Council of Charleston; [33] by Barbour in New York *v.* Miln; [34] by Story in Prigg *v.* Pennsylvania; [35] by Daniel in Veazie *v.* Moor; [36] by Grier in Marshall *v.* Baltimore and Ohio Railroad Company; [37] by Wayne in Dodge *v.* Woolsey; [38] and by Taney in Dred Scott *v.* Sanford.[39] In only five cases were the citations in concurring opinions of the justices, the first instance being the case of Satterlee *v.* Matthewson in 1829,[40] while they were cited in seventeen dissenting opinions, the first being Brown *v.* Maryland in 1827.[41]

29 Others mentioned by justices or counsel include Nos. 1, 7, 11, 12, 14, 21, 22, 27, 29, 31, 33, 34, 35, 36, 38, 39, 40, 41, 45, 46, 47, 51, 54, 63, 69, 70, 71, 78, 79, 81, 83.

30 4 Wheat. 316 at 433-435 (1819). No specific citation.

31 6 Wheat. 264 at 418-420 (1821). Articles on the Judiciary.

32 12 Wheat. 213 at 304, 306 and 329 (1827). No. 44.

33 2 Pet. 449 at 469 (1829). No specific citation.

34 11 Pet. 102 at 133 (1837). No. 45.

35 16 Pet. 539 at 616 (1842). No. 43.

36 14 How. 568 at 575 (1852). Nos. 7 and 11.

37 16 How. 314 at 326 (1853). No. 80.

38 18 How. 331 at 357 (1855). Nos. 43 and 22.

39 19 How. 393 at 447 (1856). No. 38.

40 2 Pet. 380 at 416c. No. 44 in note by Johnson, J.

41 12 Wheat. 419 at 456, Thompson, J., dissenting. No. 32.

St. George Tucker's edition of Blackstone's *Commentaries* attained some popularity as an authority in Supreme Court cases. It was cited twice in majority opinions of the court,[42] by two justices in dissenting opinions,[43] and several times in argument of counsel.[44] In all but one instance, the English edition of Blackstone is cited for references to the body of that work. The exception is the case of Governeur *v.* Robertson, in which the page in the American edition of Blackstone is cited at the same time as that in the English edition.[45] Tucker's importance as an authority is for the material in his appendixes and notes.

One of the key sections in the strict construction doctrine is quoted by Emmet in his argument for the respondent in Gibbons *v.* Ogden. After alluding to the clauses restraining the powers given, Tucker says,

> The sum of all which appears to be, that the powers delegated to the federal government are, in all cases, to receive the most strict construction that the instrument will bear, where the rights of a state, or of the people, either collectively or individually, may be drawn in question.[46]

42 By Story in Terrett *v.* Taylor, 9 Cr. 43 at 47 (1815), referring to 2 Tucker's *Bl. Com.*, App., Note M; and by Washington in Buckner *v.* Finley, 2 Pet. 586 at 591-592 (1829), referring to 2 *ibid.*, 467 note.

43 Woodbury in three cases—Waring *v.* Clarke, 5 How. 441 at 478-479, 481, 491, 499 (1847), citing I, Part 1, App., p. 432; III, 109, App. 380; Part 2, App. 99; I, Part 1, p. 383, App.; I, 250 note, in that order; Luther *v.* Borden, 7 How. 1 at 71, 72 (1849), citing I, App., p. 270; and Passenger Cases, 7 How. 283 at 526, 535, 536, 542-543, 548, 550-551, 556, 564 (1849), citing I, Part 2, App., p. 33; I, Part 2, App. 50; I, App. 231; I, App. 290; I, 249; I, 252; I, App. 3, 4, 255, 296; I, App. 109, 110; and Curtis in Dred Scott *v.* Sanford, 19 How. 393 at 578 (1856), citing I, App. 255-259.

44 In 14 cases between 1805 and 1856.

45 11 Wheat. 332 at 341 (1826). Refs. to 2 *Bl. Com.* 351 (Tucker's ed. 344) and 2 *ibid.*, 252 (Tucker's ed. 249) by Bibb for the defendant. Subsequent references to Blackstone do not give citations to Tucker's edition, but are to an English edition alone.

46 9 Wheat. 1 at 86-87 (1824). Ref. to 1 Tucker's *Bl. Comm.*, Part 1, App. D, p. 154. Other matters on which Tucker was cited include treason, corporations, naturalization, militia, inviolability of contract, commerce, copyrights,

However, Tucker went on to admit that the power to regulate commerce is exclusive with the federal government—a point which led Mr. Emmet to argue that Tucker had stated the matter regarding commerce "very imperfectly." [47]

The posthumously published commentaries of James Wilson contributed less to his fame as an authority in the Supreme Court than his single opinion in Chisholm v. Georgia.[48] His *Lectures on Law* were cited in only two cases—in 1807 and in 1849. In the first instance, Wilson is called upon in drawing the distinction between treason and levying of war, depending upon whether one adhered to an enemy or to a rebel.[49] Later, Wilson is cited for what impresses this student as his most interesting series of analyses. Hallett, arguing for the plaintiff in Luther v. Borden, sees fit to examine the problems of the nature of the state, who the people are, the location of the ultimate power or sovereignty, the right of the people to establish government, the mode in which that right may be exercised, and the difference between a change of government and a revolution.[50] In this particular case, Hallett has relied heavily on the commentators, also citing the *Federalist,* Tucker, Story, Taylor, Rawle, and Dane.

The first citation in argument of counsel to Thomas Sergeant's *Constitutional Law* was made one year after its appearance, by David Hoffman, whose own work had gone more or less unnoticed by the court.[51] This was the first of seven citations of Sergeant's volume, all by counsel. Reference was made to the first edition in 1823, 1828, and 1831, and to the second

---

force of foreign laws in newly acquired territory, war powers, slavery, English colonial law, and police power.

47 9 Wheat. 1 at 119.

48 2 Dall. 419 at 453 to 466 (1793).

49 Argument of Attorney-General Rodney in *Ex parte* Bollman, 4 Cr. 75 at 115, referring to 3 Wilson's *Lectures*, 105.

50 7 How. 1 at 21-25. Refs. to various pages in all 3 vols.

51 In argument for the defendant in Childress v. Emory, 8 Wheat. 642 at 668 (1823). Ref. to Sergeant 113, 117.

in 1833, 1838, 1840, and 1842. The points on which Sergeant was used as an authority vary widely, involving jurisdiction of the Supreme Court and the circuit courts,[52] salvage as coming under admiralty law,[53] contract,[54] and unconstitutionality of a section of the Fugitive Slave Act of 1793.[55]

John Taylor's *New Views on the Constitution of the United States* was referred to only once—by Hallett, arguing for the plaintiff in Luther *v.* Borden.[56] Hallett was seeking answers to his questions: who are the people, where is the ultimate power or sovereignty located, and do the people have a right to establish government?[57]

Most of the references in the *United States Reports* to Nathan Dane's *Abridgment of American Law* are to Volumes II and VI, and there are only three citations to the ninth volume. It has been thought valid to include all the references to all the volumes in this study, inasmuch as constitutional law is interwoven among so many other subjects. However, only points connected with constitutional law will be mentioned specifically.[58] The first time that the *Abridgment* was cited from the bench was in 1830, when Dane provided authority for Story's

52 Menard *v.* Aspasia, 5 Pet. 505 at 507 (1828), ref. to Serg. 64; Kendall *v.* United States, 12 Pet. 524 at 560 (1838), ref. to Serg., 2nd ed., ch. 15, p. 123; Suydam *v.* Broadnax, 14 Pet. 67 at 70 (1840), ref. to Serg., 2nd ed., 44, 275-278, 287-290.

53 American Insurance Company *v.* Canter, 1 Pet. 511 at 523b (1828), ref. to Serg. 207.

54 Livingston *v.* Moore, 7 Pet. 469 at 483 (1833), ref. to Serg. 352 (2nd ed., though not so indicated).

55 Prigg *v.* Pennsylvania, 16 Pet. 539 at 598 (1842), ref. to Serg. 386, 398 [2nd ed.].

56 7 How. 1 at 22-23 (1849). Title not used, just name and page.

57 Refs. to Taylor 4, 412, 413, 519, 447; 489, 490. No specific citations for the last question.

58 Therefore, the only citations of Dane's *Abridgment* in an opinion of the court is omitted as dealing with a detail of procedure: By Woodbury, J., in Jones *v.* Van Zandt, 5 How. 215 at 228 (1847), referring to 5 *Abr.* 244, sec. 8.

point that in construing a treaty, each government should be deemed entitled to the allegiance of those who were at the time adhering to it.[59]

On general points of legal interpretation, Dane was the authority in McLean's contention that grants of limited political powers were construed strictly,[60] and for the argument that when there is doubt as to the intention of the legislature, the law should be construed favorably to those who claim under it.[61]

Justice Woodbury in his dissenting opinion in Waring v. Clarke, refers to Dane's able section on admiralty jurisdiction.[62] He notes that all American admiralty law is based upon English precedent and that the authors of the Constitution referred only to what they were familiar with in establishing jurisdiction in that branch of the law.[63]

Hallett, arguing for the plaintiff in Luther v. Borden, gives the only citations to Dane's ninth volume on points of constitutional law. He is concerned with the manner in which a state constitution becomes paramount,[64] and the time when the United States Constitution became binding.[65] Also, Dane is called upon in the distinction that Hallett was seeking to draw between a change of government and a revolution.[66]

Peter Stephen DuPonceau was honored with judicial cognizance of his *Jurisdiction of the Courts of the United States,*

59 Story's dissenting opinion in Inglis v. Sailor's Snug Harbor, 3 Pet. 99 at 164, note a (1830). Ref. to *Abr.*, ch. 131, art. 7.

60 Justice McLean's concurring opinion in Charles River Bridge v. Warren Bridge, 11 Pet. 420 at 557 (1837). Ref. to 2 Dane *Abr.* 683.

61 Argument of Brant and Coxe for the plaintiff in Decatur v. Paulding, 14 Pet. 497 at 505 (1840). Ref. to 6 *Abr.* 570.

62 5 How. 441 at 469-483 (1847). Ref. to 6 Dane *Abr.* 341, 352-353, 357.

63 Same point in Daniel's opinion in New Jersey Steam Navigation Company v. Merchants' Bank, 6 How. 344 at 409 (1848). Ref. to 6 Dane *Abr.* 353.

64 7 How. 1 at 24 (1849). Refs. to 9 Dane *Abr.* 18, sec. 8; p. 26, sec. 14; p. 22, sec. 11.

65 *Loc. cit.* Refs. to 9 Dane *Abr.* p. 38, sec. 28; p. 41, sec. 32; p. 44, sec. 35.

66 *Loc. cit.* Ref. to 9 Dane *Abr.* pp. 67, 68, sec. 56.

published in 1824. The point that received the first attention in the Supreme Court was the interesting distinction that Du-Ponceau drew between the common law as a source of power and as a means for its exercise.[67] Thus, he proposed to solve one of the thorniest problems in American jurisprudence. In the two remaining cases in which DuPonceau is used, the citation is made by Justice Woodbury. All references are to points in admiralty.[68]

William Rawle's *View of the Constitution* was not noticed in the Supreme Court until 1834, nine years after it was published. At that time, Thomas Sergeant, a personal friend and co-worker of Rawle's, cited it on the copyright power.[69] No further reference appears for fifteen years. In 1849, however, Hallett, who made quite a thorough canvass of the commentators in building up the argument for the plaintiff in Luther v. Borden, referred to Rawle five times,[70] and Justice Woodbury cited him in proving that the power to discipline the militia is not exclusive.[71]

Rawle's *View of the Constitution* was used in four more cases, once in each. In two instances, the treaty-making power

67 Wheaton's note to United States v. Ortega, 11 Wheat. 467 at 475 (1826), note a; also J. R. Ingersoll, arguing for the defendants in Wheaton v. Peters, 8 Pet. 591 at 627 (1834). Ref. to DuPonceau, *Jurisdiction*, Preface, pp. xi, xiv, xv. Ingersoll also made the point in the same case, basing his contention on DuPonceau, p. 101, that federal courts, sitting in states, cannot exercise common law jurisdiction, unless national and local laws are not applicable. 8 Pet. 591 at 628.

68 Woodbury, J., dissenting in Waring v. Clarke, 5 How. 441 at 478, 481, 483 (1847), referring to DuPonceau, pp. 158, 94, 95 note, 139 and note; Woodbury's opinion in New Jersey Steam Navigation Company v. Merchants' Bank, 6 How. 344 at 436 (1848), referring to pp. 22, 23.

69 Wheaton v. Peters, 8 Pet. 591 at 640 (1834), citing ch. 9, pp. 105-106.

70 7 How. 1 at 22-25. The points are those which have been listed previously—questions on who are the people, where is the ultimate power or sovereignty, right of the people to establish government, mode in which that right may be exercised, difference between change of government and revolution. Pp. 14-17 in Rawle cited.

71 Passenger Cases, 7 How. 283 at 555-556 (1849), dissenting opinion. Ch. 9, p. 111 of Rawle cited.

was involved; [72] again it was held that Congress had the power to pass an act on counterfeiting that had been called in question; [73] and lastly, the power of Congress to establish a uniform rule of naturalization was analyzed.[74]

Kent's *Commentaries,* taken as a whole, were cited more often than any other commentaries on the same subject, but the record of the citation of the constitutional part is more modest. Of the 80 separate cases in which the *Commentaries* were noted between 1827 and 1860, Part II of the first volume is the subject of the reference in 41, or just about half. In four instances, the citations are in the opinion of the court.[75] There are also two citations in concurring opinions,[76] and four in dissents.[77] The

---

72 United States *v.* Reynes, 9 How. 127 at 142 (1850). Brent and May arguing for the appellee, citing Rawle 56, 57, that American order of survey of the land acquired in the Louisiana purchase was valid. Treaty to be regarded as speaking from the exchange of ratifications, so order of survey was expressly protected. Cross *v.* Harrison, 16 How. 164 at 173 (1853). James W. and John S. McCollok arguing for the plaintiff, citing Rawle, ch. 27, p. 237. Substantiating point that power of United States over conquered or ceded territory sovereign and exclusive except as limited by treaty or Ordinance of 1787.

73 United States *v.* Marigold, 9 How. 560 at 562 (1850), Attorney-General Johnson arguing for the United States, citing Rawle, ch. 9, p. 163.

74 Dred Scott *v.* Sanford, 19 How. 393 at 578 (1856), Justice Curtis dissenting, citing 1 Rawle [*sic*], 84-88.

75 Taney in Jecker *v.* Montgomery, 13 How. 498 at 516, 517 (1851), citing I, 359, 101, 102; Taney in Kennett *v.* Chambers, 14 How. 38 at 51 (1852), citing I, 116; Daniel in Leitensdorfer *v.* Webb, 20 How. 176 at 177-178 (1857), citing I, 177; Nelson in Freeman *v.* Howe, 24 How. 450 at 458-459 (1860), citing I, 410.

76 Barbour in Holmes *v.* Jennison, 14 Pet. 540 at 594 (1840), citing I, 351; Daniel in New Jersey Steam Navigation Company *v.* Merchants' Bank, 6 How. 344 at 409 (1848), citing I, 377, 5th ed.

77 Woodbury in Waring *v.* Clarke, 5 How. 441 at 473, 483, 486, 488 (1847), citing I, 377, 376, 357, 365 note, in that order; Woodbury in the Passenger Cases, 7 How. 283 at 555 (1849), citing I, 364; Daniel in Jackson *v.* Steamboat Magnolia, 20 How. 296 at 309-310 (1857), citing I, 376; Taney in Taylor *v.* Carryl, 20 How. 583 at 604 and 615 (1857), citing I, 380; 371 and 372, notes.

subjects upon which Kent is used as an authority are many, including bankruptcy, admiralty, contract, copyright, common law, jurisdiction, impeachment, land title, corporation law, division of powers between federal and state governments, treaties, trial by jury, necessary and proper clause, common carriers, public duty, sovereignty, *habeas corpus,* commerce, riparian rights, slavery, and interference in foreign wars.[78]

One cannot help but notice that Kent's decisions in the high courts of New York, both as Chief Justice and later as Chancellor, were cited even more frequently than his *Commentaries,* and with almost unvarying approbation. For example, Wickliffe and Johnson, arguing for the appellants in Bank of the United States *v.* Daniel, cited one of Kent's decisions with the following introduction:

> Upon this subject, the remarks of Chancellor Kent, whose decisions are almost reverenced throughout the Union, are so pertinent and just, that we could not do better than make a short extract from them.[79]

Story's *Commentaries on the Constitution* began to appear as authority in argument of counsel and in opinions from the bench within a year after their publication. As was the case with all the other works under consideration, Story was relied on more heavily by counsel than by the justices, but, nevertheless, he was cited in four cases in the opinion of the court,[80] twice in

78 Each of these subjects was referred to more than once. The list is too long to make advisable separate citations to all the points.

79 12 Pet. 32 at 41 (1838).

80 Wayne in McElmoyle *v.* Cohen, 13 Pet. 312 at 326, 327 (1839), citing 183 [*sic*]; Baldwin in McNutt *v.* Bland, 2 How. 9 at 16, 17 (1844), citing I, 70, 715; III, 1932, 1939; Nelson in Fellows *v.* Blacksmith, 19 How. 366 at 372 (1856), citing III, p. 695; Campbell in Taylor *v.* Carryl, 20 How. 583 at 598 (1857), citing III, sec. 1666 note. Citations to Story are often not clear in referring to page or section. They are given here as they appear in the court reports.

concurring opinions,[81] and eight times in dissents.[82] In all, Story was cited in 42 separate cases. A similarity to Chancellor Kent may be found in the fact that Story was cited more frequently for his judicial decisions, in the first circuit of the federal courts, and as a Supreme Court justice, than he was for his commentaries.

The subjects on which Story was used as authority cover almost the entire range of problems of constitutional law. The most frequently referred to seem to be common law rights in the states and as applicable to the Constitution, copyrights, citizenship, bankruptcy and insolvency, commerce, eminent domain, contract, powers of the executive, judiciary and jurisdiction of courts, interpretation of laws, slavery, *habeas corpus,* admiralty, necessity for direct collision between federal and state laws before the Supreme Court can intervene, philosophical questions of government,[83] war powers and militia, taxation, treaties, acquisition to territory and right to govern what has been acquired, sovereignty, " law of the land," and new states.[84]

81 Woodbury in the License Cases, 5 How. 504 at 619 (1847), citing I, 432; Woodbury in West River Bridge Company *v.* Dix, 6 How. 507 at 539 and 540 (1848), citing III, 661 and secs. 1377, 1378. Woodbury questions the last two sections cited.

82 Thompson in Wheaton *v.* Peters, 8 Pet. 591 at 685-688 (1834), citing III, 48; I, 137-140; I, 140 and note, in that order; Taney in Kendall *v.* United States, 12 Pet. 524 at 633-635 (1838), citing secs. 608-609; Woodbury in Waring *v.* Clarke, 5 How. 441 at 488, 489, 491 (1847), citing III, secs. 1659, 1667, 1639; Woodbury in Luther *v.* Borden, 7 How. 1 at 58, 60, 67, 71, 76, 77 (1849), citing III, secs. 214, 215, 120, 1325, 217, 1335, 1206 (Justice Woodbury's citations are difficult to follow, particularly when he refers to Story, and they often do not check with the original) ; Woodbury in the Passenger Cases, 7 How. 283 at 534, 555-556, 561 (1849), citing II, sec. 437, III, sec. 1202, 434 [*sic*] ; Taney in Pennsylvania *v.* Wheeling and Belmont Bridge Company, 13 How. 518 at 587 (1851), citing II, 201-207; McLean in *Ex parte* Wells, 18 How. 307 at 321 (1855), citing 346 [*sic*] ; Curtis in Dred Scott *v.* Sanford, 19 How. 393 at 578 (1856), citing III, 1-3.

83 The same ones mentioned previously in Hallett's argument for the plaintiff in Luther *v.* Borden, 7 How. 1 at 21-25 (1849).

84 Each of these subjects appeared more than once. Several others appeared also, but the list is already too lengthy to include them. All of the citations,

Another volume of Story's, *Commentaries on the Conflict of Laws*, dealt primarily with the law of nations, but much of it was applicable to relations between the states and with the federal government. Hence, before long, this volume was added to the group of commentaries that rated attention by the legal minds surrounding the Supreme Court. In fact, the *Conflict of Laws* has a higher proportion of citations by the justices than any of the other commentaries under consideration. Of the 19 cases in which it was cited, it was used in the opinion of the court in nine,[85] in three concurring opinions,[86] and in two dissents.[87]

The subjects treated include bills of exchange, international and especially judicial comity (which Story holds is the only phase of comity in operation), acceptance of foreign laws and force of law, civil law, contract, slavery, common law, bankruptcy, inheritance and administrations, and domicil.[88]

---

with one exception, are to Story's full-length *Commentaries*. There is only one reference to the Abridgment—Barry, arguing for himself in Barry *v.* Mercein, 5 How. 103 at 109 (1847), citing Sto. *Com. Abr.* 608.

85 Catron in Bank of United States *v.* Daniel, 12 Pet. 32 at 55 (1838), citing secs. 281-286; Taney in Bank of Augusta *v.* Earle, 13 Pet. 519 at 589 (1839), citing 37; Grier in Cook *v.* Moffat, 5 How. 299 at 307 (1847), citing sec. 287; Grier in Stacy *v.* Thrasher, 6 How. 44 at 58 (1848), citing sec. 522; McLean in Nathan *v.* Louisiana, 8 How. 73 at 82 (1850), citing 314; Wayne in Union Bank of Tennessee *v.* Jolly's Administrators, 18 How. 503 at 507 (1853), citing sec. 521, 3rd ed.; Curtis in Thomas *v.* Osborn, 19 How. 22 at 28 (1856), citing sec. 322b, 401-403; Taney in Brown *v.* Duchesne, 19 How. 183 at 194 (1856), citing ch. 14, sec. 541.

86 Taney in Cook *v.* Moffat, 5 How. 295 at 311 (1847), citing sec. 335 and secs. ffg., ed. of 1841 [2nd]; Woodbury in the same case, at 315 and 316, citing secs. 272-329, 281-284, 331-335, in that order; Nelson in Dred Scott *v.* Sanford, 19 How. 393 at 460, 461, 462, 467 (1856), citing pp. 24, 398, 59, 60, secs. 91, 96, 103, 104, 396a, in that order. On p. 467, Nelson refers to Story's correspondence with Lord Stowell in the *Life of Story*, I, 552, 558.

87 McKinley in Bank of Augusta *v.* Earle, 13 Pet. 519 at 599 and 604 (1839), citing 37; Woodbury in Waring *v.* Clarke, 5 How. 441 at 503 (1847), citing 423.

88 Each of these subjects involved more than one citation. Those subjects involving only a single reference are here omitted.

Henry Baldwin's *General View of the Constitution* was used as a significant part of the argument by Walker in Groves *v.* Slaughter,[89] and by Van Buren, arguing for the defendant and Justice Woodbury dissenting from the opinion of the court in the Passenger Cases.[90] The last time it was cited was in 1856, by Justice Catron, in his opinion in the Dred Scott case.[91] The points involved seem divided between those of a general constitutional interpretation and more specific points of law. An example of the former is the idea for which Baldwin is used as an authority that "Laws and acts which tend to public utility should receive the most liberal and benign interpretation to effect the object intended or declared." [92] And an example of the latter is the concrete point that measures involving police powers do not come under the cognizance of the federal government.[93]

Justice Levi Woodbury seems to have been best versed in the commentaries. Almost any opinion of his can be counted upon to be rich in textbook citations.

A tabulation of the references to all of the commentaries in constitutional cases indicates that they increased in popularity with the bench and bar until they reached a peak in the 1840's. After that they declined sporadically, apparently giving place to increased references to American judicial decisions. They did not disappear, however, and as will be mentioned in chapter x, they are not infrequently found in *post bellum* cases.

89 Arguing for the plaintiffs, 15 Pet. 449 at App. 600 and 617 (1841). Ref. to pp. 99-100, 192; 8, 9, 11, in that order.

90 7 How. 283 at 368, 377, 524, 526, 546, 556, 571 (1849). Refs. to Baldwin 29-32, 194-197, 183, 184, 188, 193. Some of these pages were cited twice or more.

91 19 How. 393 at 522 and 528, citing pp. 90, 84.

92 Groves *v.* Slaughter, 15 Pet. 449 at 617 (1841). Ref. to Baldwin 8, by Walker for the plaintiffs.

93 Passenger Cases, 7 How. 283 at 524 (1849). Ref. to Baldwin 184, 188, Woodbury, J., dissenting.

## Section III

The connections in which the commentaries have been mentioned as figuring were not the only ones in which they appeared. Joseph Story provides the examples for a few other uses. The marked similarity between the reasoning of the *Commentaries on the Constitution* and Webster's speech on the Union, delivered in the Senate a month after the three volumes were published, has already been noted.[94] And John Quincy Adams entered in his *Memoirs,* under date of January 13, 1845,

> Tibbatts, of Kentucky, made an hour speech for the annexation [of Texas] upon the constitutional question, the whole compass of which was intrepid assertion of the prior right of France to Texas over that of Spain, and misapplication of numerous extracts from Judge Story's Commentaries on the Constitution.[95]

Mention has been made of the popularity of Story's works outside the United States. George Bancroft, in his *History of the United States,* noted that " The European who would understand our form of government, must study the Commentaries of Story." [96] The merit of this idea was recognized by Alexis de Tocqueville who borrowed heavily for his *Democracy in America.* Story was aware of the fact, and mentioned it to Francis Lieber.[97] Later, Story's son wrote,

94 *Cf. infra,* ch. iv, note 146, p. 152.

95 Adams, *Memoirs,* XII, 145.

96 I (Boston: 1834), 372.

97 Story to Lieber, May 9, 1840, in Story, *Life and Letters,* II, 330. " The work of DeTocqueville has had great reputation abroad, partly founded on their ignorance that he has borrowed the greater part of his reflections from American works, and little from his own observations. The main body of his materials will be found in the Federalist, and in Story's Commentaries on the Constitution; *sic vos non vobis.* You know ten times as much as he does of the actual workings of our system and of its true theory."

It is a little singular, that though such extensive use is made of my father's Commentaries on the Constitution . . . no acknowledgment is made, and the Commentaries are scarcely referred to by name.[98]

In the southern hemisphere, various editions of Story's works appeared. And recently it was recalled that President Domingo Faustino Sarmiento of Argentina in the 1870's, had such documents as the *Federalist* and Story's constitutional writings translated into Spanish. He established schools based on the United States model, and educated his people in the political institutions of federalism, which he greatly admired.[99]

98 *Ibid.*, II, 329.

99 *Cf.* letter by George S. Wallis, Jr., to the editors of *Time*, XLIX (Feb. 3, 1947), 10.

# CHAPTER X

# POSTSCRIPT

THOUGH by the time of the Civil War, Dane, Chipman, Hoffman, Duer, Taylor, and others retained only historic or even antiquarian interest, a few of the commentators survived to be noticed in various connections after Appomattox. As might be expected, Kent and Story retained the supremacy which they had exhibited in the earlier period. References to them and to many of the others may be found in constitutional histories and in general histories of American political thought, although new commentaries were coming along to replace them.[1]

The old Tucker-Story controversy was not suffered to rest, even after the Civil War. John Randolph Tucker, in his *Commentaries on the Constitution* (Chicago: 1896), took occasion to disagree with the theories which had perturbed his *ante bellum* sire and grandsire. Later, a representative of the next generation, another Henry St. George Tucker, entered the fray. In his article on " Judge Story's Position on the So-Called General Welfare Clause," he examined in detail Story's effort to lead us to a " government of unlimited power " by means of the construction of this clause. Opposed to Story, with whom only one writer can be found to agree, Tucker sets up a long list of authorities who disagree.[2]

1 See the forthcoming monograph of Charles E. Larsen, *Commentaries on the Constitution, 1865-1900.*

2 (The list given in the *Congressional Record* is different from that in Senate Doc. 17, 70th Cong., 1st sess.) Tucker's speech was called forth by the Congressional debates over the constitutionality of the national subsidy laws. See his remarks on the Maternity Act delivered in the House on March 3, 1926. *Congressional Record*, 69th Cong., 1st sess., pp. 4931-39. The address referred to above was delivered before the Georgia Bar Association, and appeared in the *American Bar Association Journal*, XIII (July and Aug. 1927), 363-368, 465-469. See esp. pp. 468-469. This address was reprinted as Senate Doc. 17, 70th Cong., 1st sess.; and again in the *Constitutional Review* for January 1929, and discussed in the subsequent issues of April and July 1929, XIII, 13-35, 98-100, 163-164. *Cf.* Carpenter, *The South as a Conscious Minority*, p. 48 note.

In the late nineteenth century, citations of the commentaries as precedents in constitutional cases were still found in the *Supreme Court Reports.* Story was the most popular authority through 1900, and his successor, Thomas Cooley, ran him a close second. Kent more than held his own, and occasional references were found to the *Federalist,* Rawle, Sergeant, and Curtis.[3]

As a form of legal literature, commentaries were on the decline in the post-Civil War period. Relatively few new ones were written, though the best of the early volumes were kept up to date. By the beginning of the twentieth century, when time had provided a sufficient perspective to permit of judgments on their significance, editors of revisions occasionally referred to the importance of the works which they were once again bringing to the attention of the public.

The Eleventh edition of Walker's *Introduction to American Law,* published in 1904, was one in which the editor recognized the peculiar contribution of the author:

> Perhaps no greater tribute can be paid to the genius, broad views, and thorough learning of Judge Walker than to say that his recommendations, his criticisms, and the improvements suggested by him, running through every topic of the law, have been in a great degree realized in the development of the law since his day, rendering it unnecessary to repeat them. Their results appear in the growth and betterment of the science of which he was one of the ablest expounders.[4]

And the editor of the Fourteenth edition of Kent's *Commentaries* wrote,

> The masterpiece of Chancellor Kent has now become so interwoven with judicial decisions that these commentaries upon our frame of government and system of laws will doubt-

3 Tabulations supporting these conclusions are in Larsen, *Commentaries on the Constitution, 1865-1900.*

4 Clement Bates, ed. (Boston: 1905). Preface to 11th ed.

less continue to rank as the first of American legal classics so long as the present order shall prevail.[5]

Joseph Story, as the representative of all the commentators, has been given a rare and lasting tribute. In the magnificent stained-glass of the Chapel of St. Yves in the Cathedral of St. John the Divine in New York, there is a small medallion of Story, as Dane Professor of Law at Harvard University, instructing his students.[6] He is among a noteworthy company— Solon, Hammurabi, Bracton, Grotius, Marshall, and other immortals. The artist's selection of his subject's vocation as a teacher was a particularly fitting one, in view of Story's belief that his fame lay with his students. Our knowledge of men whose names have been lost to common sight, but who served in smaller spheres than did Story, leads us to regard his perpetuation for the ages in art as symbolic of the many who nobly strove for the elevation and clarification of the law.

5 John M. Gould, ed. (Boston: 1896). Preface to 14th ed. Oliver Wendell Holmes, who prepared the 12th ed. (1873), on which the 14th is based, said in his prefatory note explaining his contributions, " The great weight attaching to any opinion of Chancellor Kent has been deemed a sufficient reason for not attempting any alteration in his text or notes."

6 Edward Hagaman Hall, *A Guide to the Cathedral Church of Saint John the Divine in the City of New York* (12th ed., New York: Laymen's Club of the Cathedral, 1942), p. 64.

# BIBLIOGRAPHY OF WORKS CITED

Research for this study was conducted at the following libraries: Columbia University, New York Public, Harvard University, Middlebury College, William and Mary, the University of California, and the Library of Congress. Separate law libraries were used at Columbia, Harvard, the University of California, and the Library of Congress. Since the chief emphasis throughout has been on printed materials, relatively few manuscript sources have been consulted. However, such manuscripts as were available at the institutions mentioned were used, including the Sumner Papers (Harvard), the Kent Papers (Library of Congress), and the Lieber Papers (Huntington Library, San Marino, California).

Instruction in the exact wording of the Constitution apparently antedated any other form of training in civics or government in the United States. The main part of this study has been confined to the commentaries on the Constitution which were prepared to influence public opinion and/or to serve as textbooks for students in colleges and law schools. But there were many authors who were concerned with the proper training of younger minds and with providing works of reference for the general public. Story himself prepared two abridgments of his lengthy *Commentaries* designed for children, and many other teachers wrote original works of the same nature. The most complete study of these texts is *The Constitution in School and College*, by H. Arnold Bennett (New York and London: G. P. Putnam's Sons, 1935). Dr. Bennett's bibliography indicates, however, that he must have worked primarily with the collection in the Library of Congress. Various other texts have been located in other libraries, notably at Harvard. These works have been included here for purposes of completeness, but they cannot be discussed in detail. They are marked with an asterisk in the first part of this bibliography.

Note: The name of the publishing house is given only for volumes published within the last twenty-five years.

### COMMENTARIES AND TEXTBOOKS ON THE CONSTITUTION

Baldwin, Henry. *A General View of the Origin and Nature of the Constitution and Government of the United States.... Together with Opinions in the Cases decided at January term, 1837, arising on the Restraints on the Powers of the States.* Philadelphia: 1837. 197 pp.

*Bayard, James. *A Brief Exposition of the Constitution of the United States: with an appendix,... containing the Declaration of Independence, and the Articles of Confederation. And a Copious Index.* Philadelphia: 1833. 166 pp. 2nd ed., 1834. 178 pp.

*Burleigh, Joseph Bartlett. *The American Manual; containing a brief outline of the origin and progress of political power, and the laws of nations; a commentary on the Constitution of the United States of North America,... designed to ... impart an accurate knowledge of the nature and necessity of political wisdom. Adapted to the use of schools, aca-*

*demies, and the public.* Philadelphia: 1848. 318 pp. 55 additional pp. in Appendix. 15th ed., 1852, with different title.

Chipman, Nathaniel. *Principles of Government, A Treatise on Free Institutions, Including the Constitution of the United States.* Burlington, Vt.: 1833. 330 + 44 pp.

——. *Sketches of the Principles of Government.* Rutland, Vt.: 1793. 292 pp.

Cooper, Thomas. *Two Essays: 1. On the Foundation of Civil Government: 2. On the Constitution of the United States.* Columbia, S. C.: 1826. 71 pp.

Curtis, George Ticknor. *History of the Origin, Formation, and Adoption of the Constitution of the United States; with Notices of Its Principal Framers.* New York: 1854-58. 2 vols. Rev. ed., *Constitutional History of the United States from Their Declaration of Independence to the Close of the Civil War.* New York: 1889-96. 2 vols. 2nd vol. ed. by J. C. Clayton.

Dane, Nathan. *A General Abridgment and Digest of American Law, with occasional Notes and Comments.* Boston: 1823-24, 1829. 9 vols.

*Davis, Pardon. *The Principles of the Government of the United States. Adapted to the Use of Schools.* Philadelphia: 1823. 204 pp.

Duer, William Alexander. *A Course of Lectures on the Constitutional Jurisprudence of the United States, delivered annually in Columbia Colege, New-York.* New York: 1843, reprinted in 1845, 1868 and 1874. 419 pp. 2nd ed., Boston: 1856, rev., enl., and adapted to professional as well as general use.

——. *Outlines of the Constitutional Jurisprudence of the United States; Designed as a Text Book for lectures, as a Class Book for Academies and Common Schools, and as a Manual for Popular Use.* New York: 1833. 249 pp.

DuPonceau, Peter Stephen. *A Brief View of the Constitution of the United States, Addressed to the Law Academy of Philadelphia.* Philadelphia: 1834. 106 pp.

——. *A Dissertation on the Nature and Extent of the Jurisdiction of the Courts of the United States, being a valedictory address delivered to the students of the law academy of Philadelphia, ... on the 22nd of April, 1824.* Philadelphia: 1824. 254 pp., including other material.

*The Federalist, a collection of essays, written in favour of the new Constitution,* written by James Madison, Alexander Hamilton, and John Jay. New York: 1788, with numerous later editions.

*Fellowes, Francis. *Youth's Manual of the Constitution of the United States; adapted to classes in schools, and to general use.* Hartford, Conn.: 1835. 188 pp.

*Flanders, Henry. *An Exposition of the Constitution of the United States. Designed as a Manual of Instruction.* Philadelphia: 1860. 311 pp. Several revisions after 1860.

*Goodrich, Samuel Griswold. *The Young American: or, Book of Government and Law; showing their history, nature, and necessity. For the use of schools.* Boston: 1842; 8th ed., 1845. 282 pp.

*Hale, B. E. *Familiar Conversations upon the Constitution of the United States; designed for the Use of Common Schools.* West Bradford and Boston: 1835. 132 pp.

*Hart, John Seely. *A Brief Exposition of the Constitution of the United States.* Philadelphia: 1845. 100 pp.

*Hickey, William. *The Constitution of the United States of America, with an Alphabetical Analysis; the Declaration of Independence; the Articles of Confederation; the prominent political acts of George Washington; Electoral Votes for all the Presidents and Vice Presidents; the high authorities and civil officers of government, from March 4, 1789 to March 3, 1847;* ... 3rd ed., Philadelphia: 1848; 7th ed., 1854. 1st ed., 1846, with slightly different title.

Hoffman, David. *A Course of Legal Study, Respectfully Addressed to the Students of Law in the United States.* Baltimore: 1817. 383 pp. 2nd ed., *A Course of Legal Study, Addressed to Students and the Profession Generally,* rev. and enl. Baltimore: 1836. 2 vols. Reprinted in 1 vol., 1846.

———. *Syllabus of a course of lectures on law; proposed to be delivered in the University of Maryland; addressed to the Students of Law in the United States.* Baltimore: 1821. 91 pp.

Kent, James. *Commentaries on American Law.* New York: 1826-30. 4 vols. 14th ed., 1896.

*Mansfield, Edward Deering. *The Political Grammar of the United States; or, A complete view of the theory and practice of the general and state governments, with the relations between them. Dedicated and adapted to the Young Men of the United States.* New York: 1834. 275 pp. 16th ed., 1849.

*Mason, Charles. *An Elementary Treatise on the Structure and Operations of the National and State Governments of the United States. Designed for the use of Schools and Academies and for general readers.* Boston: 1842. 233 pp.

*McKinney, Mordecai. *The United States Constitutional Manual; being a comprehensive compendium of the System of Government of the Country; presenting a view of the general government, ... and of the Governments of the States, ... Particularly that of Pennsylvania, and their relations ... respectively to the Union, and to each other; with definitions, constructions of constitutional provisions, and explanations; in the form of questions and answers; designed for academies, schools, and readers in general.* Harrisburg, Pa.: 1845. 304 pp. 2nd ed., 1856, with slightly different title.

*Moulton, R. K. *The Constitutional Guide. Comprising the Constitution of the United States with Notes and Commentaries from the Writings of Judge Story, Chancellor Kent, James Madison, and Other Distinguished American Citizens.* New York: 1834. 143 pp.

*Oliver, Benjamin Lynde. *The Rights of the American Citizen; with a commentary on State Rights, and on the Constitution and Policy of the United States.* Boston and Philadelphia: 1832. 411 pp.

*Parker, Daniel. *The Constitutional Instructor, for the Use of Schools.* Boston: 1848. 162 pp.

*Pratt, Luther. *An Exposition of the Constitution of the United States to Which is Prefixed the Forms of Government in Different Parts of the World.* Albany, N. Y.: 1837. 55 pp.

Rawle, William. *A View of the Constitution of the United States of America.* Philadelphia: 1825. 347 pp. 2nd ed., 1829. 349 pp.

Sergeant, Thomas. *Constitutional Law. Being a collection of points arising upon the Constitution and Jurisprudence of the United States, which have been settled, by judicial decision and practice.* Philadelphia: 1822. 415 pp. 2nd ed., Philadelphia: 1830: *Constitutional Law: Being a view of the practice and jurisdiction of the courts of the United States, and of constitutional points decided.* 440 pp.

*Sheppard, Furman. *The Constitutional Text-book: a Practical and Familiar Exposition of the Constitution of the United States, and of portions of the public and administrative law of the Federal Government. Designed chiefly for the use of Schools, Academies and Colleges.* Philadelphia: 1855; reprinted in 1858. 324 pp. Abridged edition with slightly different title, Philadelphia: 1866. 210 pp.

*Shurtleff, J. B. *The Governmental Instructor, or, A Brief and Comprehensive View of the Government of the United States, and of the State Governments, in easy lessons, designed for the use of schools.* New York: 1845. 182 pp. 3rd rev. ed., New York: 1871. 193 pp.

Smith, E. Fitch. *Commentaries on Statute and Constitutional Law and statutory and constitutional construction, containing an examination of adjudged cases on constitutional law under the constitution of the United States, and the constitution [sic] of the respective states concerning legislative power, and also the consideration of the rules of law in the construction of statutes and constitutional provisions.* Albany, N. Y.: 1848. 976 pp.

*Stansbury, Arthur Joseph. *Elementary Catechism on the Constitution of the United States. For the Use of Schools.* Boston: 1828. 78 pp.

Story, Joseph. *Commentaries on the Conflict of Laws.* Boston: 1834. 557 pp. Rev. eds. in 1841, 1846, 1852, 1857, 1865, 1872, 1883.

——. *Commentaries on the Constitution of the United States; with a preliminary review of the constitutional history of the colonies and states, before the adoption of the Constitution.* Boston: 1833. 3 vols. Later eds., 1851, 1858, 1873, 1891 reprinted in 1905. 2 vols.

——. *Commentaries on the Constitution of the United States; with a preliminary review of the constitutional history of the colonies and states, before the adoption of the Constitution. Abridged by the author, for the use of colleges and high schools.* Boston and Cambridge: 1833. 736 pp.

*——. *The Constitutional Class Book: being a brief exposition of the Constitution of the United States. Designed for the use of the higher classes in common schools.* Boston: 1834. 166 pp.

*——. *A Familiar Exposition of the Constitution of the United States: containing a brief commentary on every clause, explaining the true nature, reasons, and objects thereof; designed for the use of school libraries and general readers. With an Appendix, containing important public documents, illustrative of the Constitution.* New York and Boston: 1840, with reprints in 1842, 1847, 1859, 1867, 1869, 1882, 1884, etc. 372 pp.

*Sullivan, William. *The Political Class book; intended to instruct the higher classes in schools, in the Origin, Nature, and Use of Political Power. With an appendix upon studies for practical men; with notices of books suited to their use by George B. Emerson.* Boston: 1830. 148 pp. Later eds., 1831 and 1838.

Taylor, John. *Construction Construed, and Constitutions Vindicated.* Richmond, Va.: 1820. 344 pp.

——. *An Inquiry into the Principles and Policy of the Government of the United States.* Fredericksburg: 1814. 656 pp.

——. *New Views of the Constitution of the United States.* Washington City: 1823. 316 pp.

*Towle, Nathaniel Carter. *A History and Analysis of the Constitution of the United States, with a full account of the confederations which preceded it; of the debates and acts of the convention which formed it; of the judicial decisions which have construed it; with papers and tables illustrative of the action of the government and the people under it.* Boston: 1860. 444 pp. 2nd ed., 1861; 3rd ed., rev. and enl., 1871.

Tucker, Henry St. George. *Lectures on Constitutional Law, for the use of the Law Class at the University of Virginia.* Richmond: 1843. 242 pp.

——. *Lectures on Government.* Charlottesville: 1844. 224 pp.

Tucker, Nathaniel Beverley. *A Series of Lectures on the Science of Government, Intended to Prepare the Student for the Study of the Constitution of the United States.* Philadelphia: 1845. 464 pp.

Tucker, St. George. *Blackstone's Commentaries: with Notes of Reference, to the Constitution and Laws, of the Federal Government of the United States; and the Commonwealth of Virginia. With an Appendix to each volume, containing short tracts upon such subjects as appeared necessary to form a connected view of the laws of Virginia, as a member of the federal union.* Philadelphia: 1803. 5 vols.

Upshur, Abel Parker. *A Brief Enquiry into the Nature and Character of Our Federal Government: Being a Review of Judge Story's Commentaries on the Constitution of the United States.* Petersburg: 1840. Reprint, Philadelphia: 1863. 131 pp.

Walker, Timothy. *Introduction to American Law, Designed as a First Book for Students.* Philadelphia: 1837. 679 pp.

*Williams, Edwin. *The Book of the Constitution, Containing the Constitution of the United States; a synopsis of the several state constitutions; with various other important documents and useful information.* New York: 1833. 144 pp.

Wilson, James. *The Works of the Honourable James Wilson, LL.D.*, ed. by Bird Wilson. Philadelphia: 1804. 3 vols. 2 vols. with same title ed. by James DeWitt Andrews. Chicago: 1896.

*Winchester, Elhanan. *A Plain Political Catechism. Intended for the Use of Schools,... Wherein the Great Principles of Liberty, and of the Federal Government, Are Laid Down and Explained, by way of Question and Answer. Made level to the lowest capacities.* Greenfield, Mass.: 1796. 107 pp.

*Young, Andrew White. *The American Statesman: A Political History exhibiting the Origin, Nature and Practical Operation of the Constitutional Government of the United States; the rise and progress of parties; and the views of distinguished statesmen on questions of foreign and domestic policy,... with an Appendix...* New York: 1855. 1016 pp. Other eds. in 1857, 1860, 1864, 1870, 1877.

*———. *The Citizen's Manual of Government and Law: Comprising a familiar illustration of the principles of civil government; a practical view of the state governments, and of the government of the United States; a digest of common and statutory law, and of the law of nations; and a summary of parliamentary rules, for the practice of deliberative assemblies; with supplementary notes on the government of the State of Ohio, and the Constitution of the State.* Cleveland: 1853. 336 pp. Rev. eds. in 1858, 1877.

*———. *First Lessons in Civil Government; including a Comprehensive View of the Government of the State of New-York, and an abstract of the laws, showing the rights, duties, and responsibilities of citizens in the Civil and Domestic Relations; with an outline of the Government of the United States: Adapted to the capacities of children and youth, and designed for the use of schools.* Auburn, N. Y.: 1843. 235 pp. 8th ed., 1845, apparently identical to 1st. Other eds., 1846, 1856, 1877.

*———. *The Government Class Book; designed for the Instruction of Youth in the Principles of Constitutional Government, and the Rights and Duties of Citizens.* New York: 1859. 308 pp. Other eds., 1857, 1880, 1882, 1885, 1894, 1900, 1901 rev. and enl.

*———. *Introduction to the Science of Government, and compend of Constitutional and Statutory Law: Comprehending a general view of the government of the United States; with practical observations on the duties of citizens. Adapted to purposes of instruction in families and schools.* Warsaw, N. Y.: 1835. 304 pp. Other eds., 1839, 1848.

### OTHER PERTINENT WRITINGS BY THE COMMENTATORS

Chipman, Nathaniel. *Reports and Dissertations.* Rutland, Vt.: 1793. 296 pp.

Cooper, Thomas. *Lectures on the Elements of Political Economy.* Columbia, S. C.: 1826. 280 pp. 2nd ed., 1829. 366 pp.

Dane, Nathan. Letter to Daniel Webster *re* Northwest Ordinance. Massachusetts Historical Society *Proceedings*, X (Feb. 1869), 475–480.

DuPonceau, Peter Stephen. *A Treatise on the Law of War, Translated from the original Latin of Cornelius van Bynkershoek.* Philadelphia: 1810. 218 pp.

Hoffman, David. *Legal Outlines, Being the Substance of a Course of Lectures now Delivering in the University of Maryland.* Baltimore: 1829. 626 pp. Only vol. I published.

Kent, James. *An Introductory Lecture to a Course of Law Lectures, delivered November 17, 1794.* New York: 1794. 23 pp. Reprinted in *Columbia Law Review,* II (May 1903), 330-343.

——. *Dissertations: Being the Preliminary Part of a Course of Law Lectures.* New York: 1795. 87 pp.

Story, Joseph. *A Discourse Pronounced upon the Inauguration of the Author as Dane Professor of Law in Harvard University, on the Twenty-fifth Day of August, 1829.* Boston: 1829. 60 pp.

——. *The Miscellaneous Writings, Literary, Critical, Juridical, and Political, of Joseph Story, LL.D., Now First Collected.* Boston: 1835. 527 pp. 2nd ed. by his son, W. W. Story, Boston: 1852. 828 pp.

Taylor, John. *Disunion Sentiment in Congress in 1794, A Confidential Memorandum Hitherto Unpublished, written by John Taylor of Caroline, Senator from Virginia, for James Madison.* Gaillard Hunt, ed. Washington: 1905. 23 pp. incl. facsimile of the original memorandum.

——. *Tyranny Unmasked.* Washington, D. C.: 1822. 349 pp.

Tucker, Henry St. George. *Commentaries on the Laws of Virginia, comprising the substance of a course of lectures delivered in the Winchester Law School.* Winchester, Va.: 1831, 1836-37. 2 vols.

——. *Notes on Blackstone's Commentaries for the use of students.* Winchester, Va.: 1826. 2 vols.

Tucker, St. George. *Proposals for publishing an American edition of Blackstone's Commentaries, with notes of reference to the Constitution and laws of the Federal Government of the United States, and of the Commonwealth of Virginia: with an appendix to each volume, containing tracts upon such subjects as appeared necessary to form a systematic view of the laws of Virginia as a member of the Federal Union.* Philadelphia: 1797? 4 + xxiv pp.

Wilson, James, and McKean, Thomas. *Commentaries on the Constitution of the United States of America, with that Constitution prefixed, in which are unfolded, the principles of free government, and the superior advantages of republicanism demonstrated.* London: 1792. 147 pp.

Wilson, James. *Selected Political Essays of James Wilson.* Randolph G. Adams, ed. New York: Alfred Knopf, 1930. 356 pp.

### WORKS SUPPLEMENTARY TO THE MAJOR COMMENTARIES

Adams, John. *A Defence of the Constitutions of Government of the United States of America, against the Attack of M. Turgot in his letter to Dr. Price*... London, Boston, New York, Philadelphia: 1787-88, with later editions and translations. 3 vols.

Adams, John Quincy. *An Oration Addressed to the Citizens of the Town of Quincy on the Fourth of July, 1831,*... Boston: 1831. 40 pp.

Benjamin, Reuben M. *Questions on Kent's Commentaries, with References to Illinois Statutes and Decisions, where the law of the state differs from that laid down in the text.* Chicago: 1880. 146 pp.

——. *Student's Guide to Elementary Law, consisting of Questions on Walker's American Law and Blackstone's Commentaries, with references to Illinois Statutes and Decisions, where the law of the state differs from that laid down in the text.* Chicago: 1879. 178 pp.

Blackstone, Sir William. *Commentaries on the Laws of England.* Oxford: 1765-69, with numerous subsequent editions. 4 vols.

Calhoun, John C. "A Disquisition on Government," and "A Discourse on the Constitution and Government of the United States," in *The Works of John C. Calhoun,* ed. by Richard C. Crallé in 6 vols. Charleston and New York: 1851-1870. Vol. I.

Carson, Hampton L. "The Works of James Wilson," *American Law Reporter and Review,* Vol. 44, o. s., (35, n. s.), (Oct. 1896), 633-641.

"A Course of Lectures on the Constitutional Jurisprudence of the United States"... by W. A. Duer (2nd ed., Boston: 1856). Book review. *North American Review,* LXXXVI (April 1858), 464-486.

Dickson, Frederick S. *An Analysis of Kent's Commentaries.* Philadelphia: 1875. 428 pp.

[Everett, Edward]. "Story's Constitutional Law," *North American Review,* XXXVIII (Jan. 1834), 63-84.

Fine, John. *Lectures on Law, Prepared Principally from Kent, by a lawyer for the use of his sons.* Albany and New York: 1852. 320 pp.

Johnson, J. Eastman. *An Analytical Abridgment of Kent's Commentaries on American Law, With a full series of questions for examination, adapted both to the Analysis and to the original commentaries.* New York: 1839. 389 pp.

Kinne, Asa. *The Most Important Parts of Kent's Commentaries, Reduced to Questions and Answers.* New York: 1838. 2nd ed., 1840, 249 pp. 4th ed., 1843, 266 pp.

Lieber, Francis. *Manual of Political Ethics.* Boston: 1838-39. 2 vols.

——. *On Civil Liberty and Self-Government.* Philadelphia: 1853. 2 vols. Reprinted in London: 1853. 552 pp.

——. *What is our Constitution,—League, Pact, or Government? Two lectures on the Constitution of the United States... delivered in the Law School of Columbia College, during the winter of 1860-61, to which is appended an address on secession, written in the year 1851.* New York: 1861. 48 pp.

Marshall, John. *The Writings of John Marshall, Late Chief Justice of the United States, upon the Federal Constitution.* Boston: 1839. 728 pp.

"Outlines of Constitutional Jurisprudence in the United States, by William Alexander Duer, LL.D., President of Columbia College." Book review. *American Jurist and Law Magazine,* XI (Jan. 1834), 235-236.

Review of Story's Commentaries on the Constitution. *American Monthly Review,* IV (Dec. 1833), 499-513.

Review of Story's Commentaries on the Constitution. *American Quarterly Review*, XIV (Dec. 1833), 327-367.

Stephens, Alexander. *A Constitutional View of the Late War between the States; its causes, character, conduct and results presented in a series of colloquies at Liberty Hall.* Philadelphia: 1868-70. 2 vols. in 1.

Story, Joseph. "A General Abridgment and Digest of American Law with Occasional Notes and Comments by Nathan Dane, LL.D., Counselor at Law, in 8 vols." Book review. *North American Review*, XXIII (July 1826), 1-41.

[Story, Joseph]. "A Course of legal study respectfully addressed to the Students of Law in the United States. By David Hoffman, Professor of Law in the university of Maryland..." Book review. *North American Review*, VI (Nov. 1817), 45-77.

" Story's Commentaries—Vol. I." *American Jurist and Law Magazine*, IX (April 1833), 241-288.

" Story's Commentaries—Vols. II and III." *Ibid.*, X (July 1833), 119-147.

Tucker, John Randolph. *The Constitution of the United States. A Critical Discussion of its Genesis, Development, and Interpretation.* Chicago: 1896. 2 vols. 2nd ed. by Henry St. George Tucker, Chicago: 1899. 2 vols.

Webster, Daniel. "The Constitution Not a Compact between Sovereign States," in *The Works of Daniel Webster.* III (Boston: 1851), 449-505.

### ADDITIONAL PRIMARY SOURCES

Adams, John. *The Works of John Adams, Second President of the United States,...* ed. by Charles Francis Adams. Boston: 1856. 10 vols.

Adams, John Quincy. *Memoirs of John Quincy Adams, comprising portions of his diary from 1795 to 1848,* ed. by Charles Francis Adams. Philadelphia: 1874-77. 12 vols.

"Advertisement of the Harvard Law School." *The Christian Review.* Nashville, Tenn.: Sept. 1845. Vol. II, no. 9.

Agnew, Daniel. Address to the Allegheny County Bar Association, December 1, 1888, Sketch No. 8 on Henry Baldwin. *Pennsylvania Magazine of History and Biography*, XIII (Jan. 1889), 23-29.

American Bar Association. *Canons of Professional Ethics,... Adopted by the American Bar Association.* As amended, Sept. 30, 1937. 50 pp.

*Annals of Congress.* Esp. 5th Cong., 2nd sess.; 10th Cong., 2nd sess.; 14th Cong., 1st sess.; 15th Cong., 1st sess. *Passim.*

Bennett, R. T. "Morale of the Confederate." *Southern Historical Society Papers*, XXII (1894), 81-86.

" Biographical Notice of Mr. Justice Story." *American Review, A Whig Journal*, III (Jan. 1846), 68-82.

Brown, David Paul. "Eulogium of William Rawle," delivered Dec. 31, 1836. Philadelphia: 1837. Reprinted in D. P. Brown, *The Forum; or, Forty Years Full Practice at the Philadelphia Bar.* Philadelphia: 1856. 2 vols.

Call, Daniel. "Biographical Sketch of the Judges of the Court of Appeals," 4 Call Rep. xlvi. Reprinted in Virginia Reports Annotated, V-X (Charlottesville, Va.: 1902), 627-628.

Carter, Alfred G. W. *The Old Court House: Reminiscences and Anecdotes of the Courts and Bar of Cincinnati.* Cincinnati: 1880. 466 pp.

Chipman, Daniel. *Life of Honorable Nathaniel Chipman, LL.D., Formerly Member of the United States Senate, and Chief Justice of the State of Vermont, with Selections from His Miscellaneous Writings.* Boston: 1846. 402 pp.

Cist, Charles. *Cincinnati in 1841: Its Early Annals and Future Prospects.* Cincinnati: 1841. 300 pp.

Coleman, Charles Washington, Jr. "The Southern Campaign, 1781, From Guilford Court House to the Siege of York, Narrated in the letters from Judge St. George Tucker to his wife." *Magazine of American History,* VII (July-Sept. 1881), 36-46, 201-216.

*The Constitution of the United States of America (Annotated),* S. Doc. 232, 74th Cong., 2nd sess. Washington: Govt. Printing Office, 1938. 1246 pp.

Conway, Moncure Daniel. *Omitted Chapters of History, Disclosed in the Life and Papers of Edmund Randolph* ... New York and London: 1888. 401 pp.

Curtis, George Ticknor. *Life of Daniel Webster.* New York: 1869. 2 vols. 4th ed., 1872.

——. Vol. I of *A Memoir of Benjamin Robbins Curtis, LL.D., with some of his professional and miscellaneous writings.* Ed. by his son, Benjamin Robbins Curtis. Boston: 1879. 2 vols.

Davis, Matthew L. *Memoir of Aaron Burr, with Miscellaneous Selections from His Correspondence.* New York: 1837. 2 vols.

"Death of Peter S. DuPonceau," obituary taken from the *United States Gazette. Western Law Journal,* I (May 1844), 379-380.

Duer, John. *A Discourse on the Life, Character, and Public Services of James Kent, Late Chancellor of the State of New-York; delivered by request, before the Judiciary and Bar of the City and State of New-York, April 12, 1848.* New York: 1848. 86 pp.

Duer, William Alexander. *New-York as It Was, During the Latter Part of the Last Century.* An anniversary address delivered before the St. Nicholas Society, of the City of New-York, December 1st, 1848. New York: 1849. 48 pp.

——. *Reminiscences of an Old New Yorker,* Address to the St. Nicholas Society, 1848. New York: 1867. 102 pp.

Dunglison, Robley. "Biographical Sketch of Peter S. DuPonceau." *American Law Magazine,* V (April 1845), 1-33.

DuPonceau, Peter Stephen. "The Autobiography of Peter Stephen Du-Ponceau," ed. by James L. Whitehead. *Pennsylvania Magazine of History and Biography,* LXIII and LXIV (April 1939–April 1940), *passim.*

——. "Mr. DuPonceau's Will." *Pennsylvania Law Journal,* III (1844), 297-299.

——. "Memoir of William Rawle," delivered June 3, 1837. *Memoirs of the Historical Society of Pennsylvania*, IV, part I (Philadelphia: 1840), 77-91.

Elliot, Jonathan. *The Debates in the Several State Conventions on the Adoption of the Federal Constitution* ... Washington: 1827-30. 4 vols. Vol. V, containing Madison's Notes, published in 1836.

Farrand, Max, ed. *The Records of the Federal Convention of 1787*. Rev. ed., New Haven: Yale University Press, 1937. 4 vols.

"Fitch's and Fulton's Steam-Navigation," a letter to the editor signed by "A Former Member of the Legislature." *Putnam's Monthly Magazine*, V (Jan. 1855), 103-105.

"George Ticknor Curtis," an obituary. *Harvard Graduates' Magazine*, II (June 1894), 572-574.

Gilmor, Robert. "Diary of Robert Gilmor." *Maryland Historical Magazine*, XVII (Sept.–Dec. 1922), *passim*.

Greenleaf, Simon. *A Discourse Commemorative of the Life and Character of the Hon. Joseph Story, LL.D. ... pronounced on the Eighteenth Day of September, 1845, at the Request of the Corporation of the University, and the Members of the Law School*. Boston: 1845. 48 pp.

——, comp. *Scrapbook of Eulogies of Joseph Story*. Presented to the Harvard Law School, June 9, 1846. In Treasure Room of Langdell Hall.

Hamilton, Alexander. *The Works of Alexander Hamilton; Containing His Correspondence, and His Political and Official Writings* ... , John C. Hamilton, ed. New York: 1850-51. 7 vols.

"Henry Baldwin," an obituary. *Pennsylvania Law Journal*, III (1844), 330-332.

Hillard, George S. *Memoir of Joseph Story, LL.D.*, reprinted from the Massachusetts Historical Society *Proceedings* for 1867-68. Boston: 1868. 32 pp.

Hoffman, David. [*Letters*] *To the Trustees of the University of Maryland in Relation to the Law Chair*, and letter of resignation. Baltimore: 1826 and April 21, 1836. 36 + 1 pp.

Hone, Philip. *Diary, 1828-1851*, Allan Nevins, ed. New York: Dodd, Mead, 1927. 2 vols.

Jefferson, Thomas. *Writings*, ed. by H. A. Washington. Washington: 1853-54. 9 vols.

    Ford ed., New York and London: 1892-99. 10 vols.

    Library ed., Washington: 1903. 20 vols.

    Federal ed., New York and London: 1904-5. 12 vols.

*Journal of Debates and Proceedings in the Convention of Delegates, Chosen to Revise the Constitution of Massachusetts*. Boston: 1821. 292 pp. New ed., Boston: 1853. 677 pp.

Kennedy, John Pendleton. *Memoirs of the Life of William Wirt, Attorney-General of the United States*. Rev. ed., Philadelphia: 1850. 2 vols.

Kent, William. *Memoirs and Letters of James Kent, LL.D.* Boston: 1898. 341 pp.

"Laws and Regulations, 1837," *Bulletin of the College of William and Mary.* XI (1917), No. 2. 28 pp.

Lieber, Francis. *Life and Letters,* ed. by Thomas Sergeant Perry. Boston: 1882. 439 pp.

Madison, James. *Letters and Other Writings of James Madison, Fourth President of the United States,* published by order of Congress. Philadelphia: 1865. 4 vols.

——. *Writings,* ed. by Gaillard Hunt. New York: 1900-10. 9 vols.

McMaster, J. B., and Stone, F. D., eds. *Pennsylvania and the Federal Constitution, 1787-1788.* Historical Society of Pennsylvania: 1888. 803 pp.

McRee, Griffith John. *Life and Correspondence of James Iredell, One of the Associate Justices of the Supreme Court of the United States.* New York: 1857-58. 2 vols.

Monroe, James. "Letters of James Monroe," Massachusetts Historical Society *Proceedings.* XLII (May 1909), 318-341.

Newell, William. *A Discourse Occasioned by the Death of the Hon. Joseph Story, LL.D., Delivered in the Church of the First Parish in Cambridge, on Sunday, September 14, 1845, by ... the pastor.* Cambridge: 1845. 23 pp.

Nicolay, John G., and Hay, John, eds. *Abraham Lincoln, Complete Works.* New York: 1894. 2 vols.

*Niles Weekly Register.* XI (Baltimore: 1817). *Passim.*

Peabody, Andrew Preston. *Harvard Graduates Whom I Have Known.* Boston and New York: 1890. 255 pp.

"Peter S. DuPonceau," obituary notice. *Law Reporter,* VII (May 1844), 62-64.

Pickering, John. "Peter S. DuPonceau, LL.D." *Journal of the American Oriental Society,* I (1844), 161-170.

Rawle, William. *Two Addresses to "The Associated Members of the Bar of Philadelphia," pronounced by William Rawle, Esquire, Chancellor of the Association.* Philadelphia: 1824. 52 pp.

"Report made to the General Assembly of the State of Louisiana, of the Plan of the Penal Code for the said State, by Edward Livingston, Member of the House of Representatives from the Parish of Plaquemines." *North American Review,* XVII (Oct. 1823), 242-268.

*Reports of Cases Argued and Adjudged in the Supreme Court of the United States, 1790-1860.* New York: 1882-83. Vols. 1-65.

Safford, William Harrison, ed. *The Blennerhassett Papers, Embodying the Private Journal of Harman Blennerhassett (and unpublished correspondence).* Cincinnati: 1864. 665 pp.

Scharf, J. Thomas. *The Chronicles of Baltimore; Being a Complete History of "Baltimore Town" and Baltimore City from the Earliest Period to the Present Time.* Baltimore: 1874. 756 pp.

Stiles, Ezra. *The Literary Diary of Ezra Stiles, D.D., LL.D., President of Yale College,* ed. by Franklin B. Dexter. New York: 1901. 3 vols.

Story, Joseph. *Life and Letters of Joseph Story,* ed. by William Wetmore Story. Boston and London: 1851. 2 vols.

Sumner, Charles. "The Scholar, the Jurist, the Artist, the Philanthropist," address before the Phi Beta Kappa Society of Harvard University, August 27, 1846, in *The Works of Charles Sumner*. I (Boston: 1875), 245-302.

——. "Tribute of Friendship: The Late Joseph Story," article from the *Boston Daily Advertiser*, Sept. 16, 1845, in *ibid.*, I, 133-148.

"Timothy Walker." *Monthly Law Reporter*, VIII new series (April 1856), 708-709.

Tucker, John Randolph. "The Judges Tucker of the Court of Appeals of Virginia." *Virginia Law Register*, I (March 1896), 789-812. Printed separately as *The Public Services of St. George Tucker, a Judge, and of Henry St. George Tucker, a President, of the Court of Appeals of Virginia*. N. p.: 1896. 24 pp.

Tyler, Lyon Gardiner. *The Letters and Times of the Tylers*. Richmond: 1884-85. 2 vols.

U. S. Continental Congress. *Journals of the American Congress: From 1774 to 1788*. Washington: 1823. 4 vols.

——. *Journals of the Continental Congress, 1774-1789*. Washington: Govt. Printing Office, 1936. 34 vols.

*Virginia Magazine of History and Biography.* XXIX (1921), *passim*.

Waln, Robert, Jr. "James Wilson," in John Sanderson, ed., *Biography of the Signers of the Declaration of Independence*. VI (Philadelphia: 1824), 113-175.

Walton, E. P. "Nathaniel Chipman," in Abby Maria Hemenway, ed., *Vermont Historical Gazetteer*, III (1877), 1154-1160.

Watson, John F. *Annals of Philadelphia and Pennsylvania in the Olden Time*, enlarged by Willis P. Hazard. Philadelphia: 1899. 3 vols.

*Western Law Journal*, ed. by Timothy Walker. Cincinnati: 1843-53. 10 vols.

Wharton, Thomas I. "A Memoir of William Rawle," *Memoirs of the Historical Society of Pennsylvania*. IV, part I (Philadelphia: 1840), 35-76.

*William and Mary College Quarterly.* Williamsburg, Va.: 1892-1945. 52 vols., *passim*.

SECONDARY WORKS

Adams, Henry. *History of the United States of America during the Administrations of Jefferson and Madison*. New York: 1909. 9 vols.

Adams, Randolph Greenfield. "Abel Parker Upshur," in S. F. Bemis, ed., *The American Secretaries of State and Their Diplomacy*. V (New York: 1928), 67-124.

——. *Political Ideas of the American Revolution. Britannic-American Contributions to the Problem of Imperial Organization, 1765 to 1775*. Durham, N. C.: 1922. 207 pp.

Alexander, Lucien Hugh. "James Wilson, Nation Builder." *The Green Bag*, XIX (Jan.-Apr. 1907), 1, 98, 137, 265 *et seq*.

——. "James Wilson, Patriot, and the Wilson Doctrine." *North American Review*, 183 (Nov. 16, 1906), 971-989.

Aumann, Francis R. *The Changing American Legal System: Some Selected Phases.* Columbus: Ohio State University Press, 1940. 281 pp.

Bancroft, George. *History of the United States, from the Discovery of the American Continent.* I (Boston: 1834).

Barnard, Henry, ed. Note regarding Nathaniel Chipman. *American Journal of Education*, XXVII (July 1877), 546.

Barrett, Jay A. *Evolution of the Ordinance of 1787.* New York and London: 1891. 94 pp.

Beard, Charles A. *Economic Origins of Jeffersonian Democracy.* New York: 1915. 474 pp.

——. "Time, Technology, and the Creative Spirit in Political Science." *American Political Science Review*, XXI (Feb. 1927), 1-11.

Bennett, Andrew. *James Wilson of St. Andrews, an American Statesman, 1742-1798.* St. Andrews: J. and G. Innes, Ltd., [1928]. 81 pp.

Bennett, H. Arnold. *The Constitution in School and College.* New York and London: G. P. Putnam's Sons, 1935. 315 pp.

Beveridge, Albert J. *The Life of John Marshall.* Boston and New York: 1916. 4 vols.

Bingham, Robert. "Sectional Misunderstandings." *North American Review*, 179 (Sept. 1904), 357-370. Also published as a pamphlet. Asheville, N. C.: n. d. 20 pp.

Bruce, Philip Alexander. *History of the University of Virginia, 1819-1919; the Lengthened Shadow of One Man.* New York: 1920-22. 5 vols.

Bruce, William Cabell. *John Randolph of Roanoke, 1773-1833.* New York and London: 1922. 2 vols.

Buchanan, Roberdeau. *Genealogy of the McKean Family of Pennsylvania.* Lancaster, Pa.: 1890. 273 pp.

Burdick, Francis M. "Legal Instruction at Columbia." *Columbia University Quarterly*, IV (March 1902), 120-132.

Burns, James, publr. *Selections from the Works of Joseph Story, LL.D., with a Sketch of his Life.* Boston: 1839. 219 pp.

*Cambridge History of American Literature*, ed. by William Peterfield Trent, John Erskine, Stuart P. Sherman, and Carl Van Doren. New York: Macmillan; Cambridge, Eng.: University Press, 1933. 3 vols.

Carpenter, Jesse T. *The South as a Conscious Minority, 1789-1861, A Study in Political Thought.* New York: New York University Press, 1930. 315 pp.

Carson, Hampton L. *An Historical Sketch of the Law Department of the University of Pennsylvania, read by request before the Society of the Alumni, the Law Faculty and Undergraduates of the Department, in the Chapel of the University, October 10, 1882.* Philadelphia: 1882. 37 pp.

Cassoday, John B. "James Kent and Joseph Story." *Yale Law Journal*, XII (Jan. 1903), 146-153.

Chambrun, Clara Longworth de. *The Making of Nicholas Longworth, Annals of an American Family.* New York: Ray Long and Richard R. Smith, Inc., 1933. 322 pp.

Chaney, Henry A. " Nathan Dane." *The Green Bag,* III (Dec. 1891), 548-558.

Channing, Edward. " Kentucky Resolutions of 1798." *American Historical Review,* XX (Jan. 1915), 333-336.

Chester, Alden, ed. *Legal and Judicial History of New York.* New York: 1911. 3 vols.

Chipman, Alberto Lee. *Chipmans of America.* Poland, Me.: 1904. 232 pp.

Coleman, Charles Washington, Jr. " St. Mémin Portraits: St. George Tucker, Judge of the U. S. District Court for Virginia." *Magazine of American History,* VII (Sept. 1881), 217-221.

Coleman, Mary Haldane (Begg). *St. George Tucker, Citizen of No Mean City.* Richmond, Va.: The Dietz Press, 1938. 190 pp.

Cooley, Thomas M. *Constitutional History of the United States as Seen in the Development of American Law.* New York: 1889. 296 pp.

Cordell, Eugene Fauntleroy. *Historical Sketch of the University of Maryland School of Medicine (1807-1890), with an introductory chapter, notices of the schools of Law, Arts and Sciences, and Theology, and the Department of Dentistry, and a General Catalogue of Medical Alumni.* Baltimore: 1891. 218 pp.

Craven, Avery Odell. *Soil Exhaustion as a Factor in the Agricultural History of Virginia and Maryland, 1606-1860.* University of Illinois Studies in the Social Sciences. Urbana, Ill.: 1925. 179 pp.

Crockett, Walter Hill. *Vermont, The Green Mountain State.* New York: 1921. 4 vols.

Cutting, Elisabeth. *Jefferson Davis, Political Soldier.* New York: Dodd, Mead and Co., 1930. 361 pp.

" Death of a Noted Writer on Law" (George Ticknor Curtis). *New York Herald* (March 29, 1894), p. 16.

Dexter, Franklin Bowditch. *Biographical Sketches of the Graduates of Yale College, with Annals of the College History.* New York: 1885-1911. 5 vols.

*Dictionary of American Biography,* ed. by Allen Johnson and Dumas Malone, under the auspices of the American Council of Learned Societies. New York: Charles Scribner's Sons, 1928-36. 20 vols.

Dodd, William E. " John Taylor, of Caroline, Prophet of Secession." *John P. Branch Historical Papers of Randolph-Macon College.* II (Richmond, Va.: June 1908), 214-252. Followed by the " Letters of John Taylor of Caroline," pp. 253-353.

Dudley, Edgar S. " Was ' Secession' Taught at West Point? What the Records Show." *Century Magazine,* 78 (Aug. 1909), 629-635.

Duer, William A. " William Alexander Duer, Fifth President of Columbia College." *Columbia University Quarterly,* IV (March 1902), 148-158.

Duyckinck, Evart A. and George L. *Cyclopedia of American Literature; Embracing Personal and Critical Notices of Authors, and Selections from their Writings, from the earliest period to the present day, with Portraits, Autographs and other illustrations.* New York: 1856. 2 vols. Rev. ed. by M. Laird Simons, 1882.

*Early History of the University of Virginia,* [Nathaniel Francis Cabell, ed.]. Richmond: 1856. 528 pp.

East, Robert A. "The Massachusetts Conservatives in the Critical Period." In *The Era of the American Revolution,* Studies Inscribed to Evarts Boutell Greene, ed. by Richard B. Morris. New York: Columbia University Press, 1939. Pp. 349-391.

*Encyclopedia of Social Sciences,* Edwin R. A. Seligman, editor-in-chief; Alvin Johnson, associate editor. New York: Macmillan, 1935. 15 vols.

Farrand, Max. *The Framing of the Constitution of the United States.* New Haven: 1913. 281 pp.

Flick, Alexander, ed. *History of the State of New York.* New York: Columbia University Press, 1933-37. 10 vols.

Fox, Dixon Ryan. "James Kent in Politics." *Columbia Alumni News,* XIV (April 27, 1932), 367-368.

Freeman, Douglas Southall. *R. E. Lee, A Biography.* New York and London: Charles Scribner's Sons, 1934. 4 vols.

Fuess, Claude Moore. *Daniel Webster.* Boston: Little, Brown and Co., 1930. 2 vols.

Garland, Hugh A. *The Life of John Randolph of Roanoke.* New York and Philadelphia: 1851. 2 vols.

Gettell, Raymond G. *History of American Political Thought.* New York and London: Century Co., 1928. 633 pp.

Glenn, Thomas Allen. *Some Colonial Mansions and Those Who Lived in Them with Genealogies of the Various Families Mentioned.* 2nd series, Philadelphia: 1900. 503 pp.

Haddow, Anna. *Political Science in American Colleges and Universities, 1636-1900.* New York and London: D. Appleton-Century Co., 1939. 308 pp.

Hall, Edward Hagaman. *A Guide to the Cathedral Church of Saint John the Divine in the City of New York.* 12th ed., New York: Laymen's Club of the Cathedral, 1942. 200 pp.

Hardy, Sallie E. Marshall. "Some Virginia Lawyers of the Past and Present." *The Green Bag,* X (Feb. 1898), 57-68.

Harley, Lewis R. *Francis Lieber, His Life and Political Philosophy.* New York: 1899. 213 pp.

Hazelton, John H. *The Declaration of Independence, Its History.* New York: 1906. 629 pp.

Hicks, Frederick C. "Kent's Commentaries." *Columbia Alumni News,* XIV (April 27, 1932), 369-370.

——. "A Man of Law as a Man of Letters." *New York Times Book Review* (May 27, 1923), p. 12.

——. *Men and Books Famous in the Law.* Rochester, N. Y.: 1921. 259 pp.

Hildreth, Richard. *The History of the United States of America.* New York: 1871. 6 vols.

*A History of Columbia University, 1754-1904; Published in Commemoration of the 150th Anniversary of the Founding of King's College.* New York: 1904. 493 pp.

*The History of the College of William and Mary From Its Foundation, 1660, to 1874.* Richmond: 1874. 183 pp.

Holdsworth, Sir William Searle. *Sources and Literature of English Law.* Oxford: 1925. 247 pp.

Holst, Hermann Eduard von. *The Constitutional and Political History of the United States,* tr. by John J. Lalor and Alfred B. Mason. Chicago: 1877-92. 8 vols.

Honeywell, Roy J. "Nathaniel Chipman, Political Philosopher and Jurist." *New England Quarterly,* V (July 1932), 555-584.

Horton, John Theodore. *James Kent, A Study in Conservatism, 1763-1847.* New York and London: D. Appleton-Century Co., 1939. 354 pp.

——. "Western Eyres of Judge Kent." *New York History,* XVIII (April 1937), 152-166.

Houston, David Franklin. *A Critical Study of Nullification in South Carolina.* New York: 1896. 169 pp.

Hutchinson, John. *A Catalogue of Notable Middle Templars with Brief Biographical Notices.* London: 1902. 284 pp.

Jones, E. Alfred. *American Members of the Inns of Court.* London: 1924. 250 pp.

Keppel, Frederick Paul. *Columbia.* New York: 1914. 297 pp.

Konkle, Burton Alva. *James Wilson and the Constitution, the Opening Address in the official series of events known as The James Wilson Memorial . . . delivered before the Law Academy of Philadelphia on Nov. 14, 1906.* Philadelphia: 1907. 40 pp.

Langdell, C. C. "The Harvard Law School, 1869-1894." *Harvard Graduates' Magazine,* II (June 1894), 490-498.

"The Late Mr. Justice Story" *The Law Review and Quarterly Journal of British and Foreign Jurisprudence,* III (London: May 1846), 366-388.

"The Litchfield Law School." *Albany Law Journal,* XX (July 26, 1879), 72-73.

Malone, Dumas. *The Public Life of Thomas Cooper, 1783-1839.* New Haven: Yale University Press, 1926. 432 pp.

Marshall, Carrington T., ed.-in-chief. *A History of The Courts and Lawyers of Ohio.* New York: American Historical Society, Inc., 1934. 4 vols.

McLaughlin, Andrew C. *A Constitutional History of the United States.* New York and London: D. Appleton-Century Co., 1935. 833 pp.

——. "Social Compact and Constitutional Construction." *American Historical Review,* V (April 1900), 467-490.

McMaster, John Bach. *A History of the People of the United States from the Revolution to the Civil War.* New York: 1907-14. 8 vols.

*Memorial Biographies of the New England Historic Genealogical Society.*
IV (Boston: 1885), 72-75, on Thomas Sergeant.

Merriam, Charles Edward. *A History of American Political Theories.* New
York: 1918. 364 pp.

——. *History of the Theory of Sovereignty Since Rousseau.* New York:
1900. 232 pp.

Middlebury College. *Catalogue of Officers and Students, 1800-1915.* Middlebury, Vt.: 1917. 538 pp.

——. *A Record of the Centennial Anniversary of Middlebury College, 1800-
1900.* Middlebury, Vt.: 1901. 292 pp.

Morison, Samuel Eliot. *The Life and Letters of Harrison Gray Otis, Federalist, 1765-1848.* Boston and New York: 1913. 2 vols.

Mudge, Eugene Tenbroeck. *The Social Philosophy of John Taylor of
Caroline, A Study in Jeffersonian Democracy.* New York: Columbia
University Press, 1939. 227 pp.

Nelson, Margaret V. "The Cases of the Judges, Fact or Fiction?" *University of Virginia Law Review,* XXXI (Dec. 1944), 243-255.

——. *A Study of Judicial Review in Virginia, 1789-1928.* New York:
Columbia University Press, 1947. 249 pp.

Oberholtzer, Ellis P. *The Literary History of Philadelphia.* Philadelphia:
1906. 433 pp.

Obering, William F. *The Philosophy of Law of James Wilson, Associate
Justice of the United States Supreme Court, 1789-1798.* Washington,
D. C.: Catholic University of America, [1938]. 276 pp.

O'Donnell, May G. *James Wilson and the Natural Law Basis of Positive
Law.* New York: Fordham University Press, 1937. 40 pp.

Palmer, John McAuley. *General Von Steuben.* New Haven: Yale University Press, 1937. 434 pp.

Parrington, Vernon Louis. *Main Currents in American Thought.* New
York: Harcourt, Brace, 1930. Vol. II, "The Romantic Revolution in
America."

Patteson, S. S. P. "The Supreme Court of Appeals of Virginia." Part I,
*The Green Bag,* V (July 1893), 310-329.

Pollock, Frederick, and Maitland, Frederic William. *The History of English
Law before the Time of Edward I.* Cambridge, Eng.: 1895. 2 vols.

Pound, Roscoe. "The Place of Judge Story in the Making of American
Law." *American Law Review,* XLVIII (Sept.-Oct. 1914), 676-697.

Powell, Thomas R. "Kent's Contribution to Constitutional Law." *Columbia
Alumni News,* XIV (April 27, 1932), 372-374.

Radin, Max. *Handbook of Anglo-American Legal History.* St. Paul, Minn.:
West Publ. Co., 1936. 612 pp.

Reed, Alfred Zantzinger. *Training for the Public Profession of the Law.*
Bulletin No. 15 of the Carnegie Foundation for the Advancement of
Teaching. New York: 1921. 498 pp.

"St. George Tucker." *Gentleman's Magazine,* 144 (London: Nov. 1828),
471-472.

Scharf, J. Thomas, and Westcott, Thompson. *History of Philadelphia, 1609-1884.* Philadelphia: 1884. 3 vols.

Schofield, William. "Joseph Story, 1779-1845." In *Great American Lawyers,* ed. by William Draper Lewis. III (Philadelphia: 1908), 123-185.

Schouler, James. *History of the United States of America Under the Constitution.* Rev. ed., New York: 1899. 7 vols.

Simms, Henry Harrison. *Life of John Taylor; the Story of a Brilliant Leader in the Early Virginia State Rights School.* Richmond, Va.: William Byrd Press, 1932. 234 pp.

Sloane, Paul Edward. *The Background of the Constitutional Ideas of James Wilson.* Unpubld. M. A. thesis. Berkeley: University of California, 1945. 129 numbered leaves.

*The South in the Building of the Nation.* Richmond, Va.: 1909. 12 vols.

Spaulding, Ernest Wilder. *New York in the Critical Period, 1783-1789.* New York: Columbia University Press, 1932. 334 pp.

Stone, Edwin Martin. *History of Beverly, civil and ecclesiastical, from its settlement in 1630 to 1842.* Boston: 1843. 324 pp.

Stone, Harlan F. "James Kent, Judge and Chancellor." *Columbia Alumni News,* XIV (April 27, 1932), 366.

Tate, Allen. *Jefferson Davis: His Rise and Fall, A Biographical Narrative.* New York: Minton, Balch and Co., 1929. 311 pp.

Taylor, M. Flavia. "The Political and Civil Career of Henry Baldwin, 1799-1830." *Western Pennsylvania Historical Magazine,* XXIV (March 1941), 37-50.

Tucker, Henry St. George. "Judge Story's Position on the So-Called General Welfare Clause." *American Bar Association Journal,* XIII (July and Aug. 1927), 363-368, 465-469. Also, S. Doc. 17, 70th Cong., 1st sess. (Washington: Govt. Print. Off., 1927), 21 pp. Reprinted in *Constitutional Review,* XIII (Jan. 1929), 13-35, with discussion (April 1929), 98-100; and (July 1929), 163-164.

——. "Patrick Henry and St. George Tucker." *University of Pennsylvania Law Review,* LXVII (Jan. 1919), 69-74.

Twiss, Benjamin R. *Lawyers and the Constitution: How Laissez Faire Came to the Supreme Court.* Princeton: Princeton University Press, 1942. 271 pp.

Tyler, Lyon Gardiner. *The College of William and Mary in Virginia: Its History and Work, 1693-1907.* Richmond: 1907. 96 pp.

——. *Early Courses and Professors at William and Mary College,* an address before Alpha Chapter, Phi Beta Kappa, Dec. 5, 1904. Williamsburg: 1904. 13 pp.

——. *Making of the Union.* Richmond: 1923. 39 pp.

Wallis, George S., Jr. Letter to the editor of *Time Weekly News Magazine,* XLIX (Feb. 3, 1947), 10.

Warren, Charles. *A History of the American Bar.* Boston: 1911. 586 pp.

——. *History of the Harvard Law School and of Early Legal Conditions in America.* New York: 1908. 3 vols.

——. *The Supreme Court in United States History*. Boston: 1922. 3 vols.

William and Mary College. *The History of the College of William and Mary from its foundation, 1660 to 1874*. Richmond: 1874. 183 pp.

Williams, Charles Langdon, compiler. *Statistics of the Rutland County Bar, with Biographical Notes of the Most distinguished of its Deceased Members: Also, a list of the County officers from 1781 to 1847*. Vol. I No. 5. Brandon, Vt.: 1847. 31 pp.

Winfield, Percy Henry. *The Chief Sources of English Legal History*. Cambridge, Mass.: 1925. 374 pp.

Wright, Benjamin F., Jr. *American Interpretations of Natural Law*. Cambridge: Harvard University Press, 1931. 360 pp.

——. "The Philosopher of Jeffersonian Democracy." *American Political Science Review*, XXII (Nov. 1928), 870-892.

Zane, John Maxey. *The Story of Law*. New York: Ives Washburn, 1927. 486 pp.

TABLE OF CASES

American Insurance Company *v.* Canter, 1 Pet. 511 (1828).

Bank of Augusta *v.* Earle, 13 Pet. 519 (1839).

Bank of the United States *v.* Daniel, 12 Pet. 32 (1838).

Barry *v.* Mercein, 5 How. 103 (1847).

Bollman, *Ex parte*, 4 Cr. 75 (1807).

Brown *v.* Duchesne, 19 How. 183 (1856).

Brown *v.* Maryland, 12 Wheat. 419 (1827).

Buckner *v.* Finley, 2 Pet. 586 (1829).

Calder *v.* Bull, 3 Dall. 386 (1798).

Cases of the Judges, 4 Call (Va.) 135 (1788).

Charles River Bridge *v.* Warren Bridge, 11 Pet. 420 (1837).

Childress *v.* Emory, 8 Wheat. 642 (1823).

Chisholm *v.* Georgia, 2 Dall. 419 (1793).

Cohens *v.* Virginia, 6 Wheat. 264 (1821).

Cook *v.* Moffat, 5 How. 299 (1847).

Cross *v.* Harrison, 16 How. 164 (1853).

Dartmouth College *v.* Woodward, 4 Wheat. 627 (1819).

Decatur *v.* Paulding, 14 Pet. 497 (1840).

DeLovio *v.* Boit, 2 Gallison (1st Circuit Fed.) 398 (1815).

DeVaux *v.* Salvador, 4 Adolphus and Ellis (King's Bench) 420 (1836).

Dodge *v.* Woolsey, 18 How. 331 (1855).

Dred Scott *v.* Sanford, 19 How. 393 (1856).

Fellows *v.* Blacksmith, 19 How. 366 (1856).

Fletcher *v.* Peck, 6 Cr. 87 (1810).

Freeman *v.* Howe, 24 How. 450 (1860).

Gibbons *v.* Ogden, 17 Johnson (New York) 488 (1820).

Gibbons *v.* Ogden, 9 Wheat. 1 (1824).

Governeur *v.* Robertson, 11 Wheat. 332 (1826).

Groves *v.* Slaughter, 15 Pet. 449 (1841).

Holmes v. Jennison, 14 Pet. 540 (1840).

Houston v. Moore, 5 Wheat. 1 (1820).

Hylton v. United States, 3 Dall. 171 (1796).

Inglis v. Sailor's Snug Harbor, 3 Pet. 99 (1830).

Jackson v. Steamboat Magnolia, 20 How. 296 (1857).

Jecker v. Montgomery, 13 How. 498 (1851).

Jones v. Van Zandt, 5 How. 215 (1847).

Kamper v. Hawkins, 1 Va. Cas. 128 (1800).

Kendall v. United States, 12 Pet. 524 (1838).

Kennett v. Chambers, 14 How. 38 (1852).

Leitensdorfer v. Webb, 20 How. 176 (1857).

License Cases, 5 How. 504 (1847) .

Livingston v. Moore, 7 Pet. 469 (1833).

Luther v. Borden, 7 How. 1 (1849).

Marbury v. Madison, 1 Cr. 137 (1803).

Marshall v. Baltimore and Ohio Railroad Company, 16 How. 314 (1853).

Martin v. Hunter's Lessee, 1 Wheat. 304 (1816).

McCulloch v. Maryland, 4 Wheat. 316 (1819).

McElmoyle v. Cohen, 13 Pet. 312 (1839).

McIlvaine v. Cox, 4 Cr. 209 (1808).

McNutt v. Bland, 2 How. 9 (1844).

Menard v. Aspasia, 5 Pet. 505 (1828).

Nathan v. Louisiana, 8 How. 73 (1850).

New Jersey Steam Navigation Company v. Merchants' Bank, 6 How. 344 (1848).

New York v. Miln, 11 Pet. 102 (1837).

Ogden v. Gibbons, 4 Johnson Chancery (New York) 150 (1819).

Ogden v. Saunders, 12 Wheat. 213 (1827).

Passenger Cases, 7 How. 283 (1849).

Penhallow v. Doane, 3 Dall. 54 (1795).

Pennsylvania v. Wheeling and Belmont Bridge Company, 13 How. 518 (1851).

People v. Croswell, 3 Johnson's Cases (New York) 337 Appendix (1803).

Peters v. Warren Insurance Company, 3 Sumner (1st Circuit Fed.) 389 (1838).

Prigg v. Pennsylvania, 16 Pet. 539 (1842).

Satterlee v. Matthewson, 2 Pet. 380 (1829).

Stacy v. Thrasher, 6 How. 44 (1848).

Stockdale v. Hansard, 9 Adolphus and Ellis (King's Bench) 1 (1839).

Suydam v. Broadnax, 14 Pet. 67 (1840).

Taylor v. Carryl, 20 How. 583 (1857).

Terrett v. Taylor, 9 Cr. 43 (1815).

Thomas v. Osborn, 19 How. 22 (1856).

Turpin v. Locket, 6 Call (Va.) 113 (1804).

Union Bank of Tennessee v. Jolly's Administrators, 18 How. 503 (1853).

United States *v.* Hudson and Goodwin, 7 Cr. 32 (1812).
United States *v.* La Jeune Eugenie, 2 Mason (1st Circuit Fed.) 409 (1822).
United States *v.* Marigold, 9 How. 560 (1850).
United States *v.* Ortega, 11 Wheat. 467 (1826).
United States *v.* Reynes, 9 How. 127 (1850).
Veazie *v.* Moor, 14 How. 568 (1852).
Ware *v.* Hylton, 3 Dall. 199 (1796).
Waring *v.* Clarke, 5 How. 441 (1847).
Wells, *Ex parte*, 18 How. 307 (1855).
West River Bridge Company *v.* Dix, 6 How. 507 (1848).
Weston *v.* City Council of Charleston, 2 Pet. 449 (1829).
Wheaton *v.* Peters, 8 Pet. 591 (1834).
Woodson *v.* Randolph, 1 Va. Cas. 20 (1793).
Worcester *v.* Georgia, 6 Pet. 515 (1832).

# INDEX

Abolition of slavery, attitude of commentators toward: Curtis, 114n; Hoffman, 112; Rawle, 63-64; Story, 143 and n; St. George Tucker, 176. *See also* Slavery

Adams, John, *A Defence of the Constitutions of Government of the United States of America*, 28 and n, 189, endorsed by Jefferson in 1787, 191n, Taylor's reply to, 189-91; presidency supported by Chipman, 121; member of Massachusetts Constitutional Convention (1820), 144 and n

Adams, John Quincy, on Nathan Dane, 35; supported by Story, 135n; offered seat on Supreme Court, 140; Fourth of July Oration (1831), 28, 151n, 226n; quoted, 356

Adams, Sam, 68

Admiralty law, Story and, 142 and n; Dane on, 349

Alabama, 74

Alexander, William, 97n, 104

Alien and Sedition Acts, 121, 186, 235n

"American Blackstone," Wilson's desire to be, 54-55; St. George Tucker as, 181

American Insurance Company *v.* Canter, 348n

American Revolution, philosophy of, 182, 213-14; confusion during, 18; problems settled by, 229; Story's account of history of, 310-11; significance of, 232-33, 252; lives and ideas of commentators during: Chipman, 115-16, Duer's family, 97 and n, DuPonceau, 68-69 and n, Kent, 79-80 and n, Rawle, 59, Story's family, 133, Taylor, 182-83 and n, St. George Tucker, 171-72, 197, Wilson, 46-47, 213-14

American Society for the Encouragement of Domestic Manufactures, 194 and n

Annapolis Convention, 172

Anti-federal party, DuPonceau as member of, 71, 73; in New York, 82; Dane accused of sympathizing with, 127

Articles of Confederation, Dane's

attitude on, 127, 220; Kent's attitude on, 219, 259n; Story on, 284; Taylor on, 266; St. George Tucker on, 234; Wilson's views on implied powers in, 50 and n. *See also* Confederation

Ashmun, James Hooker, 146

Bacon, Ezekiel, 138, 140, 159

Bailey, Theodorus, 83n

Baldwin, Henry

Biographical sketch, 39-40n; *General View of the Constitution*, 159, 242-45, 301-02, 355: complaint about commentaries, 211, interpretation of the Constitution, 29, 40n, 242-43 and n, on sovereignty, 243-44, criticism of Story, 244-45, cited in Supreme Court, 355; citation of commentaries while a justice, 352n

Bank of Augusta *v.* Earle, 354n

Bank of North America, 49-50 and n

Bank of the United States, First, 185, Hamilton's report on constitutionality of, 50n, 323n; Second, 168, 199, 202

Bank of the United States *v.* Daniel, 352, 354n

Barbour, Justice Philip P., 345, 351n

Barry *v.* Mercein, 354n

Beard, Charles A., opinion of Taylor, 189, 195-96

Benson, Egbert, attorney-general of New York, 81, 82

Bentham, Jeremy, 20

Benton, Senator Thomas Hart, 126, 178n

Blackstone, Sir William, 17-20, 335; *Commentaries on the Laws of England*, 17-20, 24, 346, criticism of, 18-19 and n, American edition of, 18, 21, use in training of lawyers, 22-23, 336, 337; studied by Wilson, 44n, Kent, 80 and n, 81, 94, Story, 134; used by St. George Tucker, 175-76; on sovereignty, 213-14, 217, 218, 223; definition of law, 214, 248, 256, 282; definition of compact, 282n, 283. *See also* Tucker, St. George, *Blackstone's Commentaries*; "American Blackstone"

72
74
75
76
77
79
81
83
85
88